RADIO
BROADCASTING

RADIO BROADCASTING

AN INTRODUCTION TO THE SOUND MEDIUM

EDITED BY

ROBERT L. HILLIARD

REVISED AND ENLARGED EDITION

CONTRIBUTORS

ELIZABETH S. CZECH
GEORGE L. HALL
WILLIAM HAWES
ROBERT L. HILLIARD
EARL R. WYNN

A COMMUNICATION ARTS BOOK

Hastings House, Publishers   New York 10016

To Lee, Zeke, Stu

Second Edition, Revised, January 1976
Second Edition published, August 1974
First Edition published, September 1967
Second Printing, June 1969
Third Printing, October 1969
Fourth Printing, June 1970
Fifth Printing, October 1970
Sixth Printing, November 1971
Seventh Printing, May 1972

Library of Congress Cataloguing in Publication Data
Hilliard, Robert L   Radio Broadcasting
    (A Communication arts book)
    1. Radio broadcasting. I. Czech, Elizabeth S. and others
PN1991.5.H5   1974   384.54   73-22487
ISBN 0-8038-6331-4
ISBN 0-8038-6332-2 (pbk.)

Published simultaneously in Canada
by Saunders of Toronto, Ltd., Don Mills, Ontario
Printed in the United States of America

42,939

CONTENTS

PREFACE

SINCE THE PUBLICATION OF *Radio Broadcasting* in 1967 those of us who contributed to the book have been told frequently by students whom we have met socially, professionally and in other non-academic situations that they have used or are using the book in class. At professional meetings and social gatherings teachers and professionals in the broadcasting field have told us that they use the book in their classes, or at their stations for reference and for training newcomers who enter their organizations. Many foreign visitors who come to my office in Washington ask whether I am the same person whose name appears on *Radio Broadcasting*, which they use as a basic text/reference in their respective countries. I appreciated a recent postcard from Lesotho from an official of a major American broadcasting company, who wrote: "Here I am in south Africa and what do I see but your book, *Radio Broadcasting*, on the library shelf. It's like meeting an old friend." We are grateful.

Radio *is* an old friend that in its stability and aging may sometimes be taken for granted, temporarily replaced by a more glamorous medium. But, like a beneficent Hydra, radio always seems to get its head together and comes back as an essential and dependable part of our life. In many emerging countries of the world, radio, rather than television, is the principal medium of mass communications — including, as it does, information, entertainment and motivation. In the United States, as pointed out in Chapter 1, radio has grown in the past decade, despite a retrenchment following the

7

sudden bursting forth of television some two decades ago. When some of its functions were cut off by television, which performed them more attractively, radio grew new heads and reoriented itself to new major areas. Radio and television are not, as some once thought, competing media. They are complementary. Even when the content may be essentially the same, such as news and sports, their target audiences, including place and time of reception, are largely different. Now, in the summer of 1974, the number of radio stations in the United States exceeds 7,600, with some 25,000 stations in operation throughout the world.

We look forward to the not-too-distant future when every person in the world will have the advantage of multi-media reception, including radio and television, and when satellites will permit all peoples and all cultures to communicate with each other and to understand each other's needs and values. But right now, in most countries of the world, radio is the dominant and, in some cases, the only viable mass medium.

When we put this book together for the first time almost ten years ago we wanted to provide a single, comprehensive source for learning about radio for the student, for the beginning professional, for the practitioner and for the lay person. Our aim was to be more humanistic than technical, yet at the same time to help people learn "how-to" *do* as well as to understand the various things that go into the development, operation and programming of a radio station. We hoped to combine the descriptive and the didactic: the use of radio and all its facets to meet the needs and serve the purposes of the people who listen. We sought to achieve a combination of ethics and action, of ascertainment and fulfillment.

In his Publisher's Letter in *Television/Radio Age* of January 21, 1974, S. J. Paul wrote that "A half century ago, the communications hero in small town America was the editor of the country weekly, or the small town daily. He wrote much of the paper, solicited the ads and supervised the printing. He was also usually his own circulation manager. He was the town chronicler. Today that individual has been replaced in local influence by the manager of the local radio station. . . . He is usually his own program director, sales manager and many times the chief announcer and news director. He belongs to just about every service organization in the town and he is involved with his community in a personal way, as well as through his station."

If we may add "she" to the "he" above, we would say that the initiator, protector and chronicler of an enlightened country and of a thinking country can and should be, to a large extent, the radio professional — the manager, the writer, the announcer, the technician, the performer, the producer — all those who are responsible for keeping the radio station on the air and for what goes out over the air. We hope this book can be helpful to them.

We also hoped to show enough of the basic concepts and applications of radio to make the book useful beyond the United States and we have been pleased that it has been used in many countries, in part through a French language edition published in 1970 by Nouveaux Horizons of Strasbourg and Paris as *La Radio: Une Carrière* and distributed by the U.S. Information Service in French-speaking lands.

I am grateful to my collaborators, Betty Czech, George Hall, Bill Hawes and Earl Wynn for their dedication and cooperation in the difficult job of revising and updating, to Gertrude Barnstone for her proofing and editorial suggestions, to Yuri Tanaka for her gracious and dependable typing, to Russ Neale for his tactful combination of patience and exhortation, to his assistants at Hastings House, Jim Moore and Lee Tobin, to the broadcasters and agencies who cordially and cooperatively provided updated scripts and other materials, and to the many people who have used *Radio Broadcasting* and whose comments and suggestions over the years were so helpful in arriving at this new edition. Although this book was completed entirely on my own time, with my own equipment and supplies, and with no use of any government materials not available to the general public, I am appreciative to those of my colleagues at the Federal Communications Commission whose publicly-available resources and comments were also made available to me. Their help to me reflects their same good service to the public.

When we began writing the first edition of *Radio Broadcasting* many people were saying that radio was dead. It wasn't then and it isn't now. It is, indeed, very much alive and we feel privileged to have been and to be, through this book, a part of its life.

ROBERT L. HILLIARD

Washington, D.C.
August, 1974

R A D I O
BROADCASTING

ROBERT L. HILLIARD

*Chief, Educational Broadcasting Branch
Federal Communications Commission*

• *Radio Broadcasting* is among Dr. Hilliard's four books for Hastings House Communication Arts series. The first edition became the leading work of its kind and in 1970 was printed in France as *La Radio: Une Carrière* and distributed in Africa by the United States Information Agency. His *Writing for Television and Radio* is also the leader in its field, and his *Understanding Television* is a companion work to this book. He is co-author with Hyman Field of *Television and the Teacher*. Dr. Hilliard has also published more than 25 articles on communications and education in professional journals. He has worked in both the commercial and educational mass media fields as a writer, producer and director, has been the recipient of several playwriting awards and has had his plays produced in university and community theatres. His newspaper background includes five years as a drama and film critic in New York.

Dr. Hilliard received the B.A. degree from the University of Delaware in philosophy and political science, the M.A. and M.F.A. degrees from Western Reserve University, and the Ph.D. degree from Columbia University. He began his teaching career in 1950 at Brooklyn College, subsequently taught at Adelphi University and was Associate Professor of Radio, Television and Motion Pictures, University of North Carolina at Chapel Hill, prior to joining the FCC staff in 1964. He has been active in professional associations and has served as chairperson of committees and projects for national and regional organizations. He has been consultant on television in higher education for New York State and special consultant on television for the Council of Higher Educational Institutions in New York City. He is Founder of The International University of Communications, Washington, D.C., the first institution to combine the individualized learning and project approach with the use of communications to directly solve critical human problems. In 1970 he served as a consultant and lecturer on communications and education in Japan, assisting in the planning for the Open University, and he visited officials of eight other Asian nations on behalf of the U.S. government.

In addition to his position as Chief of Educational Broadcasting for the FCC, Dr. Hilliard founded the Federal Interagency Media Committee in 1965 and has been re-elected chairperson of that organization every year since then, and was also instrumental in the founding of the FCC's National Committee for the Instructional Television Fixed Service, of which he served as executive vice-chairman. He is a frequent speaker to professional meetings and citizen groups and has received several awards for his work in education and communications.

---

* Dr. Hilliard has written this chapter in his private capacity. No official support or endorsement by the Federal Communications Commission is intended or should be inferred.

1

BEGINNING,
GROWTH
AND REGULATION

BY ROBERT L. HILLIARD

THROUGHOUT history people have sought ways of achieving instantaneous mass communications. From ancient Athens where a speaker on a platform reached the total population at once in one place, to early America where an Indian sending smoke signals reached all the people of his tribe at once scattered over a wide area, the instant medium has been a most significant factor in the conduct of human relationships. It was only in this century, however, that a medium that was truly instant and mass, capable of reaching the total population of the world as well as of a country or a region or a community, came into being.

That radio has had tremendous impact on society, affecting attitudes, behavior and motivation, is undeniable. Mussolini was quoted as saying that without radio he would not have been able to achieve the solidification of and the power over the Italian people that he did. In the United States, from a different ideological viewpoint, the Fireside Chat over radio is frequently thought of as having vastly strengthened President Franklin D. Roosevelt's popularity and influence with the American people. Who of us who heard them will ever forget the tremendous excitement and impact of the Fireside Chats? What an indication of radio's power when we realize that the total number of Fireside Chats F.D.R. gave was only *four*.

In the United States radio's impact on the economy, on business and industry, on marketing, on the entertainment field has been great, in some instances revolutionizing selling and buying practices and corporate organization. In 1974 advertisers spent $60 million on network commercials, $387 million on national and regional spot announcements and $1.31 billion for commercials on local radio stations for a total of $1.76 billion — up 6.6% from the previous year. Increased expenses caused a leveling off of radio profits to $90.2 million. This was, we must remember, some 20 years after radio supposedly died. With the growth of national network television in the early 1950's, prognostications were that radio's demise was not far off. The harbingers were partly correct. Net radio profits, which were $61 million in 1952, dropped to $29.4 million in 1961. However, with radio revitalizing itself with new formats and organizational approaches, net profits rose to $87.3 million by 1966 and reached a pre-1972 peak of $113.4 million in 1968. Total revenues increased from just under $469 million in 1952 to $872 million in 1966 and went over the billion mark, to $1,023 million, in 1968. The contributions of FM radio to the medium's generally increased popularity was reflected in the more than 25% increase of FM revenue in 1974 over 1973.

In October, 1975 there were 7,958 radio stations on the air in the United States: 4,424 commercial AM, 2,713 commercial FM, and 821 noncommercial public or educational stations. In 1975 more than 96% of the population over 12 years of age — some 155 million people — listened to radio during the course of any given week, for an average total of over 26 hours per week. Some 98.6% of the homes in the United States had one or more radio sets. Over 400 million sets were in use, including homes, automobiles and public places.

The Beginning

But radio did not come full-blown on the American scene, although in the measure of history its growth has been as instantaneous and rapid as its function. It was only in 1920 that the first professional public broadcasting took place — a remarkably short time ago for the growth it has achieved when we consider the great number of people now alive who were alive then. In fact, radio is still being run by many of its "first generation"!

Theoretically, radio was discovered in the 1860's by James C. Maxwell, a Scottish physicist who worked out the formulas that predicted the existence of electromagnetic or radio waves. The first person to create what we now call radio waves was German physicist Heinrich Hertz who in the 1880's and 1890's projected rapid variations of electric current into space in the form of waves similar to those of light and heat, proving Maxwell's theories correct. It is Hertz' name that we now use internationally to describe the number of cycles per second of radio frequencies. Guglielmo Marconi, the inventor of the wireless telegraph, is credited with sending and receiving the first wireless signals in 1895. These were flashed just a short distance, across his father's estate in Bologna, Italy. By 1899 Marconi was able to send the first wireless signal across the English channel and in 1901 successfully spanned the Atlantic Ocean, with the transmission of the letter "S" from England to Newfoundland.

Two inventions of tubes marked the next significant steps in the development of radio: the diode rectifier tube in 1904 by Englishman Sir John Fleming, and the audion or vacuum tube, a triode amplifier with a filament, plate and grid in 1906 by American Lee de Forest, considered by some to be the "father" of radio.

At first all transmissions sent through the air by "radio" were telegraph signals. There are conflicting claims for the first broadcast of speech sounds over the air. Historians generally acknowledge the first voice transmission to be by Reginald A. Fessenden in 1906 from Brant Rock, Massachusetts. Nearby ship operators were surprised to pick up the sound of the human voice on their receiving equipment. One claim dating back to 1892 is the reported transmission, "Hello, Rainey," from Nathan B. Stubblefield to his neighbor Rainey T. Wells in a wireless demonstration near Murray, Kentucky.

Early in 1910 voice transmission received great impetus when the voices of Enrico Caruso and Emmy Destinn were transmitted from backstage at the Metropolitan Opera House in New York by de Forest radiophone and were heard by a radio operator on the S.S. Avon at sea and by amateur operators in Connecticut. The value of radio was dramatically proven in 1912 when wireless signals from the S.S. Titanic were received by young radio operator David Sarnoff in New York and helped save 705 lives. The first practical application of radio was for ship-to-ship and ship-to-shore telegraphic communication. This new communications medium was first known as "wireless." American use of the term "radio" began in 1912 when the Navy, believing that "wireless" was too inclusive, adopted the term "radiotelegraph." The British still continue to use "wireless." The word "broadcast" stems from early United States naval reference to the "broadcast" of orders to the fleet. In 1915 the Bell Telephone Company of Arlington, Virginia conducted the first transatlantic voice experiments.

There were many early experimental audio transmissions, but it was not until after World War I that regular broadcasting began. The "first" broadcasting station is a matter of conflicting claims, largely because some of the pioneer stations developed from experimental operations and it has been difficult to ascertain when experimental transmission left off and public broadcasting began. Two of the earliest experimental stations began at the University of Wisconsin in 1915 and in Pittsburgh in 1916. The Pittsburgh operation became KDKA and is generally credited with beginning the first regularly scheduled broadcasting with the Harding-Cox presidential election returns on November 2, 1920. Claims are also made for WWJ, Detroit, as having started regular broadcasting on August 20, 1920. The first station to be issued a regular broadcasting license according to the records of the Department of Commerce, which then supervised radio, was WBZ, Springfield, Massachusetts, on September 15, 1921.

An important technical advance in making radio available for the public was the demonstration in 1922 by inventor Edwin H. Armstrong of the superheterodyne as a broadcaster receiver. It wasn't long before the commercial value of radio was realized. At first many of the stations were operated by colleges and universities, with information and educational programs, including newscasts, weather reports and farm news as the principal programming. The costs of radio operation began to put many of these stations out of operation. Many stations were operated by newspapers in order to promote the newspapers. Some stations were used principally to sell the receiving equipment manufactured by the station's owner. Businessmen, however, looked for some better financially stable use of the new medium. Their answer came on August 28, 1922, when WEAF, New York City, broadcast the first sponsored program. When the sponsoring real estate firm's two advertised buildings in the Borough of Queens were sold through the radio ads, commercial radio was born.

As early as 1922 there was experimental network operation, using telephone lines. In that year WJZ (later WABC), New York, and WGY, Schenectady, broadcast the baseball World Series. Early in 1923 WEAF, New York, and WNAC, Boston, jointly picked up a football game. On June 21, 1923, a speech by President Harding was broadcast simultaneously in St. Louis, New York and Washington, D.C. to an unprecedented audience of some one million people. Later that same year WEAF and WGY were connected with KDKA and KWY, Chicago, to carry talks made at a dinner in New York. President Calvin Coolidge's message to Congress was broadcast by seven stations in late 1923. Limited networks carried the 1924 Republican convention in Cleveland and Democratic convention in New York. "Chain" broadcasting, as it was then called, soon extended across the country, and in 1925 a 24-station transcontinental hookup carried President Coolidge's inaugural to some 30 million people.

Network growth during this period, however, was limited by the American Telephone and Telegraph Company's control over long distance lines. It did not permit stations other than those joining its own radio network to use these lines for interconnection. It wasn't until AT&T withdrew from radio broadcasting in 1926 that network radio was able to develop. AT&T sold its radio properties to the Radio Corporation of America, which established the first regular network that year with 24 stations. It started with two key stations, WEAF and WJZ, both in New York. As the National Broadcasting Company, it firmly established the network concept on January 1, 1927 with a play-by-play description of the Rose Bowl football game from Pasadena, California over its first coast-to-coast hookup of 19 stations. Finding itself with two sets of stations, the ones it purchased from

AT&T and the stations it had been developing as an RCA network, NBC formed two networks, naming them the Red and the Blue after the colors of the sheaths covering the wires of each of the networks. In 1927 the Columbia Broadcasting System was organized with a basic network of 16 stations.

Radio grew wildly during its formative years, in terms of a proliferation of stations, the development of networks and advertising support, and technically culminated in the first around-the-world broadcast from Schenectady in 1930. Its unchecked growth, however, resulted in chaos over the airwaves, with the new medium virtually choking itself to death. By the mid-1920's it was clear that federal regulation was necessary if radio was to survive.

EARLY REGULATION

The first federal law relating to radio was the Wireless Ship Act, enacted by Congress in 1910. It dealt solely with the use of radio by ships, at that time the only serious use of the wireless medium. The first law to regulate radio in general was the Radio Act of 1912. In anticipation of the growth of radio, it gave the Secretary of Commerce and Labor (combined in one Department at that time) the responsibility of licensing radio stations and operators. Inasmuch as commercial or public stations as we now know them did not develop until after World War I, for some years the new regulations were applied principally to ships, which were required to have wireless stations and operators for safety purposes, and to the forerunners of stations, the experimental radiotelephone operations. As in World War II in the case of television, civil radio development stayed at a plateau during World War I as the United States government took over all the wireless stations with the exception of a few high-powered ones.

Following World War I radio broadcasting received its first federal impetus when the experimental radiotelephone operations were permitted to operate as "limited commercial stations." With the licensing of the first regular operating station in 1921, radio grew rapidly, even then presaging the proliferated use of the airwaves that would soon result in chaos and require strong regulatory action.

In 1922 the Secretary of Commerce assigned the wavelength of 360 meters — approximately 830 kilocycles per second — for the transmission of "important news items, entertainment, lectures, sermons and similar matter." The need to develop rational guidelines for the growth of the new industry prompted the government to call a first National Radio Conference in Washington in 1922. The recommendations of the Conference resulted in further regulations being established by the Secretary of Commerce; a new type of broadcast station was developed, with two AM frequencies, 750 and 833 kilocycles per second, assigned for program transmission, and a minimum power of 500 watts and a maximum power of 1,000 watts — 1 kilowatt — set. During that year more than 500 new stations were licensed. A remark of prophetic irony at the 1922 conference by then Secretary of Commerce Herbert Hoover, under whose jurisdiction broadcasting regulation was placed, received little attention. Reflecting the Conference attendees' unfavorable attitude toward the possibility of advertising over radio, Hoover said: "It is inconceivable that we should allow so great a responsibility for service to be drowned in advertising chatter."

It was through subsequent National Radio Conferences in 1923, 1924 and 1925 that a broadcasting regulatory body was established. With the continued deluging of the airwaves, with stations springing up all over the country, the Department of Commerce, acting on recommendations from these conferences, attempted to develop some sort of orderly development through piecemeal rulings, such as the allocation of 550 to 1500 kilocycles per second as the broadcasting frequency and the authorization of power up to 5000 watts (5 kilowatts). It didn't work.

By 1925 broadcasting had grown to such proportions that there was absolute chaos on the air. Stations changed frequencies, increased power and went on and off the air as they wished. It was virtually impossible for any station to be heard clearly except in a limited area. The interference threatened to result in mass suicidal strangulation for radio, and the Fourth National Radio Conference in 1925 asked the Secretary of Commerce to regulate broadcast times and power and to assign specific frequencies. Because court decisions had held that the Radio Act of 1912 did not give such authority to the Secretary of Commerce, new legislation was needed if radio was to survive, and in 1926 President Coolidge urged Congress to take action. Because both Coolidge and Hoover indicated displeasure with the possibility of a strong, independent regulatory commission, a compromise bill, the Dill-White Bill, proposed an independent bipartisan commission of five members to function for just one year to try to solve the problems of the airwaves. The Radio Act of 1927 established the Federal Radio Commission, and subsequent amendments continued to prolong its life until, in the Communications Act of 1934, the Federal Communications Commission was established as a permanent regulatory agency.

Public Interest, Convenience and Necessity

"Fairness" and "renewal" have become key words in broadcast regulation. Although they are only two of the implementational tools of the federal regulatory agency, they are symbols of its power and duty to protect and serve the "public interest, convenience, or necessity." The first statement of the broadcast regulatory agency on this subject was made in the context of the renewal process and issued on August 23, 1928. The Federal Radio Commission stated:

The Commission has been urged to give a precise definition of the phrase "public interest, convenience, or necessity . . . The Commission is convinced that the interest of the broadcast listener is of superior importance to that of the broadcaster and that it is better that there should be a few less broadcasters than that the listening public should suffer from undue interference. It is unfortunate that in the past the most vociferous public expression has been made by broadcasters or by persons speaking in their behalf and the real voice of the listening public has not sufficiently been heard. . . . While it is true that broadcasting stations in this country are for the most part supported or partially supported by advertisers, broadcasting stations are not given these great privileges by the U.S. Government for the primary benefit of advertisers. Such benefit as is derived by advertisers must be incidental and entirely secondary to the interest of the public. The emphasis must be first and foremost on the interest, the convenience, and the necessity of the listening public, and not on the interest, convenience or necessity of the individual broadcaster or the advertiser.

The degree to which the FRC and its successor, the FCC, effectively applied these principles is a matter of controversy and may be judged by an evaluation of FRC and FCC actions through the years.

The Federal Radio Commission

The FRC was given the authority to issue station licenses, allocate frequency bands to various radio services, including broadcasting, assign and require individual stations to operate on specific frequencies, and to limit power. Strong, immediate action by the FRC resulted in some 150 of the 732 stations on the air in 1927 relinquishing their licenses. The Radio Act of 1927, however, put part of the regulation of radio under the Secretary of Commerce, including the authority to inspect radio stations, to test and license radio operators, and to assign call signs for stations.

For its first year of existence the FRC foundered, without staff or space and without, indeed, a full Commission. The ties to vested interests, including those who would be regulated by the FRC, resulted in difficulties in getting Senate confirmations of nominees. It wasn't until March, 1928, with the appointment of Ira Robinson as chairman, that there was a full Commission.

Even during its first year the FRC considered approaches that reflected the drastic measures needed. These included the banning of commercials and taking action against the air "pirates" — those who went on the air on any frequency they wished without being licensed, similar to the wave of air "piracy" that struck Europe in the 1960's. The FRC issued licenses for 60-day periods only, and in 1928 held its first "renewal" hearings, for 164 stations. The FRC received praise for straightening out the chaos, but was criticized for the manner in which it did so. For example, in setting up

24 clear channel stations, the FRC assigned 21 to network stations. Educational stations, which up to that time constituted a large segment of radio broadcasting, were given limited hours of operation, mostly in the daytime hours, removing them from effective competition with commercial stations. Although the sense of Congress and other government officials who had been responsible for the FRC was that radio should not become an advertising medium, the FRC took no action in that direction, and by 1932 the Senate was impelled to pass a resolution concerning the growing dissatisfaction with the use of radio and even suggested an exploration of the "feasibility of government ownership and operation" of radio. The FRC's answer was that self-regulation was the best approach. The FRC did, however, strongly regulate educational stations — those licensed to colleges and universities — and arbitrarily shifted them about, in some instances deliberately to make room for commercial stations. Coupled with the economic depression, the FRC action caused these stations to go off the air in increasing numbers and resulted in the almost complete disappearance of educational broadcasting until the post World War II FM boom. There were efforts in 1932, following the formation of foundation-supported educational radio national committees, to obtain reserved channels, but the FRC accepted the strong opposition of the commercial interests to such a plan. As one FRC Commissioner, Harold A. LaFount, stated: "Commercialism is the heart of broadcasting in the United States. What has education contributed to radio? Not one thing. What has commercialism contributed? Everything — the life blood of the industry."

In 1933, after completing a six-month study of radio, including its advertising system, the FRC reported to Congress that "any plan . . . to eliminate the use of radio facilities for commercial advertising purposes, will if adopted destroy the present system of broadcasting."

At the same time, the FRC was taking action in specific cases that established the concept of "fairness" in content and was upheld by the courts on the question of its right to deny a license to a station that it deemed was not operating in the public interest, convenience or necessity.

Other precedent-setting actions by the FRC in the few years preceding the Communications Act of 1934 included deletion of licenses based on the Davis Amendment of 1927, which gave the Commission authority to allocate stations according to zone and state quota systems; requiring station breaks only every 30 minutes; and issuing regulations for the orderly transfer of licenses. In addition, an early question of station responsibility for content was established when the Nebraska Court ruled in 1932 that a station is equally liable with the speaker for any libelous statement broadcast over its facilities. The Interstate Commerce Commission ruled that same year that broadcasting stations were not public utilities and that the ICC had no authority to regulate their advertising rates. In 1933 Congress passed a Broadcasting Code setting minimum wages for radio broadcasting personnel, many of whom had worked at little or no pay in order to break into the growing and competitive medium. During those years frequent attempts were made to develop a practical frequency-sharing plan among the United States, Canada and Mexico, and though agreements were arranged with Canada, problems increased with across-the-Mexican-border broadcasting, a problem that was to take some 40 years to be resolved.

With the election of President Franklin D. Roosevelt in 1932, the development of a New Deal toward utilities, quasi-utilities and regulatory agencies, the economic crisis at home, the growing turmoil in Europe, and the realization by the President of the significant role communication plays in all human affairs, the groundwork was laid for a new, permanent communications regulatory body. The Communications Act was passed on June 19, 1934, with a Federal Communications Commission replacing the Federal Radio Commission on July 1.

The Federal Communications Commission

On July 11, 1934 the Federal Communications Commission began operating with E. O. Sykes, a member of the old FRC, as chairman. Some of the seven commissioners seemed determined to make it an entirely new organization. Commissioner George H. Payne publicly stated that, "There is a belief that our predecessor, the old Radio Commission, was dominated by the industry it was supposed to control. I am very happy to say that such is not now the case."

The FCC major areas of control of radio were in issuing licenses and renewals. The FCC allocates the use of spectrum space, determining what frequencies are to go to non-broadcast as well as broadcast services. Within the broadcast area are AM radio, FM radio, non-commercial FM radio, and television, as well as translator and auxiliary services. In 1934, however, the major concern was with what technology had developed up to that time: AM radio. In 1975, as this is being written, the license period is three years, with Congressional bills being considered that would extend that period. In 1934, however, licenses had to be renewed every six months. Much as does the FCC today, the early determinations of renewals were based principally on complaints filed against any given station and on programming summaries that were evaluated in terms of their meeting the local interest, convenience or necessity. The categories used in the early reports were "educational," "agricultural," "religious," "fraternal" and "entertainment." The Commission used the threat of a hearing on license renewals when it felt that it could not arbitrarily censor certain programming practices that it believed were clearly not in the public interest. Such threats resulted in the disappearance of lotteries (which were later prohibited by an amendment to the Communications Act) and liquor advertising, among other things.

Within a few years what was developed into and became known as the Fairness Doctrine became a significant and controversial issue. Shortly after its establishment in 1934 the FCC on several occasions affirmed the concept of "fairness," to the consternation of most of the broadcasting industry. In 1938 the FCC denied an application for a construction permit because the applicant refused to let its facilities be used by persons holding any viewpoint it did not hold. In 1940, in its Sixth Annual Report, the FCC stated that, "In carrying out the obligation to render a public service, stations are required to furnish well-rounded rather than one-sided discussions of public questions." And in the landmark *Mayflower* case in 1941 the FCC said: "Freedom of speech on the radio must be broad enough to provide full and equal opportunity for the presentation to the public of all sides of public issues . . . In brief, the broadcaster cannot be an advocate." In 1949 the FCC overrode the *Mayflower* decision to the extent that the broadcaster could be an advocate by editorializing, but that such editorializing must be within the bounds of "fairness" and "balance."

In April, 1935, under new chairman Anning S. Prall, the FCC seemed to move into a consumer-oriented activist stance, including warnings to stations about accepting medical advertising which was deluging the public with fraudulent cure-alls; the FCC emphasized the need for the broadcast industry to adhere to the rules and regulations; the FCC reflected the growing public concern about good taste in broadcasting and called a meeting with network heads on that subject; it called a national meeting to try to work out ways of establishing better relationships between the radio industry and education, which had by then lost, in great measure due to adverse FRC action, virtually all its stations. In October of 1935 the FCC indicated its desire to meet the public interest by issuing only temporary renewals to a large number of stations pending its investigation of those stations' programming that it considered questionable. In 1936 the still fledgling FCC dealt with regulatory areas ranging from changing the requirement for announcements of recordings and transcriptions to only one per quarter-hour, to setting up hearings on new allocations of frequencies and power as a result of the repeal of the Davis Amendment to the Communications Act. The Davis Amendment had required the equal division of radio facilities among five geographical zones and among the states within each of the zones. With its repeal the way was opened for more stations and higher power. A Supreme Court decision with special portent for the future of broadcasting held that broadcasting was interstate, as opposed to intrastate, commerce. In 1938, establishing a policy that would be reflected in the multiple ownership rules of more than 30 years in the future, the FCC announced that it would not grant a licensee a second station in the same community unless it was clearly shown that such a license would be in the public interest. After a number of years of pressure by educational and citizen groups, the FCC in 1938 allocated 25 channels for "curricular" use by educational institutions. In that same year the FCC began asking stations to submit financial reports.

In 1939, in continuing efforts to determine the need and direction of regulation over the growing industry, the FCC sent 30-page questionnaires to all stations, asking for detailed information on their operations. Also in 1939 radio's long sought-for license extension was achieved when the FCC extended the period from six months to one year. An Appelate Court ruling shortly afterward put a new light on the issuing of licenses. Despite strong FCC objections, the Court ruled that economic interests and open competition must be considered important factors in licensing stations.

1940 brought the entire broadcasting industry closer to a new realignment, as both war and television loomed larger. The FCC attempted to establish more comprehensive approaches to licensing, delving into legal, economic, programming and engineering aspects of proposed stations. Its new application form of 42 pages caused consternation in the industry. The FCC also established FM radio in 1940, authorizing commercial FM operations on 35 channels in the 43 to 50 megacycle band. By the end of 1941 the two major events that were to change broadcasting had occurred: the entry of the United States into World War II and the authorization on July 1 of commercial television operation. It was a year of many decisions for the FCC, including a strong stand on monopoly, in which it ordered public hearings on newspaper ownership of broadcasting stations — an issue still strong more than 30 years later; the adoption of an order prohibiting multiple ownership of stations in the same market; the opening up of the legal development of broadcasting to the public by permitting any person, not only an applicant, to petition for a change in the rules of practice or procedure; and the extension of the license term for broadcasting stations from one to two years. Within months after Pearl Harbor, however, radio and all areas of communications were put under the jurisdiction of the Defense Communications Board, and the FCC froze broadcast assignments and station construction for the duration of the war.

At the same time, the importance of radio to the war effort was recognized by the FCC in easing operator requirements to keep stations on the air, and by the Selective Service System in declaring broadcasting an essential industry. Radio had reached a zenith that it would not again regain — at least not in the same way or direction. But what it had accomplished, in making people, programs and products an integral part of the fabric of American society, was beyond all expectation. The years following the Communications Act of 1934 to the freeze of 1942 were indeed fabulous years.

Radio's Heyday

The salon orchestras, political and sports reporting and voices of famous people that began the programming development of radio in the early 1920's "segued" (seg-wayed) into entertainment personalities who provided some of the greatest comedy and variety produced in America. In the 1930's Ben Bernie, Rudy Vallee, Eddie Cantor, Amos n' Andy, Burns and Allen, Fibber McGee and Molly, Jack Benny and Mary Livingston, Joe Penner, Edgar Bergen and Charlie McCarthy, Bob Hope, Ed Wynn, Fred Allen and countless more became better known than they had in theatre, the films or vaudeville.

There was considerably more than comedy and variety. For the first time drama came right into the home, alternating between pop mystery and adventure such as "The Shadow," "The Lone Ranger" and "Big Town" and the serious, excellently produced drama of such programs as "The Lux Radio Theatre," "Dupont Cavalcade of America," and Orson Welles' "Mercury Theatre." The "Mercury Theatre" production of "Invasion from Mars" in 1938 proved the power of radio to affect not only the minds and emotions of people, but also their actions, causing near-panic in many places in the country.

Great writers emerged, with radio developing to a high point of art through the efforts of people such as Norman Corwin and Archibald MacLeish, and providing a creative base for new writers such as Arthur Miller.

The "soap opera" became endemic to American culture, with the characters on "Ma Perkins," "Mary Noble, Backstage Wife," "Young Dr. Malone" and so many others becoming extensions of real families throughout the country.

The openness with which controversial issues were discussed, through a modified form of debate presenting a variety of viewpoints, made "Town Meeting of the Air" a program yet to be equalled.

Every child knew the format, characters, theme song and commercials of "The Singing Lady," "Uncle Don," "The Horn and Hardart Children's Hour," "Let's Pretend," "Little Orphan Annie," "Jack Armstrong" and "Chandu the Magician."

And the quiz and expert and audience participation shows, creating a new form of entertainment and to many a convoluted concept of education and intelligence! No one who has ever heard them will forget the sense of anticipation of "I have a lady in the balcony, Doctor"; the call of "Johnny presents . . ." to the strains of the Grand Canyon Suite; "Can You Top This"'s topper: ". . . three men were floating down the river on a marble raft . . ."; "The Quiz Kids"; and the forerunner of its famous and infamous television counterparts, "The $64 Question" — it was during the depression of the 1930's and the weekly cry "You'll be sorry" meant that the $32 lost equalled a month's rent.

And how many youngsters (and oldsters) went on to stardom from the votes of the transfixed weekly listening public of "Major Bowes Amateur Hour": "Round and round she goes . . ."!

Radio became indispensable for special events, some planned and some on-the-spot. President Franklin D. Roosevelt's "Fireside Chats," the Zeppelin Hindenburg disaster, the trial of Bruno Hauptmann, the abdication of King Edward VIII, the opening of the New York World's Fair of 1939, the Olympics of 1936, the professional championship prizefights which seemed to be on almost every week, the reports from a war-primed Europe, including the voices of those who would affect the lives of all of us listening over here — Churchill, Hitler, Mussolini. The individual personalities who became experts and demi-gods through a disembodied voice bringing "the word" to America: Ben Grauer, Red Barber, Arthur Godfrey, Graham McNamee, Gabriel Heatter, Walter Winchell, Lowell Thomas, Fulton Lewis Jr., Elmer Davis, H. V. Kaltenborn, among others.

Along the way the successful formats became fixed — the comedy-variety show, the mystery-adventure drama, the gag-situation comedy, the star drama, the quiz-experts show, the live orchestra or band, the news commentator. Some new styles developed, some emulated successfully — anyone alive then will hum with youthful nostalgia to their dying day the theme from Martin Block's "Make Believe Ballroom," which launched the disc jockey and d.j. program as a staple of American radio. Some programs remained virtually one of a kind — there was hardly a teen-age party which was not scheduled around the Saturday night "Lucky Strike Hit Parade."

It is significant that the revival of "old-time radio" in the early 1970's — increasing numbers of both commercial and non-commercial radio stations were broadcasting programs from the 1930's and 1940's — appealed as much to young people who had never heard the originals as to those of middle-age who listened as much for nostalgia as for entertainment.

The growth of radio — that is, the economic base to make possible entertainers of stature and high salaries — paralleled and was due to the growth of networks. By guaranteeing a certain number of affiliates, networks could guarantee the financial resources for high-cost productions. As noted earlier, AT&T's withdrawal from network control resulted in the establishment of the NBC Red Network in 1927, the conversion of the RCA-Westinghouse-General Electric chain to the NBC Blue Network, the development of the CBS Network out of the Columbia Phonograph Recording Company, and the establishment of the Mutual Broadcasting System in 1934. In 1945 the government required NBC to divest itself of its multi-network operation, and it sold the Blue Network, which became ABC, the American Broadcasting Company. A number of regional networks were developed, some failed and some remained. New national networks were tried, but none succeeded. The four national networks, NBC, MBS, CBS and ABC steadily grew.

With the advent of television and the gradual disappearance of the personality program, networks had less to sell to individual stations, and many stations found little value in network affiliation. The early 1950's found networks readjusting rates, and seeking formats and economic bases to regain or add affiliates. By 1975, with the development of new programming and organizational approaches, the coming-of-age of FM radio, and a dramatic rise in the number of local stations throughout the country, network affiliates had reached a relative stability, with NBC having about 240, CBS about 250, MBS about 660 plus a Black network of over 90, and ABC, as a result of a four-network organization in 1968, some 1,400. In addition, National Public Radio served about 175 stations, and the National Black Network about 75.

During World War II radio increased in prestige and popularity, with the American public eager to know immediately — before the newspapers could edit, print and distribute the information — what was happening in the war, particularly from correspondents on the scene, such as the reports of Edward R. Murrow from bomb-wracked London.

Sometimes the on-the-spot coverage made it a truly "You Are There" experience. On September 13, 1943 General Dwight D. Eisenhower himself broadcast the news of Italy's surrender, the first time such an event was first announced by radio.

Because television, which had begun public broadcasts in 1939, was suspended in 1942 for the duration of the war, radio continued after the war for several years as strongly as it had before. It wasn't until the operation of regional TV networks in the late 1940's and national live TV networks in the early 1950's that radio suddenly found itself the "second" medium and went into a decline, having to reorganize its operations and programming format. Its immediate post-war contributions, still and all, were among its greatest, including such productions as "On a Note of Triumph," "Ballad for Americans," and the popularity of personalities who took special advantage of the medium's potentials, such as Henry Morgan and Bob and Ray.

The war and its ending also brought the federal government, principally through the FCC, into the metamorphosis of radio.

WORLD WAR II: TRANSITION AND CHANGE

The FCC was attacked from many quarters. In 1943 Georgia Congressman Eugene Cox called the FCC the "nastiest nest of rats in this entire country" and the House approved his resolution to investigate the FCC. Later that same year the Supreme Court upheld the FCC's authority to regulate broadcasting, including its network monopoly rules. The FCC that year banned multiple ownership of standard broadcast stations in the same market and extended the license period to three years. For several years the FCC had been considering the possibility of a rule concerning newspaper ownership of stations, but in early 1944 decided against it; it would be 25 years before the issue would be full blown again.

FM operations, which were authorized to begin January 1, 1941 after extensive public hearings, were frozen during the war as was all radio construction, although the 40 stations on the air continued to serve about 400,-000 receivers. Shortly after V-E day the FCC moved FM to a more desirable part of the spectrum, 88 to 108 MHz, and provided 80 channels for commercial use and 20, in the lowest part of the band, for non-commercial educational purposes. Later that year the FCC issued a tentative allocation plan that would accommodate some 1,500 commercial FM stations throughout the country.

As radio grew so did regulatory requirements. Even as the war was ending in 1945 the FCC set forth new requirements for ownership and financial reporting by stations, and late in the year the Supreme Court ruled that the FCC was required to have hearings on all mutually exclusive applications before granting a construction permit. The most famous regulatory document, the FCC "Blue Book," was issued in March of 1946. This report, "Public Service Responsibility of Broadcast Licensees," stated that the FCC would give "particular consideration" to certain kinds of programming for renewal of station licenses, including sustaining programs, local live programs, and programs devoted to discussion of public issues. It also listed the elimination of advertising excesses as a factor in license renewal. It suggested an 80% commercial — 20% sustaining time ratio. The National Association of Broadcasters led a generally shocked radio industry by stating that the basic freedoms of radio were at stake.

Despite the doom predicted by many because of stronger regulation, radio grew and by the end of 1945 over 1,000 stations were licensed. Within another year some 93% of all American homes had radio sets, a jump of some 20% from the pre-war year of 1940. With the power and effect of the media growing, the concept of fairness began to evolve and in 1949 the FCC approved editorializing by stations within as yet undefined limits of "fairness" and "balance." A year later it clarified this decision by adding that stations have "an affirmative duty to seek out, aid and encourage the broadcast of opposing views in controversial questions of public importance."

On the broader scene, however, conformity of thought and opinion was being officially sanctioned by networks and stations, cooperating fully with the suppression of dissent, real or imagined, that became known as "McCarthyism." The first prominent artist blacklisted was Jean Muir, fired from "The Aldrich Family" by General Foods. Literal "blacklists" and then "graylists" were used by networks, stations and advertising agencies in hiring all personnel, including actors, writers and directors, and it became sufficient for someone merely to be accused of "communism" to frighten the radio industry into barring them from making a living. Before the end of 1950 blacklisting became a way of life in broadcasting, including NBC inquiring into its employees' past political party affiliations and CBS requiring all employees to sign loyalty oaths. The blacklist was to continue for many years, well past the death of Senator McCarthy, and was to destroy careers, reputations and lives.

Even as radio grew, television began to create meaningful competition, and radio started to make adjustments. At the beginning of 1950 there were more than 2,000 AM and more than 700 FM stations on the air. Although only about 100 television stations were in operation, their rapid increase within the next few years, coupled with regional and national interconnection, began to draw advertisers away from the older medium. In 1951 a series of rate-cuttings began in radio that was to continue for many years and would include changes in network option time, in allowing advertisers to pick specific markets as opposed to the previous policy of "must buys," and in providing top talent for local sales by local stations. Recognizing the "prime time" changes, radio began to drop nighttime rates substantially and to raise daytime and morning rates.

Television grew so quickly that 1953 was the last year in which radio revenues ($474.6 million) were larger than television's ($431.8 million). Through ebb and flow radio revenues increased only to 591.9 million in 1960 and $776.8 million in 1965 (it wasn't until 1964 that radio's income climbed back to where it had been in 1952), while TV revenues quickly passed the billion mark and reached $1,268.6 million in 1960 and $1,964.8 million in 1965, going over $2 billion the following year. By 1955, 439 TV stations were on the air, virtually saturating the large-city VHF spectrum; by 1960 growth had slowed, with 573 TV stations on the air; in 1965 there were 586. Radio, on the other hand, increased voluminously, with 2,669 AM, 552 FM and 122 non-commercial FM stations in operation in 1955; 3,456 AM, 678 FM and 162 non-commercial FM in 1960; 4,012 AM, 1,270 FM and 255 non-commercial FM in 1965; 4,447 AM, 2,678 FM and 770 non-commercial FM in 1975.

The first major overhaul of the Communications Act of 1934 was the McFarland Bill in 1952, which permitted the FCC to issue cease-and-desist orders in addition to revoking licenses, and to prohibit broadcasters from charging more for political advertising than for regular business advertising; required the FCC to explain to Congress any delay of over three months after filing or six months after hearing on a case; prohibited staff members from recommending actions to Commissioners; required the FCC to prove that a licensee was not qualified for renewal; deleted FCC authority to revoke licenses of stations found guilty in federal court of antitrust violations; permitted protests against grants for up to 30 days after a grant, and required the FCC to answer protests or petitions for a rehearing within 15 days; and forbade Commissioners from practicing before the FCC for one year following a resignation.

Broadcasting became so profitable and its influence so great that many abuses began to creep in, including the infamous "payola" and "plugola" scandals of 1958 and 1959 in which some disc jockeys were bribed by record companies and distributors with more than $250,000 to promote their records. Both the FCC and the FTC went after the wrongdoers, and Congress passed legislation against the practice. One of the consequences was an FCC emendation of the sponsor identification requirements to include on-the-air announcement of all free program material and how it was acquired.

In the early 1960's radio was boosted by several technical developments: multiplexing, stereophonic broadcasting, and the mass distribution of transistors. One FCC action in 1961 presaged requirements of a decade later: an FM station applicant was denied a grant for failure to ascertain local program needs.

Faced with uncontrolled growth of radio, the FCC in 1962 put a freeze on AM construction and began a revision of FM rules, including the designation of more classes of stations, tighter mileage separations, and the issuance of a proposed FM table of allocations. A little-noted, but significant milestone that was to result in a nationwide network 10 years later was the hook-up in the fall of 1962 of eight non-commercial educational FM stations in the northeast into the Educational Radio Network.

In 1964 the FCC lifted the AM freeze, setting new rigid technical requirements. It also limited FM duplication of AM programming, a standard practice by AM-FM owners, to 50% in cities of 100,000 or more population. Advertising continued to grow, and in 1967 the NAB radio code board removed its self-imposed 18-minute per hour limit on commercials for "good cause" in "special circumstances." 1967 was a landmark for non-commercial radio with the Public Broadcasting Act covering both television and radio and including radio for the first time in the matching grants facilities program of the U.S. Office of Education.

RECENT FCC REGULATION

The late 1960's and early 1970's was a time of re-evaluation of the status of radio and the beginning of re-regulation.

In 1967 the FCC put a new freeze on AM radio, which it lifted partially in 1973 and somewhat more in 1975, accepting applications for new daytime, unlimited time and nighttime-expansion facilities in communities having fewer than two independent stations during the proposed period of service, and from applicants who would provide first-time primary service to at least 25% of their coverage area.

In 1969 the FCC required broadcasters to establish equal employment opportunity programs for every aspect of station employment policy and practices. The following year the FCC proposed rules to bar an owner of any full-time broadcasting station (AM, FM or TV) from acquiring another station in the same market. In the late 1960's and early 1970's a plethora of regulatory action related to protecting the public interest was taken by the FCC, much of it based on court decisions, pressures from citizen groups, Congressional laws and new technical developments. The nature of the entire broadcasting field began to change.

Perhaps the most significant event was the WLBT case of 1964 in which the FCC renewed the license of the Jackson, Mississippi television station after documented protests by the United Church of Christ that the station was blatantly segregationist in employment and programming, despite a 45% Black population in the station's viewing area. Following court appeals by the United Church of Christ, the United States Appeals Court ruled in 1966 that the FCC should have taken into consideration the findings and interests of the citizen group, although it was not a direct party to the renewal proceeding, and thus established the principle that responsible and representative public groups should be allowed to participate as parties to FCC proceedings. This led to subsequent participation by many minority groups, including Blacks, Spanish-surnamed and women, in complaints and challenges against applicants and stations, and included "strike" applications — that is, filing on top of a licensee at renewal time. The pressures resulted in stations and networks beginning to change employment and programming policies and opening broadcasting's doors to minorities. Many groups began to emulate the United Church of Christ in its efforts to achieve greater citizen participation in the business of broadcasting, including the National Citizens' Committee for Broadcasting; Black Efforts for Soul in Television (BEST); the Citizen's Communications Center; the Communications Task Force of National Organization for Women; the Stern Community Law Firm and, in the area of children's programming, Action for Children's Television (ACT).

The FCC recognized the need for regulatory action in this area and in early 1971 issued a "Primer for Ascertainment of Community Needs," in which all commercial stations, both television and radio, were obliged to determine, in consultation with community leaders and organizations, the needs of their respective communities and the way in which their programming could meet those needs. The 1969 rules prohibiting licensees from discriminating in their employment practices with respect to race, color, religion and national origin also required stations to establish and maintain equal employment opportunity programs. Subsequently, stations with five or more employees were required to file annual reports, and in 1972 women were included as a minority group. Whether the FCC adequately enforced these rules was an issue raised by a number of sources at subsequent renewal times.

In 1972 the first Black to be a Commissioner, Benjamin L. Hooks, was appointed to the FCC. In 1973 the term of Commissioner Nicholas

Johnson, who had been the severest critic of the FCC in regard to its public interest actions, expired.

The civil rights ferment of the early 1960's, the subsequent militant attacks on radio's public service and employment practices, and the citizen challenges to license renewals contributed to a new programming phenomenon in the early 1970's: ethnic radio. Although there had been many Black-oriented stations before, few were owned by Blacks. More and more stations began to program for minorities, and even a Black network was established.

The Fairness Doctrine became a significant and controversial issue. The *Mayflower* decision of 1941 provided the base for the FCC standard, that a station provide comparable time for other sides of an issue of a controversial nature in a community where the station had presented only one side of that issue. In the *Red Lion* decision, dealing with the Red Lion Broadcasting Company's station in Media, Pennsylvania, the Supreme Court unanimously ruled in 1969 that the FCC's personal attack and political editorial rules were both Congressionally authorized and constitutionally valid and that the Fairness Doctrine regulations "enhance rather than abridge the freedoms of speech and press protected by the First Amendment." The Court held that licensees "must give adequate coverage to public issues . . . and coverage must be fair in that it accurately reflects the opposing views." The FCC revoked the Red Lion station's license. The debate over the concept of "fairness" was on again, however, as it had been more than three decades before, and many important segments in and out of the broadcasting industry clamored for an end to the Fairness Doctrine.

The "Equal Time" rule for political broadcasts became an issue, too, with the broadcasting industry in general pushing hard for repeal of this rule. During presidential election years, in order to encourage stations to provide time for the major candidates and not, as the equal time provision would require, for all, including minority party candidates for a particular office — which stations were reluctant to do, thus reducing the amount of time offered to major candidates — Congress regularly suspended the rule for presidential and vice-presidential races. Relatively little free time was provided by commercial networks and stations for actual campaigning — although most candidates received a fair amount of news coverage, and some educational stations devoted many hours to presentation of all candidates for one or more offices in their communities — and in the 1972 election campaigns candidates for all offices spent a total of $59.6 million on broadcast ads, $37.5 million of which was for radio.

A most significant action, with portent for affecting the entire advertising structure of broadcasting, was the 1970 passage by Congress of the Public Health Cigarette Smoking Act of 1969, which included the prohibition of broadcast advertising of cigarettes after January 1, 1971. The issue had been raised several years earlier by an individual citizen, John F. Banzhaf, who was responsible for a milestone when the FCC agreed with his complaint that cigarette commercials presented only one side of a controversial issue, smoking, and that the Fairness Doctrine applied, requiring presentation of a contrary view.

In the early 1970's, however, a series of decisions by the FCC that the Fairness Doctrine did not apply to commercial announcements (e.g. a citizen's group concerned with ecology sought time to respond to gasoline commercials; a businessmen's group attempted to place paid advertising against the war in southeast Asia) was upheld by the courts.

Multiple ownership rules were strengthened in the late 1960's and early 1970's, again much to the displeasure of most of the leaders of the broadcasting industry. Common ownership is limited to seven AM, seven FM and seven TV stations, no more than five of which may be VHF. In addition, common ownership of different broadcast services in the same market is prohibited with the exception of AM-FM combinations, and with the grandfathering of existing cross-ownership prior to the March 25, 1970 order.

Some FCC actions created unexpected controversy of considerable proportion. One was the 1971 order requiring stations to review the lyrics of all records played to avoid any promotion, through such lyrics, of drugs. In 1973 the FCC fined a station for its so-called "topless" radio format — a phone-in format in which women, particularly, were encouraged to discuss their sex lives — and, through thinly veiled threats against other stations, successfully eliminated that short-lived but highly popular programming approach. The question of obscenity had been raised on a number of occasions and in two important cases — including a nominal fine of a noncommercial educational station which had aired a program containing profanity — the FCC had sought a test case in the courts. It wasn't until 1975, however, that Pacifica became the first licensee to carry their case to the courts.

Since the growth of television the FCC had frequently treated both media more or less as a unit, with overall regulations developed for television generally applied as a package to radio as well. For example, pressure built up in the late 1960's and early 1970's for new procedures for renewal of station licenses, the need evolving principally in terms of television and spurred by the increasing number of petitions challenging renewal applications. In May, 1973 the FCC ordered renewal applications to be filed four instead of three months prior to expiration of the license in order to provide more time for the public to file opposition, such opposition having to be in at least one month prior to the expiration date. The new rules also required licensees to make more public announcements on the impending renewal and on how the public could file comments with the FCC. The rules also alleviated some of the paper work and forms required for renewal filings.

But even as this kind of approach to regulation continued, administration spokesmen and the broadcasting industry in the early 1970's were campaigning to treat radio as a separate entity. Dr. Clay T. Whitehead, Director of the Office of Telecommunications Policy, suggested in 1971 that radio be considered more like magazines than like television, and that it be "de-regulated." The FCC subsequently set up a "re-regulation" Task Force and by mid-1973 had begun changing a number of rules specifically for radio, making station operations easier, such as permitting third class instead of first class operators to carry out routine operations of certain kinds of radio stations. The Task Force clarified and simplified a number of rules in terms of the state of the art in the early 1970's and eliminated a number of rules that no longer applied. Checking equipment, notifications and reporting, keeping records and a number of on-the-air operations such as rebroadcasting material from another station, mechanical reproductions and station-break requirements were made easier. Other major changes included a Further Notice of Inquiry on ascertainment, and a new short form for renewals, in 1975.

In the 1970's technical innovation began to motivate significant change for broadcasting, some evolutionary, some revolutionary. After decades of planning and discussion, an agreement with Mexico was finally concluded, allocating frequencies along the border states, and a new agreement with Canada seemed likely by the late-1970's. The development of cable (CATV) was beginning to prompt entirely new approaches on the part of the television industry, and CATV's plans for two-way and multi-way interconnections, including voice channels, suggested entirely new approaches for radio as well in the not-too-distant future. International and domestic satellite agreements and authorization also presaged important changes for broadcasting, including radio as we knew it in the early 1970's. The needs of business radio, mobile services, inter-city relay and other growing areas of use required reevaluation of spectrum allocations.

Although not yet, and probably not in the near future, a serious competing force for commercial radio, non-commercial educational radio (or, as it is also called, public radio) began to grow, with 821 educational/public radio stations on the air in late 1975. The establishment of National Public Radio, a national network, in the early 1970's solidified the status and aided the growth of this service.

Licensing Procedure

Although seemingly complex to the layperson, the process of obtaining a radio station license is a relatively simple one, provided the applicant accurately meets the engineering, legal, financial and programming requirements.

AM and non-commercial FM applicants must make their own search for a frequency which will not cause or receive interference from existing stations. Commercial FM applicants must find an unused channel from the nationwide city-by-city table of allocations. An application for a construction permit is filed first, in which the applicant demonstrates fulfillment of the legal qualifications for licensing, including citizenship; financial qualifications, including sufficient funds on hand to build and equip the station and operate it for at least one year; engineering qualifications, including transmitting apparatus to be used and antenna and studio locations; programming qualifications, including clear indication that the service proposed will meet the community's needs. All applicants, including those making major changes in existing stations, selling a station or filing for renewal of license, must give public notice of their intention so that any interested party may have time to file comments. Applicants and stations must also keep reference files available to the public.

The FCC cannot take action on an accepted application prior to a 30-day statutory period. This provides time not only for comments, but for competing applications to be filed. Presuming the application is in good order and there are no competing applications or valid protests, the FCC processing system usually grants a construction permit in about three months time. If there is a serious question the application may go to hearing. A hearing is mandatory for valid competing applications. The hearing procedure takes place initially before an Administrative Law Judge, but then may be heard by the FCC Review Board and, finally, by the Commission. Ultimately, the case might even be taken to the courts.

After receiving a construction permit, the permittee must complete construction of the station and file for a license within 12 months. If delayed, the permittee may apply for an extension of time. When all the terms and obligations set forth in the construction permit are complied with, a license may be applied for, at which time the permittee can request authority to conduct program tests. With the granting of this authority the station is, in effect, on the air.

Commercial stations are subject to a fee schedule: 1) a filing fee, which is payable when the application is submitted; 2) a grant fee, which is payable when the application is granted; and 3) an annual operating fee. Filing and grant fees are based on the type of station and operating fees on the station's highest commercial announcement rate.

Programming

With the competition of television in the late 1940's and early 1950's radio had to change its programming policies and techniques drastically.

For a short while some of the personalities of the 1930's and 1940's continued their 30-minute and 60-minute programs on radio. Then came a transition period of dual programs, on radio and TV both, then the gradual dropping of the radio program for the TV series. New personalities, such as Milton Berle and Sid Caesar, went into television, not radio. Formulas began to change, the music-news approach becoming a quick substitute for the personality program on radio in the early 1950's. Give-away programs still tried to hold listeners. "Rock 'n roll" and the Beatles came into being and provided a charged, new music for the d.j. program. NBC sought an entirely new format and the "Monitor" magazine concept developed. By the early 1960's the general approach of radio had changed from that of mass listening to the personalized concept, with specialized programs and the gradual growth of highly specialized stations, such as the all-news format. Experiment and change were constant, and even as country music, the "Nashville sound," became popular in 1963, that same year, after 33 years, CBS ended its Philharmonic radio concerts. News began to grow, boosted by surveys which showed listeners placing higher and higher value on radio as a prime news source. "Talk" radio was headlined by several trade publications in 1966 as the "newest route to profits." All through this period, from the initial displacement of radio by television through the late 1960's, there was constant change based on the recognition that the radio "program" was dead and that the "formula" was the new way of life. Stations attempted to orient their programming to a day-long listener loyalty that transcended individual programs or personalities. The "Top-40" formula, for example, became widely prized and saved many stations from bankruptcy and made others more successful than they had been before. In more recent years MOR, "Middle-of-the-Road," has become a staple formula for radio. In every community each station finds "its own thing." With the number of radio stations growing at an unprecedented rate each station seeks its own type of specialization in order to attract and hold a concrete, loyal segment of the potential audience of its listening area.

Owners, managers and personnel of a radio station are faced with a two-sided decision today: economics require them to determine which format is going to enable the station to "make it" in its particular market; public interest, convenience and necessity require them to determine which programming is going to meet the real needs of the people to whom they broadcast. It is a wise and fortunate operation which does both.

FCC Rules Summary

The FCC periodically issues a general summary of rules and regulations entitled "The FCC and Broadcasting." The following is from the March, 1975 bulletin:

1(a). *What the Commission Does.* Congress created the Federal Communications Commission in 1934 for the purpose (among other things) of "regulating interstate and foreign commerce in communication by wire and radio so as to make available, as far as possible, to all the people of the United States a rapid, efficient, nation-wide, and world-wide wire and radio communications service . . ." Thus, the Commission regulates not only all broadcasting stations in this country, but also all interstate and foreign telephone, telegraph and cable service, and communications by satellite. The Commission regulates certain aspects of cable television (CATV) systems, although the franchising or licensing of such systems in the first instance is a matter for determination by municipalities according to local law. The

FCC also licenses and regulates more than 1,800,000 stations which you cannot hear on the regular broadcast bands, including public safety and industrial services, air, land and water transportation communications, and the amateur and citizens bands. In 40 years the number of Commission licensed stations has increased by over 3,500 per cent. At present, in 1975, approximately 8,300 radio and television broadcasting stations are on the air and several hundred more have been authorized. Most of these are licensed for commercial operation, and are supported by advertising revenue. However, there are approximately 750 noncommercial FM stations, 25 noncommercial educational Standard (AM) stations and about 250 noncommercial television stations operating. In order to provide better broadcasting service to the American people and a greater variety of programming, the Commission has consistently encouraged the expansion of all forms of broadcasting, including educational (noncommercial) broadcast services. The Commission does not regulate closed-circuit television operations, and, accordingly, does not control what events may be carried by closed circuit or the prices that may be charged. Furthermore, the FCC has no regulatory authority over the promoters of prize fights or other sporting events, bullfighting, rodeos or other exhibitions, as such, and cannot direct them to offer or refrain from offering such events to any person or persons for exhibition, including networks or broadcast stations. Arrangements for exhibitions of this kind are the subject of private contractual agreements between the owners of the rights and other parties thereto. The Commission does not license Canadian, Mexican or other foreign stations nor does it regulate any aspect of the operation of such stations. The names and addresses of the government agencies of Canada and Mexico which regulate broadcasting in these countries are listed in the Addendum hereto. Such monitoring of broadcast stations as the Commission is able to do is directed principally to detection of technical violations, such as operation with unauthorized power or on a frequency other than the one assigned. A frequently misunderstood matter is the fact that standard transmissions cover greater distances at night, and therefore many stations in the standard (AM) broadcast band must limit their operating power at night, or cease operating altogether, to avoid interference with other stations on the same or adjacent frequencies. Licenses for daytime operation were originally sought by the applicants with the knowledge that requests for operations of full time facilities cannot always be granted because of serious electrical interference with established nighttime stations. FM and TV stations are authorized to operate unlimited hours. The Communications Act provides that the Commission "may grant construction permits and station licenses, or modification or renewals thereof, only upon written applications therefore received by it."

1(b). *Licensing and Operating of Educational Stations.* Under the Communications Act, the Commission licenses educational radio and television stations to provide non-profit, non-commercial broadcast services, although under a special rule, FM educational stations may charge for authorized educational material transmitted by sub-carriers simultaneously with main channel programming (multiplexing), provided funds retained by the station licensees do not exceed actual costs incurred by the stations in the presentation of the program material. Educational stations may transmit educational, cultural and entertainment programs and programs designed for use by schools and school systems, but may not engage in editorializing or support or oppose any candidates for political office. Section 326 of the Act prohibits Commission censorship of broadcast matter, and the Commission does not attempt to direct either its commercial or noncommercial broadcast licensees to present or refrain from presenting specific programs.

1(c). *Construction Grants and Special Funding; The Corporation for Public Broadcasting; Retention and Availability of Certain Broadcast Matter; Educational Broadcasting Organizations.* The construction of noncommercial educational broadcasting facilities is assisted by matching grants of federal funds under the administration of the Department of Health, Education and Welfare, as provided in the Communications Act. In 1967, by amendment to the Act, the Congress established the Corporation for Public Broadcasting declaring "that a private corporation should be created to facilitate the development of educational radio and television broadcasting and to afford maximum protection to such broadcasting from extraneous interference and control." The CPB is a nonprofit corporation and is not an agency or establishment of the United States Government. The FCC believes it was the intent of the Congress to keep the Corporation free from government control [Communications Act, Sec. 398] and the Commission holds that it would not be warranted in attempting to oversee the Corporation's execution of its duties. CPB contributes to the growth and development of educational broadcasting by, among other things, assisting in financing programs for such broadcasting from its funds, which come from congressional appropriations and private sources. Under an amendment to the Communications Act, each licensee receiving assistance from CPB is required to retain for 60 days a recording of the sound portion of its broadcast of any program in which any issue of public importance is discussed, and during the period make a copy of such recording available to the FCC upon request and to any other person upon payment to the licensee or its designated entity of its reasonable cost of making such copy.

2(a). *Licensing of Broadcasting Facilities and Licensee Responsibilities; FCC Cannot Censor; Audience Expression.* The Commission is prohibited by law from censoring broadcast matter, does not attempt to direct broadcasters in the selection or presentation of specific programming and is not the arbiter of taste. However, no application for the construction of a broadcast station (or for the licensing or renewal of license of the same) will be granted unless the Commission finds that the public interest, convenience and necessity will be served by such a grant. Applicants are expected to show what they have done to ascertain the problems and needs of the people in the communities to which the stations are to be licensed and other areas undertaken to be served, and what broadcast matter is proposed to meet those problems and needs as evaluated. A copy of the Commission's "Primer on Ascertainment of Community Problems by Broadcast Applicants" is available upon request. Commercial television station licensees are also required to file with the Commission an Annual Programming Report showing the amount of time and perecentage of total operating time devoted to various types of programs other than entertainment and sports. Concerned persons are urged to express their views on programming, preferably in writing, directly to stations and networks. (See Section 4 below regarding "The Public and Broadcasting — A Procedure Manual.")

2(b). *Printed Matter, Films and Recordings; Audience Survey, News Gathering and Music Licensing Organizations; Certain FCC Licensing and Programming Policies Under Continuing Study; Network Formation and Affiliation.* Since the Commission at times receives comments, inquiries and complaints concerning motion pictures, newspapers, magazines and other forms of printed matter and the manufacture and sale of phonograph recordings, it should be made clear that persons or firms engaged in motion picture production or exhibition, in publishing, or the manufacture or distribution of recordings, as such, are not subject to regulation by the Commision, nor does the FCC assign ratings (R, X, etc.) to films. However, persons or firms engaged in these activities may hold ownership interests in licensees of broadcast stations which are subject to the provisions of law and appropriate Commission policies. The FCC has no jurisdiction over news gathering organizations, including press associations, and thus cannot direct them in servicing their publishing and broadcast licensee clients with news and comment. Similarly, the Commission cannot direct music licensing organizations, such as ASCAP, BMI and SESAC, as to their licensing procedures. The Commission has no regulatory authority over survey firms that measure the size and other characteristics of broadcast audiences although it would be concerned if broadcast station licensees were to disseminate false or deceptive information or claims regarding audiences, geographical coverage, station power or other aspects of their service. The FCC has under review its policies regarding concentration of media control, broadcast ownership by so-called "conglomerate" firms, and of major TV network ownership of programs. The Commission does not attempt to direct any person to form or refrain from forming any network nor does it direct any of its licensees to affiliate or refrain from affiliating with any network or networks. Network organizations are not licensed by the Commission except insofar as they may be owners of individual broadcast stations.

3. *Public Inspection of Applications and Other Material.* Each broadcasting station is required to maintain for public inspection during regular business hours in the community to which it is licensed a "public file" with copies of most applications filed with the Commission, reports of station ownership, the FCC's pamphlet, "The Public and Broadcasting — A Procedure Manual" (see Section 4 below), and certain other material. Also, commercial radio and television stations are required to retain in the file for three years, with certain exceptions, mail and other written comment

from the public regarding station operation and programming efforts. Additionally, commercial television station public files must contain copies of the Annual Programming Report referred to in 2(a) above as well as an annual listing of (no more than 10) problems and needs of the area served and typical and illustrative programming broadcast in response to them in the preceding twelve months. Members of the public need not make appointments to inspect the public file of a station nor are they required to examine its contents only at times most convenient to the licensee or members of his staff. Copies of all applications, as well as various other documents, also are available for public inspection in the Commission's headquarters in Washington.

The FCC has adopted regulations requiring television stations to make program logs available for public inspection and prescribing the circumstances under which they would be made available for inspection and reproduction. These regulations differ significantly from those governing the contents of the "public file" and access thereto as summarized above. Also, Commission Rules have been amended to permit machine reproduction on request made in person of records and materials maintained locally for public inspection by television station applicants, permittees and licensees, provided the party pays the reasonable costs.

4. *Length of License Period and Notices of Applications; Public Comment and Participation; Procedure Manual Available.* Broadcast licenses are normally granted for a three-year period, and the licenses of all stations in a given state expire at the same time. Applications for license renewal contain information regarding station programming and commercial practices, both past and proposed, and must be filed four months before date of expiration. Six months prior to the expiration date all broadcast stations begin announcing information regarding the expiration of their licenses, the availability for inspection of their applications, the dates by which members of the public should file comments with the FCC regarding station operations and the availability of further information concerning the renewal process in the station's public file or from the FCC at Washington. "The Public and Broadcasting — A Procedure Manual" may be studied in the public files of stations or may be obtained from the FCC. It contains, among other things, information helpful to community groups and members of the public generally in filing comments concerning station performance.

However, as stated in Section 2(a) above, concerned persons are urged to make their opinions know to their local stations. Every effort should be made by all parties to resolve differences at the local level. Frequently citizens will find that broadcasters welcome suggestions from members of the public as to possible ways to improve their service.

5. *Non-Discrimination in Broadcast Employment.* The Commission has adopted rules which provide that "equal opportunity in employment shall be afforded by all licensees or permittees of . . . standard, FM, television or international broadcast stations . . . to all qualified persons, and no person shall be discriminated against in employment because of race, color, religion, national origin or sex." In addition, Commission Rules require that broadcast licensees employing five or more persons file annual reports indicating employment in certain job categories of persons belong-

ing to national minorities, and subdivided as to sex. Also, such licensees must file information regarding affirmative equal employment programs for minorities and women. The Commission does not attempt to direct a licensee in its selection of an individual employee or performer for a particular program or announcement.

The Commission's rules regarding nondiscrimination in employment are, in a sense, an affirmation of federal, state and local legislation in this field, and they are also in accord with the public interest standard established by the Communications Act. Title VII of the Civil Rights Act of 1964, as amended, which prohibits employment discrimination because of race, color, religion, sex, or national origin, is applicable to employers of 15 or more persons, and similar State and local legislation in many instances covers employers of lesser numbers of persons. Under the Civil Rights Act, primary consideration for a complaint of discriminatory employment practices is given to a State or local agency having jurisdiction in the matter. In the absence of such an agency, the United States Equal Employment Opportunity Commission assumes responsibility for processing the charge. Complaints of employment discrimination by broadcast stations because of race, color, religion, sex, or national origin may be brought first to the attention of the District Office of the U.S. Equal Employment Opportunity Commission serving the area in which the station is located, or — if the address of the appropriate EEOC District Office cannot be ascertained locally — directed to the EEOC's headquarters, at 1800 G Street, N.W., Washington, D.C. 20506. All such complaints should include the request that the FCC be advised of the final determination made by the EEOC or any other agency having jurisdiction in the matter. If the EEOC determines that a complaint comes within the jurisdiction of a State or local agency, it will advise the complainant of that fact. In the event that neither Federal, State or local legislation is applicable to an individual complaint concerning a broadcast station, specific and detailed allegations indicating violations of the rules referred to in the first paragraph of this section should be addressed to the Broadcast Bureau, Federal Communications Commission, Washington, D.C. 20554, where a determination will be made as to what action may be appropriate in the matter.

Complaints alleging discrimination because of age should be filed with the nearest local Wage and Hour Office, listed in telephone directories under U.S. Department of Labor, Employment Standards Administration, Wage and Hour Division, with the request that the Broadcast Bureau of the Federal Communications Commission be advised of the Wage and Hour Office's findings in the matter. Information concerning the location of such offices may also be obtained from the U.S. Department of Labor's Employment Standards Administration, Wage and Hour Division, Washington, D.C. 20210.

6(a). *Acceptance, Rejection, Scheduling, Cancellation and Duplication of Program Matter; Color and Stereo Broadcasting; Adherence to Published Program Schedules.* The Commission is prohibited by Section 326 of the Communications Act from censoring broadcast matter and from taking any action which would interfere with the right of free speech by broadcasting. It should also be stated that the FCC is not the arbiter of taste. The licensee is responsible for the selection of programming based on what he learns about the problems, needs and interests of his community of license. Thus, the Commission does not direct him to broadcast one program or cancel another, or as to the time of day when programs or announcements should be presented. This policy applies to many programming matters, such as discontinuance of a particular program over a station or network or the deletion of certain portions of a program for reasons of taste or propriety, to avoid offending the sensibilities of members of the audience, or for other editing purposes. It is also applicable to the selection of religious programs, motion pictures and sports programs (including wrestling exhibitions and bullfights) and specific types of public service programs. Whether to present public service announcements for any specific purpose or on behalf of any particular public or private organization is a matter for determination by the individual licensee. The same policy covers decisions by networks or stations to present simultaneously the same or similar sports or news events, or other types of programs. The FCC will not substitute its judgment for that of the broadcaster in the selection and presentation of material for programs of news and comment. (See Section 12 below.) There is no regulation requiring licensees to present television programs in color or FM programs in stereo when stations are equipped to broadcast such programs. Licensees of FM stations in cities of over 100,000 population may devote no more than 50 per cent of the average FM week to programs duplicated from an AM station owned by the same licensee in the same local area.

Publications setting forth the Commission's policies regarding the depiction of violence as well as programming and advertising directed to children are available upon request.

Complaints are received that some stations do not always adhere to program schedules as published. The Commission has no authority to regulate the listing of programs in magazines and newspapers. Changes in programming plans sometimes occur after listings have been sent to the press and it may not always be possible to submit corrected listings before the deadline for changes, particularly in the case of weekly publications, such as TV Guide and supplements in Sunday newspapers. However, citizens are urged to make their views known to the stations involved so that stations will become more fully aware of the opinions of their audience, and attempt to the best of their ability to eliminate such sources of dissatisfaction.

6(b). *Access to Broadcast Facilities, Program Guests and Freedom of Speech; Licensee Programming Judgment and Audience Reactions; Advisory FCC Opinions; Submission of Program Ideas and Material.* Section 3(h) of the Communications Act states that a broadcaster shall not be deemed a common carrier and therefore is not required to accept all matter which may be offered to him for broadcast. There is no provision of the Constitution or of any statute or regulation guaranteeing to any particular person the use of a microphone or TV camera for the presentation of broadcast material and therefore, except under special circumstances, the broadcast licensee is under no obligation to have any particular person as his guest or to present that person's remarks.[1] It is not the Commission's policy to review material prior to its broadcast.

Persons wishing to market program ideas or scripts, or to have their recordings or other material broadcast, should deal directly with producers, stations or networks, as the Commission cannot serve as a clearing house for talent or programs. The FCC cannot direct any person or firm as to their procedures for the disposition of material submitted to them and will not intervene in the private disputes which may arise in this regard.

6(c). *Licensee Business Practices and Advertising Rates.* While the Commission would be concerned if any practice of a licensee might be in restraint of trade, result in unfair competition or otherwise not be in accord with law, the licensee is not required to submit his advertising rates for Commission approval and the rates he may charge a given sponsor are a matter for negotiation between the sponsor and the station. Licensees authorized to operate commercially are not required to charge or refrain from making a charge for broadcast time. Rates charged by broadcasters for the use of stations by candidates for public office are governed by special provisions of federal law as set forth and explained in Commission publications available upon request.

7. *Fairness Doctrine; Retention of Material Broadcast.* The Commission does not attempt to substitute its judgment for that of the broadcast licensee regarding "open mike" or other programs in which the editorial views of the licensee himself are set forth. We should explain, however, that the Commission believes that licensees are obligated to give the public more than one viewpoint on a controversial issue of public importance. The Constitutionality of this policy, known as the fairness doctrine, has been upheld by the Supreme Court. The policy requires a licensee who presents one side of a controversial issue of public importance to afford reasonable opportunity for presentation of opposing viewpoints on that issue. The fairness doctrine does not require exact equality of time for opposing viewpoints, and should not be confused with the law governing use of broadcasting stations by candidates for public office. What the fairness doctrine requires is that a broadcast licensee, having presented one side of a controversial issue of public importance, make reasonable efforts to present opposing sides of the issue in his over-all programming. Opposing views need not be presented on the same program or even in the same series of programs, so long as an effort is made in good faith to present contrasting views in the station's overall programming. With the exception of certain circumstances involving political editorials of licensees, personal attacks as defined by the Commission's Rules and a provision of law affecting non-

---

[1] When one qualified candidate for public office has been permitted to use a broadcasting station, Section 315 of the Communications Act requires that the station "shall afford equal opportunities to all other such candidates for that office. . . ." The Commission's Rules also require that with certain exceptions a person who is the subject of a personal attack shall be afforded an opportunity to respond. A personal attack is defined as an attack "upon the honesty, character, integrity or like personal qualities of an identified person or group, which occurs during discussion of a controversial issue of public importance."

commercial educational stations [see Section 1(c) above], licensees are not required to make, maintain or provide to the general public scripts, tapes or summaries of program material broadcast.

8. *Other Aspects of Fairness; Editorializing and Scheduling of Editorials and News Comment.* It should be stressed that the purpose of the fairness doctrine is to protect the right of the public to be informed, not to provide broadcast time to any particular person or group. Having broadcast one side of a controversial issue of public importance, the broadcast licensee has an obligation to attempt to present contrasting viewpoints, but it lies within his discretion to select the particular format to be used in such presentations as well as the particular individual to express the various viewpoints — provided, of course, that the licensee appears to be acting reasonably and in good faith. A more detailed statement of Commission policy regarding the fairness doctrine, including examples of the way it has been applied to particular factual situations, is contained in a booklet on that subject which is available upon request. In June of 1971 the Commission instituted a comprehensive review of all aspects of the fairness doctrine. The Commission also has prepared a detailed explanation of the way the so-called "equal time" law applies to candidates for political office, which also is available upon request. Editorializing by broadcast licensees is encouraged under the Commission's policies, subject of course to the requirements of the fairness doctrine. In this regard, it should be noted that there is no law or rule which requires editorial or news comment (or, indeed, any kind of broadcast material) to be labeled or announced as such, or which requires that it be separated or distinguished in any way from other program matter.

9. *Profane, Obscene or Indecent Language or Material.* The Commission's authority in the area of broadcast matter which may be complained of on the grounds that it is profane, obscene or indecent is governed by federal statutes and by decisions of the courts in interpreting them. On the one hand, Section 326 of the Communications Act specifically prohibits Commission censorship of broadcast material. On the other, Section 1464 of the United States Criminal Code provides criminal penalties for uttering "any obscene, indecent or profane language by means of radio communication." While criminal prosecution under this section is solely within the jurisdiction of the Department of Justice, the Commission is authorized under provisions of the Communications Act to revoke a broadcast license or impose a fine upon the licensee for violation of Section 1464 regardless of whether criminal prosecution has been initiated.

The courts have held in many cases that material that may be offensive to some people is not necessarily obscene as a matter of law. The United States Supreme Court adopted the present standard for determining whether a particular printed work is obscene in the case of *Miller* v. *California* (June 21, 1973). That standard is "(a) whether the average person, applying contemporary community standards, would find that the work, taken as a whole, appeals to the prurient interest; (b) whether the work depicts or describes in a patently offensive way, sexual conduct specifically defined by the applicable state law, and (c) whether the work, taken as a whole, lacks serious literary, artistic, political or scientific value." The Court has applied the same standard to motion pictures and to violations of federal laws other than Section 1464. The Court has not specifically ruled on whether a particular work may be regulated because it is "indecent" in contrast to "obscene," although in one case concerning motion pictures, the Court has indicated that it might construe the word "indecent" as being the equivalent of "obscene" for Constitutional purposes. However, the Court has never specifically interpreted Section 1464 or any other statute with specific reference to the *broadcast* of questionable material, in contrast to its presentation in print or in motion pictures. The Supreme Court has ruled that nudity alone is not enough to make material legally obscene under the *Miller* standards.

In April of 1970 and April of 1973, Notices of Apparent Liability were issued to the licensees of Stations WUHY-FM, Philadelphia, Pennsylvania and of WGLD-FM, Oak Park, Illinois, respectively, proposing to fine the stations for the broadcast of obscene and/or indecent language, but stating that the Commission would welcome court review of its actions. In each case the licensees elected to pay the fines.

In July of 1973 the Commission denied an application by the Illinois Citizens Committee for Broadcasting and the Illinois Division of the American Civil Liberties Union for remission of the $2,000 fine against the licensee of Station WGLD-FM. The two groups appealed the Commission's decision to the United States Court of Appeals for the District of Columbia Circuit, essentially urging that the Commission had erred in assessing the fine. On November 20, 1974 the Court ruled, in effect, that the FCC does not act unconstitutionally when it determines that broadcast discussions in daytime radio call-in programs of ultimate sex acts in a titillating context are obscene; but the Court in this case established no standards applicable to broadcast matter different from those presently applied to printed material or to motion pictures. Moreover, because the Court found the material broadcast by WGLD to be obscene, it did not reach the question of the constitutionality of the Commission's interpretation and application of the term "indecent."

On February 12, 1975 the Commission issued a declaratory Order concerning the use of indecent language on the public airwaves. The Commission defined "indecent language" as "language that describes in terms patently offensive as measured by contemporary community standards for the broadcast medium, sexual or excretory activities and organs." This definition differs from the definition of obscenity in that the latter also requires a showing that the material appeals to the prurient interest. The Commission further stated that at hours when it is likely that children will be in the audience, indecent language "cannot be redeemed by a claim that it has literary, artistic, political or scientific value." However, when the number of children can be expected to be at a minimum, such as late-night hours, the Commission "would also consider whether the material has serious literary, artistic, political or scientific value, as the licensee claims."

The Commission submitted its *Report of the Broadcast of Violent, Indecent and Obscene Material* to the Congress on February 19, 1975. The report summarized discussions with representatives of the three major commercial networks with respect to reducing the "level and intensity" of violent and sexually-oriented programming. (The response of the networks has been to propose the establishment of a "Family Viewing" period during the early evening hours of network television programming starting in the fall of 1975.) In its *Report* the Commission also sought from the Congress clarification of the statutory language that prohibits the broadcast of obscene and indecent language to assure the applicability of the statute to television and to cable television.

Profanity. The intention of the speaker has governed in key cases involving language commonly regarded as profane ("hell," "Damn," "God damn it," etc.), the test being whether there were uttered "words importing an imprecation of divine vengeance or implying divine condemnation, so used as to constitute a public nuisance." Complaints of such language unaccompanied by evidence of the indicated intention do not normally furnish a basis for Commission action.

10. *Criticism of Laws or Government.* The courts have held that the First Amendment to the United States Constitution guarantees free speech with certain very limited exceptions, such as expressions which "constitute a clear and present danger of serious substantive evil." Thus, broadcasts of views opposing existing laws or criticizing social conditions, government activities or officials, including the President, are protected by Constitutional guarantees of free speech.

11. *Programs Which Reflect Upon Religion, Race or National Background.* Programs containing criticism, ridicule or humor concerning the religious beliefs, race or national background of persons or groups are sometimes the subjects of complaints received by the Commission. Such broadcast matter, however offensive it may sometimes be, also enjoys the protection of the Constitutional guarantees of free speech. As the Commission stated, in part, in its Memorandum Opinion and Order of January 22, 1964, concerning the license renewal of the Pacifica Foundation stations:

> "We recognize that as shown by the complaints here such provocative programming as here involved may offend some listeners. But this does not mean that those offended have the right, through the Commission's licensing power, to rule such programming off the airwaves. . . . No such drastic curtailment can be countenanced under the Constitution, the Communications Act, or the Commission's policy, which has consistently sought to insure the maintenance of radio and television as a medium of freedom of speech and freedom of expression. In saying this, we do not mean to indicate that those who have complained about the foregoing programs are in the wrong as to the worth of these programs and should listen to them. This is a matter solely for determination by the individual listeners."

12. *News Programs.* The Commission sometimes receives allegations that a network, station or newscaster has distorted or suppresed news, or unduly emphasized certain aspects of the news, or has staged, instigated or fabricated news occurrences. The Commission will not attempt to substitute

its judgments of news values for those of a licensee, but the deliberate distortion, slanting or "staging" of news by broadcast stations would be patently inconsistent with the public interest and would call for remedial action by the Commission. However, the Commission in order appropriately to commence action in this sensitive area must receive significant extrinsic evidence that the news was deliberately distorted or fabricated. Were this Commission to proceed upon the basis simply of what was said over the air, it would be in the position of determining the "truth" of each factual situation, evaluating the degree to which the matter complained of departed from the "truth," and, finally, calling upon the licensee to explain the deviation. The Commission believes that such activities on its part would be inappropriate for a Government licensing agency.

13. *Violence and Crime in Programming; Narcotics and Dangerous Drugs.* This Commission will cooperate in every feasible way with the work of government entities and other organizations studying the possible influence upon human behavior of the depiction of crime or violence in broadcast programs, and will take cognizance of any findings that may result from these studies. Publications setting forth the Commission's policy regarding the depiction of violence as well as programming and advertising directed to children are available on request.

The Commission receives complaints alleging that some broadcast material, and particularly certain songs, encourage or glorify the illegal use of narcotics or dangerous drugs. On March 5, 1971, the Commission issued a Public Notice reminding licensees of their responsibility to acquaint themselves with the nature of their programming, including lyrics of songs. Four years earlier the Commission had issued a similar reminder with reference to foreign language programs. In its Notice of March 5, 1971, the Commission did not state that a licensee should not broadcast any particular type of record, and made clear the fact that selection of records was a matter for the licensee's judgment. Because the Public Notice was widely misconstrued as a directive not to play certain kinds of records and because a number of petitions for reconsideration of the Notice were received, the Commission on April 16, 1971, issued a Memorandum Opinion and Order treating the matter in greater detail and constituting the Commission's definitive statement on the subject.

A number of government agencies, including the Departments of Justice and of Health, Education and Welfare, are cooperating with the National Association of Broadcasters and individual broadcasters in presenting material designed to acquaint young people with the dangers of narcotics.

14. *Tobacco Products: Cigarette and Little Cigar Advertising; Depiction of Use of Tobacco Products in Programs.* Section 6 of the Federal Cigarette Labeling and Advertising Act of 1965 (Title 15 of the United States Code, Sections 1331-1340), as amended by the Public Health Cigarette Smoking Act of 1969 and further amended by the Little Cigar Act of 1973, states: "After January 1, 1971, it shall be unlawful to advertise cigarettes and little cigars on any medium of electronic communication subject to the jurisdiction of the Federal Communications Commission." Cigarettes are defined in the Act of 1969 and little cigars in that of 1973. The law does

not prohibit the broadcast advertising of such tobacco products as pipe tobacco or cigars not defined as "little cigars" in the legislation referred to above; nor does it prohibit the incidental use of any tobacco product in television programs by actors, announcers, etc.

15. *Alcoholic Beverages.* The Commission has constantly taken the position that prohibition of broadcast advertising of alcoholic beverages is a matter for legislative determination by the Congress. The Congress has enacted no law in this regard. The Commission is prohibited by the Communications Act from censoring any broadcast matter and does not direct licensees to accept or reject such advertising or in the depiction of the use of alcoholic beverages in dramatic or other types of program matter. The National Association of Broadcasters' codes, which are aspects of self-regulatory activities among broadcasters, forbid the advertising of hard liquor and establish guide-lines for advertising wine and beer as well as for the depiction of the use of alcoholic beverages in television programs. Membership in the NAB and subscription to its codes are entirely voluntary on the part of broadcast licensees.

16. *Other Advertising Complaints and Inquiries.*

(a). *Amount of Advertising.* There is no statute or regulation which limits the amount of commercial material which may be broadcast in any given period of time. However, when applying for a license or renewal thereof, the applicant is required to state the maximum amount of commercial matter he proposes normally to allow in any 60-minute segment. If the applicant proposes to permit this amount to be exceeded at times, he is required to state under what circumstances and how often this is expected to occur, and the limits that would then apply. In addition, each applicant for renewal of license is required to inform the Commission of the amount of commercial matter per hour actually broadcast during his past license period. Commercial time is measured in total minutes per clock hour rather than by number of announcements. Public service announcements are not computed as commercial time, nor are unsponsored time signals, routine weather announcements, and station or program promotion announcements.

(b). *Advertising in Bad Taste.* In matters of questionable taste or propriety, the Commission urges concerned citizens to make their views known directly to the broadcasters of the particular advertisements which are considered offensive.

(c). *False or Misleading Advertising; Food and Drug Products Advertising.* The Federal Trade Commission (Pennsylvania Avenue and Sixth Street, N.W., Washington, D.C. 20580) has the primary responsibility for determining whether advertising is false or deceptive and for taking appropriate action against the sponsors of such material. The FCC, however, holds broadcast licensees responsible for exercising reasonable diligence to prevent the use of their facilities for false, deceptive or misleading advertising, and takes cognizance of FTC findings in this regard. The two Commissions have established liaison procedures under which they will exchange information and maintain regular staff contacts on matters of mutual concern. The FTC has been studying the role in our national life, as well as the advertising, of such products as non-prescription stimulants, calmatives and sleeping aids, and the National Association of Broadcasters has adopted guidelines for the advertising of these three classes of drug products. Complaints and inquiries regarding food or drug products believed to be dangerous or unsafe should be addressed to the Food and Drug Administration, Department of Health, Education and Welfare, 200 C Street, S.W., Washington, D.C. 20204.

(d). *Loud Commercials.* The Commission also receives complaints that certain broadcast advertising is objectionably loud. The Commission has made extensive inquiries into this problem and has concluded that although no method apparently has been developed whereby the objectionable quality of "loudness" can be measured objectively, many factors pertaining to "loudness" can be controlled by broadcasters. Accordingly, the Commission amended its rules to this end. It also issued a policy statement setting forth the various methods by which "loudness" can be controlled, and requested broadcast licensees to take appropriate measures to adhere to the policy. Following these actions by the Commission, there has been a marked decrease in the number of complaints received on this subject. However, the Commission makes inquiry into each such complaint it receives if the complainant states the call letters of the station which broadcast the commercial, describes the commercial or lists its sponsor, and specifies the date and approximate time of the broadcast.

(e). *Subliminal Advertising.* The Commission receives complaints regarding the supposed use of subliminal techniques in television advertising. Such complaints usually concern words and pictures flashed briefly on the screen but of which the viewer is consciously aware. However, subliminal advertising is designed to be perceived on a subconscious level only. The FCC has held that the use of subliminal techniques is inconsistent with the obligations of a licensee and has made it clear that broadcasts employing such techniques are contrary to the public interest, adding that, whether effective or not, the broadcasts are clearly intended to be deceptive.

17. *Private Controversies; Miscellaneous Claims Against Stations; Contests; Lotteries; Solicitation of Funds.*

(a). *Controversies and Claims.* The Commission does not attempt to resolve private controversies involving broadcasting stations, and generally leaves the enforcement of individual claims to the parties involved. It cannot, for example, collect contest prizes for participants, secure delivery of merchandise ordered through broadcast stations or enforce claims against stations for payment of wages or other debts. However, it is the Commission's duty to consider practices which might reflect upon either the character or financial qualifications of a broadcast licensee or which could adversely affect the ability of the broadcast industry to serve the public interest. The Commission will consider comments, inquiries and complaints which may raise questions regarding the qualifications of licensees with the view to taking such action as may be deemed appropriate.

(b). *Improperly Conducted Contests; Program Matter (Hoaxes, Scare Headlines and Certain Types of Contests and Promotions) Which Adversely Affects the Public Interest.* It is a violation of law to prearrange or predetermine the outcome of any purportedly bona fide contest of intellectual knowledge, intellectual skill, or chance with the intention of deceiving the broadcast audience regarding such contest (Section 509 of the Communications Act). The FCC also will give careful consideration to complaints that its licensees have engaged in any of the following practices in the conduct of contests: dissemination of misleading or deceptive information regarding the nature of a contest, the prizes to be awarded or the qualifications for participation by members of the public; failure to broadcast or publish complete and clear information regarding the rules for a contest or to provide the public with full and timely information concerning a change in a contest, its premature termination or decision not to award announced prizes.

The Commission is also concerned that licensees refrain from broadcasting contests, promotions or hoaxes which may alarm the public about imaginary dangers; infringement of public or private property rights or the right of privacy; annoyance or embarrassment to innocent parties; hazards to life and health, and traffic congestion or other public disorder requiring diversion of police from other duties.

(c). *Lotteries.* A lottery is a game, contest or promotion which combines the three elements of (1) a prize, (2) dependence in whole or in part upon chance in determining winners, and (3) the requirement that contestants purchase anything or contribute something of value in order to compete (consideration). If any of these elements is absent, there is no lottery. Generally, Section 1304, Title 18, United States Code, prohibits the broadcast of advertisements for or information concerning lotteries [raffles, bingo, etc.]. However, Title 18 does permit a station to broadcast information, advertisements and lists of prizes of lotteries conducted by the state in which the station is located, and information, advertisements and lists of prizes of lotteries conducted by adjacent states.

(d). *Solicitation of Funds.* There is no law or regulation which prohibits the broadcast solicitation of funds for lawful purposes (including appeals by broadcast licensees for contributions to defray station operating expenses) if the monies or other things of value contributed are put to the announced purposes. Where use of the mails is involved in this area, enforcement of relevant law is the responsibility of the United States Postal Service. Whether to permit solicitation over his facilities is a matter within the discretion of the individual licensee. Section 1343 of Title 18, United States Code, provides criminal penalties for fraud by wire, radio or televison.

50 RADIO BROADCASTING

BIBLIOGRAPHY

Barnouw, Erik. *A History of Broadcasting in the United States* in three volumes. Published by Oxford University Press. The most comprehensive work to date, revealing and evaluating ideas, individuals and events as well as facts.
A Tower in Babel, 1966. Broadcasting up to 1933.
The Golden Web, 1968. Broadcasting from 1933 to 1953.
The Image Empire, 1970. Broadcasting from 1953.

Chester, Giraud, Garnet Garrison and Edgar Willis, *Television and Radio*. New York: Appleton-Century-Crofts, 1971. Updated edition concentrates on place of media in society and on studio operations.

Devol, Kenneth S., ed., *Mass Media and the Supreme Court*. New York: Hastings House, 1971. Anthology of cases relating to First Amendment issues.

Emery, Walter, *Broadcasting and Government: Responsibilities and Regulations*. East Lansing: Michigan State University Press, 1971. Updated edition concentrates on FCC jurisdiction and rules and includes FTC role in broadcasting.

Head, Sydney W., *Broadcasting in America: A Survey of Television and Radio*. Boston: Houghton-Mifflin, 1972. Updated edition includes history, economics, regulation and impact on society of broadcasting.

Jennings, Ralph M., *Guide to Understanding Broadcast License Applications and Other FCC Forms*. New York: United Church of Christ, 1974. Simplifies public participation in licensing process.

Kahn, Frank J., ed., *Documents of American Broadcasting*. New York: Appleton-Century-Crofts, Rev. Ed., 1973. A collection of laws, codes and historical documents relating to broadcasting.

Lichty, Lawrence W. and Malachi C. Topping, *American Broadcasting: A Source Book on the History of Radio and Television*. New York: Hastings House, Publishers, 1975. Covers technical, stations, networks, economics, employment, programming, audiences, regulation.

Skornia, Harry and Jack Kitson, eds., *Problems and Controversies in Television and Radio: Basic Readings*. Palo Alto: Pacific Books, 1968. Various viewpoints on corporate and public responsibility.

Stanley, Robert H., ed., *The Broadcast Industry: An Examination of Major Issues*. New York: Hastings House, 1975. A report on the IRTS Fourth Faculty/Industry Seminar.

Steinberg, Charles S., ed., *Mass Media and Communication*, 2nd rev. ed. New York: Hastings House, 1972. Impact of mass media on society.

Federal Communications Commission Publications. Available free on a limited basis from the Office of Public Information, Federal Communications Commission, Washington, D.C. 20554.

"FCC Publications and Where They May Be Obtained" — ED Bulletin No. 1.
"How To Apply for a Broadcast Station" — INF Bulletin No. 1-B.
"Broadcast Services" — INF Bulletin No. 2-B.
"What You Should Know About the FCC" — INF Bulletin No. 3-G.
"Radio Station and Other Lists" — INF Bulletin No. 4-G.
"Station Identification and Call Signs" — INF Bulletin No. 13-G.
"Frequency Allocation" — Bulletin No. 15-G.
"Field Engineering Services" — INF Bulletin No. 19-G.
"Educational Radio" — INF Bulletin No. 21-G.

In addition, application forms may be obtained from the FCC: Form 301 — Application for Authority to Construct a New Broadcast Station or Make Changes in an Existing Station (Form 340 for non-commercial stations); Form 302 — Application for New Broadcast Station License (Form 341 for non-commercial stations); Form 303 — Application for Renewal of Broadcast Station License (Form 342 for non-commercial stations). The FCC also issues an annual report on AM-FM Broadcast Financial Data, a biennial Survey of Political Broadcasting, plus other documents, a comprehensive list of which may be found in its "FCC Publications" bulletin. As a result of the increased participation of the public in the licensing procedure, the FCC also makes available "The Public and Broadcasting — A Procedural Manual," which describes how interested citizens may take part in the FCC application and licensing process.

FCC Rules and Regulations are obtainable from the Superintendent of Documents, U.S. Government Printing Office, Washington, D.C. 20402. Volume II, Part 73 covers Radio Broadcast Services. It is available on a subscription fee basis.

A list of non-government publications containing data, news and commentary about broadcasting, including such publications as *Broadcasting Yearbook* and *World Radio-TV Handbook*, may be found in the FCC bulletin "Radio Station and Other Lists."

RADIO NETWORKS AND ASSOCIATIONS

Broadcasting Yearbook regularly includes a section containing the names, addresses and officers of networks, associations and other organizations involved in radio broadcasting affairs. Some of the major groups are:

NATIONAL NETWORKS

American Broadcasting Company
1330 Avenue of the Americas
New York, N.Y. 10019

Columbia Broadcasting System
51 West 52nd Street
New York, N.Y. 10019

Mutual Broadcasting System
135 West 50th Street
New York, N.Y. 10020

National Black Network
1350 Avenue of the Americas
New York, N.Y. 10019

National Broadcasting Company
30 Rockefeller Plaza
New York, N.Y. 10020

National Public Radio
2025 M Street, N.W.
Washington, D.C. 20036

NATIONAL ASSOCIATIONS

American Association of Advertising
  Agencies (AAAA)
200 Park Avenue
New York, N.Y. 10017

American Federation of Television and
  Radio Artists
1350 Avenue of the Americas
New York, N.Y. 10019

American Women in Radio and Television
1321 Connecticut Avenue, N.W.
Washington, D.C. 20036

Association of Public Radio Stations
1730 Pennsylvania Avenue, N.W.
Washington, D.C. 20006

National Association of Broadcasters
1771 N Street, N.W.
Washington, D.C. 20036

National Association of Educational
  Broadcasters
1346 Connecticut Avenue, N.W.
Washington, D.C. 20036

National Association of FM Broadcasters
420 Madison Avenue
New York, N.Y. 10017

National Association of Television and
  Radio Artists
1408 South Michigan Avenue
Chicago, Illinois 60605

Station Representatives Association
230 Park Avenue
New York, N.Y. 10017

OTHER ORGANIZATIONS

Corporation for Public Broadcasting
1111 - 16th Street, N.W.
Washington, D.C. 20036

National Association for Better Broadcasting
373 North Western Avenue
Los Angeles, California 90004

National Citizens Committee for Broadcasting
1914 Sunderland Place, N.W.
Washington, D.C. 20036

Radio Advertising Bureau
116 East 55th Street
New York, N.Y. 10022

ELIZABETH SHIMER CZECH

Associate Professor of Communications
University of Kansas

• Dr. Czech has worked in commercial and noncommercial radio and has taught broadcasting. She holds an FCC First Class Radiotelephone license and immediately prior to coming to the University of Kansas she supervised installation of educational station WSHA (FM) in Raleigh, North Carolina, served as station engineer, and trained operators for air work.

Originally a music education major, Dr. Czech received the B.A. degree *magna cum laude* from Georgian Court College, New Jersey, the M.A. degree from Lehigh University and the Ph.D. degree in Mass Communications from Ohio State University. She has taught music at Georgian Court College, speech, drama and English at Bethlehem High School, Pennsylvania, served as head of the Radio-TV Department at Centenary College for Women, New Jersey, where she also supervised the operation of WNTI (FM), one of the original members of the Educational Radio Network, and established and developed a Radio-TV Department and FM station at Shaw University, North Carolina. Although she has taught a variety of media courses, Dr. Czech's major areas have been management, audio production, performance, mass media and society, and writing for television and radio. She has been at the University of Kansas since 1972.

Her first broadcasting experience was with WGPA, Bethlehem, Pennsylvania, first as a singer, harpist and on-the-air interviewer, and then over a period of eight years in local-live production, traffic, community and school programming and as assistant to the station manager.

Dr. Czech has also been active as a drama coach and actress, musical director in the theatre, counselor for the emotionally disturbed, and consultant to business and industry. She has published articles on communications in professional journals and has addressed broadcasting and management groups.

Active in minority affairs, Dr. Czech is currently serving as Chairperson of the Minority Education and Training Committee of the Association for Professional Broadcast Education. She has also written several papers focused on methods to prepare young Black men and women for decision-making media positions.

2

STUDIO
AND OPERATING
FACILITIES

BY ELIZABETH S. CZECH

ACCORDING to the Communications Act of 1934, broadcasting is defined as the dissemination of radio communications intended to be received primarily by the public. In order to provide room in the radio spectrum for all public and non-public users of radio waves, the Federal Communications Commission (FCC) allocates particular bands and frequencies to certain uses, granting licenses to qualified applicants in a manner designed to assure equitable distribution of radio spectrum among all parts of the United States.

The International Telecommunications Union, an organization with a membership of approximately 130 countries, agrees how to carve up and use all portions of the radio spectrum and designates which bands will be utilized on a world basis for a particular function — such as radionavigation, satellite communication and any other frequency usage which might interfere with each nation's broadcasting. The individual member nations determine how to allocate frequencies within such assigned bands. The ITU also assigns initial letters to be used for radio call signs throughout the world, designating the letters "W," "K," "N," and part of the "A" series to the United States. Except for certain pioneer stations which were in existence before the current rules were adopted, American broadcasting stations located west of the Mississippi use four-letter call signs beginning with the letter "K," and those east of the Mississippi are identified by the letter "W." The FCC approves selection of each station's call letters in order to prevent duplication of letter combinations.

Spectrum space is in great demand for many services beyond public-oriented radio and television broadcasting, namely: aeronautical, maritime, amateur (ham), international, citizens band, land-mobile and space research. Land-mobile assignments encompass police, fire and hospital public safety communication services in addition to communication needs of business, industry and various utilities.

Because the quality and types of programs are determined to some degree by the technical capabilities and limitations of the AM or FM distribution systems, it is necessary for a broadcaster to understand the fundamentals of the nature of sound and its electronic transmission.

In its original form sound is a wavelike motion of air, measurable by its pressure and velocity. A sound which completes one wave per second is said to have a frequency of one cycle per second. The higher the pitch, the shorter the wave length and the more frequent the number of cycles per second. A tone of 1,100 cycles per second has a wavelength of one foot. If we keep in mind that a conversational human voice ranges around 1,000 cycles per second and the highest note a musical instrument (the violin) can produce is approximately 16,000 cycles per second, we can visualize the approximate wave lengths and number of cycles per second generated by talk and music. We find, however, that we need waves of much greater frequency to project natural sounds into the ether.

The frequency of a radio station corresponds with its location on the dial of the receiver, with the exception of the final zero which is deleted for lack of printing space. A station licensed to operate at a frequency of 1,240 kilocycles per second will be located at 124 on the AM dial and will issue its signal on a carrier wave that oscillates at a rate of 1,240,000 vibrations per second. Because Heinrich Hertz was the first person to generate, transmit, receive and measure radio waves, scientists now honor him by assigning his name, Hertz, to represent the electronic unit of cycle per second: usually abbreviated to "Hz" or "hz." The operating frequency of the station just described would, therefore, be identified as 1,240 kilohertz (KHz).

As seen in Fig. 1, sound entering a microphone is changed to electrical energy, referred to as audio current. That current passes into the control board where it is made stronger (amplified) before it is fed to a transmitter by means of an "equalized" telephone wire — sometimes aided by a microwave system to complete a difficult studio transmitter link (STL).

At the transmitter, an oscillator generates a carrier wave at the frequency assigned it by the FCC. The sound, acting as a modulator, shapes the carrier wave and becomes radiated energy emitted by the transmitter in form of radio frequency (RF) which is broadcast through the air in a random manner.

The receiver's antenna, responsive only to the set of frequencies to which it is tuned, filters from the atmosphere the radio frequency it seeks, and feeds it to the detector unit which filters out the carrier waves, leaving

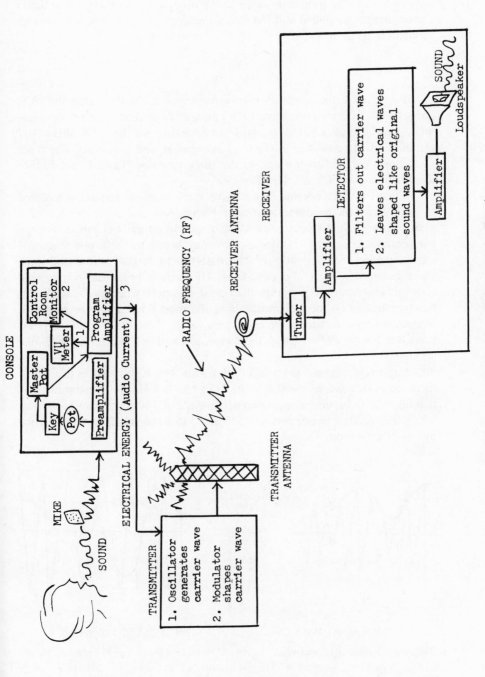

Fig. 1: The Transmission of Sound from Source to Receiver

only audio current similar in shape to the original sound waves. The audio current is then amplified and fed into a loudspeaker from which it emerges as sound in its initial state.

AM

Responsible for spectrum management in the United States, the FCC has set aside 107 medium-wave (MF) frequency channels for use by amplitude modulation (AM) standard broadcasting stations. Of these 107 channels, 60 are classified as clear, 41 as regional, and 6 as local. The types of stations assigned to use one of the three types of channels are further identified as either Class I, II, III or IV.

Class I stations operate on exclusive, clear channels and are considered to hold dominant positions with their high power and exclusive use of a clear channel. Class II stations may also operate on clear channels, but are considered "secondary" insofar as they may broadcast with power assignments varying from as little as 250 watts up to 50,000 watts, and must share clear channel frequencies. Class III stations broadcast on regional channels and have less coverage than clear channels, whereas Class IV stations, operating on local channels, have the most limited service contours. Because of their restricted coverage area, more than 1,000 local AM stations operate on one of the 6 local channels without interfering with one another.

Each AM channel is 10,000 cycles wide (10 KHz) and is located in the band of frequencies ranging from 535 to 1605 KHz. To illustrate: a station licensed to broadcast at a center frequency of 540 KHz is authorized to utilize the spectrum space between 535 and 545 KHz, free from interference by any other station.

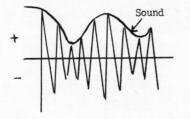
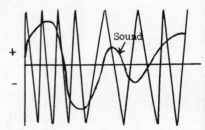

Fig. 2

AM RADIO WAVES

Distance (frequency) between waves remains constant. Amplitude (height) is changed to duplicate the pattern of original sound waves.

FM RADIO WAVES

Distance (frequency) between waves changes according to pattern of original sound waves. Amplitude remains constant.

In amplitude modulation (AM) the sound of the program being transmitted modulates (increases or decreases) the amplitude (height) of the carrier wave. Amplitude may be perceived as power, strength or intensity.

In frequency modulation (FM) the amplitude of the wave remains constant, but the frequency (wave length) changes. (Fig. 2.)

The steel tower of an AM radio station antenna emits radio waves in all directions, even straight up. Antenna height is determined by the wavelength of a station's assigned frequency, with the most effectiveness at .58 of the particular wavelength. If a station has a directional pattern assigned by the FCC in order not to interfere with the service pattern of another station, it will have two or more towers as part of its antenna system. The station with a single tower, sometimes called a "stick," covers all directions with three kinds of waves: ground, direct and sky.

Ground waves follow the curve of the earth and, aided by direct waves, provide the AM station's primary service area free of fading. The ground wave of an AM station is supported by a ground system of wide copper bands buried in the ground, extending in a circular pattern from the base of the antenna. Band lengths and number are determined by FCC engineering guidelines in proportion to the wave length emitted by the antenna.

Direct waves are those propagated by line of sight and go in a straight line from transmitter to receiver, limited by the curvature of the earth. In AM they may be considered to be part of the ground system.

Sky waves provide a station's secondary coverage and consist of medium frequency (MF) and high frequency (HF) waves which are reflected back to earth from several different layers of the ionosphere. Other waves pass through the ionospheric stratum. Active after sunset, when the Kennelly-Heaviside layer of ionized particles gather at a height of approximately 68 miles above the surface of the earth, sky waves make long-distance nighttime AM coverage possible; but they also create potential interference with other stations. To prevent overlapping signals, the FCC requires certain AM stations either to discontinue broadcasting at sunset or to change to arrays of directional antennae or to reduce their power. Not as dependable as ground waves, sky waves are the cause of fading AM reception.

As a rule, the greater the power the greater a station's coverage. Additional favorable factors which may contribute to increased AM coverage and which are taken into account by the FCC when a license is issued include: (1) a high antenna location, (2) absence of local obstructions such as high buildings or mountains, (3) moist soil at the antenna site, (4) favorable climate, free of natural or man-made static.

As seen in Fig. 2, the center frequency bisects two side bands, each of which duplicates the other. The AM signal, therefore, can actually propagate a maximum signal of only 5 KHz rather than the 10 KHz bandwidth it occupies. When we recall that some musical instruments, such as the violin, flute and oboe have fundamental frequencies from 14 to 16 KHz, we recognize that AM broadcasting denies the listener the full range of the musical spectrum.

FM

Frequency modulation (FM) propagates signals of greater frequency and smaller waves than does AM. Consequently the FCC has allocated to FM a portion of the very high frequency (VHF) electromagnetic spectrum and has set aside 100 FM channels in the frequency band from 88 to 108 MHz. The first 20 channels, 88 through 92, are reserved for educational FM; the remainder are open to qualified commercial applicants.

FM stations are classified by the FCC according to their power and antenna height. Class C FM stations are the most powerful and are allowed to transmit a maximum effective radiated power (ERP) of 100 kilowatts (Kw). Class B FM stations are limited to no more than an output of 50 Kw ERP, whereas Class A FM stations are restricted to no more than 3 Kw ERP. Ten watt educational FM stations are identified as class D.

Since FM signals are propagated only by direct line-of-sight, or an approximate maximum distance of 50 miles from antenna to horizon, an FM station obtains distance by placing its antenna as high as possible above average terrain. Mountains, high buildings, even trees may obstruct FM signals. The range of an FM station, therefore, is determined by its power and antenna height as assigned by the FCC. The interaction between transmitter, power and height of antenna control the maximum transmitting range of each station. In frequency modulation the only function of the tower is to elevate and support the small circular or elliptically shaped FM antenna. The configuration of FM antennae depend upon whether they are intended to broadcast horizontal or vertical signals or a combination of both. Polarized antennae provide better local reception, particularly in car radios, although they may have to sacrifice some distance for the assured local coverage over difficult terrain. Because FM antennae project neither ground nor sky waves, only under infrequent atmospheric conditions (such as those which cause temperature inversions) might sporadic long-distance FM broadcast propagation occur. FM's waves are so short that they penetrate, rather than bounce off the ionosphere. On the other hand, an FM station's coverage remains stable and consistent day and night, free of fading. Instead of overlapping, as AM signals may do, the stronger FM station completely blanks out the straying signal of a weaker station.

FM is superior to AM in several ways, the most outstanding difference being FM's freedom from static. Because FM sound waves ride in a protected fashion within the envelope of the FM carrier wave's edges, neither lightning nor man-made static can piggyback on the signal as it does in AM. For example, the next time an airplane passes over your residence while you are viewing something on your television set (which uses AM for video and FM for audio) note that the plane's proximity will momentarily distort the picture but not the sound. High fidelity is an additional asset of frequency modulation. Because of its wider channel (30 KHz), an FM transmitter can duplicate musical frequencies up to 15 KHz on each sideband, contrasted to AM's maximum sideband capability to transmit frequencies no greater than 5 KHz. For this reason classical music stations are usually FM. It should be noted that high fidelity means full frequency range of sounds, not loud volume.

The width actually reserved for each FM channel is 200 KHz — a much broader band than AM's 10 KHz. Normal FM broadcasting, however, uses only 30 KHz in each band, freeing the remaining spectrum space in its channel for a variety of uses, including multiplexing and broadcasting in stereo or quad. Multiplexing is the simultaneous transmission of two or more signals on a single carrier. Licensees must obtain FCC permission to multiplex auxiliary services by applying for Subsidiary Communications Authorization (SCA). Examples of multiplexing include music fed to stores, doctor's offices or restaurants, specialized talk program services for the blind, doctors' state-wide conferences to keep up to date on medical advances and instructional services for home-bound children. Aural material may also be multiplexed, with FCC permission, by television relay systems. Recipients of multiplexed programs need specially tuned FM receivers in order to pick up the programs which are transmitted on a portion of a station's sideband.

Just as in AM, normal FM broadcasting duplicates the signal on both sidebands. To air stereo, the licensee transmits a different signal on each of its two sidebands. Quad, which is discussed later in this chapter, is broadcast through an adaptation of the stereo principle. Even visual material, such as sketches or photographs, can be reproduced by a slow scan method on FM. The recipient, of course, needs a special video receiver attached to the FM radio in order to receive the transmitted pictures.

In communities with cable television service, FM stations are frequently fed to subscribers' homes on one or more of the unused television channels. Cable systems sell extra taps to enable subscribers to hook up either their FM radios or second TV sets to the cable line. FCC authorization is required for FM to be extended in this manner. Some college carrier-current campus stations are similarly fed in order to reach students who live off campus, beyond the range of the low-power transmitting systems.

TRANSMITTERS

Transmitters may be either tube type or transistorized — or a blend of the two. Their power may be as low as 10 watts or as great as 50 kilowatts. All but certain low-powered stations must have a first class radiotelephone operator in full-time employment, but may use second class and third class licensed operators to perform certain routine operations of the transmitting system. The chief engineer is responsible for maintaining the equipment in accordance with technical standards established by the field engineering bureau of the FCC and supervises the other engineers.

Because modern equipment is more stable than older transmitters, the FCC in 1972 and 1973 began easing some of its transmitter watch and engineering regulations. The latest regulatory information can be obtained from the FCC Field Engineering Bureau.

CONTROL ROOM: FUNCTION

A radio station may have more than one control room, depending upon its size and the number of live programs it produces. It will, however, have one master control room through which all programs are ultimately fed. In the small station a single control room may have to function both as master control and production room. Some stations can broadcast from several control points, rather than going through master control, and use such auxiliary areas for back-up purposes in case of failure of equipment in a major control room. All control rooms contain the same basic pieces of equipment even though their size, quantity and quality may vary.

The average control room contains a control board (console), a minimum of two turntables, tape and cassette recorders, cartridge tape units, and a jack panel with which to patch in programs from remote sources beyond the studios. It also includes equipment for monitoring the Emergency Broadcast System (EBS). Appropriately located loudspeakers and headphones enable the operator to monitor what is on the air or being auditioned, to cue up tapes or records and to receive messages from personnel elsewhere in the station. If the station is partially or fully automated there are also racks of appropriate equipment — which are discussed in detail later.

The Console

The control board, also referred to as the console, is a combination of input-output toggle switches, volume controls and volume indicator meters. Basic audio control principles remain the same whether a station broadcasts in monaural, stereo or quad. Rather than memorize the operation of any particular console, an operator should study the board to locate components according to their functions: input, output, monitor or internal communications.

Source selector toggle switches enable the operator to bring in or send out anything he wishes to cue, audition or broadcast. Often two different sources may be controlled by the same toggle switch. Considered "dead" in its middle position, the switch may be "keyed" to the left to bring in one source or keyed to the right to bring in a different source. In similar manner, toggle switches may be keyed to determine whether material will be heard only in the control room through the audition line or keyed to feed material to the transmitter through the line marked "program." Toggle switches are also used to activate whichever remote lines the operator needs to audition or air. (A in Fig. 3) Keying operations should be brisk but controlled. Hitting switches with excessive force may cause internal board problems or damage a switch.

Any source of audio feed is designated as input, whether the sound is fed directly into the console through permanent lines or indirectly through patch cords or remote sources. Studio microphones, turntables, tape recorders and cartridge machines are usually wired permanently into the console and are clearly identified as to channel number and function. Temporary program sources that can be patched into the board through a jack panel are usually activated by one of the remote input switches (G in Fig. 3). Sound sources may be aired as individual units or mixed with a combination of live or recorded sounds fed into the console through microphones, records, tapes, network feeds or remotes.

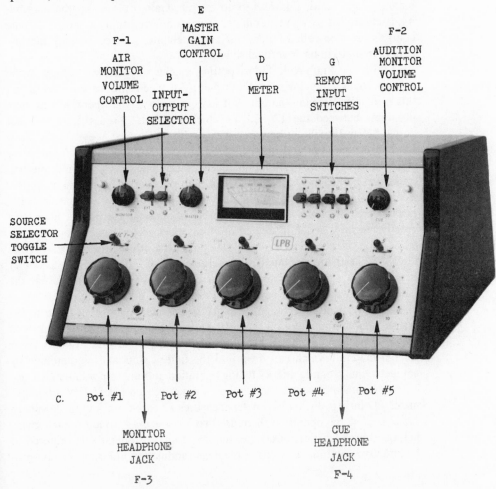

Fig. 3: 5-channel Mono Console

Courtesy of LPB, Inc., Frazer, Pa.

After the volume level of each input is preset and the material is cued to start at the proper spot when aired, the operator prepares material for output on the air by keying the input-output selector to the "Pgm" position (B in Fig. 3). Selector switches may be located elsewhere on boards different from the one used in this illustration. A guide to tight board operation is to preset as many keys and pots possible immediately after cueing material for air. The mnemonic code "PPP" can remind a new operator that in order to put something on the air and to monitor it he should: (1) *Pot* up, (2) throw source selector toggle switch to *Program*, (3) set monitor output selector switch to *Program*.

Volume Control

The act of adjusting the sound level is known as "riding gain." It is the constant responsibility of an operator to ride gain aesthetically as well as to balance it electronically. He or she must not depend upon built-in automatic volume limiting devices to do the job. Gain, or signal-gathering ability, is controlled by a potentiometer, usually referred to as a "pot." Volume controls are also called faders, mixers, attenuators, or pads; they may be either circular knobs or vertical sliders.

With the knob-style fader, potting clockwise increases volume while potting counter clockwise reduces gain. All electronic knobs operate on this principle. Viewing the pot as if it were a clock, the operator airs most programs between the 12 and 3 o'clock positions. As a rule, any signal potted below 12 will not have presence and sound potted above 3 may blast. Potting out one line and immediately fading up another line is referred to as a "segue" (seg-way). Simultaneously potting one line down and one line up so that both signals are heard when both pots are at 12 o'clock is known as a cross-fade. These operations may occur in musical or special dramatic productions. Because the opening levels of musical recordings may vary greatly, music is generally potted in unless an operator has had opportunity to audition the record or tape and has preset the pot for the proper volume level. For aesthetic reasons it is preferable to pot out music. On the other hand, speech should always be keyed on and off in order to prevent the fading effect which would occur with a slow pot.

The vertical slide fader (Fig. 4) is operated by sliding it up to increase volume and sliding it down to decrease gain. Care must be taken to assure that slide faders are kept free of dust, cigarette ashes or any other foreign material which can drop into the fader's slots and contaminate its contacts, thus creating a jerky fading operation and uneven volume changes.

Percentage of sound modulation is registered on a VU (volume unit) meter (D in Fig. 3). A VU meter measures all input and output levels. In the case of stereo operation there are two VU meters — one for each channel; quad broadcasting, of course, requires four. An operator is required to be attentive continually to the percentage modulation indicated on the pro-

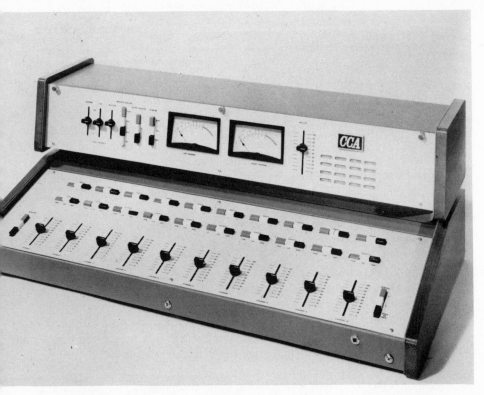

Fig. 4: Stereo Console

Courtesy of CCA Electronics Corp., Gloucester City, N.J.

gram VU meter, regardless of other control room duties. As a rule, the loudest portions of musical selections should peak no higher than 100% and no lower than 85%. There can be no set rule concerning peaks because the timbre and type of tone affects the way the VU meter responds. Usually the more sustained the music or sound — such as a single, pure violin tone — the higher the VU meter should peak. Because of mechanical inertia a VU meter's needle cannot physically move as rapidly as do volume changes in complex sounds such as speech; therefore a peak of 85% should be sufficient for the human speaking voice. It must be kept in mind that the meter registration is only an indication of the average intensity, not an absolute measure. It is for this reason that the audio operator must use his ear to achieve good balance, presence and signal fidelity.

Distortion of sound results when a signal rides above 100% modulation. Although stations install limiters to cushion overload at the transmission point, the signal will still go out distorted if it has been overmodulated at the console. In addition to "bending the needle" and creating a muddy sound when a signal is aired above 100% modulation on the VU meter, "riding in the red" illegally increases the coverage area of AM stations but reduces the maximum coverage area of an FM signal. Because riding gain improperly at too high a level can create such adverse situations, the FCC has regulated that material peak no lower than 85% and no higher than 100% on negative peaks of frequent occurrence. There are, consequently, practical, legal and aesthetic reasons for knowing when and how to adjust volume levels.

The master gain pot (E in Fig. 3) simultaneously controls all other pots (submixers) in a console. The master gain is set by the chief engineer to deliver the best possible sound from the console in relation to background noise and sound fidelity, measured as the signal-to-noise ratio. Under normal operating conditions the master gain should never be changed. In certain emergencies, however, such as the need to pull in a program of low volume, to tone down an excessively loud input or to compensate for component failure in the board, the master gain may be altered. It should be returned to its original setting as soon as the emergency is over, and all operators should be alerted to the emergency change since it will affect all their other potting operations.

All electronic equipment generates heat and needs a certain amount of ventilation to prevent overheating and premature wear on components. If a console is designed for top ventilation, operators must be cautioned never to place on top of the console anything which will reduce the flow of air. Records placed on hot equipment can warp and plastic tapes can lose their resiliency.

A stereo console contains the same components as a monaural board with the exception that two separate channels are aired at once. In Fig. 4 we see a modern stereo console with slide attenuators. This particular board can accommodate 10 inputs, switchable to 6 faders for easy multiple mixing. Notice the separate VU meters for the left and right channels of the stereo system.

THE CONSOLE OPERATOR

An effective console operator is part artist, part logician and part engineer. Through the audio control board comes the mix of live and recorded sound, voices and music — all of which blend to create the life of the radio station, the sound which attracts and keeps listeners. Artistic sound mixing and aesthetic pacing identify the professional audio operator. The console operator not only must be manually adept at technical operations, but also must develop a sensitive ear in order to judge proper balance of sounds and to originate a signal which creates for the listener the sensation of a live performance — a quality referred to in broadcasting as "presence."

As the major human link between studio and transmitter the console operator performs a variety of roles. As a production coordinator the operator must plan far ahead to cue up tapes and records, to prepare live talent's microphone setups and levels, to air everything at the exact second scheduled and to present everything in the correct sequence. In addition, the operator must ride gain in a manner that seems natural so that the listener does not have to adjust the volume on the receiver.

The operator must know FCC rules and regulations pertinent to accurate log keeping, when and how to give station breaks (ID's) and how often to log FCC-required meter readings. The latest official information on such matters is always available in the station's copy of the FCC rules and regulations, usually kept in the office of the chief engineer. In the role of producer the operator at a small station is usually expected to arrange studio furniture and microphones for live programs, to take talent voice levels and to run the board during the broadcast. The operator may also be expected to handle similar responsibilities for local remotes at area stores, supermarkets, fairs and other out-of-studio events. In the small or automated station the console operator may be the only person on duty and, in such circumstances, also fills a public relations role representing the station when answering the phone, greeting station visitors, conducting interviews, setting up studios or speaking on the air. Particularly in the small station, the console operator functions as a "combo" person — simultaneously serving as a disc jockey-announcer. These duties are analyzed in Chapter 7, Performing.

Finally, it is extremely important that the operator be familiar with all equipment in the control room and studios. Knowing that identical models do not necessarily respond the same electronically, the operator is careful to learn the idiosyncracies of each piece of equipment, knows which microphone to use at what time, can transfer sound to tape, and can edit tape both manually and electronically.

Unions

There are approximately 56 unions affiliated with aspects of broadcasting. Of these, many serve only television personnel. The major unions associated with creative aspects of radio and television include the American Federation of Television and Radio Artists (AFTRA), the American Federation of Musicians (AFM), the Writers Guilds of America and the Directors Guild of America. Technically oriented unions with members employed by networks and stations are the International Brotherhood of Electrical Workers (IBEW), the National Association of Broadcast Employees and Technicians (NABET) and the International Alliance of Theatrical Stage Employees (IATSE).

AFTRA is the union for live talent and among its members are actors, announcers, masters of ceremonies, quizmasters, disc jockeys, singers, sportscasters, reporters and any other others who sing or speak professionally for radio or television. AFTRA also serves professionals who perform for radio transcriptions, commercials and phonograph records. Almost all musicians who play on the air belong to AFM. If a musician also wishes to sing, it may be necessary also to join AFTRA, SAG or both. The Screen Actors Guild serves talent appearing in filmed television programs and commercials as well as members of the motion picture industry.

IBEW originally organized only radio engineers but expanded to include additional technical and craft personnel. Approximately 12,000 broadcast employees hold membership in IBEW. NABET (AFL-CIO) covers engineers, technicians and specified nontechnical people, with a membership of about 8,500. The International Alliance of Theatrical Stage Employees (IATSE) mainly serves persons working in visual media as electricians, carpenters, grips, prop handlers and in similar backstage jobs. About 10% of broadcasting stations employ IATSE members.

At unionized stations only union members may perform certain operations. The nonunion employee must know what he or she is and is not permitted to do.

Time

Time is the essential component of broadcasting. Programs and announcements must be accurate to the second. Network feeds must be joined on cue, with no dead air and no clipped content. Material must be aired and logged at the precise times scheduled. In other words, an audio operator must be a professional "clock watcher."

Wall-mounted clocks with clearly visible numbers and a large, red second sweep hand have been standard equipment in virtually all radio stations. Such clocks should be positioned so that the operator can read the time accurately from any working position. Originally used as an adjunct to automated equipment, the 6-digit display clock has been gaining favor in a number of stations. Available in either 12- or 24-hour modes, digital clocks may report real time or production time. Some models may be used as a stop-watch or an elapsed time indicator. Those made especially for production may contain the added feature of holding the count when the clock is reset to 00:00:00. The advantage of 24-hour clocks is that they eliminate possible confusion between the AM and PM log entries required by the FCC. Twenty-four hour time is commonly used in scientific work, in Europe and in the American Armed Forces. With this system the day begins at midnight (indicated either as 0000 or 2400) and the hours are numbered 0 through 24. The colon is frequently omitted. To illustrate: 6 AM is written as 0600, 6:42 AM is 0642, 6 PM is 1800, 6:42 PM is 1842, and 10:15:03 is 221503.

Techniques and Procedures

Hand signals. When the operator is responsible for airing live studio programs he or she needs to know and use standard broadcast hand signals. These are described in Chapter 6. In order to avoid hitting the mike when thrusting a hand forward to give talent the "you're on" signal, it is suggested that one use the hand farthest from the mike as the cue hand and do all the board operations with the remaining hand. In this way the operator can maintain a constant "ready for air" hand signal as well as feel free to make a definitive hand cue the instant the studio mikes are keyed to the air position.

Speaking over music. Announcers must frequently speak over a theme, fill music or selected background music. The easiest way to assure proper balance between speech and music is for the console operator to pot the music down to about 20 and to pot the announcer's mike at normal voice level. In this way the music will enhance but neither dominate nor obscure the message. The decision to use music under speech should be made only when the music makes an important contribution to the message. Habitual use of musical background weakens the effectiveness of the technique. Background music should be instrumental only; a combo-man should never attempt to speak over a vocal. Listeners want to hear the song and resent announcers whose chatter overrides the voices of their favorite singers.

If it is station policy to approve use of fill music, the music director usually selects music to match the mood and style of the various blocks of programming. Often such music is prerecorded on cartridges for this purpose. Fill music should be instrumental because it may be necessary to pot the music out before the selection is concluded and it is easier to pot out an instrumental than a vocal.

Control room etiquette. Control room etiquette, infrequently discussed in books, contributes to cordial working relationships and prevents distractions that can cause errors. As a rule, nobody should be in the control room except the operator. When it is necessary for station personnel to enter the control room during air time, business should be completed as quietly and quickly as possible. On such occasions the operator should alert others in the control room to maintain silence prior to each live announcement by respectfully but firmly stating, "Hold it!"

Most stations have a firm policy forbidding visitors in the control room at any time. This not only prevents distractions but also guarantees that equipment or records are not inadvertently damaged or uncued by interested but careless guests who might accidentally jostle a cued record, bump and unseat a turntable arm or dislodge a switch or button. Even the chief engineer should be considerate enough to avoid undue conversation or noise which may distract the operator.

Before the end of each shift an operator should make certain that log entries have been completed accurately and that upcoming tapes, records and cartridges have been cued for the convenience of the next person. Such courtesies ease the opening of each new shift, prevent mistakes, and help build team spirit among staff members.

Legal responsibilities. Persons who operate the console for broadcasting must hold and post a valid FCC third class broadcast-endorsed radiotelephone operator's license. Although such operators do not need a detailed knowledge of electronics, they are required to know the basic laws, terminology and operating standards of AM and FM, enter required FCC information on logs, calibrate meters and make specified external adjustments to the transmitting equipment. To obtain this license an operator must pass three separate examinations consisting of 20 questions each and referred to as Elements I, II and IX. Such examinations are given in FCC regional offices across the country. Study guides are available either from the FCC or commercial publishers.

Remotes

Any broadcast which originates outside the studios is termed a remote and requires special remote equipment and lines. A remote may be as close as the building next door or as far away as a satellite. Remotes may be conveyed either by microwave relays which feed special telephone wires leased from AT&T, or via remote equipment set up at the remote site from which the program is fed through special telephone wires to the radio station's patch panel. Remotes can also be fed by means of a special voice coupler or a portable conference telephone, both of which permit the use of regular telephone lines which are adequate for voice transmission for broadcast purposes.

Remote telephone lines of broadcast quality are usually ordered at least several days in advance of their anticipated use. They are normally checked out by the station engineer and personnel sent to the remote site to make certain that all hookups function properly. One bad connection or weak component can prevent the signal from reaching the studios. If a program is scheduled to originate at a spot where there is no telephone wire installation, a remote may be fed by short wave transmission via portable walkie-talkie units which send the signal to a mobile remote truck which is wired to relay the remote program to the main studios.

In the control room there is provided for the console operator a set of run-down sheets containing the order of events, the cues for transferring control and, sometimes, a checkout system to make certain the lines are fully operational both ways. During the period just before air time the control room operator and the remote engineer synchronize levels on both consoles so that the VU meters register the same percentage of modulation for the same sound, usually using "woof" as the test word. Every microphone at a remote location is tested and identified by a prearranged system, usually by number so that the console operator can know which voice or event to expect on each microphone. The final leg of any remote may be brought into the control room by means of short "patch cords" which serve the function of audio extension cords. The double male phone plugs of the cords are inserted into the appropriate female jacks in the control room jack panel, feeding the sound into any of the console's remote lines chosen by the operator, who can then either audition or air the program in the same manner as if it were originating in the studios (Fig. 5). Recently developed equipment eliminates patch cords by using modular pushbutton units to distribute signals from or to various sources.

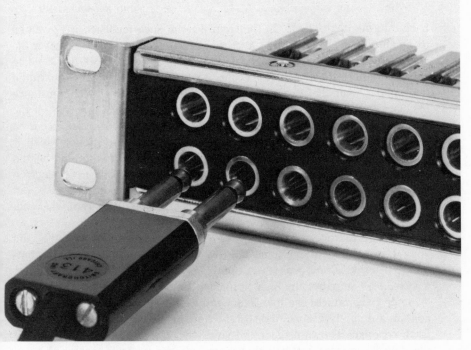

Fig. 5: Jack Panel

Courtesy of Switchcraft, Chicago, Illinois

THE CONTROL ROOM

Monitors

A monitor is a loudspeaker or headphone which enables an operator to hear what is being cued, auditioned, or broadcast. A monitor has its own selector switch to permit the operator to choose whatever needs to be heard. It is important to remember that the monitor volume control never affects the volume of what is on the air, only what is being heard on the control room monitor (see F-1 and F-2, Fig. 3). When not cueing or auditioning material the operator should maintain the monitor in the air setting so as to audit both the level and content of what is being broadcast. By setting the monitor pot at approximately one o'clock position the operator should be able to hear but not be dominated by the broadcast signal. This is particularly important if headphones are used for monitoring rather than loudspeakers (F-3 and F-4, Fig. 3). Because sound seems much louder through headphones than it actually is, an operator can misjudge level unless he coordinates his listening with vigilant observation of the VU meter.

There are occasions when monitors can contribute to feedback. Feedback is a howling sound which occurs when the sound which has entered a microphone exits from a loudspeaker that is close enough to feed the sound back into the microphone. In the control room such feedback is prevented by an automatic cut-off which mutes the control room monitor whenever the control room microphone is activated. The same device does the same to studio monitors. Feedback can occur, however, if there is an open studio microphone near the area of the control room door. In this circumstance feedback may occur when the control room door is opened, especially if the loudspeaker monitor volume is potted high. Feedback can also occur in situations where a remote broadcast originates in a large room which is equipped with a public address system. If the PA monitor is located behind the PA microphone, feedback will occur if the PA microphone is potted too high. To kill feedback the operator should momentarily completely pot out either the offending microphone or loudspeaker and then raise the gain cautiously to a lower level.

A third reason why monitor loudspeakers should not be potted at full volume is that excessive volume can fracture or burn out loudspeaker components. Inside a loudspeaker box are two or three cones. The smallest cone, a "tweeter," amplifies the high frequency treble tones; the largest cone, a "woofer," reproduces the low frequency bass tones. Quality speakers also contain a dome-type cone to distribute tone in the middle frequency range. Each cone has its own magnet and voice coil. Excess volume can overheat the delicate loudspeaker coil that surrounds the magnet, causing the coil either to drag, burn out or break loose from its cone; a volume overload can also fracture the cones' edges.

Internal Communications

Talk-back communication between control room and studio is possible either through the audition system or a special intercom built into the console. Some consoles feature a push-to-talk (PTT) button to enable operators to communicate with the next studio. Shouting can shatter the small loudspeakers inside the unit and hand signals are preferred.

Disc Recordings and Turntables

Most broadcast discs are intended to be aired at either 45 or 33⅓ revolutions per minute (RPM); older records and transcriptions rotate at 78 RPM. An electrical transcription (ET) is a long-playing disc designed solely for broadcast purposes and intended to be aired only a few times. It does not have the durability for long usage, is more subject to damage through scratches and use of incorrect styli than are standard records and may also be unable to produce extreme frequency ranges. Transcriptions may contain complete programs or series of spot announcements and are usually distributed free by public service or foreign organizations. Most stations immediately transfer transcribed material to tape or cartridges, particularly announcements that are scheduled for frequent airing.

Modern turntables may be either 12 or 16 inches in diameter, with three-speed selectors conveniently located near the front of the mounted unit. The platter upon which the discs are placed is dynamically balanced, propelled by a drive system that produces rapid starts and uniform operating speed. To prevent rumble, the drive motor is mounted on a separate mounting plate, isolated from the turntable chassis by rubber shock mounts. Professional equipment also has neutral positions for the speed selector in order to prevent the formation of "flats" on the rubber idler wheel during periods of non-use.

The design of the turntable determines which mode of record cueing should be used. On some models the entire turntable can be backwound when the power is off; on other models the turntable remains stationary and the felt platter cover or the disc moves during backwinding. Attempting to backwind a turntable not designed for such an operation will damage the equipment. An operator's fingers should never touch the grooves of a record, since the natural oil of the hands can contaminate the grooves and attract dust which will scratch the groove walls each time a record is played. Holding the disc by its edges and supporting it, if necessary, by placing the thumb on the center label, the operator positions the disc upon the platter with the appropriate side up. Sides may be labeled either 1 and 2, or A and B. Each album selection is identified by its cut number. If the music to be aired is on the first side and the fifth cut from the edge, it would be identified as S-1 C-5 on a script. On some consoles a record is cued through the audition line, with both the source selector switch and the monitor set at "Aud." If the console has a separate cue system, the appropriate hardware must be set at "Cue."

Cueing. To cue a record, after positioning the appropriate keys and pots, the operator tries to place the stylus (needle) on the smooth section before the cut to be aired. A "clunk" sound indicates that the needle has been improperly placed on the audio portion of the cut. Absence of sound assures that the stylus is properly located on the silent band between cuts. At this time the speed selector should be adjusted to conform with the speed indicated on the record label. With the right hand the operator either spins the turntable or activates the turntable motor, depending upon the turntable's design. Meanwhile the free left hand should be suspended above the record in order to stop the disc or turntable as soon as the opening sound is audible. After the record is stopped the left hand should gently backwind the disc (keeping fingers clear of grooves) until there is silence. To prevent wow-in when the record is aired, there should be additional backwinding — about 1/8 revolution for a 33⅓, 1/4 revolution for a 45, and 1/2 revolution for a 78 disc. New equipment provides satisfactory starts with only 1/16 revolution.

During the cueing process, where VU meters permit, volume level should be observed and the pot adjusted accordingly. After the record is cued as described, the pot level may be retained and the turntable's toggle switch keyed to the air position. The record is ready for air in this mode and will be broadcast whenever the turntable motor is activated. If, however, there is no time to audition volume level, the record should be started on the air with a dead pot and then brought up to the proper volume. If there are no remote starting buttons for the turntables, the operator should practice locating the turntable power switch by feel rather than sight, sliding the hand backward using the edge of the turntable mount as a guide. This technique enables the operator to start the turntable instantly after presenting a live announcement from the control room. A technique known as a "slip cue" can provide a quick and tight method of airing material that occurs within the middle of a cut. In this method the record is cued as close as possible to the opening sound and is *not* backwound after cueing. Prior to airing the disc, the operator places one finger firmly on the edge of the record, pressing hard so that the record does not move when the power is turned on, at which time the turntable but not the record should rotate. Pressure applied at the outer edge of the record is most effective. At the appropriate time a quick release of the finger will provide instantaneous sound from the middle of a cut. Slip cueing demands practice but is a skill worth developing. It is often necessary in a pseudo-interview — when the operator asks live questions of a famous personality whose remarks are prerecorded on a disc.

The technique of backtiming enables an operator to coordinate the last note of a record with the final second of an announcement or program. By subtracting total running time of the musical cut from the total planned program time, the audio operator determines exactly when to begin the record with a *dead* pot. Then, when needed, the music can be faded up to the desired level and held there until the program ends. For example: if a cut runs 2:13 and the script calls for the final 1:24 of that musical cut to be heard under the last 1:24 of a 13:30 program, the operator starts the disc with a dead pot after the program has run 11:17 (13:30 minus 2:13). By fading up the pot after 12:06 elapsed program time (13:30 minus 1:24) the audio operator will synchronize music and program to end simultaneously.

Styli. The air quality of discs depends greatly upon the type and treatment of turntables and their component arms, cartridges and styli. Modern records have sound impressed on the sides of the grooves (laterally) whereas older records and transcriptions were recorded on the bottom, producing a hill-and-dale (vertical) motion. In stereo recordings the left channel is impressed on the left wall of the groove and the right channel on the right wall. A stylus (needle) must be flexible, strong, extremely sensitive to delicate sounds and able to pick up sounds in phase. Stylus weight and thickness are, therefore, critical. A stylus of one mil (1/1,000 inch) is required for microgroove recordings (33⅓ and 45), but a thicker stylus of either 2.5 or 3 mil is necessary for playing old 78's. Some pickup tone arms have reversible cartridges, flip style, containing several styli of different thicknesses for different types of records. Not only must a stylus be the proper diameter, but it must have the correct angle for high-fidelity reproduction. Such an angle can be disastrously altered if the stylus is accidentally dropped on a record or if the tone arm is jostled from its rest.

The stylus is mounted in a phono cartridge set into the tone arm. The cartridge as well as the stylus follows the tiny zig-zag path of the record groove and converts mechanical energy to electrical energy. Unless the cartridge follows the path of the groove accurately, the original sound will not be reproduced, in which case "compliance" is said to be poor. The cartridge should be able to follow the groove yet exert minimum pressure on the record. The lighter a cartridge's tracking weight, the less wear on the record. Some turntables have anti-skate controls which equalize the pressure on both walls of a record groove. The predominant type of phono cartridge is magnetic, which is more sensitive than the ceramic style cartridge. If a control room is equipped with magnetic cartridges, these should be protected from exposure to bulk erasers. Whereas some styli may be removed from the cartridge, others are a permanent part of the cartridge and, if damaged, necessitate replacement of the entire cartridge.

Tonearms. Just as important to the production of high fidelity response is the arm which holds the cartridge and stylus. Unless the arm tracks correctly, the life of the stylus will be short. In a correct tracking pattern the stylus is not in full contact with the sound source in the groove of the record. Because the groove walls of the record must do the major work related to stylus movement, a heavy stylus assembly can crush through and smooth out the delicate high-frequency engravings on the soft groove walls. Low tracking pressures demand that the design and maintenance of the pickup arm be devised to critical tolerances. A perfectly balanced arm moves freely in both vertical and lateral directions and, on a level turntable, should not swing on its own toward either edge of the record. An arm which is pulled toward the center spindle as a result of imbalance of forces due to friction between the stylus tip and the record surface is said to "skate." An unseated tone arm can distort the normal glide path of a stylus and place undue pressure on one of the walls of the record groove. For this reason an operator should never risk unseating an arm by raising it higher than its operational design permits. The light weight of modern turntable components result in delicate assemblies which are easily damaged.

TAPE RECORDERS

The magnetic tape recorder is an outgrowth of the magnetic wire recorders developed during World War II. Three forms of tape recorders are common at most radio stations: reel-to-reel, cartridge and cassette. Some stations use a series of decks rather than complete recorders. A tape deck is a tape machine which has no built-in power amplifier or loudspeaker of its own and is intended to be fed into a separate system — in this case, a console. Using 1/4-inch tape, standard open-reel tape machines are available in one-, two- and four-track configurations. Multiple track machines with additional configurations are designed primarily for recording studios rather than for day-to-day broadcasting. Whereas many open-reel tape recorders are portable, the most sophisticated are often mounted in permanent racks in the control room; they may also be mounted in permanent or rolling consoles for production work.

As seen in Fig. 6, the key components of a tape recorder include: the supply reel (1) which is positioned on the supply hub (2); the take-up reel (3), on the take-up hub (4); a tension roller (5) to equalize pressure on the tape; the erase head (6), record head (7) and playback head (8); a capstan (9) and a rubber pressure roller (10) which pushes the tape against the capstan. The capstan, which is the heart of a tape recorder, is a power-driven drum that provides consistent speed by handling the changes of tension from reel to reel. Only its post is visible during operation; the complex set of drives, clutches, and drags are concealed within the cabinet.

Tape recorder speeds begin at a rate of 15/16 inches per second (ips) and then double progressively to speeds of 1⅞, 3¾, 7½, 15 and 30 ips. As speed increases, so does quality. A sound impressed on 30 inches of tape every second will have more fidelity than a sound compressed into 15/16 of an inch every second because on the longer segment of tape there is more magnetic compound to pick up the many frequency vibrations. The standard speed used for broadcast tapes is 7½ ips, although with current scientific strides in miniaturization of electronic components contributing to improved quality at slower speeds, some stations approve usage of tapes recorded at 3¾ ips if they were made on a recorder with superior reproducing qualities. For easier editing, as well as for quality, professional music tape recordings are prepared and aired at 15 ips and master tapes in recording studios at 30 ips.

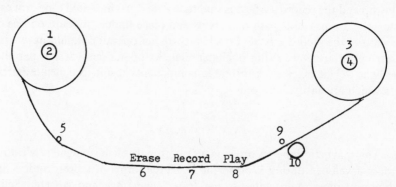

Fig. 6: Key Components and Threading Pattern of a Tape Recorder

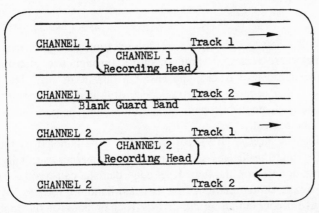

Fig. 7: Sketch of a Two-Channel, Four-Track Tape Recorder Information Flow.

The recording process. The process of recording is the impressing of magnetic variations of sound upon the iron oxide side of a tape. Carefully milled particles of iron oxide are suspended in a resin binder and applied to one side of plastic recording tape. Each minute speck of iron oxide is made up of many small magnets in the shape of needles. The recording head, which is a strong electro-magnet, pulls all the magnets into a sound pattern without disturbing the oxide itself. A weak sound impresses a weak current, which lines up only a few magnetic needles. A strong volume creates strong currents which line up all the magnets and produce a quality signal. Monitoring the VU meter on the tape recorder is just as important as monitoring the volume indicator on a console. Ideally, the tape recorder should have a VU meter synchronized with the one on the console. During the recording process, even if the sound passes through the console, the final gain should be controlled on the tape recorder. The current in the erase head is stronger than the current in the recording head; consequently, it rearranges the nice pattern imposed by sound and scrambles the tiny magnetic needles into random polar patterns found on new, unrecorded tape.

Tracks and channels. There is an important distinction between channels and tracks. A channel is a single, complete through-path, as from a microphone to a loudspeaker. A track is the information impressed on a tape from one channel of information. Only one track can be made at one time, from one input. The more tracks that are impressed on one tape, the narrower the width of each track. If a one-channel tape recorder has two tracks, each track will take up slightly less than half the width of the tape. If a one-channel machine has four tracks, each track is proportionately narrower since all four tracks, plus guard bands, must fit on the 1/4-inch width of standard recording tape.

Fig. 7 illustrates the arrangement of a two-channel (stereo), four-track recording head. Notice that each channel has two tracks; track 1 is recorded during the first run of tape, left to right. If the tape is not rewound but is removed from the takeup hub and placed on the supply hub, it then will record on track 2, left to right. For a stereo operation both #1 tracks then both #2 tracks, are recorded simultaneously, through two microphones. The fewer the number of tracks, the easier a tape is to edit. The sound quality is also richer because a full track recording is able to contain twice as many magnetic elements as a half track. Editing may be performed either manually or electronically.

Operation techniques. Open-reel tapes should be handled by the hub, not the flanges, and the flanges should never be squeezed, especially when they are being mounted on the hub. Reel edge damage can wrinkle tape as well as lead to tape contamination. Just as when handling records, an operator should avoid contaminating either the front or back of the tape with fingerprints. Dirt deposits attracted by body oil not only transfer to the next wrap on the reel, but can also spread oil and contamination to the tape recorder heads and guides, thus depositing abrasive material on other tapes. Each such deposit appears as a sound dropout when the tape is run.

The tape should be threaded according to instructions that accompany the particular model. It is advisable to permit a foot or more of tape to feed on to the take-up reel before starting to record. In case of accidental breakage during a fast rewind, no sound will be lost. As a protection against accidental erasure some tape transports require that the "record" and "play" buttons be pressed simultaneously in order to record. With such equipment both buttons should be pressed with equal intensity, not jabbed haphazardly. If only one of the two buttons remains depressed, no recording will occur. In order to avoid jamming high speed equipment, it is good practice to activate the "stop" button between every operation. This is particularly important between the "fast forward" and "fast rewind" operations. Some tape transports have lifters that automatically pull tape away from recorder heads during "fast forward" and "fast rewind." If equipment does not have lifters, volume should be lowered during these fast modes, otherwise the very high frequencies which result from fast tape speeds can ruin a tweeter speaker.

Even when using tapes of identical reel size there are constant tension changes as the tape feeds during playing. As mentioned previously, the job of the capstan is to equalize such tension. When using reels of mixed size, such as feeding a 5-inch reel to a 7-inch reel, tension changes are even more drastic. If the tape transport is not equipped with tension equalizers which can be set to compensate for unequal reel sizes, an operator should try to use reels of similar size.

In order to preserve full frequency response, good tape recorder heads are designed with an exceptionally small gap tolerance to handle high frequencies. Abrasive action by unlubricated tapes cause tape heads to wear; several mils of wear can open the tiny head gap by a few thousandths of an inch and cut frequency response as much as a full octave. Better tapes have a lubricant such as silicone impregnated throughout the oxide in order to decrease the clogs which may form in the gaps as tape passes over them.

To maintain clean magnetic tape recorder heads and to sustain a signal of high fidelity, it is recommended that heads be cleaned after every 10 hours of use with a cotton swab and cleaning liquid designed for the purpose. Regular demagnetizing of tape heads with special equipment protects tapes from partial erasures or noise insertions which can be caused by magnetic deposits on the heads.

When recording from a microphone that is more than 30 feet from the tape recorder, it is advisable to use low impedance cable. This will reduce the possibility of hum pickup by the cable from power lines, electric lights in the room or even the tape recorder's own motors and transformers. Professional microphones are usually low impedance and therefore more sensitive. The impedance of the microphone and cable should match, otherwise a poor signal will result.

Use of a form such as that in Fig. 8 helps identify the content and routing of a tape and provides opening and closing cues for the operator.

```
+-------------------------------------------+
|      PLACE INSIDE BOX ON TOP OF TAPE      |
|           THIS SIDE FACING UP             |
|                                           |
|  Tape #____  Side #_____  Speed _____    |
|                                           |
|  Date to be aired      Time to be aired   |
|  _____      _____   |
|                                           |
|  Length: _____Minutes _____ Secs.       |
|                                           |
|  RECORDED ON:                             |
|     Ampex _____    Wollensak___           |
|     Left to right___  Right to left___    |
|     Full track _____  Half track _____  |
|     Monaural _____  Stereo _____      |
|     Other _____  |
|                                           |
|  Program or event taped_____  |
|  _____  |
|                                           |
|  Person or persons on tape _____    |
|  _____  |
|                                           |
|  Opening Words _____  |
|                                           |
|  Closing Words _____  |
|                                           |
|  Recorded by _____  |
|                                           |
|  Date Recorded _____                |
|                                           |
|  Remarks or instructions about airing:    |
|  _____  |
|                                           |
|  DISPOSITION OF TAPE AFTER AIRING:        |
|  ____  Permanent hold                     |
|  ____  Temporary hold                     |
|  ____  Erase                              |
|  Route to _____  |
+-------------------------------------------+
```

Fig. 8: Tape Recording Information and Disposition Form.

Tapes. First quality tapes never lose tonal quality, even if played thousands of times, unless they are played on equipment that impresses additional, unwanted noises on them. "Economy" tapes may contain "clumps" of magnetic needles that can accelerate head wear, degrade high-frequency response, appear on the tape as noise and prevent some sound from being recorded. A warped tape may wander up and down on the recorder head; a super-thin tape may stretch and alter the sound or length of a program.

Tapes vary in types of base, thickness, coating emulsions and length. Manufactured with acetate or polyester plastic bases, tapes may be .5, 1.0 or 1.5 mil thick. The thicker the tape, the more durable; therefore, professionals prefer to use 1.5 mil tape for standard usage. Acetate-base tape becomes brittle and may break more often than does polyester. It breaks clean, however, and can be spliced easily. Polyester base tape is preferred for long term storage because it is immune to temperature extremes and humidity and will not dry out or become brittle as it ages.

A 7-inch reel of 1.5 mil tape will hold 1,200 feet of tape and provide 30 minutes of playing time at a speed of 7½ ips. The same size reel will hold 1,800 feet of 1 mil tape (extended play) or 2,400 feet of .5 mil tape (double play) with comparative extended playing times. At a speed of 3¾ ips the 7-inch reel of 1.5 mil tape provides 60 minutes of playing time; 1⅞ ips on the same tape provides 120 playing minutes. Thinner tapes, while holding more program material, are also more likely to stretch and to develop a condition known as "print through" in which sound from one layer leaks through the thin plastic and impresses its sound on the next layer of iron oxide, creating a magnetic "echo" which usually cannot be removed. If discovered quickly, "print through" may be diminished by the playing of the tape several times. Storing tapes with the tail out also helps prevent this condition because, if leakage should occur, it then occurs as post-print which is less troublesome than pre-print, since it may be masked by the original signal.

Tape storage. Tape should be stored at room temperature, in metal cans sealed with pressure-sensitive tape or in an area where humidity is controlled to between 40-60%. Tape stored in temperatures above 80 degrees may become brittle as a result of evaporation of the plasticizing agents. Such tape might be restored for limited playback if it is placed in a closed vessel with a wet sponge for 24 hours, avoiding direct contact between the tape and sponge. Unboxed reels of tape are stored best on their edges; boxed tapes may be stored flat on individual shelves. Stacking unboxed reels on top of one another can warp them for further use. Tape also becomes distorted if it is wound too loosely or too tight. A tight wind can stretch the tape's edge because the edges are exposed to humidity while the center is not. A loosely wound tape contains space between winds, will crinkle in storage and will not feed back with even tension when placed on a playback unit. Tapes should be kept in boxes to protect them from dust

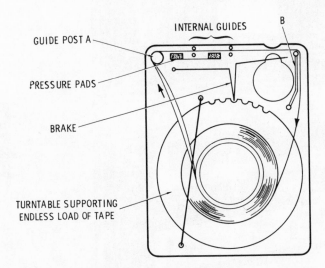

Fig. 9: Drawing of an NAB type A Standard Cartridge.

and physical damage. Tapes should not be stored near sources of strong magnetism, because stray magnetic fields can partially erase or impress themselves upon the sound. Three inches distance from most magnetic sources affords adequate protection; the distance, however, from powerful demagnetizers or motors should be at least several feet.

Cartridge Recorders

A cartridge tape is a continuous loop of tape of specified length, sealed in a plastic cartridge in a manner so that the operator's hands never touch the tape itself (Fig. 9). Because of its loop design, a cartridge tape only feeds forward and has no rewind mode. Some recently designed cartridges can be loaded on standard open-reel tape recorders as well as placed in commercial cartridge loaders. There are a variety of cartridge tape machines. Some only play back; some only record; others can perform both functions and can even duplicate themselves on a "slave" cartridge machine. Cartridge decks can be rack-mounted (Fig. 10) or stacked on top of one another. Older models handle cartridges up to 5 minutes in length; new equipment accepts cartridges ranging from a few seconds long up to programs of 10½, 16 and 31 minutes.

Cartridge tapes offer partial or full automation and are the heart of many automated systems — often supplemented with automated reel-to-reel equipment. Because a cartridge requires no hand threading and is self-cueing it is especially useful for the "panic periods" of multiple short announcements which occur between programs and during station breaks. All that is required is that the operator activate the start button. At the conclu-

Fig. 10: Rack-Mounted Tape Cartridge System.
A basic system, Criterion 80 series, monaural. Combination record/play-back, monaural or stereo models interchangeable.

Courtesy of Gates Radio Company

sion of the announcement or program, the cartridge continues to run silently until it cues itself up for the next message and then it automatically stops itself. Such cueing is done by means of a 1 KHz "stop" tone which is automatically impressed on the tape at the time the message is recorded. Some cartridge tape recorders also can impress a second cue tone (200 Hz) for "end of message" switching which will automatically start another machine. In addition, a third random cue tone (5 KHz) can be incorporated into some systems to activate additional equipment such as slide projectors and similar devices.

Cartridges are an advantage for airing a sequence of short station breaks. A series of seven 10-second ID's can be recorded on one 70-second cart and played in sequence. The same procedure can be utilized to handle a package of rotated commercials for the same client. If cartridges of unusual length are needed or if the tape in old cartridges is worn out and needs replacement, cartridges can be rewound on a special tape-cartridge winder. This is usually done by the station engineers, manufacturers or firms which provide special services to broadcasters. There is no erase head in some cartridge machines and the operator must use a bulk demagnetizer to remove an old recording from a cart before he can again record on that cartridge.

Premature activation of the "stop" button after a cartridge has been aired will prevent it from cueing itself up. There is no need to utilize this button during normal playback operations. Cartridges should be handled gently, not only because the plastic might break if a cart is dropped, but especially because such a jolt could unseat the tape alignment guide which controls the tape angle necessary to keep the machine in phase.

Many stations utilize color-coded labels to identify whether the recorded material is commercial, sustaining, promotional, a special feature or a station ID. Color-coding not only cuts down possible board errors, but also provides a double check on spots and programs for traffic, sales and program departments. Information that can be written on the labels includes the start and expiration date of each message, the title of the program or name of the client, and the identification number by which it is referred to on the log.

Cassettes. Cassettes are smaller, differently designed versions of cartridge tapes, consisting of two spools of ⅛-inch width magnetic tape sealed in plastic housings. They can be rewound; cartridges cannot be. Originally geared for the home audiophile, because of their small size and light weight cassette tape recorders were found useful by broadcast journalists who use them in the field for actualities, interviews and note-making. As program sources cassettes may be transferred to tape and edited before airing, or patched directly into the console. In emergencies or to meet deadlines, operators have been known to air cassettes simply by playing them on their own recorders through an open microphone suspended a few inches above the cassette player.

The standard cassette speed of 1⅞ ips, normally considered unsatisfactory for air use, has become acceptable through improved equipment. New model cassette recorders can accommodate a speed of 3¾ ips. Some recent cassette machines exhibit frequency response capable of handling tones evenly over the entire musical spectrum. The slower speed of cassette recordings does permit a high level of background hiss. Addition of noise-reduction systems such as the Dolby or ANRS help repress the natural noisiness found in tape and the circuitry of its recording equipment in order to produce a signal of broadcast quality. The many varieties of tape used in cassettes can be classified into two basic groups — the brown or dark-grey iron-oxide type and the blue chromium-dioxide class. Although the chromium-dioxide tape has the potential to provide better performance, much depends on the specific cassette deck. Chromium-dioxide tape can be used only on machines which have special bias switches. A cassette tape recorder's characteristics will determine which type of tape will provide most satisfactory results.

A major deterrent to expanded use of cassettes in broadcasting is the absence of control room hardware to accommodate cassettes on a professional scale — a role currently being filled by the cartridge tape. The gap is narrowing. Some cassette tape recorders are presently designed to handle three different cue tones in accordance with the standards established by the National Association of Broadcasters Engineering Department, which sets up specifications for all kinds of tapes and tape-recording equipment.

The Studio

Microphones

Microphones have come a long way from the time when they were often wrapped in asbestos or cooled with water so as not to singe the lips of performers who got too close!

At small stations the console operator is frequently expected to set up equipment for studio interviews, discussions and taping sessions. He must, therefore, be familiar with microphone types, capabilities and patterns as well as fundamental studio acoustics. A properly-equipped radio station will have several types of microphones, each with its advantages and disadvantages. Basic microphone pickup patterns and their configurations are as follows:

PATTERN CONFIGURATION	CONE OF ACCEPTANCE	BEST USES
Unidirectional	M ∢45° Live / Dead	Announcing, narration, tight instrumental and vocal pickup
Bidirectional 100°	Live ⟩M⟨100° Live / Dead	Across-the-table interview, two facing music sources
Omnidirectional	(M) 360° Live	Remotes, news, sports, hand held, interviews, large music group
Cardioid	M ⟨face⟩40° Live	Announcing, narration, desk microphone for talk shows (avoids monitor feedback and unwanted audience noise)
Shotgun	M ∢Live	Picking up sound from long distance

There are many variations and combinations of the preceding fundamental patterns as well as different degrees of microphone response. Some mikes have a screw at the base (or side) with which the pickup pattern may be changed. A number of microphone models contain a response selector switch in order to provide selectivity of high or bass frequencies. A "push-to-cough" button is available on some models. The more directional the pattern, the less chance there is of unwanted background noise. Cardioid microphones are especially good in preventing feedback in a broadcast setting where a large audience and a public address system are potential sources of feedback.

Microphones are also classified within their types as to how and where they are to be used: for music or speech, for close or distant pickups, wired or wireless, stand-mounted, held in the hand, worn around the neck. Broadcast-quality microphones are classified too, according to the type of internal construction which affects their response to particular kinds of sounds. Of the five fundamental types, only three are used in broadcasting: the dynamic, velocity, and condenser. (Fig. 11.) Unacceptable for broadcasting because of their high impedance and limited frequency response are the piezoelectric (crystal and ceramic) and carbon types.

Dynamic microphones. The most rugged and most used is the dynamic microphone, which operates on sound pressure and is noted for its bright, articulate quality. In response to sound pressure the motion of the diaphragm in the dynamic microphone causes a small coil (sometimes a straight conductor) to move back and forth in the field created by the magnet surrounding the diaphragm. Open to free air pressure on only one side, the diaphragm is moved by the difference in internal pressure between the front and rear of the microphone (Fig. 11a).

These microphones are constructed with one or a combination of all pickup patterns. The "shotgun" microphone, used to select sound from distant sources, is a class of dynamic microphone with a super-cardioid pattern and a more limited directional pattern than the usual cardioid. The dynamic microphone is a favorite choice for use on remotes because it is less likely to pick up outdoor wind noises or the sound of heavy breathing. Older model dynamics are susceptible to excessive "s" (sibilance) and "p" (plosive) sounds and tend to "pop" when performers' speech contain such phonations. New dynamics, however, have been designed to eliminate the popping problem. In addition, microphones intended for outdoor use are provided with foam rubber wind screens which can be slipped on the microphone at breezy locations to cut down wind noise. If no wind screen is handy, a handkerchief or even a foot sock will suffice!

When used indoors, the dynamic microphone is most effective in a quiet studio which has good reverberation. If worked too close, however, it will provide a thin quality. This may also occur if the studio acoustics are too live. The dynamic microphone is favorable to heavy voices because it

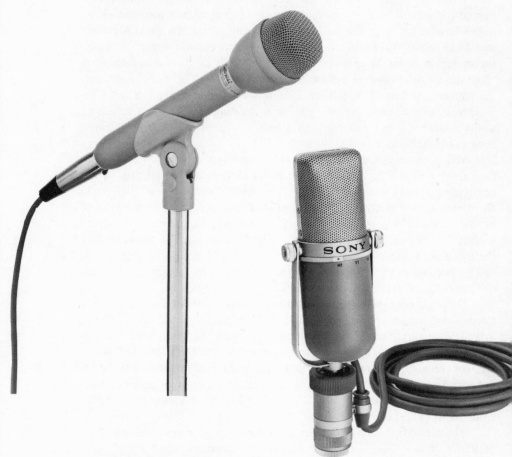

Fig. 11a: Dynamic Omnidirectional
Microphone.
Electro-Voice RE 50 "Noiseless
Hand & Stand." For vocals, inter-
views, instruments and recording.
Courtesy of Electro-Voice

Fig. 11b: Variable-Directivity Condenser Microphone SONY C-37P.
Courtesy of Superscope

screens out some of the muddy low tones and brings out the high frequencies in the voice. Although they are normally used for speech, better quality
dynamic microphones are also used for music.

Condenser Microphone. The condenser microphone is a type of dynamic microphone because it is activated by pressure, but it contains a different and more sensitive type of device. A tiny piece of mylar film stretched
over a solid backplate, with an air space separating the two, forms a variable capacitor inside the microphone. In fact, condenser is the old name for

capacitor. Sound waves hitting the mylar cause it to move toward and away from the backplate, thus changing the capacitance and causing the electrical signal which is amplified for distribution. Condenser microphones are manufactured with any one of the possible directional characteristics or may have four switchable patterns built into one: omnidirectional, bidirectional, cardioid and super-cardioid (Fig. 11b).

Noted for their extremely wide and smooth high frequency response as well as low noise level, condenser microphones are most frequently used for high-quality studio and recording work. In the past they were confined to studio usage because they needed a bulky power-supply box and cable to supply the high voltage power needed to polarize the diaphragm. A vacuum tube built into the microphone also added to its cumbersomeness and fragility. Ways of eliminating the inconvenience of the separate and expensive power supplies have been achieved through use of small transistors to replace the vacuum tube and dry batteries to replace the power supply box. Some modern condensers use penlight batteries; others use batteries which provide over a year's power. Such technological advances have enabled the condenser microphone to move beyond the confines of the studio and to be used for purposes demanding an extremely responsive instrument (Fig. 11c).

Fig. 11c: High Directivity Short Shotgun Condenser Microphone Model CK-8.
Courtesy of AKG Products, North American Philips Corp.

Velocity microphone. The principal component of the velocity microphone is a corrugated aluminum ribbon suspended between the poles of a
powerful horseshoe magnet. The velocity (speed) of the sound entering the
microphone moves the ribbon which vibrates within its magnetic field to a
very faithful reproduction of the original sound. Its full range of sensitivity
and its ability to produce a warm, mellow quality make the velocity the
preferred instrument for music pickups.

Because of the delicate nature of its internal "ribbon," the velocity
microphone is extremely sensitive to shock or sudden gusts of wind. Even

Fig. 11d: Velocity Bidirectional Microphone Model 300, symmetrical
front and rear pickup.

Courtesy of Shure Brothers, Inc.

Fig. 11e: Velocity Unidirectional
Microphone SM33 super cardioid
ribbon microphone. Polar pattern is
more directional than conventional
cardioid. Rejects background noise
extremely well.

Courtesy of Shure Brothers, Inc.

a close, loud cough can damage the component. It is, however, less likely to pick up sibilants and plosives and should be used by performers with such speech problems. The normal working distance from a velocity microphone should be two feet, in a very quiet studio. Performers who wish their voices to sound richer or lower choose the velocity microphone. The closer one is to a velocity microphone, the more the bass frequencies will be emphasized.

Although generally bidirectional, in a figure 8 pattern, a velocity microphone may be directional or contain a switch which provides a variety of pickup patterns and cones of acceptance. A performer must be careful not to address the dead "beam" sides of a bidirectional microphone unless attempting a distant off-mike effect for dramatic value. A recently developed velocity microphone (Fig. 11e) has a super cardioid pattern and is lighter in weight than the usual velocity microphone which, because of its large magnet, has been the heaviest of the microphone types and had to be stand mounted.

Wireless microphones. Wireless microphones, designed for use where presence of cords or lack of electricity would impede production, are cardioid dynamic types. They operate through a built-in transmitter which can be picked up a short distance away by any good tuner and then patched to the broadcast control point.

Lavalier microphones. Although originally designed for television usage, small lavalier microphones which hang around the performer's neck have also proved useful in radio, especially when airing a program which involves many people in a large room. These small dynamics, which may be either omnidirectional or cardioid, usually contain a built-in response which compensates for the slightly "off mike" location and enables them to respond without "chestboom."

Additional features. Some microphones may contain built-in blast filters to reduce possible damage from gun blasts and other violent noises likely to occur in dramatic presentations. For personnel who "chew the mike" there are external "pop" filters. Microphone stands come in many shapes and sizes. They may be of standard or anti-shock design; they may be floor booms on rolling wheels, vertical stands, or rigid or flexible desk stands. Shock-mounted stands help to isolate the microphone from spurious, unwanted noises; some microphones themselves contain shock mounts, especially necessary in hand-held equipment.

Acoustics

Studio shape, height, wall treatment, size, floor coverings and furniture affect microphone response. Walls with smooth, hard surfaces are considered "live" because sound bounces off them and continues to travel. An acoustically treated wall will absorb sound to some degree and/or refract it to prevent excessive reverberation. Acoustically absorbent materials include draperies with a thick pile, wall tile designed to absorb sound and shag-type rugs hung on the wall. The composition of a fabric determines whether it will absorb or reflect sound. For example, certain high-density polyester rugs will not absorb sound; on the contrary, they will increase the live quality of a studio. Felt is often used on table tops to deaden sound.

Untreated parallel walls are most likely to create acoustical problems and some studio designers break up the shape of one or more walls with angular or round projections which prevent some of the sound from bouncing around the room and back into the microphone. The ideal studio has some live and some dead walls, seeking to provide proper reverberation while avoiding unnatural echoes.

Placement of Microphones and Performers

The general rule for setting up a studio for a large number of people or instruments is to use as few microphones as possible. Although this requires more audition time during the rehearsal, the advantage which results is a more natural sound and affords less chance of "spill-over" from one microphone to another. For example, one good omnidirectional microphone is satisfactory to cover four or five people seated around a small table. If more than one microphone is necessary, the second microphone and persons using it should be as far as possible from the first group so that the operator can isolate and control the individual microphones with their individual pots. If performers have voices of varying strengths, those with light voices should be grouped as close as possible around one microphone while those with stronger voices should be grouped farther away.

Unnatural echoes and reverberation can be caused by many things, including low voices, performers and microphone being too close to the glass window partitioning the studio from the control room, and a hard, glossy table top. Felt table coverings help control these reverberations and those that occur if a performer/guest drums nervously on the table or tries to slide the mike across the table to another speaker. In a makeshift studio, as may be necessary at remote sites such as department store windows, poor acoustics can be partially overcome by the hanging of sound-absorbent curtains on rods suspended by cup hooks, or by placement of folding screens covered by thickly napped fabric (a gobo board).

Some announce booths are so small that incorrect microphone placement can create problems. To cure the barrel effect which can occur if a microphone is too close to the studio wall, suspend the microphone a few feet over the announcer's head rather than attach it to a desk stand. To pick up the performance of a large musical group such as a choir or orchestra, one good omnidirectional microphone hung about 12 feet above the center of the group will produce fine results. To record stage presentations of a dramatic nature, placing the microphone just a fraction of an inch above the floor will minimize the hollow sound caused by floor reflections. Special microphone stands are manufactured for this purpose. Since there are so many variables affecting microphone response, an operator experiencing difficulty should experiment with microphone locations, height, angle, and distance — or, try a different microphone.

TECHNICAL MAINTENANCE AND REPAIR

The efficient audio person should be able to perform a number of practical operational and maintainance functions.

Microphone Cables and Connectors

Microphone cables contain delicate internal wires. A cord that has been stepped on might break down at the most inopportune time. If cords must be on the floor during a performance, they should be arranged so that they are not in the path of foot traffic. Cable damage also occurs when a cable connector is incorrectly disengaged from its mated plug or a wall receptacle. Cables should be detached only by means of depressing the lock switch on the connector; the wire itself should never be pulled. Some station engineers permit only engineering personnel to handle microphones and related cables.

Improper coiling is an additional source of cable damage. To coil a cord properly, start at the attached end. Holding the left edge of the cable with the left hand, use finger and wrist motions of the right hand to shape the coils in a clockwise manner. The longer the wire, the larger the coils in order to prevent kinking when the cable is later extended. Since cables tend to retain their curves, it is easier to match existing curves than to create new ones. Coiled cables should be hung on appropriate hooks, either on the microphone stand or on the wall.

Other victims of cable abuse are headphones, particularly those intended for stereo. When adjusting "cans" on his or her head, an operator should be cautious in bending the delicate wires feeding into each earpiece. Hastily tossing "phones" on the console at the end of a shift or dropping them on the floor can shock and demagnetize the magnet in the equipment. To unplug a headphone, the operator should grasp the plastic sleeve of the phono plug — never the wire itself.

Erasing Tapes and Cartridges

Large magnetic erasers, called degaussers, are standard equipment wherever tape recordings are made. Although each tape recorder contains its own erase head which automatically "cleans" a tape of sound before accepting a new signal, an audio operator can be sure of working with an unrecorded tape by removing all old signals with the aid of a bulk magnetic eraser. The eraser, a large electromagnet, demagnetizes the tape by returning the microscopic polarizations in the tape to a scrambled, random, soundless state. Degaussers erase cartridges, reel-to-reel tapes, magnetic film sound strips as well as demagnetize record and playback heads of tape recorders, tools, surfaces and instruments that have been magnetized. They are designed in a variety of strengths and sizes and may be either hand-held or table-top models. Bulk erasing before recording is particularly necessary if a tape was previously recorded on a machine with a different number of tracks than the one to be used for the new recording. For example, the erase heads of a four-track recorder would not be able to erase all the signal previously impressed by a two-track recorder because track locations and guard spaces between heads on the two machines would not be fully compatible.

Operating instructions, which are printed on each degausser, must be followed explicitly as to sequence of events and the number of seconds necessary to erase each side. On all models it is important to activate the power switch *before* the tape is placed on the degausser — otherwise the sudden surge of energy may impress a loud, unerasable sound on the tape. After the power is on, the tape should be rotated slowly within the degausser's magnetic field for the recommended length of time. Then, with power still on, the tape should be withdrawn from the field. Only then should the power button be released. To prevent the possibility of fire from an overheated degausser as well as to provide the operator with complete control, the power button of most degaussers is designed so that the operator must continually exert manual pressure to hold it down during the erasing process. When not in use, degaussers should be stored in a semi-protected area so that the power button cannot be accidentally activated by somebody's placing a book or other item on top of the unit. Powerful degaussers should be operated a reasonable distance from any equipment which contains magnets; the degausser might otherwise accidentally demagnetize components in microphones, headphones, loudspeakers, tone-arm cartridges and tapes. When working with a hand-held degausser, an operator will find it more convenient to hold the heavy unit in a stationary position and to move the item to be erased.

Splicing Tape

Correct splicing of audio tape is an art. A good production person not only knows how to isolate and remove (or switch) sound, but also knows how to cut the tape and splice it in a manner which will maintain full tape strength as well as avoid overlaps of sticky adhesive which later can cause magnetic tape to jump or to break at the site of the splice. Because the sound is on the dull side of the tape, the tape should be spliced only on the shiny side, using a pressure-sensitive type designed especially for the purpose. Transparent mending tape or masking tape should never be used because their adhesive softens under operating conditions and contaminates adjacent layers of recording tape. Use splicing tape of a width slightly less than that of the tape to be mended. This eliminates the need to trim and the danger of edge overlap. Standard 1/4-inch audio tape, therefore, is spliced best with 7/32-inch splicing tape. Units designed to hold and trim tape during splicing are useful, but not necessary. Some models contain their own cutting blades, others have slots to guide razor blades. A disadvantage of the former type is that the blades soon become dull. Satisfactory hand splices can be made with a good pair of scissors and a steady hand.

To splice, first identify exactly what you wish to add or remove from a recording. If you can physically see the tape playback head, you can locate the cutting area more precisely; if not, rock the tape back and forth (in free edit mode) until you can identify what precedes and follows the section you wish to delete. Then, with razor or china marking pencil, cut or mark that spot. (Although aiding visual identification, china marking pencils can clog tape heads if used excessively because the marking rubs off during the running of the tape.) After removing the unwanted material with a vertical cut, overlap the two edges of the tape to be rejoined by approximately 1/2 inch; then cut an angle. This will provide two matching pieces which will join perfectly. An angle cut is stronger than a vertical cut and is less likely to be audibly noticeable when the splice is completed. Abut the two angled edges on a flat surface or in a tape guide. Apply the splicing tape to one side at a time, trying to avoid touching the adhesive portion because finger oil can cause small bubbles and weaken the contact. Rub out any such bubbles with a fingernail or with the handle of the scissors. A 3/4-inch length of splicing tape is sufficient for a satisfactory splice.

Should the splicing tape be wider than the recording tape, the extra width must be removed to prevent its contaminating other edges of audio tape with adhesive. A long, gentle curve, no deeper than 1/16-inch on both sides, will achieve this. If scissors are used, the middle portion will produce a more satisfactory result than will the points of the instrument. Illustrations of this technique are printed on boxes of quality audio tape. A good splice is not visually noticeable on the audio side of the recording tape. A poor splice can cause audio tape to stick in the feed roll of the tape player and to break. Cutting of tape should not be performed directly above a tape recorder or other equipment with openings because the small particles can fall inside and cause equipment malfunctions. Timed leader tape spliced to the opening portion of the recording makes visual cueing easier as well as prevents possible loss of the first portion of a program by breakage caused by fast rewinding. Timed leader tape is also used between segmented parts of a recording when it is necessary to have a specified number of seconds of silence between recorded events.

There are also electronic methods of editing, including erasing a portion of tape by running it through the record mode with the pot dead and then recording over that segment of tape, transferring desired portions of audio by recording only those sections on a different tape, and using pause control to eliminate unwanted content during the original recording process without having to take the tape recorder out of the record setting.

LOGGING

A log is any record of an action completed, whether technical or non-technical. In broadcasting there are three types of logs which must be kept current: the *maintenance log,* kept by the engineer in charge; the *operating log,* kept either by the first class transmitter engineer or the console operator with a third class, FCC broadcast endorsed license; and the *program log,* kept either by the operator on duty in the control room or by the transmitter control engineer. Although logging has usually been done by hand or typewriter, computer advancements have introduced equipment which enables a station to handle all its required logging through automated systems.

There are technical and managerial reasons for log keeping. The FCC requires a log to verify that stations operate within the technical specifications established in their licenses, not intruding upon the signal of another station. Maintenance and operating logs serve this purpose. Program logs list the names and types of every program and announcement broadcast, including sponsors of commercial segments or donors who provide programs or expenses of program production for noncommercial educational FM stations. The log must be divided into hourly segments and indicate the exact starting and concluding time of each program. Although it is not required to enter the starting and concluding time of each announcement, many stations choose to do so for purposes of record keeping. Although program logs are prepared primarily to satisfy FCC requirements, they are also of value to station management. All logs must be retained for at least two years, and portions of program logs are necessary as evidence of programming performance-vs-promise at license renewal time.

Keeping the program log is often the duty of the console operator, who must be fully knowledgeable of how and when to make entries. Prepared in advance of air time, the program log is assembled in the traffic department in cooperation with the program and sales departments. The program log acts as a schedule, informing the operator what to air, and also serves as a form of verification of how closely the day's broadcasting conformed to the prepared log. The FCC requires stations to identify and log programs according to eight main types, plus three sub-categories. Entries also indicate whether a program's origination was local, network, or recorded. The FCC log legends are usually printed on every page of a program log. (See Fig. 12.)

Fig. 12: *Courtesy of National Association of Broadcasters*

MAIN CATEGORIES		
A — Agricultural	S	— Sports
E — Entertainment	O	— Other programs not falling in the above categories
N — News		
PA — Public Affairs	SUB-CATEGORIES	
R — Religious	EDIT — Editorials	
I — Instructional	POL — Political	
	ED — Educational	

STATION WXXX DAILY PROGRAM LOG

Chevrolac Broadcasting Co., Inc.

Littletown, Plainstate

page 1

day Monday

date 10/6/73

time EST

6. Commercial Matter or Announcement Type: Commercial Matter (CM); Public Service Announcement (PSA); Mechanical Reproduction Announcement (MRA); Announced as Sponsored (√).
7. Program Source: Local (L); Network (Identify); Recorded (REC).
8. Program Type: Agricultural (A); Entertainment (E); News (N); Public Affairs (PA); Religious (R); Instructional (I); Sports (S); Other (O); Editorials (EDIT); Political (POL); Educational (ED).

Station Identification Time 1	PROGRAM TIME Begin 2	End 3	PROGRAM TITLE — SPONSOR 4	Commercial Matter or Announcement Duration 5	Type 6	PROGRAM Source 7	Type 8
8:00	8:00	9:00	RHYTHM MELODIES			REC	E
			James Brothers	60	✓ CM		
			XYZ Laundry	60	✓ CM		
			Alan Tires	60	✓ CM		
			ABC Ice Cream	30	✓ CM		
			Red Cross		PSA		
			Sureway Food	60	✓ CM		
			Stop-Start Driver Training School	60	✓ CM		
			Shady Hill Summer Theatre	60	✓ CM		
8:30	8:30	8:35	NEWS HEADLINES - Country Journal	1:30	✓ CM	L	N
			John's Donut Shop	60	✓ CM		
			Blackacre Real Estate	60	✓ CM		
			Wright Insurance	60	✓ CM		
			Rong Shoe Store	60	✓ CM		
9:00	9:00	9:14	JOE SMITH DEM. County Democratic Com.			L	PA-POL
			Cosmo Drugs	30	✓ CM		
	9:15	9:28	FARM REPORT Coles' Tractor Co.	3:00	✓ CM	L	A
	9:29		Local Notice per Sec. 1.580				
9:30	9:30	9:59	LITTLE ORPHAN PUNJAB			MBS	
			Mechanical Reproduction Announcement		MRA		
10:00	10:00	10:29	LITTLETOWN LIBRARY TOPICS			L	I-ED
			Petite Clothes	60	✓ CM		
10:30	10:30	10:44	HEAVENLY MOMENTS - Coun. of Churches			L	R
			Lehi Beverage Co.	EM 30 60	✓ CM		
	10:45	10:59	MAN ON THE STREET Ford's Used Cars	3:00	✓ CM	L	PA
			John's Garage	60	✓ CM		
11:00	11:00	11:24	COKE MELODIES	3:30	✓ CM	REC	E
			Tony's Pizzeria	60	✓ CM		
	11:25	11:29	MORNING HEADLINES -			L	N
			Sta. Promo - Sports Windup (Schmaltz Beer)	10	✓ CM		
11:30	11:30	11:59	JOHN'S OTHER LIFE			MBS	
			Ray Hay Rep. Back Hay Com.	20	✓ CM		
			Weekday Religious Education		PSA		
12:00	12:00	12:14	MID-DAY NEWS			MBS	
	12:15	12:30	AIR FORCE TUNE TIME			REC	E
			Air Force Recruiting		PSA		
12:30			Air Force Recruiting		PSA		

On	Operator or Announcer	Off	Operator or Announcer
8:00	Jim Cue	12:32	Jim Cue

COMMENTS: ABC Ice Cream spot was not run during Rhythm Melodies and log-keeper forgot to delete entry. *Bob West, Program Manager WXXX 10/7/73*

Every program must be identified in one of the main categories. Such information enables a station to determine the percentage of program types it airs. A program may be further identified in a sub-category. For example, a news program with an editorial viewpoint would be logged as N EDIT. There is a difference between the terms "Instructional" and "Educational." The former refers to programs produced to teach a specific subject or skill and is either part of required in-school listening or is offered for course credit. An "educational" program may consist of non-formal enrichment or appreciation material, such as a discussion.

Program source identification and explanation is coded as follows:

L — Local program employing live talent more than 50% of the time and originated or produced by the local station.

NET — Any direct or delayed broadcast originated by a national, regional, special or tape network. Each must be identified according to network (i.e. ABC, CBS, NBC, MBS, etc.).

REC — A recorded program not otherwise defined above. Includes recordings, transcriptions, tapes and disc jockey programs consisting mainly of recordings.

Commercial continuity refers to the advertising message of the sponsor of an entire program. A commercial announcement is the advertising message of the client who bought announcement time; this may also include bonus spots, trade-out spots, and promotional spots which mention a client's name. All commercial matter may be logged as CM and includes both commercial continuity (CC) and commercial announcements (CA). In such a case the total duration of all commercial matter in each hourly segment (beginning on the hour) may be shown in one entry. Licensees may continue to break down commercial matter according to CC and CA and to identify the time duration of each commercial message if they wish. It is required, however, that the log must be divided into hourly segments in either method.

Non-commercial announcements are identified by the following.

PSA — Public Service Announcement (does not include time signals or routine weather announcements).

PRO — Non-commercial spots which promote a program.

Additional codes which help identify material are:

MRA — Mechanical Reproduction Announcement (intended to prevent misleading the public by airing taped, filmed or recorded material in which time is of special significance).

SI — Station identification which is not sold as part of a commercial announcement.

SA — Sustaining announcement (non-commercial announcement not fitting into above categories).

T   — Tape
ET   — Transcribed
M   — Live music
S   — Speech
D   — Drama
V   — Variety

These codes are normally part of the program log prepared by the traffic department. If, however, there is a change in programming or announcements during an air shift, the operator must log the appropriate legends as well as the titles of substitute programs or announcements. Other items which must appear on a program log are the name and political affiliation of every candidate for whom an announcement is made; the names of persons who paid for announcements or sponsored a program; the name of any person or firm who may have furnished materials or services in exchange for air time or mention of their name. Noncommercial educational broadcasting stations may not engage in editorializing nor may they support or oppose any candidate for political office.

The logs of noncommercial educational stations must also contain an entry briefly describing each program broadcast — such as "music" (M), "drama" (D), "speech" (S) — together with the name or title of the program plus the name of any donor. If a speech is made by a political candidate, the name and political affiliation of such speaker must be entered. Logging regulations pertaining to standard broadcasting (AM) are found in part 73.1 of the Code of Federal Regulations; FM logging requirements are found in 73.2 of the Code of Federal Regulations; and noncommercial educational station logging requirements are detailed in 73.5 of the Code of Federal Regulations.

Both the signature and starting time of duty must be entered on the log by each operator. Similarly, the signature and exact time the operator goes off duty must be entered in the appropriate space. If there are several log pages intervening, the operator may initial each succeeding page in the space indicated "operator." Some stations provide a cover sheet for the log keepers' signatures and duty times, in which case the operator need only initial each page of the log covered during the period of duty. If material was run at the scheduled time, the FCC permits the operator to place a check mark beside the entry to verify that it ran as planned, as illustrated in Fig. 12. An operator should keep the log current to the second and not rely upon memory to log items at the end of a shift. There are FCC prohibitions against false log entries.

If changes or corrections on a log are necessary, the operator must follow procedures prescribed by the FCC. Erasures on logs are never permitted. Logs should be typed or kept in ink. To make a change, the operator should strike out the item to be altered with one line in a manner which retains the legibility of the original entry, then enter the change or correction above the line, writing legibly and neatly, and initialing the end of each change. If the correction is made during the shift, it need not be dated. If, however, the log is corrected later, not only the date but the reason for the change must be added. Items excluded from this procedure are entries which are needed for the billing department or to cue automatic equipment.

FCC log regulations also require that the page of every log be dated and consecutively numbered. The log must show local time — e.g. EST, EDT, CST, CDT, etc. It is also required that any abbreviations or codes used by a station to identify announcement or program types and origins be printed on each day's log. If it is necessary to announce that a program has been mechanically recorded (MRA), such an announcement should be made prior to airing the program. No broadcasting station shall rebroadcast the program, or any part thereof, of another U.S. broadcasting station without the express authority of the originating station. The same restriction applies to retransmission of subcarrier background music and other FM multiplex subscription services.

A number of stations now use automatic transmitter and studio logging, either tied in with certain existing automated systems or as separate units. Thus program and operating logs may be automatically produced in some areas. Part of an automated log contains a verification tape imposed by the control circuitry and part comes from the voice cue track on each automated cartridge. Such a method provides double verification and the announcer-operator merely signs the automated log and tape. Audio and visual warnings are usually built into automated equipment to attract the attention of attendant personnel when there is no audio coming from the transmitter. In such a case the printer automatically prints the time the silence occurs and then it cancels all further logging functions until the transmitter is reactivated.

"Re-regulation"

Broadcast equipment is much more stable than in radio's early years, when FCC operational requirements first began to be develoeped. As a result, in 1972 the FCC began a deliberate process of re-regulation which was still in process as this was being written in early 1974.

The most significant changes thus far to note are:

(1) Meter readings are to be read and entered into the operating log at the beginning of the operation and at intervals of three hours (or less).

(2) Operating and maintenance logs may be combined on one technical log, with certain conditions.

(3) Station identification (call letters and geographic location) must be made at the beginning and end of an operation and also as close to the top of each hour as feasible, at a natural break in the program.

(4) In case a taped, filmed, recorded or rebroadcast program may mislead the public to assume a program is live, appropriate announcements must be made by the station to reveal the delayed status of the show (logged as MRA — Mechanical Recorded Announcement).

(5) Transmitter equipment must be inspected at least once a week, with an interval of not less than five days between inspection.

(6) If a station wishes to rebroadcast the program of another station, it still needs the written consent of the originating station, but need not request FCC authority or notify the FCC of such consent.

AUTOMATION

Automation developed in the middle 1960's created out of the need of FM broadcasters to satisfy FCC requirements for at least 50% separate programming on AM-FM combination stations in markets over 100,000. Automation is a combination of open-reel record/play tape decks or recorders plus a bank of cartridge carousels or decks with everything controlled by a form of memory bank which can range in complexity from a simple cart directing each sequence to a computer that will do the directing, logging, engineering and even sales billing. By adding carousels and more open-reel units the most complicated format can be controlled and aired. Stations may be partially automated or may be automatically programmed for a full day's operation. (See Fig. 13.)

Fig. 13: Sequential Automated System.
Courtesy of Systems Marketing Corporation

Not just a "luxury" intended for large stations only, automated programming frees talent to produce more creative production for small stations, thus providing a quality sound. Local announcements, commercials and programs can be pre-recorded, assuring an error-free sound. Many stations produce their local and state news slightly ahead of air time, then load the program material into an automatic cart player which is remote-mounted in the newsroom. The local news cart cues the delayed network news and afterward automatically cues in the entertainment portion of the schedule.

Not only is local material aired via automated or semi-automated gear, but remotes, network programs and closed-circuit feeds may also be recorded for delayed broadcast and programmed by automation. A station may even have "automated" turntables with a system that automatically segues from a commercial on cart to music on a record. Variables built into automated systems enable an operator to have manual control and, when necessary, to advance the sequential operating program. He or she can stop a system at completion of a program and insert a special event such as a news bulletin upon completion of material then on the air.

Some automated systems are designed to produce complete program logs, verify actual airing of all logged entries, produce client invoices complete with time notations, produce profit-and-loss statements, prevent scheduling of competitive announcements in close proximity to one another, produce billing breakouts by salesmen, account and product category, figure commissions and issue statements, produce a daily FCC report for the general manager and program director, and break down the number of minutes devoted to commercials, public service announcements and promotional material.

Automated logging is generally recorded on open-reel tapes at unusually slow speeds. One such piece of equipment can provide as much as twenty broadcast days of broadcast logging on one 10½ inch reel at a speed of 15/32 ips on 8 channels of .5 mil tape. The two basic types of system control are either computer-guided or are directed by some form of matrix selection system. Matrix systems may use either programming panels, plastic cards, thumbwheel or rotary switches. Programming panels look like large peg boards, and insertion of pegs in appropriate holes act as cues (Fig. 14).

Used in digital computercasting, heavy duty plastic prepunched cards the size of a credit card are used to program events, one card to each program event. Cards are loaded in the same order as the items scheduled on the log and can be changed even while a system is on the air. With such a system a disc jockey can provide the traffic department with a music play-list, traffic codes it on plastic memory cards, and the cards are fed into the reader to be cued by either the digital clock or the operator. The use of

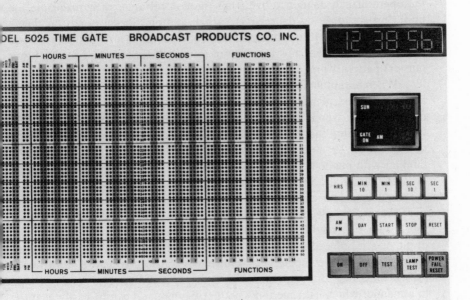

Fig. 14: Programming Panel.
Courtesy Broadcast Products Co., Inc., Rockville, Md.

manual, punched tape and magnetic tape memory loading is another method of triggering program events.

Among recent developments in automated equipment is a broadcast cartridge that provides reversible, continuous-loop operation with full-length program capability. This eliminates the need for reel-to-reel production with later transfer to cartridge. In every type of automation there is a warning device called a silence sensor, designed to alert the operator if there is silence or a malfunction. The sensor can be adjusted to operate between a range of 2 to 40 seconds. The process of automated tape reversal or pauses in music selections may take up to 10 seconds, so sensors are generally not set to operate for less than this length of time. If a station wishes to log program content, it may install "aircheck" recorders which automatically operate whenever the FM or AM announce microphones are on the air.

The Operator's Role in an Automated System

Far from depriving the operator of the opportunity or capability to insert the human dimension into a program, automation adds to the personal touch. In fact, stations installing automated or semi-automated consoles are usually "personality" operations which use the human/automation approach to utilize the best features of both. In a human/automated system the operator can announce live from the control area, then reactivate the music programmer by depressing a single button. Special tones on theme carts allow provision for an announcement to come in over the theme. The announcer may select any sequence of music, thus preventing a repetitious musical pattern which may become too familiar and boring to the listener.

Whereas automation cuts down the number of needed disc jockeys and announcers, it also increases the demand for an all-round audio production person who is capable of voicing and recording tapes and cartridges for air, preparing the master music tapes, and manning the console during air shifts. To be able to meet such responsibilities an operator must be familiar with methods by which to impress cue tones or cue voice tracks on program material and announcements. In some systems, music tapes are mastered on a four track, 1/2-inch tape — utilizing the first two tracks for stereo recording, placing the cue tones on track three and the voice on track four. With this method the music portion need not be rerecorded in the event of a misplaced tone of voice track. Voice tracks are also used with systems that have computer log print-outs. The station with a fixed music format finds that automation enables it to prerecord selected tunes on tape in a manner which uses cue tones so that the material can be easily adapted to request-type programs.

Ways to impress cues. There are two dominant types of cue mechanisms involved in transfer of audio to an automated tape or cartridge — the fixed delay and the variable delay. Fixed delay turns off a tape deck and advances the sequence a fixed time after the cue tone appears. This type is used predominantly by middle-of-the-road (MOR) stations, which do not demand an extremely tight sound. The variable delay, used by progressive rock and Top-40 stations, turns off a tape deck and advances the sequence in a manner that permits overlap of events so that openings and closings can come on top of the music. To impress a cue tone in this system, the operator must activate the cue tone insert switch about one second *before* the change should occur and should maintain the cue tone until after the selection has faded out. A one-second delay, however, is necessary when the mechanical components of the system cannot stop instantly.

Digital systems require that an operator set the control digits on an encoder for the specific code assigned to the recording. When the audio recording begins, the digital information is automatically pulsed onto the control track of the tape cartridge; during playback the pulsed codes are read out through a decoder and fed to a printer which simultaneously accepts information from a digital clock, printing time and code number within the first ten seconds of broadcast audio reproduction.

LOOKING AHEAD

From Stereo to Quad

Because FM channels can reproduce the best range of musical frequencies, FM stations have been the choice of broadcasters who wish to
offer their music in stereo. By the end of the 1960's a great number of FM
stations were stereocasting. During the 1960's a number of battles raged
between monaural and stereo LP recording companies. Some firms, seeking to ride the stereo wave but owning only monaural property, "bootlegged"
monaural recordings by rechanneling them into pseudo-stereo, breaking
down the original, single monaural track into two tracks — a left track that
emphasized high frequencies and a right track that emphasized the lows.
With addition of more reverberation, the resultant "stereo" discount-priced
recording, although not of pure stereo quality, helped whet the public ap-
petite for the two-channel sound. Audiophiles soon purchased types of two-
channel equipment with which to experience the new dimension in music
available on records and on the air.

In 1970 stereo broadcasting expanded to a new double-version of
itself — referred to as quadrasonic, four-channel stereo, and "surround
sound." That was the year when quad broadcasts were experimentally aired
via specially prepared four-channel tapes, broadcast on paired-up FM
stations which were tied together with a pair of high-quality telephone
lines and arranged for one station to air the first two channels while the
second station aired channels three and four. Because this method permits
the airing of four separate channels over a full range frequency spectrum of
15 KHz per channel, it is referred to as a "discrete system." To receive the
four channels broadcast by a discrete system a listener needs two complete
FM systems with the speakers arranged so that two are in front and two
behind. Utilizing the FM sidebands in this manner required Subsidiary
Communications Authorization (SCA) from the FCC.

Matrixing is another method of four-channel stereo approved by the
FCC. Several manufacturers have designed matrix systems that encode a
four-channel course, broadcast the four on a two-channel system to a listener who has a decoder (the opposite matrix) which recovers and feeds
the four-channel information to four separate power amplifiers and four
speakers. With this system quad can be broadcast over stereo broadcast
bands, provided the listener has the equipment to receive it. Quad music
was originally available only on tape. Other music was soon converted to
quad discs, however, because most major recording firms normally cut their
masters on eight channels and, therefore, only had to remix their eight-
channel masters to create a quad release. As early as 1973 quadrasonic
records and tapes were outselling stereo albums, particularly in MOR and
classical music. Because of the rising interest in quad, a National Quadra-

phonic Radio Committee was set up in early 1973 to work with the FCC to establish standards for quadraphonic broadcasting. By May of that year there were at least a half-dozen predominant matrix systems of quadraphonic transmission on the market, each claiming to be superior, yet none compatible with any other.

An FM stereo station which wishes to use the matrix system does not need much additional equipment. Other than the encoding system, it needs appropriate monitoring equipment in the control room: a decoder, two more amplifiers, and two more loudspeakers (or a quad headphone). If it airs a pre-encoded matrix disc, it does not need an encoder; it can simply transmit the two signals which are decoded at the receiving end as previously described. By mid 1973 there were some 100 FM stations broadcasting in quad and the public was avidly purchasing FM receivers and speakers designed for matrixed quad reception. If quadraphonic broadcasting is a station's mode of transmission, there is a significant change for operators: they have to monitor four of everything.

Binaural Recording

Binaural recording is an audio technique still in the experimental stage in 1973. It is similar to, yet different from stereo. Used primarily in radio drama to date, the binaural method (as does stereo) utilizes two microphones and two separate channels when recording. However, binaural (which means "two-eared") differs from stereo in microphone placement and mode of listener auditing. To reproduce the variables of sound as it approaches or leaves an individual, binaural recordings are made with the microphones positioned just far enough apart to simulate the distance between an individual's ears. Exceedingly realistic in effect — especially in recreating aural space — binaural recordings are designed to be listened to only through headphones. It is not unlikely that in the mid-1970's new radio equipment may be designed for binaural broadcasting in addition to quad.

BIBLIOGRAPHY

Ennes, Harold E. *AM-FM Broadcast Operations*. Indiana: Howard W. Sams & Co., 1967. Written for broadcast technicians and announcer-operators. Procedures for handling modern sound equipment in the studio, on remotes, and at transmitter sites. Practical, readable, well-illustrated.   .

Mankovsky, V. S. *Acoustics of Studios and Auditoria*. New York: Hastings House, Publishers, 1970. Focuses on noise control, sound insulation and acoustics in studios and places of public performance. Most thorough book on subject. Includes theory and design information. Valuable reference.

Nisbett, Alec. *The Technique of the Sound Studio*. New York: Hastings House, Publishers, 1972. Third ed., revised and enlarged. Written in non-technical language. Covers operational techniques of broadcast studio and microphone operations, sound effects, echo and filter techniques, tape and film sound editing. Basic book for radio technician and console operator.

Nisbett, Alec. *The Use of Microphones*. Hastings House, Publishers, 1974. In the publishers' *Media Manuals* series, this is more compact than the author's complete text (above). It focuses on some 70 topics, each page complete and self-explanatory with facing-page visual diagrams, covering: Sound — Microphones — Speech balance — Sound & picture — Music balance — Control — Glossary.

Olson, Harry F. *Modern Sound Reproduction*. New York: Van Nostrand Reinhold Co., 1972. Describes systems and methods used in high quality sound reproduction, characteristics of human ear related to sound reproducing systems, acoustical designs of rooms used for sound reproduction. Includes monaural, monophonic, binaural, stereophonic and quadraphonic sound systems.

Oringel, Robert S. *Audio Control Handbook*. New York: Hastings House, Publishers, 1972. Fourth, revised edition. Emphasis on broadcast equipment and techniques for controlling sound for radio, film and television production. Many pictures and illustrations. Excellent beginner's book.

Schwartz, Martin. *Commercial Radio Operator's License Guide — Elements 1, 2 & 9*. New York: Ameco Publishing Corp., 1973. Questions and answers format to prepare beginning operators for 3rd class, broadcast endorsed FCC exam. Includes basic theory, practice questions.

Swearer, Harvy F. *Commercial FCC License Study Guide*. Pennsylvania: Tab Books, 1972. Study guide and reference manual. Theory, applications, practice questions and answers to aid preparation for 1st, 2nd and 3rd Class FCC Radiotelephone license exams plus broadcast and radar endorsements.

U.S. Code of Federal Regulations Title 47 — Telecommunication Parts 70 to 79. 1972. Contains all general FCC rules and regulations applicable to radio and television national and international broadcast services as printed in the *Federal Register* through December 31 of the preceding year. Issued annually. Includes definitions of terms, administrative procedures, facility allocations, equipment specifications, technical operations, licensing procedures and policies, logging requirements, political broadcasting, lotteries, fairness doctrine issues and equal employment procedures.

Periodicals which provide current information about the state of the art of broadcast and audio electronics include:

Audio. North American Publishing Co., Philadelphia, Pa., and *High Fidelity*, Billboard Publications, Inc., New York, N.Y. Both contain informative articles and schematics of new sound equipment, trends in sound recording, record reviews and applications of new sounds to broadcasting. Monthly.

Broadcast Engineering. Kansas City, Mo.: Intertec Publishing Corporation. Technical news, schematics, theory, current FCC regulations and interpretations, new technical literature and book reviews. Of particular interest to broadcast engineers. Monthly.

Broadcast/Management Engineering. New York: Broadband Information Services, Inc. Geared to serve management's need for engineering information and application as well as interests of the engineering staff. Equipment information, sources of technical literature, design problems and solutions applicable to radio, TV, cable and CCTV. Also contains non-technical features pertinent to current industry concerns and new FCC rules and regulations. Monthly.

Broadcasting. Washington, D.C.: Broadcasting Publications. The newsweekly of broadcasting and allied arts. Regular features about key people in broadcasting, broadcast advertising, media, cablecasting, broadcast journalism, equipment and engineering, programming, music, current FCC station actions and license authorizations, employment information. Weekly.

Broadcasting Yearbook. Washington, D.C.: Broadcasting Publications. Directory of station facilities, owners, frequencies, summary of broadcast history and current FCC rules and regulations; sources of equipment; NAB codes, program services; station representatives, networks, government agencies, professional groups, unions, advertising agencies, consultants. Annual.

3

FORMAT

BY ROBERT L. HILLIARD

SPECIALIZATION

THE CONCEPT of specialization took hold in the late 1960's and within a few years had become the cardinal principle of station programming and image. It is likely that format changes during the next two decades of radio will not be as drastic or frantic as in the past two. A *Television/Radio Age* survey at the end of 1973 showed that the "overwhelming majority of . . . stations were not undergoing any significant changes in the type of music they presented." Radio did not initiate these changes so much as it was forced into them. In the popular areas of entertainment it could not hope to compete with television and was left with a more limited field — principally news, sports, weather, recorded music, discussions and interviews, and certain types of special features. What radio did, in effect, was to retrogress to its strength: local origination. Most of the network shows in the 1930's and 1940's had come from local stations and then developed into national programs. Morris S. Novik, one of radio's pioneers, has stated that:

> Pre-war consisted of the old stations, the pioneers, the foundations of the great networks. There were the regional and local stations that gained prestige and influence because they were network affiliates, and the small independent low-powered stations. The small stations . . . played their tunes to their special audiences; mountain and western music, jazz, classics, spirituals . . . The networks broadcast programs with big stars, symphony orchestras, variety shows, worldwide news and comment programs and even soap operas . . . [It] was diversified radio. The listener had a choice . . . With the end of the war the freeze was lifted and many more local stations were licensed. . . .

The trend, of necessity and circumstance, turned back to local programming and local need, and the format or formula approach to radio broadcasting grew.

In 1963 John E. McCoy, vice president of the Storer Broadcasting Company, described what was happening in radio:

> . . . independent radio stations discovered a "formula" for programming that revitalized radio in the field of national spot and local sales, at least for stations which did not have a network affiliation. This formula was based on the discovery that audience habits had changed. Television stations now attracted the bulk of the audience that wanted drama, comedy, variety, westerns, murder mysteries, games, and similar "talk" programs. But radio stations could still provide a service the public wanted in the form of music, news, and sports events, which were not available on television, or which the audience wanted to hear in their automobiles or at the beach in places where television was not available. The most successful of these "top 40" or "formula stations" generally provided a 24-hour service of current popular music interspersed by brief newscasts and sport news.
> . . . It is practically a maxim today that to be successful a radio station must have a consistent "sound" so that anyone who tunes to the station knows what to expect and gets it substantially all day long.

As Dr. Sidney W. Head has stated, ". . . most radio stations . . . now serve specialized, limited publics almost exclusively. The radio station with the full range of programming for all segments of the public has become an anachronism."

Station Size and Trend

By the early 1970's, while most stations had reached the point of being specialized even within a particular type of format, the largest and most successful stations were moving in the opposite direction. An ARB (American Research Bureau) survey in the fall of 1972 showed that the stations in the top 50 markets which had the highest quarter-hour audience shares for the longest time were those which had several types of programming, including news, talks, features and two or more types of music. These "full-service" stations were the ones that have continued to dominate their markets over the years. In the largest metropolitan areas news and talk stations are predominantly the most successful; as the size of the market grows smaller, music stations become the leaders. Next to the full-service stations in popularity in the largest markets are contemporary or "top-40" stations, then MOR ("middle-of-the-road," providing popular-standard music).

As the mid-1970's, with a tightening economy, approached, there began a levelling-off of format approaches for middle-sized and smaller market stations, too. Many aimed at broadening their audience, reaching out to more than one principal demographic or specialized group. Individual station formats were beginning to blend elements of other types of music into the primary one, mixing "contemporary" (including rock), "MOR," "country" and "good music."

The demographic breakdown of target audiences for major types is illustrated in the results of the *Television/Radio Age* late-1973 survey, showing the percentage of each type of station aiming at specific age and sex groups:

	CONTEMPORARY	MOR	COUNTRY	GOOD MUSIC
Adults 18-49	47.3%	39.5%	59.5%	30.3%
Adults 25-64	5.3	39.5	18.9	48.5
All adults	4.3	23.2	8.1	27.2
All listeners	12.9	13.9	21.6	12.1
Adults 18-34	32.2	0.0	2.7	3.0
Teens, young adults 12-24	20.4	0.0	0.0	0.0
Women	3.2	4.6	5.4	3.0
Men	3.2	4.6	8.1	0.0
Teens	11.8	0.0	0.0	0.0
Other	9.6	10.0	8.1	3.0

Source: TELEVISION/RADIO AGE survey, November, 1973: prime target preferences as reported by stations. Percentages in each column may add up to more than 100% due to multiple answers. Demographics listed in order of overall importance to all four formats.

A point to note is that even the stations with multi-programming approaches attract specialized audiences, appealing to the age or interest group that happens to be listening at the particular time of the day. This is further reflected in the increase of local radio advertising during the late 1960's and early 1970's over national spot advertising, particularly in the largest markets. Local growth is attributed to several factors, including greater promotion by local stations, the growth of shopping centers and discount and department stores, and the specialized formats reaching specific audiences such as businessmen, women and teenagers.

FM Stations

When FM was young most listeners equated it with so-called "good music," specifically the classical music and extended news-talk shows that few AM stations found profitable enough to program. As FM radio grew it still retained its aura and, in large degree, practice of providing specialized programming for minority tastes, but in fact grew more and more competitive in the popular-taste market. In the early 1970's its format began to change as it began to fulfill the predictions of many that the next revolution in radio, with AM having become somewhat stabilized, would be in FM. Although in the early 1970's the "beautiful music" stations were still highly successful FM operations, many FMers began to reach toward the young listener, and progressive rock, for example, was the fastest growing FM format type. Some stations have found that many young listeners will switch stations if there are too many commercial interruptions, and one New York station began promoting "101 minutes of non-stop music." This, of course, requires ingenuity in order to make the balance sheet come out in the black.

A 1972 survey by the National Association of FM Broadcasters (NAFMB) showed that the major FM format was MOR, middle-of-the-road, the programming approach of 21.4% of the stations, showing a slight decrease from its previous survey in 1970. Beautiful music was second in format approach, 19.3%, showing about a 40% jump, and country and western was third, 10.6%, about the same percentage of stations as before. Other leading formats, in order, were MOR combined with beautiful music or contemporary, hard rock, progressive or underground rock, religious, classical, semi-classical, diversified music, jazz, ethnic, rhythm and blues.

The changing nature of music formats is emphasized by NAFMB's comment that definitions of music are constantly changing, with MOR having a different connotation in the early and mid-1970's than it had in the late 1960's. It noted that contemporary music, for example, means the music of living composers to some programmers, but is limited to current hit songs for others.

MUSIC AND RECORDS

Music both reflects culture and builds it. It is the dialogue of youth, providing a sense of psychological freedom for the listener and a sense of artistic freedom for the performer. Pop music is a sociological phenomenon, partly because it reflects the flexibility, growth and change of society, particularly young society. It was only some ten years before this was written (perhaps a long time for the young, but a remarkably short period for those old enough to begin to have a sense of their own history) that, in 1963, a group of young men came out of Liverpool to become the Beatles and change the face of modern popular music *and* the attitudes and behavior of youth. The Beatles motivated an escape from the traditional formulas, and their music was not music alone of bodily rhythm, but music of ideas, the communicating of unspoken and spoken meanings that were vital and forceful to the young people who eagerly pursued them. The basic concept was not new. The blues of the 1920's and '30's, the soul music of the 1950's all had meaning. But the Beatles put it all together, combining and adding as all true innovators do to create what seems like something fresh and new. Combined with the inexpensive availability of the transistor radio receiver, the new music made radio the link between creative artistry and creative reception as never before.

Records and radio had become interdependent in Martin Bloch's very first "hour of sweet romance," only they — records and radio — never really acknowledged it. On one hand, some program directors felt that their duty was to carefully choose music that would raise the level of cultural understanding and strengthen the country's common bonds. On the other hand, other program directors believed that radio was merely a carrier and that its role was not as an arbiter of taste, but only as an interpreter. Even while many record promoters demeaned radio as a technical tool unrelated to the important world of artists (as indeed, radio became unrelated when live programming disappeared and artists became only voices on discs) they courted and bribed radio to promote their wares.

At one time, in the late 1930's, the feeling was that radio's use of records gave the listener a continuing "freebee," and that the listeners would not pay money to buy the records or the sheet music of a given song. ASCAP (American Society of Composers, Authors and Publishers) controlled music performance rights exclusively until the beginning of the 1940's when BMI (Broadcast Music, Inc.) broke their monopoly. A monitoring system determined the division of income from statutory fees to be distributed to the composers of songs used over radio. It wasn't long, however, before it was discovered that radio, rather than hampering record sales, actually promoted them. Radio became the major form of exposure for new records — although artists themselves frequently made their reputations through live concerts before their records reached wide distribution over radio. Radio became a showcase for records, and record companies began to pressure program directors and disc jockeys to play their products. At the same time, radio stations found these records a virtually free source of material. Because the record business is highly competitive, from time to time record companies have resorted to almost any effective means to get their records played — as evidenced by the d.j. payola scandals of the late 1950's in the United States and of the early 1970's in Great Britain. In mid-1973 the U.S. federal government was looking into new allegations of plugola between record companies and radio stations.

The responsible radio program director or d.j. resents the promoter who tries to "hype" the station on virtually every new record, and prefers to deal with the record rep who every few months or so will honestly promote a legitimately new and hot item. It is sometimes like jungle warfare between record companies and radio stations. When a performer is hot the record company dictates the product. When the personality business is slow the radio station calls the shots.

Record companies and radio stations do, however, agree on the "democratic" aspect of radio/record music. They both feel they are serving the desires of the public. Occasionally the question arises as to whether wants are the same as needs, and whether the "democratic denominator" may be a euphemism for the "lowest common denominator"? In any event, record companies and radio stations have found that "democratic" and/or "lcd" are broad in scope and that one cannot be all things to all listeners. Thus, the development of specialization, and within the area of music alone a number of major formats.

Top-40

In the late 1940's radio was facing the need for a new approach. Post-war growth in the number of stations was almost completely local, and local revenues began to exceed those of the networks. Music programming on local stations had become affinity blocks; that is, 15-minute or half-hour segments devoted to a particular band or vocalist. Selection of records was pretty much what the program director, d.j. or music librarian decided upon for the day. In many local stations the d.j. would sign on in the morning with piles of records already waiting, prepared for that day's programs by the music librarian the night before, and the d.j. might not even know what the music for each show was before it was played.

Then came "Top-40," an attempt to reflect and to appeal to the tastes of the listeners by choosing records on the basis of record popularity as judged by sales charts, juke box surveys and record store reports. Top-40, at the beginning, was eclectic, with stations playing the same 40 most popu-lar selections, with principally the personality of the d.j. and the other ser-vices of the station, such as news or features, providing a reason for listener choice of station. Soon, however, many stations began to seek specialized audiences by concentrating on certain kinds of music. Top-40 still prevailed, and in many instances was adapted to the country and western, rock, soul and other formats.

With the emphasis on research and the music sound itself, the d.j. became less important and the between-record patter that had become a staple for the audience and the means to stardom for the radio personality began to fade. By the late 1960's the Top-40 stations were in trouble. Flexi-ble formats, such as those of the emerging FM rock stations ("rockers") were providing a serious challenge. The single record concept of the Top-40 was no longer valid, with albums making up some 85% of all retail record sales. Artists no longer made "hot" singles, but aimed for hit albums, with single cuts from the album used only to promote the entire album. Many Top-40 stations had become almost mechanical (not to be confused with automated, although that followed, too), with virtually no disc jockey patter, a playlist of only the most popular records (shortly after the rise of Top-40, some playlists would go as high as 100 records; after a while some playlists were down to 10) and quick "segues" from record to record.

One of the most effective approaches to rejuvenating Top-40 was to bring back emphasis on the d.j., providing "warmth" between records and more flexibility in format. Personality became important again and stations today are wedding personality with the station sound. Flexibility also grew in terms of audience, with record companies sensing the pulse by bringing back former recording stars. In the fall of 1972 five of the top six hits on the charts at one point were by Chuck Berry, Curtis Mayfield, Johnny Nash, Ricky Nelson and Elvis Presley, all of whom had had their first hits in the 1950's. Even FM, which was thought to be the province of specialized music, particularly progressive rock in the pop field for a select sophisticated audience, began to accommodate Top-40 formats.

By 1973 Top-40 had revived itself and was still the leader, with number "one" ranked stations in six of the top 15 markets, and number "two" in seven of the 15.

MOR

MOR, or Middle-of-the-Road music, continued to be the most popular "sound" into the middle 1970's. Although many station representatives are selling an 18-49 audience and claim that the demographics of radio are rapidly changing, the basic audience breakdowns still hold. 12-17 age span for contemporary Top-40, 18-24 for progressive rock, 25-49 for MOR and over 49 for good music. The largest age span and most active product-purchasers are in the MOR category: the "middle" of the demographic "road."

MOR is, essentially, "adult" music. It is programming without extremes, either in volume, rhythm, timing or technique. But because adults change, MOR music also changes. To one generation MOR is Frank Sinatra, Peggy Lee and Nat King Cole. To another generation also in the adult demographic road — remember that the people who grew up on Rock and Roll are now over 30 — MOR is the Beatles and The Fifth Dimension. Adult tastes are different because the adults are different and, to some degree, even contemporary rock can now be considered MOR. The 1973 *Television/Radio Age* survey verified the blending of different types of music — including elements of contemporary-folk, modern-country, rock-country, classical-jazz, country and western — into the continually evolving MOR formats.

The MOR station, flexible in its approach, does not concentrate on music alone, as do some other specialized stations. MOR programming usually combines good portions of news, features, information and talk. MOR is a personality-oriented format and announcer-deejays at MOR stations are likely to become local and even regional celebrities (see the d.j. profiles in Chapter 7), sometimes with the deliberate promotion of their stations.

Golden oldies. MOR is probably the least specialized of the specialized formats and in the early 1970's began to incorporate an approach that was successful enough to threaten to become a station format in itself: "oldies" or "golden oldies." Oldies are MOR records, but they usually are limited to popular music of some 15 to 30 years vintage. The popularity of oldies is hard to analyze; the obvious answer, but one given as a reason for almost all shifts to nostalgia, is discontent of the people with the events of their times. Musically, the initial excitement of hard rock may have worn off and the disappearance of the Beatles and the lack of personalities to equal their creativity and innovation may have turned many people away from hard rock and back to the earlier, now golden oldies, rock and roll music. Some formats concentrate on oldies, with many leading AM adult stations in the early 1970's playing golden oldies some 50% of the time. Some formats mix oldies with more current MOR, alternating, for example, an Elvis Presley hit of the mid-1950's with a Sammy Davis, Jr. recording of just a few years ago.

The rise of the oldies in the early 1970's can be traced in *Billboard* magazine, where some 20 oldies regularly made the list of the "hot 100" most popular records. Some record companies began to re-record former stars and to hire new groups to remake old hits. Some collectors were paying as much as $100 for records that originally sold for 79 cents.

Beautiful music. Encompassing as it does almost all sounds that are soothing to an adult ear, MOR is frequently the basic format for stations that play predominantly "beautiful music" or "semi classical" or "dinner" music. For a time this kind of music, lush with strings, was almost exclusively the province of FM, but in the mid-1970's it began to infiltrate the AM field, in part in MOR formats and in some stations as the entire format. This is the music of Mantovani, Percy Faith, Andre Kostelanetz and Ray Conniff. It is mood music and programmers choose it carefully to fit the different moods and tempos of different times of the day. It is estimated that some 20 to 25% of the radio audience listens to beautiful music. The format has become standardized into one-quarter hour segments, each segment cohesive and providing a consistent mood in itself. News and spot announcements fit in between the quarter-hour blocks for some six to eight interruptions each hour.

Rock

When rock was new, it was easy to categorize. In the 1950's the unfamiliar screaming sounds coming from portable radios were those of a new phenomenon, Rock and Roll. Ten years later the more involved and sophisticated beats were those of hard rock, the new music of the Beatles. Less than ten years after that the FCC was so upset by the drug lyrics of the socio-political oriented underground rock that it required licensees to review records before they were played to be certain the records did not promote illegal drug use. In general, however, radio stations maintained a liberal attitude toward lyrics and the mid-1970's saw not a holding back but a trend toward letting the music on radio "tell it like it is."

Although there does seem to be a new trend in rock in the mid-70's, it is not yet definitive. Contemporary rock can fit MOR formats. Golden oldie formats frequently feature Rock and Roll revivals. Generally, listeners seem to prefer a softer sound, moving away from the dissonance of the mid- and late-1960's; soft rock instead of hard rock. In some cases the music is secondary, the listener attitudes reflecting principally their prejudices toward the life-style or dress of the people associated with acid or underground rock. They reject all "modern" rock, not realizing that progressive rock in many instances requires the soft sound in order to make clear to the listener the socio-political nature of the lyrics. Originally, sound and tempo were predominant; now with youth more and more concerned with the state of the world and its effect upon their lives, ideas are most significant. Reflecting the traditional music with meaning, folk and jazz rock have begun to grow and many artists have moved successfully into combinations of country music and rock.

One of the reasons for the success of rock is that the kids who grew up with progressive rock are now executives in agencies and stations, and their understanding and affinity to it make it easier to sell.

Country Music

Country music took radio by storm in the early 1970's and has become one of its major formats. For example, full-time country stations grew from only 81 in 1961 to 796 in 1972 and to 1,008 only one year later, 1973; stations programming three or more hours of country music daily rose from 1,046 in 1972 to 1,447 in 1973. When country music broke into New York City in 1973 — with its adoption by WHN — it knew it had really made it.

Country music represents three distinct types: modern or "soft" country, standard country and western or "hard" country, and the popular "Nashville sound." Country music came out of the people, out of the pioneers and the heritage many of them brought from England and Scotland and Wales, with their homemade instruments, their songs with clean, simple lines and music, and the narrative lyrics telling of the hard life in work and love and play. A focal point for the growth and popularization of country music outside of the rural south was the "Grand Ole Opry," which WSM, Nashville, first began programming in 1925. The progress country music began to make, particularly reaching non-southern youth who suddenly found themselves listening to country music radio stations during World War II, abruptly stopped in the early 1950's when it was supplanted by Rock and Roll; indeed, many country singers, such as Conway Twitty and Elvis Presley, turned to rock.

In the mid-1960's there were virtually only a handful of country music stars and the modern or "soft" country style that transcended the south and appealed to other areas of the country was limited to hardly more than a half dozen stations as a major format. But Nashville caught the mood and the need and through performers such as Glen Campbell began to turn out more and more "soft" country.

By the late 1960's the new Nashville sound began to be a bonanza for radio stations everywhere. The audience, too, was diverse: the working people of the rural south, who had always been country music fans and who identified with its simplified ideas and values; and, in the early 1970's, the growing number of sophisticated professionals, the bankers and lawyers and scientists who boasted about their conversion to country music, perhaps seeking escape from the ever increasing stresses of their everyday urban world through the simple songs of the simple life.

Country music stations vary in format: some emphasize one of the three major types; others cross types but, as do some MOR stations, concentrate on the oldies mixed with traditional-sounding new songs; some find excellent audience reaction to a combination of country with a different music type, such as the alternating of one country and one pop or, a successfully growing format, mixing country with soft rock as the station sound. As are other "hard" sound stations, such as "rockers," country music stations are trending toward the incorporation of a "softer" sound into their formats.

These are only a few of the music formats of stations today, and within these categories there are endless variations and adaptations to the individual station's market and listening audience. One thing is sure: the listening audience *cares* what sound it hears. It reflects its interest most obviously by the numbers that tune in any given station and through the sales records of the products advertised on that station (provided the commercials are effective enough to influence the buyer). Sometimes the audience makes its interest known in more dramatic ways. The FCC, especially during the last few years, has received many complaints, and citizen groups have even filed suits to keep a certain format from being changed by a station, ranging from progressive rock to classical.

NEWS AND TALK

Although radio was made by news — elections and sports events in the early 1920's — and throughout the years virtually all stations continued to carry at least a minimum of news (the FCC generally requires at least 5% when it reviews renewal applications), the late 1960's and early 1970's saw changes in news approaches as well as in other formats. Some stations expanded news coverage, others reduced it, but all seemed to experiment with new techniques and organization, whether they were music stations carrying filler news or whether they were all-news stations.

In both kinds of stations producers went after more actuality coverage, prompted in part by the continuing development of low-cost portable equipment. News presentation was less formal, with less reliance on the studio "anchorman." Anchor jobs themselves changed, with some large stations putting two people on, creating an informal "Chet-David" dialogue, and with more and more stations hiring women for the single or team studio positions. New approaches to news coverage were also tried, in some instances going into depth on a given story with a combination of actuality, interview and comment. With the increasing proliferation of professional athletic teams, sports coverage expanded. Many stations use specialized news segments, such as teen news in the late evening; news, weather and local events programmed in the early morning hours for truck drivers; news discussion and analysis, in addition to straight news, for the "intellectual"; local news only; semi-documentary news concentrating on particular problems in the community.

Generally, news coverage tends to fit the station sound. For example, a contemporary station may play up in content and manner of presentation the excitement and drama of the news, while a beautiful music station may have a low-key presentation while editing out disturbing elements of the news.

The format also determines the scheduling of the news. The traditional 15-minute newscasts have largely disappeared except in the top 10 markets. "Freeform" news approaches came into being in the early 1970's, news inserted wherever and whenever it was deemed desirable. Some classical stations have stayed with the standard five-minute news presentation every hour, while others, if the FCC permitted, would eliminate all news, and program uninterrupted (except for commercials) music only. Some stations have developed expanded blocks of news at commuting times. Others have concentrated on news blocks of several hours duration one or more times per day. Still others brought in one-minute news breaks, meeting the five-minute-per-hour standard by counting up the total news time during a complete broadcast day.

All-News Stations

In 1972 six of the top ten markets had at least one all-news station. An N. W. Ayer survey of the 12 all-news stations involved showed that though they comprised 5% of the total number of stations in those markets, they had 9% of the total audience, and 14.5% of the audience in the six cities in which they were located. Listenership was primarily in the over-50 age category and from middle and higher income brackets.

The growth of all-news stations and the reorientation of other stations toward news may be prompted by surveys which show that radio is the principal source of morning news for people — over television and newspapers. Another reason may be that all-news stations have found that they attract a greater diversity of advertisers than other stations. But all-news formats are expensive and the most successful operations have been those of CBS and Group W, which have ready-made sources in their international, national and local news bureaus.

Techniques of presentation and organization of content vary within all-news stations. Generally, the pace of the news is adapted to the time of day — fast in the morning and more leisurely and in depth at night. Some all-news stations have moved more and more to specialized reporting, with segments emphasizing areas such as the arts, business and science. Feature material relating to such things as local citizen events, child care and consumer information is used. Some stations have revived the local documentary with great success. In commuting areas, traffic reports are essential. "Talk" segments have grown within all-news stations, including the telephone format (topless radio flew high for a few years before FCC disapproval in 1973), interviews and the male-female conversation team.

The success of all-news stations has prompted some observers to predict that AM is heading for all-talk and FM all-music by the end of the 1970's decade.

Talk. The essence of "talk" stations is that most of the talking is done by the listeners, not the studio personalities. One of the most successful all-talk stations in the early 1970's was New York's WMCA's listener-participation format 24-hours a day. Two or more listeners can talk with each other, as well as panelists in the studio being able to talk with listeners. As with all telephone formats, it is important to hold on to callers (a stacking system for incoming calls can be used) and to screen or be able to momentarily cut off callers who are obscene or libelous. As noted above, there are various types of talk formats which can be incorporated into all-news stations, and these same formats can be adapted and expanded for all-talk, limited-news stations. The success of such stations was noted in an ARB survey shortly after WMCA's conversion to all-talk, which showed three of the top six stations in New York being all-news or all-talk, with a fourth one of the six being very heavily talk.

ETHNIC

There have been many euphemisims for ethnic in radio. At one time a number of New York stations were oriented in greater or lesser degree to foreign language programming, reflecting the "old-country" languages of large immigrant and foreign, particularly European, ethnic groups in the New York City metropolitan area. More recently ethnic became a euphemism for Black, as the civil rights struggles led to more and more recognition by and access to communications media of minority, particularly Black, groups. In the early 1970's Spanish-language programming began to emerge strongly. As noted in Chapter 1, citizen action, court decisions and FCC rulings began to open up radio to minority and ethnic groups.

Black Stations

Although in the mid-1960's there were more than 100 radio stations (sometimes called "soul" stations) programming to Black audiences, only six of these stations were Black-owned. By 1973 there were more than 300 stations programming for Black audiences, some 50 of them full-time, and only 21 were Black-owned. It is estimated that some 78% of America's Black population are within range of a Black-oriented station, and that Blacks listen to radio more hours a day than do whites. The combination of Black consciousness-raising concerning media and the growing purchasing power of Blacks (Black population in top urban markets is two-and half times the Black population percentage in the country as a whole) combined to increase the number of Black-oriented stations and to force a change in the traditional "soul" format.

The traditional soul station format has been a combination of rhythm and blues backed by strong personalities oriented toward the need and style of the particular community, with a secondary and frequently minor stress on news and public affairs. News on soul stations was principally a "rip-and-read" affair. Blacks, through citizen groups and organizations, wanted more say over programming affecting their lives, reflecting the increasing demand by Blacks during the 1960's for control over their own affairs. Blacks wanted more social and political materials over the media, desiring information that could assist, in the view of many Black leaders, in effective community action. The complaints began to read: "soul music is not enough."

Although by the mid-1970's soul music and personalities were still the dominant approach, more and more Black-oriented stations became diversified, adopting the "Black progressive radio" approach. This attempted to encompass all of the Black experience by reflecting the diverse interests of the Black population. Pop music, gospel singing, jazz, African music, classical and other forms of music related to Blacks were added to rhythm and blues. News and commentary increased, oriented to community needs.

The growth of Black stations resulted in the development, as noted in Chapter 1, of the Mutual Black Network. Many Black stations began expanding their news services using the network's news service and that of the Black Audio Network and the Third World Network. They were able to get stories of special interest to Blacks that white stations and program directors frequently ignored or missed. The National Black Network of New York, called the first Black-controlled and Black-oriented news service in the country, began operation in July, 1973 and later that year became the fifth national radio network in the NAB membership.

The exclusivity of Black and, as "white" stations are called, general market stations, is gradually fading, with many general market stations carrying Black programming, and many Black stations reaching out to white suburbia. Many Black stations, in fact, state that their high ratings are due in great measure to the listenership of white suburban teenagers. Some concern has been expressed that as soon as Black stations begin to make money they will begin to accept the commercial outlook of the general market stations and forget what some people feel is their primary responsibility.

Spanish-Language and Other Stations

Latinos comprise the second largest minority in the United States, and their increased buying power combined with complaints and filings on the part of Latino, especially Chicano, groups against stations not adequately serving Spanish-language communities, has resulted in increased Spanish-language stations and service. Latinos comprise three principal audience groups: Chicanos, located mainly in the southwest; Puerto Ricans, primarily in New York; and Cubans, concentrated in Miami. Other Latinos are scattered in smaller numbers in many cities.

Language itself is an important factor, with some estimates suggesting that perhaps 80% of Latino families in the country speak only or principally Spanish in the home. In addition, official recognition is growing for bilingualism, with voter registration, school curricula, driver's tests and similar official activities including Spanish as an acceptable language. The musical formats of Spanish-language stations concentrate on Latino and Spanish artists; sports are a major part of programming, reflecting the emphasis on sports in many Latin-American countries; serialized novels are popular and, through increased pressures by the Spanish-surnamed community, news programs stress information on jobs, schools, housing and other matters of civic concern. Community involvement is further served by panel and hot-line formats on many Spanish-language stations. In 1972 the beginnings of real growth were just visible with number one stations in two markets and stations among the top five in several other markets.

In addition to foreign language programming in those cities where there is a significant population of a given language background, some stations, specifically on the West Coast, continue to provide programming for people of Asian, particularly Oriental, background. A new movement in the early 1970's began to develop radio stations to serve the educational and informational needs of American Indians. Several stations, particularly non-commercial FM's, were established or in the process of establishment in 1974 on several Indian reservations in the west.

ONE STATION'S APPROACH: A CASE HISTORY

How does an individual station put together the various programming approaches that constitute a format? How does it relate its principal component, music (unless it is an all-talk or all-new station), to its demographic target audience? What is the place of other program elements such as news, sports and public affairs in its total format makeup?

Terry P. Hourigan, program manager of WMAL-FM, Washington, D.C., prepared a statement on format and programming objectives for his staff, which provides a clear overview of the approach of one individual station. (You may wish to develop a similar guide for the station you work for or listen to or hope someday to build.) Mr. Hourigan's statement in its entirety:

Basic Objective

WMAL-FM has as its basic programming objective the achievement of the largest 18 to 34 year old audience in the Metropolitan Washington area. This will, in turn, allow us to accomplish two essential goals; making our station a dominant force on the FM band and increasing our contribution as a profit center in the Evening Star Broadcasting Company.

We approach this task with a very positive outlook. The timing is right, the goal is realistic and our approach is sound. Our plan of attack centers around the market key to this 18 to 34 year old audience, the 25 year old, highly educated young professional. He or she is our specific target. If we can attract the 25 year old we have zeroed in on the person of highest influence in our demographic group. Persons on the younger end of the spectrum all wish to be thought of as being "really adult," while many of those over that age are clinging to the "with it" image of the younger man or woman.

These people all coalesce in their radio listening desires. Brought up on a steady diet of top-40 and hard rock music, they have grown accustomed to its rapid pace and brevity of expression, but have been educated past the point of being able to accept the banality of top-40 or the non-musical noise of hard rock radio. There exists, therefore, a potentially huge market of untapped listeners waiting to be claimed — waiting for a station or sound they can call their own. The station is WMAL-FM. The sound is *"The Soft Explosion."* What follows is our game plan.

The Market

Washington, D.C. is a community dominated by relatively affluent young professionals. The metropolitan area is experiencing an explosive growth in population. Rapidly expanding Federal Government facilities continue to attract highly educated younger families to move into expensive homes in the metro area where an extremely high percentage of the more affluent families are located. The following facts make Washington unique among the nation's 10 largest cities. Washington metro area has an average median age of 24.1 years, with 34.7% of the population under 18 years of age and only 6.0% over age 64 — youngest by far in the country.

The average household income is $12,477 annually, the *largest* in the United States:

> Washington ranks #1 in household income.
> Washington ranks #1 in population increase.
> Washington ranks #3 in value of homes.
> Washington ranks #2 in annual purchase of FM sets.
> Washington has 431,300 metro area men 18-34.
> Washington has 468,800 metro area women 18-34.
> Washington is the nation's youngest, fastest growing market.

Personalities

Our on-the-air personalities are now, and will continue to be, aware of the unique opportunity they have to help mold the thinking and tastes of the 18 to 34 year old audience, and of the corresponding burden of responsibility this entails. They have uppermost in their minds the thought of projecting a positive, warm image — the thought that the station cares very much that the listener has chosen to listen to us. We feel, as broadcaster Chuck Blore said, "If you're programming a radio station and someone tunes into your frequency, they've given you everything they have to offer, their ears and their minds. And if you're *programming* that radio station, you have to give them something in return, and we try to give them reward after reward after reward for tuning to our place on the dial."

We believe our personalities can do just that. Their job is to communicate with the audience, to project the image that they are happy in their work, that it is truly pleasurable to present our programming, that the listener deserves the very best we have to offer and that the very best is exactly what he or she is getting.

Music

A most essential ingredient in programming for the 18-34 listener is music. While very careful control must be exercised over the selection and presentation of music, it must not sound too structured. Our morning show has been used for the past four months as a testing place, a proving ground for our new music mix. It has proven successful beyond our fondest hopes. Our audience growth in this period of tightened programming control has been 60% over the last two rating books, and our demographics almost entirely 18-34. The music formula has been devised for simplicity of implementation. This simplicity adds to our control, making more effective our ability to hold control of our music in the face of changing audience tastes. In effect, it makes us "fad-proof."

We play a mix composed of three ingredients:

1. *Contemporary Hits.* Those of the current contemporary best-sellers which fall within the parameters of the taste of our 25 year old; no "bubble gum," no non-musical noise, only good solid hits, songs which have achieved mass favor with young-adult listeners.

2. *New Album Cuts.* These songs are selected by our music director as the best efforts of the best contemporary artists, only the best one or two tracks in the best of the new albums. (This keeps us ahead of the "hit" game. In recent years the former music industry trend has been reversed and today albums are released months ahead of the singles.)

3. *FM Oldies.* These are simply hits by groups which have become the "standards" of modern rock music. Included are people like The Beatles, The Byrds, Blood, Sweat & Tears, Carole King, etc. These are chosen carefully and mixed for best maximum effect.

These three ingredients, carefully selected, imaginatively showcased, are the entirety of our music formula. Nothing gets on the air which has not met these established criteria.

News and Public Affairs

1973 will be a year of departure from the previously accepted standard of formal, "structured" newscasts. Our air personalities will integrate news items, with particular emphasis given to the local news, throughout the entire hour. There will be no "aside" comments by the announcers, no personal opinions about the news stories, just a good, brief, positive delivery of information, as smoothly integrated into the overall program flow as a commercial.

WMAL-FM will continue its effort to broadcast programs in the public interest, but they must take a new form. The line uppermost in our minds must be *"Eliminate Turnoffs!"* We feel a line of demarcation must be drawn between informing and educating the listener, and boring him or her. "Mini-specials" will be the order of the day, with all our personalities brought into the effort. These mini-specials will always be attempting to accomplish something positive — getting our audience personally involved in the areas we explore. Ours is the most socially-conscious audience in the history of radio and we would not be living up to our responsibility as broadcasters if we failed to stimulate this force to the best of our ability.

Public Service and Special Programming

Our increased commercial success has not lessened our commitment in the area of public service. We retain on our staff the position of public service director and have a continual dialog with a wide number of community groups and interests, resulting in their knowledge that WMAL-FM knows their problems and is ready to give almost instant help in informing the community. We have also undertaken major campaigns designed to help combat drug abuse, fight the growing VD epidemic and inform the public about sickle cell disease. We have participated in three-station campaigns on behalf of the United Givers Fund, The Black United Fund and the Salvation Army.

Washington Redskins. WMAL-FM is the Redskins station on FM. Our involvement with and promotion of the Skins great championship drive, our daily talk show with Jerry Smith, daily conversations on the air with Steve Gilmartin, "The Voice of the Redskins," have made us the leading FM sports station in Washington.

In Concert. Our broadcasts of these 90-minute rock specials, simulcast with WMAL-TV, has created an enormous audience for late night weekend programming. The acceptance by our audience of this, the most innovative new idea in entertainment programming in recent years, has opened the way for alternate week specials as well. The Music Festival, with John Lyon, is a locally produced 90-minute rock special featuring major artists recorded in concert settings.

Other Specials. Black Gold ran in April, 1973, as a 12-hour special featuring the greatest black musicians in pop music of the past 20 years. A cooperative venture informing the public about Howard University's Center for Sickle Cell Disease research, *Black Gold* was underwritten by Safeway Foods. *Beatles '72* was a five hour concert exploring the influence in music and life style of the most dominant force in the history of rock music. *Tommy* was a specially showcased presentation of the rock opera.

FORMAT RESPONSIBILITIES AND RESTRAINTS

A station cannot simply change a format at will — technically, anyway. First, in applying for a construction permit, a station must make a showing of how its proposed programming will meet the needs of the community. At renewal time the FCC checks the station's representative programming during the license period to see if the station has lived up to its promises. If it has not, it is expected to justify its change in programming.

In addition, citizen groups are increasingly making their wishes known to stations and to the FCC on programming formats. The FCC prefers to give the broadcaster, whether a licensee making a change or a purchaser proposing a new format, considerable flexibility. The FCC has stated that "Unless it is shown or appears to the Commission that the format choice is not reasonably attuned to the tastes and general interests of the community of license, we will not question the licensee's judgment in these matters." Court decisions, however, have established the public's right to have its views considered in any substantial change of format. In 1973 the U.S. Court of Appeals stated in the case of The Citizens Committee to Keep Progressive Rock:

> . . . the public has an interest in diversity of entertainment formats and therefore . . . format changes can be detrimental to the public interest. . . . The Commission must consider format changes and their effect upon the desired diversity. . . . In essence, one man's Bread is the next man's Bach, Bacharach, or Buck Owens and the Buckaroos, and where 'technically and economically feasible,' it is in the public's best interest to have all segments represented. . . . If no objection is raised to a format change the Commission may properly assume that the format is acceptable and, so long as all else is in order, it may grant the application. When the public grumbling reaches significant proportions . . . the format change becomes an issue for resolution and hearing procedures are applicable if issues of fact are in dispute. Questions regarding the extent of support for the format themselves may be material, and if substantial then the proper procedure is either a survey of the area residents or a hearing on the issue. Once the factual disputes are exposed and a hearing held the Commission's decision regarding the public interest must be reasoned and based upon substantial evidence. Failure to hold a required hearing or failure to render a reasoned decision will be, as always, reversible error. No more is required, no less is accepted.

In many instances, rather than going through the FCC or the courts, citizen groups have found it more efficient to work directly with the broadcaster, and a number of incipient complaints and suits have been settled outside of government channels.

BIBLIOGRAPHY

Johnson, Joseph S. and Kenneth K. Jones, *Modern Radio Station Practices*. Belmont, California: Wadsworth, 1972. Profiles of 14 different kinds of stations in different markets illustrate principles of station operations.

Lichty, L. W. and J. M. Ripley, *American Broadcasting: Introduction and Analysis*. Madison, Wisconsin: College Printing, 1969. Programming and audiences of radio.

Passman, Arnold, *The Deejays*. New York: MacMillan, 1971. A history of music on radio.

Sanger, Elliott M., *Rebel In Radio: The Story of WQXR*. New York: Hastings House, Publishers, 1973. How what is now the Radio Station of the *New York Times* "broke the rules" in pioneering good music, by its co-founder.

Taylor, Sherril W., ed., *Radio Programming in Action*. New York: Hastings House, 1967. An analysis of major radio formats in practice by officials of representative stations throughout the country.

Broadcasting Yearbook. In addition to general data on stations, agencies, representatives, program producers and other pertinent areas, *Broadcasting Yearbook* contains a special section (Section D in the 1973 edition) which lists stations according to format, ranging from Adult to Variety and including popular formats such as Black, Classical, MOR, Progressive, Top-40 and less popular formats such as Big Bands, Farm and Gospel.

Because of the changing nature of radio formats and programming, professional journals in the broadcasting field are the best source of information and analysis (next to carefully monitoring the radio stations receivable in your community). Among the publications which frequently carry articles on radio formats are *Billboard, BM/E (Broadcast Management Engineering), Broadcasting Magazine, Journal of Broadcasting, Public Telecommunications Review, Television/Radio Age* and *Variety*.

GEORGE L. HALL

Director of Telecommunications
for the State of Virginia

• After almost 17 years in commercial radio and television, George L. Hall entered the field of educational broadcasting in 1960. He is currently Director of Telecommunications for the State of Virginia. Immediately previous to his appointment to this position in 1972 he was, since 1967, Research and Development Officer and Associate Director of Professional Services for the National Association of Educational Broadcasters in Washington, D.C. Prior to that he served as director of the Teaching Resources Center at the University of Delaware. In that position his responsibilities involved supervision of an elaborate program of instructional technology as well as regular lecturing on broadcasting and related subjects.

An alumnus of the University of Virginia, Mr. Hall entered radio work in 1946 as a writer and announcer. Beginning in 1951 he served for five years as program director for WRAL-AM-FM and for the regional Tobacco Network. In 1956, after participating in the hearings that resulted in WRAL's receiving an FCC license for a television station, Mr. Hall became program director of WRAL-TV. His interest in the field of education prompted him to accept the position of program director at the Chapel Hill studios of educational station WUNC-TV in 1960. The following year he was appointed to the faculty of North Carolina State University at Raleigh as director of television. During his four years in that post, he helped N.C.S.U. develop a strong program in ITV, served as an instructor on mass communication in the department of sociology and acted as faculty advisor to campus radio station WKNC.

As a writer, Mr. Hall has had his plays produced in community and educational theatre, and on television and radio. In addition to newspaper and periodical articles, he is the author of a handbook for the United States Weather Service on Hurricane-Alert broadcasting for multi-state radio networks. He has been active in both educational and commercial broadcasting associations and is a frequent speaker, panel participant and workshop director. He has conducted special studies of broadcasting systems in Asia, Africa, Europe, the West Indies and the South Pacific, as well as in the United States.

4

PROGRAMMING
AND
MANAGEMENT

BY GEORGE L. HALL

This chapter is divided into four sections. The first concerns definitions of radio programming; the second, programming techniques; the third, station organization and management of program operations; and the fourth, radio advertising.

PROGRAMMING DEFINITIONS

Radio Programming is Communication

Basically, *communication* is the social process through which one person (the communicator) elicits responses from another person (the communicant) by the use of symbols. The communicator in radio programming is far more apt to be a group than an individual. Radio broadcasting is customarily an ensemble task in which numbers of people have a part: announcers, musicians, engineers, writers, publicists and others. The communicant in radio programming is almost always a member of a large group — the audience. (Some characteristics of audiences will be investigated later.)

Symbols are stimuli produced by a communicator and received by a communicant. They carry meanings which are more or less shared by both parties. (Words, pictures and gestures are kinds of symbols.) Only aural symbols can be used in radio communication. This is a limitation of sorts. Most people are more used to aural-visual symbols, notably those in the speech-with-gesture category. Even so, radio can employ the rich and varied symbol categories of music and speech-without-gesture.

Meanings are the similar responses which both communicator and communicant would customarily make to particular symbols when presented in similar contexts.

Responses are the specific behavior elicited by symbols. Sometimes such behavior is overt: a communicant moves, smiles, frowns or otherwise reacts in a way which can be observed by the communicator. At most times, however, response behavior is covert: a communicant thinks, imagines or feels without manifesting any physical reaction which can be observed by the communicator. When a communicator observes — or somehow discovers — overt response behavior by a communicant, he* is said to be receiving feedback from his* symbols.

Feedback enables a communicator to ascertain whether or not his symbols have elicited from the communicant (or listener) the responses he intended. It can also help a communicator find out if he and the listener are sharing the meanings of the symbols employed. Feedback is difficult to obtain in radio programming because the communicator/group is physically separated from the large audience. Overt response behavior by individual members of the audience usually cannot be observed directly by the broadcasters. Instead, feedback is sometimes obtained by various, complex methods of statistical discovery. For example, a small "sample" group of listeners will be asked to report on their own response behavior, particularly in regard to which programming they actually tuned in. Statisticians will convert the resulting data into figures by which the broadcasters may infer the response behavior of the whole audience.

Broadcasters, like personal communicators, are apt to let feedback help determine their courses of future action. Positive feedback, indicating that the communicator's intentions have been realized, is interpreted as a sign of success and is likely to cause continuance of that programming. Negative feedback may not represent a communicator's failure so much as indicate the need for the communicator to try again. This often leads to programming revision or repetition.

Revision involves a communicator's trying a different set of symbols to elicit the desired response. He may decide to choose symbols which have a certain redundancy. *Redundancy* is the term given the use of several different symbols which carry a common meaning, as with synonyms. Sometimes redundancy is inadvertent and unwanted. *Repetition* involves a communicator's trying the same symbols all over again after receiving negative feedback. This technique is often employed when the communicator suspects that the communicant did not receive the symbols on the initial try. Symbol reception is an essential aspect of communication.

Reception of symbols through the aural and visual channels is most important for most people in their everyday communication. Symbol re-

---

* The words "he" and "his" are used in this chapter as impersonal pronouns, recognizing as we do that positions in broadcasting are held by men and women both.

ception may be adversely affected when some physical block or extraneous stimulus (like noise) interferes with the symbols themselves. Still another cause of inadequate reception can result from a communicator's failure to attract or hold the attention of the person with whom he wishes to communicate.

Attention-attractants are particularly significant in broadcast communication. A communicator can attract attention in several ways. He may cause his symbols to have high stimulus *intensity;* that is, he may make them very loud, fast, large, bright, and so forth. Low stimulus intensity can also be an effective attractant technique in certain situations. Perhaps the most potent attractants are those symbols which serve as *psychological triggers.* People tend to pay quicker and closer attention to symbols which they associate with their basic drives and needs.

The basic needs of people also underlie the four social functions of communication: surveillance, prescription, cultural transmission and entertainment.

Surveillance is the label applied to communication which reports on happenings in the environment. In radio broadcasting it is manifested in such informational program types as newscasts and weathercasts. *Prescription* refers to communication giving advice or directions about measures which communicants might take in reaction to environmental conditions. Health talks and commercial announcements are likely to show this function. *Cultural transmission* is the imparting to new members of the community the beliefs and attitudes of the older members. Church sermons and educational lectures are broadcasts of this nature. Symbols used for amusement reflect the *entertainment* function. Disc jockey shows and quiz programs are obvious examples of entertainment.

Radio is a Medium of Communication

Basically, a communications *medium* is any material or device used to extend symbols over space or through time. There are many media available to modern communicators. Print, cinema, television and radio are the dominant media in our culture today.

Radio and television, as electronic media, are dependent on complex electromagnetic devices and associated materials. The symbol output of radio and television broadcasting is called programming. The broadcasting media usually extend their symbols over long space but not through long time. Their symbols are not usually re-used as are those in the print, photographic and film media, although various electronic recording devices can store the symbols for future use.

Radio Can be Used for Mass-Communication

Basically, *mass-communication* occurs when symbol materials are di-

rected through a medium toward a relatively large, scattered and hetero-
genous audience.

In radio broadcasting, a relatively large audience is that number which
represents a significant percentage of the population living in the geographical area which a station or network serves. Its significance is dependent upon
such factors as the day of the week, the hour of the day and the number of
persons living in homes that are equipped with radios. For example, an
audience of 30 percent of the population might be considered "large" on a
snowy Sunday afternoon in a community of 30,000 where many homes are
radio-equipped. In that same community, an audience of 1 percent might
be "large" if the program being measured were broadcast at 3:30 a.m.,
Monday, when 97 percent of the population was asleep. The fact that a mass
audience is scattered (that is, the individual members are not gathered together in one place) has much to do with the difficulty of feedback in radio
programming. An even more consequential aspect of mass-communication
for the radio programmer is that of audience heterogeneity.

Mass audiences are composed of people who are different from each
other in a great many respects. These differences may be social, educational,
economic, psychological, cultural, ethical, religious, political, physical or
intellectual. This wide diversity of backgrounds, skills and attitudes produces
problems for mass-communicators. In addition, audience members receive
programs in a wide variety of different locales, each with a certain level of
distractions present. Receiving sets of differing sound qualities are used, with
a considerable risk that forms of technical distortion may interfere in some
degree with program symbols. The immediate activity of a listener during
reception is still another factor. Some people may sit and concentrate on a
program while others may let the radio serve more-or-less as a source of
background accompaniment to work or reading.

It should be remembered that the basic media — print, cinema, television and radio — can be used for private as well as mass communication,
and it is only when radio is used for the latter that the process is termed
broadcasting.

As noted earlier, the success of any communication is determined by
the response behavior of the listener or viewer. Responses generally are
intended to fall into two broad categories: attending and reacting. *Attending*
responses occur when a communicant simply pays attention to the symbols.
In radio, that means simply listening. Of course, even before listening can
occur, a program must be tuned in on a receiving set. Therefore, tuning-in
is also a kind of attending response. Another kind is found in the immediate, affective behavior of the communicant during symbol reception itself:
laughing, crying, shuddering, or such. *Reacting* responses occur some time
after the reception of a program. The range of desired behavior is varied.
The programmer may wish audience members to do such things as buy
the product advertised, make a contribution to a charity which was pro-

moted, drive more safely, or make a pudding with the recipe which was described.

Attending responses are primary in radio programming. Above all else most broadcasters wish mass audiences to tune in and listen to their programs. This is not to say that certain reacting responses are not also very desirable, particularly the subsequent purchase and consumption of advertised goods. However, such complex reacting responses are difficult to elicit from a mass audience because of its heterogeneity. Of course, broadcasters do not really attempt to elicit the same responses from all members of a mass audience. (Mass-communicators have long recognized the impracticality and impossibility of such a task.) Instead, they aim at what might be termed the *widest-possible-consensus.*

Although every member of a mass audience is genuinely unique, each is likely to have some characteristics which are similar to those of a number of other members of that audience. These characteristics may sometimes take the forms of attitudes, interests, prejudices, preferences and opinions. The individual audience members who have such characteristics in common are said to be "in a consensus." There exist many consensuses formed around many values in any mass audience, but only those which include relatively large numbers of people are generally important to broadcasters. The radio broadcaster seeks especially to find sizeable consensuses which result from common attitudes that can indicate which sorts of programming are most apt to be listened to. The wider the consensus numerically, the larger the probable audience for the programming in question. Years of positive feedback have confirmed the general worth of this strategy for programmers. The widest-possible-consensus includes listeners who are frequently designated "average." A program preference established by this kind of consensus is usually sanctioned by broadcasters as reflecting "popular taste."

The widest-possible-consensus is valuable not only in helping programmers elicit attending responses (tune-in and listenership) but also in assisting them to predict the probable success of obtaining various sorts of reacting responses. This knowledge (imprecise as it is) allows radio broadcasters to be fairly realistic about probable audience reactions to commercials and other messages.

Radio Programming Reflects a Variety of Social Forces

The total population of a community is a mass audience which contains a great number of attitudinal consensuses. However, attitude is not the only factor which can unite individuals into groupings. Other groups may emerge because of similarities in the roles, authority and possessions of persons. These might be called *status* groups because their very nature tends to rank them into a social hierarchy with the more powerful at the top and the less powerful below.

The groups at the top of this hierarchy are often referred to as the *power structure*. The individuals constituting the power structure tend to control the dominant economic, cultural and political resources of a community. It is important to note that the power structure is rarely gathered together in one consensus. Instead, there may be many different consensuses among numbers of its members. Some of these are even apt to be in disagreement or in conflict with others. These internal divisions weaken the power structure so that its control of dominant community resources is not rigidly directed by a single fixed attitude or philosophy. Nevertheless, there are enough consensuses to represent a general power structure philosophy about economics, education, politics, art and the like. More often than not these beliefs have come to be widely regarded as worthy standards for the community as a whole.

The status groups which are not included in the power structure fall into two distinct categories: the *bulk population* and *minorities*. The bulk population is composed of those people who tend to form the widest-possible-consensuses on a wide range of values and issues. While bulk attitudes might sometimes differ with those of the power structure, sharp conflict between them is not often present. The bulk population is customarily the "average" component of the social hierarchy. Minority groups differ in status or attitude from both the power structure and the bulk population. These differences may be broadly classified as being cultural, economic and political, although other terms like ethnic and religious are also applied. The members of some minorities are so unlike others in the community that they are said to constitute a *sub-culture*. This is notably true when the differences include language, manner of dress and such. Although some minorities are cruelly discriminated against, most actually blend into the general community life except when some sensitive attitude is at variance with that of the larger group.

Radio programmers have special relationships with the power structure, the bulk population and some minorities. These relationships have a direct bearing on the program output itself.

The power structure views broadcasting as an instrument for community good. People in these leadership groups regularly seek involvement in serious content areas about which they feel particular concern: religion, commerce, politics, education, public morals, property, medicine and such. Programs treating with these matters are almost certain to originate with the power structure or, at least, to receive its attention and sanction. This does not mean that the power structure exercises a blunt, external censorship *per se* over such programming. Instead, it means that the broadcast programmer tends to be so closely allied with the leadership elements of the community that their attitudes are also often his. Entrepreneurs constitute a significant status group within the power structure. They have established that the media of mass-communication can contribute to the economic growth of a community through the inclusion of advertising content to stimulate consumption and the sale of goods. Consequently, entrepreneurs — acting as advertisers — have taken a guiding role in the operation of the mass media, radio among them.

The importance of the bulk population to the radio programmer has already been noted in the discussion about the widest-possible-consensus. It is necessary to add here only that the power structure generally accepts this approach because the technique does result in attracting large audiences, which are deemed necessary for effective advertising and perhaps also for other kinds of prescriptive programming. The program preferences of the bulk population and those of the power structure sometimes may be in disagreement. As a general rule, the numerically wider consensus will be allowed to prevail except where strong objection from a relatively unified power structure over-rides.

Broadcasters take minorities into account in several ways. First, some broadcasters regard certain, larger minorities as total audiences for their programming. This is notably true in metropolitan areas where the high number of competing stations may reduce the widest-possible-consensuses for a few stations to such relatively limited audience numbers, concentrating, for example, on Spanish language programming. Second, broadcasters must take the interests and needs of minorities into account, as required by FCC rules and regulations for station ascertainment of community needs. Third, when points of view of minorities are attacked or challenged in programs, rebuttal opportunities must be provided under the provisions of the FCC's "Fairness Doctrine." Fourth, broadcasters legally, as well as morally, are obligated to employ minority persons on their staffs as required by the FCC's 1971 Equal Employment Opportunities program. The FCC rules concerning ascertainment of community needs, fairness and equal employment are discussed in Chapter 1.

Critics of broadcasting have sometimes expressed concern that many of the essential differences between the program preferences of the power structure, the bulk population and minorities have become too blurred over the years. Nowadays, they say, practically everybody tends to like the "limited" kinds of programming based on the widest-possible-consensus among the bulk population. Whatever the reason, such programming, often labeled "popular entertainment," is certainly the dominant type in American broadcasting today.

PROGRAMMING TECHNIQUES

Length

The programming output of a station is usually broken up into a sequence of individual units which vary in length. Those which last from a few seconds to three minutes are customarily called *announcements* or *"spots."* Units of greater length are referred to as *programs.* Program lengths are ordinarily stated as round figures which are multiples of five minutes. However, in actual practice such programs will often last for 30 to 60 seconds less than the stated length. For example, a so-called 15-minute program might actually last on the air for only 14 minutes or 14 minutes, 30 seconds. This enables the broadcaster to insert one or more announcements before the start of the next program. It is customary to include in this kind of transitional interval a brief announcement which identifies the station by call letters and location. The Federal Communications Commission requires these "station breaks" at regular times in a schedule, generally on the hour and at the half hour. Occasionally these may fall between parts of a longer program.

The written schedule from which a station actually operates is called a *program log.* (See Fig. 1.) Conforming to certain regulations of the FCC, a program log is prepared in advance by staff traffic specialists and later signed by announcers, engineers or production technicians who can vouch for its accuracy as a record of programming actually broadcast.

In the days before television, most radio programs were neatly 15 or 30 minutes in length (i.e. 14:30 or 29:30). Nowadays the tendency is for stations to schedule programs which last for several hours, although brief news-type programs may be interspersed at convenient intervals. The longer units are apt to be recorded music shows: disc jockey, background music, classical concert.

Frequency

Most broadcasters keep track of their program schedules by drawing up a "traffic board" with seven vertical columns to represent the days of the week. Horizontal lines are drawn across the chart to represent the hours of the day (and perhaps shorter intervals as well). The names of programs (and announcements) are entered in the appropriate spaces. The traffic board is the primary source of information necessary to prepare the program log each day. (See Fig. 2.)

Radio programming usually operates in daily and weekly schedule patterns. The five weekdays tend to show a common scheme, with Saturday and Sunday showing separate schemes. Programs which recur in the same broadcast day show a *vertical* relationship because they appear in the same vertical column on the traffic board. News, weather and comparable "service" programs often have vertical relationships. Programs which recur at the same hour on different days of the week show a *horizontal* relationship. When there is a week-to-week program recurrence, the relationship is *cyclic.* In radio, many programs have vertical, horizontal and cyclic relationships. If the horizontal relationship involves all five weekdays, the programs are said to be scheduled "across the board." Nowadays strong patterns of frequency relationship in programming seem to contribute to listener convenience and habit.

RVA PROGRAM LOG

WRVA   RICHMOND, VA.

DAY   DATE

WEDNESDAY   3/21/73

| PROGRAM TIME | | | PROGRAM TITLE — SPONSOR | ALPHA ORGIN | COMM'L MATTER OR ANNC'T | | PROGRAM | | STAT. |
BEGIN	END	I.D.			LENGTH	TYPE	SOURCE	TYPE	IDENT.
6:00:00	6:05:00		WRVA NEWS & WEATHER				L	N	
6:05:00	6:30:00		ALDEN AAROE SHOW				REC	E	
			Note: please aircheck Ritt Cons/Hazel Ritt between 6:45 & 6:55 am						
			Courtesy Lincoln	LMC	CT :60	CM			
			Glenwood Gardens	GG	:60	CM			
			S&H/Colonial	SG	CT :60	CM			
6:15:00	6:20:00		VA MUSEUM/HAZELTINE	TAPE			L	I3	
			Social.Sec. Adm. (HEW)	CT	:30	PSA			
			B. C. Remedy	BD	CT :60	CM			
			Loretta Lynn Rodeo	LLL	CT :30	CM			
			Cadillac Plastic	CP	CT :60	CM			
			TH Spring Campn.	THS	CT :60	CM			
			Airborne Freight Corp	AF	CT :60	CM			
			Giant Food	GF	CT :60	CM			
6:30:00	6:35:00		WRVA NEWS & WEATHER				L	N	
			Rich. Ford Dealers	RFD	CT :60	CM			
6:35:00	6:56:00		ALDEN AAROE SHOW				REC	E	
			Trafficopter Promo		CT :40	SPA			
			Revco Housecleaning	RVS	CT :60	CM			
			United Va.	UV	CT :30	CM			
			Amer. Dairy Asso.	ADA	CT :60	CM			
			Sweet 'n Low	CPC	CT :30	CM			
			Sears Automotive	SRA	CT :60	CM			
			Chevrolet Div/Cap.	GMC	CT :30	CM			
6:45:00	6:46:00		WRVA HEADLINES				L	N	
		aircheck	Esskay Meats	SK	:60	CM			
			Ritt cons/Vogel Ritt	RCT	CT :30	CM			
			Amer Home/Prep H	AH	CT :60	CM			
6:57:00	6:59:00		WEATHERGRAM--OPEN+CLOSE		CT		LOG	N	
			*Vepco	VEP	CT 1:30	CM			

| OPERATOR OR ANNOUNCER | OFF | ON | OPERATOR OR ANNOUNCER | OFF |

Fig. 1

WRVA PROGRAM LOG

WRVA RICHMOND, VA.

DAY   DATE

WEDNESDA   3/21/73

PROGRAM TIME		☆ PM	PROGRAM TITLE — SPONSOR	ALPHA ORGIN	COMM'L MATTER OR ANNC'T		PROGRAM		STA
BEGIN	END	I.D.			LENGTH	TYPE	SOURCE	TYPE	IDE
7:00:00	7:05:30		NBC NEWS				NBC	N	
			Network Matter		1:30	CM			
7:05:30	7:14:00		WRVA NEWS & WEATHER				L	N	
	(5 - m)		*With CT Intro/Close & CT Spot Pennzoil Motor Oil PMO *CT*		1:30	CM			
			7-11 Stores SES *CT*		:60	CM			
			Yager's Liniment YD *CT*		:60	CM			
7:14:00	7:30:00		ALDEN AAROE SHOW				REC	E	
			Richmond Ind. Loan RL		:60	CM			
			Universal Motor Co. UM *CT*		:30	CM			
			Heritage(2:00) Woody Funeral Home WF CT		:60	CM			
			Sears Eager I SRE		:60	CM			
			Bill May/Zenith BMZ		:60	CM			
7:30:00	7:35:00		WRVA NEWS & WEATHER				L	N	
			With *CT* Intro/Close & CT Spots *Richmond Fed. Sav. RF		1:30	CM			
7:	7:		TRAFFICOPTER REPORT REM				L	N	
			$Altair Airlines AAL *CT*		:30	CM			
7:37:00	8:00:00		ALDEN AAROE SHOW				REC	E	
			Hanover Tire Co. HTC (instead of 3/21/73)		:60	CM			
			Mercer Rug MCC		:60	CM			
7:	7:		TRAFFICOPTER REPORT REM				L	N	
			$Internat'l Harvester III		:30	CM			
			Sears Home Fashions SRH CT		:60	CM			
7:	7:		TRAFFICOPTER REPORT REM				L	N	
			($Rich. Metro. Auth. RMA *CT* (AM *CT*		:60	CM			
			New Virginians CT		:60	PSA			
7:	7:		TRAFFICOPTER REPORT REM				L	N	
			$HarmonFisher/Marcm. HF *copy #2*		:60	CM			

Note please attached Complete 8am newscast.!!!!

7:	7:		TRAFFICOPTER REPORT REM				L	N	
			$United Va. UV *CT*		:30	CM			

N	OPERATOR OR ANNOUNCER	OFF	ON	OPERATOR OR ANNOUNCER	OFF

Fig. 1 (*Continued*)

	MONDAY	TUESDAY	WEDNESDAY	THURSDAY	FRIDAY	SATURDAY	SUNDAY
6:00 a.m.	Alarm Clock Club – – – – – – – – – – – – – –					– – – – – – –	Hymns of Faith
7:00	News – – – – – – – – – – – – – – – – –					– – – – – – –	– – –
7:05	Alarm Clock Club (continued) – – – – – – – – –					– – – – – →	Music for Sunday
7:30	News – – – – – – – – – – – – – – – – – –					– – – – – →	Music for Sunday
7:35	Alarm Clock Club (continued) – – – – – –					– – – – – →	Music for Sunday
7:45	Sportsnews – – – – – – – – – – – – – –					– – – – →	Religious Newscast
7:50	Alarm Clock Club (continued) – – – – –					– – – – →	Religious Newscast
8:00	News – – – – – – – – – – – – – – – – – –					– – – – –	↑
8:05	Alarm Clock Club (concluded) – – – – –					– – – – →	Organ Melodies
9:00	News – – – – – – – – – – – – – – – – – –					– – – – –	↑
9:05	Homemaker Harmonies – – – – – – – – – –					→ Hits in Review	– – – Choir Time
10:00	News – – – – – – – – – – – – – – – – – –					– – – – –	↑
10:05	Homemaker Harmonies (continued) – – – – – –					→ Hits in Review (continued)	Melodic Cameos
11:00	News – – – – – – – – – – – – – – – – –					– – – – –	↑
11:05	Homemaker Harmonies (concluded) – – – – – –					↑ Teen Time	Church Remote
12:00	News Roundup (International) – – – – – – – –					– – – – –	↑

Fig. 2: Typical Traffic Board Layout (omitting detailed data about announcements, origin, release, etc.)

135

Juxtaposition

Obviously, programs fall ahead and behind one another in the daily schedule. These juxtapositions are an important matter for programmers. Stations must attract and hold audiences. Several techniques can be employed to keep audiences tuned in from one program to another.

Often broadcasters juxtapose two or more similar programs. The presumption is that audiences sometimes prefer variations of the same content to an outright change. These "sound alikes" are most likely to be scheduled during well-defined activity periods like mid-morning (when women do their housework) or late afternoon (when commuters are en route home by car). On other occasions broadcasters may deliberately break the flow of such cognate materials by scheduling a *marker* program. Markers are apt to appear at times of day which "mark" a significant change in audience activity patterns. The insertion of comprehensive newscasts and other talk materials at noon and around the dinner hour frequently constitutes marker programming. When a broadcaster finds it necessary to change programming during an audience activity period, he may choose to buffer the two very dissimilar broadcasts with a short *bridge* program. Bridges are generally talk materials of wide appeal, like news, weather, sports or Hollywood gossip.

Nowadays stations tend to program in cognate *blocks*: early morning (around 6:30 a.m.-9:00 a.m.), mid-morning (around 9:00 a.m.-12:00 noon), afternoon (around 1:00 p.m.-4:30 p.m.), late afternoon (around 4:30 p.m.-6:00 p.m.), evening (around 7:00 p.m.-11:00 p.m.), and late evening (around 11:00 p.m.-1:00 a.m.). In addition to being scheduled during the luncheon and dinner periods, shorter markers are also used to separate the other cognate blocks. Bridges are rarely needed, since radical program changes within activity periods are very few.

Placement

The placement — or time scheduling — of programs is largely dependent on patterns of audience activity. Having first established which groups are probably available as listeners during a given period (families, housewives, teenagers, etc.), the broadcaster then must decide which kind of programming is most likely to suit that group's activity pattern at the time. In this way most radio stations find and fit programs to clock-hours.

Nowadays, a number of strong placement tendencies can be observed in American radio. The *early morning block* is apt to be given over to family-appeal programming: bright, recorded music interspersed with time and weather announcements, brief news reports, meeting notices and the like. The *mid-morning block* is usually beamed to the housewife: popular music compounded with household hints, shopping tips and other such informational items. The *luncheon period* carries marker programming of a fairly serious journalistic character: comprehensive news summaries, weather analyses, editorials and commentaries. The *afternoon block* is often cognate with the mid-morning, except that the recorded music is perhaps less "brisk" and the household hints may give way to short features about movie stars, women in the news and other human interest topics. Telephone quiz "gimmicks" are also frequently included in these housewife-appeal programs. The *late-afternoon* block shifts emphasis to the commuting motorist: light recorded melodies interwoven with traffic advisories, news "quickies," sports scores and comparable elements. The marker programming scheduled during the *dinner hour* is like that of the luncheon period except that its tone may be even more serious-minded, presumably because more men are in the audience. For the same reason, stock market reports and business summaries are often found in these end-of-day marker sequences. The *evening block* is very apt to be aimed at the teenager and young adult: recorded "hits" and danceable music with relatively few talk elements added. On the other hand, the *late evening* block may veer off in quite a different direction. Many stations now schedule "adult level" interview programs with an accent on controversial personalities and issues. However, many other stations offer soft, romantic background music aimed at late "readers" and courting couples.

It must be remembered that these observations are about general placement tendencies. There are many striking exceptions, particularly in metropolitan areas. There, listeners can choose among stations which offer such general service, as well as tune to other stations which program a variety of specialty services: all-news, "hard rock," classical music, telephone talk shows, background music, foreign (i.e., non-English) materials, to note just a few examples. Metropolitan FM stations are especially likely to cater to minority and other special needs.

Counter-placement

Virtually all radio stations in the United States operate in competitive markets; thus, most broadcasters must be sure that their scheduling strategy takes their competitors' programming into account. On a day-to-day basis this is accomplished in three ways.

A station may attempt *cross-programming* its competitor. For example, Station A starts an especially attractive one-hour offering at 8:00 p.m., following a fairly routine program which begins at 7:30 p.m. Station B cross-programs by starting a strongly appealing one-hour offering at 7:30 p.m. Listeners presumably would be loath to tune from B to A in the middle of a "good" program at 8:00 p.m., thus injuring A's listenership. A second strategem is *scooping*. For example, Station A offers sports scores each evening at 11:00 p.m. Station B then offers the same scores at 10:30 p.m., thus "scooping up" A's audience ahead of time. The third technique is probably the best competitive approach: *monopolizing*. This is the exclusive offering of unique programs of greatly superior appeal.

Role

Programs and announcements are either *commercial* or *sustaining*. Commercial programs are *sponsored* or *participating*. A sponsored program is paid for by a single advertiser (although sometimes various portions of a single program may be sponsored by several different advertisers). A participating program is one divided into a number of convenient segments in order to permit the insertion of various commercial announcements. Stations assume the cost of sustaining announcements, which are most frequently devoted to such public service topics as highway safety, Savings Bonds, military recruitment and fund raising for charities. Some sustaining messages promote programs to be broadcast by the particular station.

Format

The organizational form(at) of a program stems from the application of function to content. As noted earlier, function includes surveillance, prescription, cultural transmission and entertainment. Content is limitless, encompassing all aspects of life including commerce, industry, agriculture, health, politics, geography, foreign affairs, crime, romance, rhythm, urbanism, religion and so forth. As pure content, "weather" doesn't say anything. But applying the surveillance function to weather produces the familiar "weathercast." If we apply the prescriptive function to weather, we might get a discussion program in which several participants give advice about safe driving on icy roads.

Another aspect of format has to do with the kinds of symbols employed in presenting content. There are three sorts available to the programmer: speech, music and sound effects. Speech symbols can elicit very precise audience responses. Music symbols carry a wide range of emotive, ambiguous "meanings." Sound effects are aural symbols that sound like noises to which some fairly specific meaning is readily attributed. Of course, all three of these symbol forms are encountered in present-day programming, although sound effects are less important than they were in pre-television days when radio drama was a significant format type.

Nowadays certain format types reappear again and again as "carriers" of a great variety of content. The principal of these are disc jockey shows, newscasts, weathercasts, sportscasts, talks, interviews, panel discussions, telephone chats, concerts, actualities (including sports events), quizzes, background musicales and variety shows. (Analyses of format types may be found in Chapters 3, 5 and 6.)

Appeal

A wise broadcaster makes every effort to see that his programming strongly appeals to the potential audience. In so doing, he strategically applies attractant techniques like intensity and psychological triggering — techniques which can be colloquially translated into the term *showmanship*.

He also keeps in mind that some aural symbols are understood by almost anyone who might hear them while others are really meaningful only to a small intellectual elite. Most radio programming nowadays reflects a sophistication level which is neither the lowest nor the highest, a practice in keeping with the dictates of the widest-possible-consensus.

Value

Content may be treated as being good or bad, right or wrong, real or fantasy, serious or trivial. As a general rule, the value accorded any content element will reflect the attitudes of the power structure, and probably the bulk population as well.

Pace

If the rate of presenting program material over a given time period is too fast, the audience may become confused and tune out. If it is too slow, the audience may become impatient and also tune out. Obviously, neither extreme is desirable. Nowadays, a tendency to fast pacing is compensated for by a considerable use of repetition and redundancy.

Figure

Most radio programs involve the (vocal) appearance of one or more persons: announcers, commentators, politicians, home economists, preachers or the like. Each such figure can be identified as having a certain role. The role he, or she, fills — or plays — carries with it a certain set of behavioral expectations. For example, we have come to expect a sportscaster to sound confident and knowledgeable. An announcer whose voice sounded hesitant and unsure while describing an athletic contest would probably prove unpopular with an audience. In equivalent ways, disc jockeys, newscasters, quiz masters and home economists are also expected to adhere to certain requirements of their separate roles. Because voice quality is so often (mis)-taken as an indication of role, broadcasters tend to choose program figures largely on the basis of vocal characteristics. This is not to say that a figure's "knowledgeability" is altogether ignored, of course.

To a considerable extent, local programming must be built around available figures. For example, a station without a "mature, manly and authoritative" sounding voice on its announcing staff may be forced to de-emphasize serious news and commentary programs which require a figure with such vocal characteristics. However, the same station might capitalize on disc-jockey programs for teenagers because its staff includes two or three "bright and youthful" sounding announcers who demonstrate an enthusiastic knowledgeability of popular recorded music.

Origin and Release

A radio program is a kind of aural "happening." The location of the "happening" is the origin of the program. A great variety of origins is possible: local and network studios, exterior locations in the community, remote points any place in the world — or even in space. Many programs designed around the use of recorded music can be said to originate in "radio-space"; that is, although the immediate origin of the program is the studio, the content may come from other sources, seemingly extending the studio to include outside entertainment or recording spots.

Many programs are stored on audio-tapes or disc recordings for *delayed* release. Sometimes the release is *live,* the program transmitted simultaneously with its production. In either case, as explained in Chapter 2, the programming expert is dependent upon the proper use of a great deal of mechanical and electronic equipment.

MANAGEMENT

Radio station management involves the coordination of a number of specialized activities: engineering, sales and promotion, production and programming, business administration, and (sometimes) research. But programming is central to all the others. It is the primary management responsibility in every broadcasting station.

The investments in land, buildings, equipment, materials, labor, licenses, services and so on are all made in order to construct and operate an efficient means for the saleable production and distribution of attractive programs to the public. Every management decision revolves around some aspect of this complex communications activity. All the other activities, important though they are, are subsidiary to it. Transmission and studio engineering apparatus, even with the power turned on, is not really a system of communication until somebody causes it to transmit meaningful sounds, such as those of language or music, to listeners. Sales work also lacks purpose in and of itself. It requires the exchange of a commodity or a service for money or other consideration of value. Programs (including spot announcements) are part commodity, part service and are the things to be sold — in spite of the jargon which speaks of selling "time." Promotion departments exist primarily to publicize and exploit programming to achieve increased consumption and increased sales. Business administration concerns itself largely with providing the accounting, rights clearance and clerical support necessary for program operation. Research, when carried on in a systematic way by a station, is based on the study of programming and questions closely related to it. Production is simply a term used for the "manufacturing" phase of the broad programming activity.

In most station organization plans the Program Department is on a level with all (or most) of these other specialized divisions. Yet if it is genuinely central to the rest, why should it not occupy a special position of rank? This is because programming is really an activity of common concern, in which each of the departments shares a certain part. Management must supervise and harmonize these parts into a coherent and effectively operating entity. It is the collective "programmer."

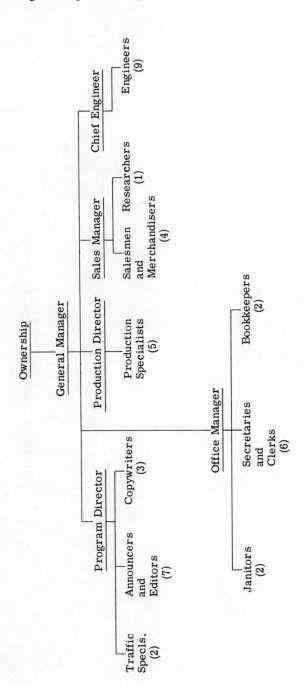

Figure 3
Staff Organization of a Station in a Medium-Sized City

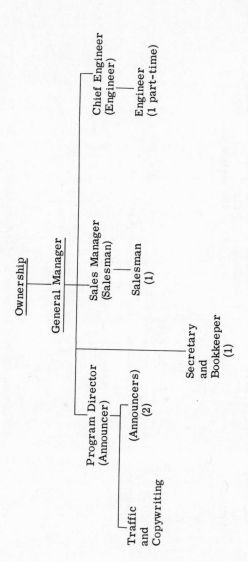

Figure 4
Staff Organization of a Station in a Small Town

The Program Department itself is simply that element of organization which is peculiarly responsible for executing management's decisions and policies about programming as a finished product. The head of the department, usually called the program director, is the executive who takes the most active role in making daily programming decisions within a context of long-range policies set by ownership, the station manager and the executive staff as a whole.

Staff Organization

The organizational patterns in broadcasting vary with the size of stations. In large stations, individuals are apt to hold single, specialized positions. In small stations, an individual may hold many positions — production, sales, management — at the same time.

Rank in a station is not necessarily an indicator of status factors such as income, seniority and prestige. For example, in a given situation, an announcer may enjoy very high status but may have an intermediate rank in the organizational structure of the station. The office manager in the same station may have a higher position of rank but may be making less money and enjoying far less prestige than the announcer. Conflicts sometimes arise between rank-holders and status-holders. A prestige announcer may resent being ordered around by a program director of higher rank but lesser status. In a well-managed station such problems rarely occur.

The organizational relationships within a radio station are, basically, similar to those of any large organization. There are collaborative relationships where people of comparable rank work at comparable jobs under the same authority. (For example, several transmitter engineers working under the leadership of the chief engineer, or several announcers supervised by the chief announcer.) A problem in large stations frequently comes from institutional relationships; that is, where people in different departments using different skills may have few direct relationships with each other, but whose totality of work must be integrated for effective functioning of the station as a whole.

One of the most important positional relationships in broadcasting is that of the "team," specifically in program production, where each person must play a particular role in a smoothly coordinated whole. For example, the team leader at a remote pick-up point might be a newsman who directs the work of several other persons of higher rank, such as the chief engineer, production director and chief announcer. In effectively completing such team efforts, normal organizational relationships are temporarily abandoned. Radio veterans will tell you that such occasions constitute "moments of truth" in which the real, professional relationships of the staff are revealed far more accurately than any study of organizational charts or observation of routine, everyday station operation.

Job Descriptions

There is no standard organizational pattern for radio stations in the United States. Therefore, the job descriptions which follow show general tendencies rather than any definite plan. The same limitation holds true for the sample organizational charts of large and small radio stations shown in Figures 3 and 4.

General Manager

Duties: 1) articulates the policies of the licensee-owner; 2) coordinates and guides the departments comprising the total station staff; 3) is responsible for the relationship of the station to the outside community and to all external institutions and organizations; 4) devises and maintains efficient business procedures for the station as a whole and as a collection of individual departments; 5) oversees and evaluates the work of department heads reporting to him; 6) is in charge of that part of the station's staff called "administration," including financial, personnel and managerial assistants.

Requisites: general, working knowledge of business administration, FCC regulations, NAB Code, radio advertising practices, copyright laws, personnel management, public relations techniques, radio programming and production, broadcasting technology, salesmanship and showmanship techniques.

Program Director

Duties: 1) supervises all units and employees of Program Department; 2) executes policies set by general manager and/or ownership; 3) is responsible for the daily scheduling of all local and network programming; 4) supervises all broadcasting talent not actually attached to the Program Department; 5) has primary supervision of "public service" and "public affairs" programming; 6) assists in the development of commercially exploitable programs and announcements; 7) supervises the auditioning and selection of program materials.

Requisites: broad working knowledge of FCC regulations, NAB Code, radio advertising practices, copyright laws, radio production, traffic procedures, showmanship techniques, broadcasting technology and journalism.

Position: supervisory; responsible to general manager; collaborates with production director in supervision of program execution; collaborates with sales manager in overseeing the design and scheduling of commercial materials.

Production Director

Duties: 1) supervises all employees of the Production Department; 2) executes policies set by the general manager and/or ownership; 3) is responsible, with program director, for overseeing the physical execution of all local programming; 4) is responsible, with chief engineer, for planning studio and remote equipment needs for program production.

Requisites: working knowledge of broadcasting technology; specialized knowledge of broadcasting showmanship techniques.

Position: supervisory; responsible to general manager (or sometimes program director).

Chief Engineer

Duties: 1) supervises all units and employees of the Engineering Department; 2) executes policies set by the general manager and/or ownership; 3) is responsible for overall technical operation of the station; 4) is in charge of maintaining necessary technical records for FCC inspection; 5) works with production director in planning program equipment needs.

Requisites: professional knowledge of radiotelephony and FCC regulations; First Class Radiotelephone license.

Position: supervisory; responsible to general manager.

Sales Manager

Duties: 1) supervises all employees of the Sales Department; 2) executes policies set by the general manager and/or ownership; 3) maintains liaison with national sales representatives and networks; 4) meets with prospective and actual clients; 5) plans overall sales strategy; 6) works with program director in creating and scheduling commercials.

Requisites: complete, working knowledge of radio advertising practices, sales procedures, public relations techniques, radio programming and production.

Position: supervisory; responsible to general manager.

Announcer

Duties: 1) speaks and reads on the air; 2) plans and performs specific programs; 3) keeps (i.e. "fills out") the official program logs; 4) selects recorded music for use in programs; 5) compiles newscasts from wire services teletype copy.

Requisites: pleasant voice and personality; reading ability, fluency, poise; working knowledge of recorded music, current affairs and broadcasting showmanship techniques.

Position: responsible to program director (sometimes through a chief announcer); collaborates in program execution with other announcers, production specialists, newsmen, music librarians, copywriters and staff talent.

Production Specialist

Duties: 1) operates studio and remote control equipment during the assembly of programs and broadcast materials; 2) edits and files audio tape recordings; 3) devises sound effects of various sorts.

Requisites: skilled knowledge of broadcasting technology and showmanship techniques.

Position: responsible to production director; collaborates in program execution with other specialists, announcers, newsmen, music librarians, copywriters, staff talent and engineers.

Engineer

Duties: 1) operates and maintains transmitter, studio and remote equipment; 2) keeps engineering logs and records; 3) helps design, build, or install new equipment arrays for special program purposes.

Requisites: thorough knowledge of radiotelephony and FCC regulations; First Class Radiotelephone license usually necessary.

Position: responsible to chief engineer, collaborates with other engineers and production specialists in setting up remote broadcasts and studio equipment for program execution.

Salesman

Duties: 1) sells advertising to local and regional clients; 2) services existing commercial accounts; 3) helps plan commercial materials.

Requisites: thorough, working knowledge of radio advertising practices, sales procedures, public relations techniques, and radio programming and production principles.

Position: responsible to sales manager; collaborates with other salesmen, copywriters, traffic specialists, publicity planners and research people in mapping out and waging advertising campaigns.

Traffic Specialist

Duties: 1) prepares daily schedules and types daily logs; 2) maintains information relative to availability of program and announcement times for commercial or other scheduling.

Requisites: knowledge of FCC logging regulations; thorough set of clerical skills.

Position: responsible to program director; collaborates with other traffic specialists, copywriters and salesmen in various matters related to program scheduling and logging.

Copywriter

Duties: 1) writes commercial and sustaining announcements not externally supplied; 2) writes program continuity scripts except news; 3) maintains an orderly system for filing copy for daily broadcasting use.

Requisites: knowledge of radio advertising and showmanship techniques; high verbal skill; ability to type efficiently.

Position: responsible to program director; collaborates with other writers, traffic specialists, salesmen, production specialists, announcers, music librarians and staff talent in planning and designing various broadcast materials.

Many station organization plans include a number of other staff-specialists: newsmen, women's editors, sports editors, farm editors, music (record) librarians, publicists, audience and sales researchers, sales merchandisers, office managers, secretaries, bookkeepers and chief announcers. The work of some of these people is examined in more detail in later chapters.

In recent years, minority programming has taken on a more clearly institutionalized character in the large, metropolitan markets, especially in connection with the concerns of the ethnic and racial minorities. This has resulted from the political awakening of many groups which had been economically, socially and politically repressed by dominant "white" populations for many decades. These groups now demand a "share" in the offerings and control of the mass media, including radio.

In response to direct audience pressures as well as bureaucratic "nudges," many radio stations in densely populated urban communities have set up special minority programming mechanisms. These include such forms as minority program advisory committees, minority program affairs departments and affirmative action employment campaigns.

The advisory committees seek to bring minority concerns and aspirations to bear on corporate policies, notably as they affect program content and directions.

Since the promulgation of the FCC rules concerning ascertainment of community needs and equal employment opportunities in 1971, many stations, depending on size, have established additional positions such as director of community relations and ascertainment, and equal employment program director. Sometimes the duties of these positions are simply added on to those of someone already performing one of the other jobs for the station.

The minority affairs departments which have been set up in some of the larger stations have the regular responsibility of ascertaining community needs and developing apposite program projects. The principal staff persons assigned these tasks are customarily minority persons themselves.

Affirmative action employment campaigns are usually entrusted to the station's chief personnel authority. In smaller operations this is likely to mean the general manager; in larger ones, a designated administrative officer. Such campaigns aim at hiring more minority persons and in training minority personnel to take on more consequential duties.

Visits to stations — local and regional, independent and network — would be extremely helpful in learning about their varying organizational patterns, job responsibilities and requisites, and intra-station relationships. Such visits will also clearly show that all management patterns focus on the central task of effective programming.

ADVERTISING

It was virtually an historic inevitability that the dominant sectors of American society should have initially perceived broadcasting as an instrument of *commerce*. Even before direct advertising was attempted on the air back in the 1920's, the U.S. Department of Commerce was chosen to be the "logical" governmental mechanism for licensing and regulating the then-new radio stations. Societies elsewhere around the world looked to their ministries of post, defense, culture or interior for such stabilizing authority. But, to recall a familiar presidential observation from the period, "the business of America is business." It seemed altogether fitting that radio stations, like newspapers and other organs of mass communication, should serve the pervasive goals and purposes of commercial life.

Even so, it was also assumed from the very beginning that such commercial services which were dependent on the franchised use of a publicly owned spectrum should be "in the public interest, convenience and necessity." (This somewhat ambiguous phrase was originally drawn in a 19th century congressional statute aimed at regulating the commerce-bearing operation of canals and waterways. Interestingly enough, the same wording found its way into a central provision of the Federal Communications Act of 1934, which created the Federal Communications Commission to regulate broadcasting as well as a variety of "common carrier" technologies like telephone and telegraph. The Department of Commerce had been relieved of these growing burdens a few years earlier.)

While American society has moved away from some of the intense commercial preoccupations of its past, advertising remains a prominent (if not dominant) feature of U.S. broadcasting. It is still the way by which most radio broadcasting service in the country is paid for.

Advertising involves the use of communications techniques to stimulate commercial activity, especially the mass consumption of goods and services. It is a vital aspect of the competitive marketing system and a critical component of a dynamic industrial economy. Advertising can be employed strategically to create desires for new products as well as to reinforce or modify established patterns of consumption.

Advertising practice depends on three functional elements: marketing research, media placement and media design.

Marketing research has to do with those various activities by which entrepreneurs try to determine: a) needs for new products and services, b) attitudes about existing goods and merchandising schemes and c) patterns of consumption and buying among various publics.

Media placement concerns the selection of appropriate media "channels" by which advertising messages can be efficiently directed to particular clienteles and audiences. It requires careful empirical analyses of the circulation and appeal characteristics of various media (newspapers, magazines, radio stations, TV networks, billboards and the like). It also necessitates continuing research studies into the media behavior of particular groups of people, including the bulk and minority population components discussed earlier.

Media design is that field within the advertising trade in which the creative message specialists do their work. Any advertisement must attract the favorable attention of the readers, viewers or listeners to whom it is especially directed. Its symbol content must skillfully manipulate psychological factors so as to excite a desire to consume, reinforce or redirect a competitive purchasing habit or channalize latent buying impulses. The design of such messages is an art, indeed.

Local radio stations are centers of intensive advertising activity, in spite of the fact that much of their commercial traffic often originates and is managed from "outside" by advertising agencies located on Madison Avenue (in New York City) or elsewhere.

On a station's staff are people assigned the important job of surveying local, regional and national marketing phenomena in order to know when and where to go after new advertising accounts. These specialists, usually called "time salesman," must be able to identify dynamic business undertakings that are likely to require advertising stimulation. They are also responsible for collecting and organizing favorable data about the circulation and appeal of their station's programming efforts. These data are employed to persuade media placement agencies (and local advertisers who do their own advertising placement) to make contract use of the broadcast facility for getting messages across to desired audiences.

Station Organization and Practice

Not surprisingly, these advertising sales activities are carried on much more informally in a small station which serves a rural market town than in a large facility located in a major metropolitan area. At the small station, market surveys may merely involve the salesman's scanning local newspapers or auditing competitive stations to see which advertisers are currently active. Armed with such helpful knowledge, he will try to divert some of their business to his own station. Or he may decide to go out after competitive accounts.

In stations of all sizes, salesmen are customarily assigned a number of potential advertising accounts to check routinely for possible business. Once any of these potentials signs up as his customer, the salesman will set aside a regular time to "service" the new account, although this may represent nothing more elaborate than a casual personal visit to pick up information for a revision of advertising copy. Rarely does the salesman at a small station have to resort to more "scientific" sales methods to keep his clients satisfied and under contract.

The contrary is true in a larger, more highly organized station. There, time sales is apt to be an enterprise requiring professional management and acumen. Most accounts originate with advertising agencies which represent manufacturers, distributors or large-scale retailers. These agencies have media placement experts who insist on buying time "scientifically." Stations must be prepared with a wealth of facts and figures about their coverage, circulation, audience characteristics and program popularity ratings. Rate indices like the "cost per thousand (listeners)" are often of paramount importance in these negotiations. Salesmen must become highly skilled to deal effectively with such sophisticated concepts. Fortunately, the contract sums involved in these transactions are frequently very sizable, with corresponddingly attractive payments for the salesmen, agencies and other parties included.

The larger stations are likely to have sales departments of considerable scope, with a variety of skills attached. In addition to the salesmen themselves there might be market analysts, statisticians and sales promotion specialists. Many stations undertake to do more for their advertising clients than merely sell them programs and air time. They accept responsibility for helping the advertisers merchandise the products featured in an air campaign — placing special point-of-scale advertising displays at retail outlets, designing and mailing out promotional pieces to affected dealers, setting up special sales meetings for the advertiser's own field personnel, and the like.

Radio stations also maintain staff capacity in the highly specialized media design field. Copywriters are employed to think up and write sonically attractive and psychologically appealing commercial announcements to lure listener-consumers to the sponsor's product. Staff producers, engineers, musicians and announcers get into the creative act by serving as talent for the artful production of these aural advertisements.

In a very small station these production efforts might well involve every staff member in some capacity or other. A typical situation might be the following: the receptionist-traffic clerk types up the scripts which have been written by the copywriting sales manager; the chief engineer operates the tape recorders while all three full-time announcers provide voice characterizations; a second engineer-technician manipulates the turntables, cartridge machines and audio board; the general manager himself serves as timer and producer-director.

By contrast, a prestigious station in a cosmopolitan market might employ a number of "free-lance" writers, announcers, musicians and production experts to implement the creative design of a number of announcements to be employed in running an important advertising campaign. Meanwhile, the station's regular staff would devote all its energies to the production and airing of appealing programs into which these new spots could be scheduled.

It should be clear by now that the *programming* of the station is the real means by which an adverting announcement reaches both bulk and minority audiences. It is most unlikely that many people would consistently tune in a radio station which broadcast nothing whatever but advertising materials, one after another. The programs provide the attractant context for commercial "pitches."

Revenue Sources

Radio stations earn revenue from their advertising activities in several different ways. Foremost is the direct income received for the sale of air time to advertisers or their agencies. Often stations also generate revenue from production fees assessed advertisers who need to have new aural materials created for broadcast. There may also be extra charges attached to the placement of "spots" inside, or adjacent to, certain popular programs. In the instance of outright program sponsorship, the advertiser may be required to reimburse the station for the full cost of the program, totaled into a figure which usually includes a profit factor.

Not all gross income from advertising stays in the station's own bank accounts. Even before direct expenses are met, the station usually has to pay out various *commissions*. These are fees computed as relatively minor percentages of specific advertising income promised under contract to the particular salesmen, media placement and advertising agencies responsible for "bringing in the business." Consequently, the charge rates set by a station for its advertising services are proportionately increased to allow these deductions to be made without jeoparding profit margins.

Advertising is a hard and often frustrating business. It is highly speculative in nature. There are no guarantees or warranties possible for those who "buy in." Every advertising campaign, even the most deliberately planned and executed, is in the final instance nothing more than a calculated gamble. Competition among the media is fierce, and sometimes the economic consequences seem unreasonably harsh to the individuals involved. Yet, because advertising is a deeply-rooted element of most broadcasting activity in the United States, those who intend to work in the field, especially at the management level, would do well to learn as much as possible about practical advertising techniques and procedures.

Station Process

As a work process, radio advertising is likely to involve several steps.

It begins with an analysis of the advertising potentials of a commercial firm not already on the air, or not represented in the accounts of the station in question. This sort of analysis is customarily made by the sales manager.

Once a prospect is identified and "sized up," the account is assigned to a salesman. He works up a presentation for the potential client in which time rates, audience shares and copy themes are attractively packaged.

The presentation often takes place in the store, office or plant of the respective sponsor, although larger accounts in metropolitan markets usually pay advertising agencies to work out their advertising and media campaigns. Where the latter is the case, the presentation may take on more formal proportions.

Once the sale is made and a contract signed, the salesman calls in the traffic and copy departments to work out the details. The traffic department sees to it that the announcements or programs are properly logged into the schedule. The copy department has the job of "creating" announcement themes and advertising texts. Except where advertising agencies handle copy-writing, the station must arrange to have the writer visit the client's place of business to collect information on the goods or services to be promoted.

Back at the station the copy is prepared, checked with the client (usually by telephone) and then, where necessary, produced on a tape cartridge. The production department and announcing staff become involved at this point in converting words on paper into an electronic message.

Advertising charges are based on length (air time), frequency and time of placement of the commercial announcement and, frequently, on the type of program in which it is placed. All this is shown on a "rate card" which is made available to prospective advertisers. A typical rate card is that of WRVA, Richmond, Virginia. (See Fig. 5.)

Computer

It will be noted elsewhere in this book that radio is still undergoing significant technological changes in its methods of operation. This is true not only in respect to production and transmission. It is to be observed in the programming and management sectors as well.

Computers are beginning to make a heavy impact on the ways in which a radio station keeps business accounts, prepares sales reports and program logs, analyzes audience data and inventories its technical supplies. While as yet few local stations actually own their own computers, numbers of them nowadays arrange to "tap in" to large computers operated by data system firms. An ordinary teletypewriter connected to the computer bank by telephone lines is used to "converse" with the distant computer on a "time-shared" basis. A specially trained station employee is given regular responsibility for feeding information to the computer and for signaling the machine to analyze and retrieve data units.

Where this kind of direct connection is impractical or too expensive, some stations simply lease weekly computer time from a nearby data firm. A station employee travels to the computer center at various intervals to "input" new information and to ask the computer to print out various sales analyses, equipment inventories and accounting records which are needed.

It is very likely that before too many years computers will be used for

SECTION I-ANNOUNCEMENTS:

Per Week	"AA" Min.	30	"A" Min.	30	"B" Min.	30	"C" Min.	30	"D" Min.
1	65	52	55	44	35	28	25	20	10
6	63	50	53	42	34	27	23	18	9
12	60	48	50	40	33	26	21	17	8
18	57	46	47	38	31	25	19	15	7
24	54	43	44	35	29	23	17	14	6
Per Year									
500X	50	40	40	32	26	21	15	12	5

10 SEC. 50% OF MINUTE RATE—(2) COUNT AS (1) FOR FREQUENCY.

SECTION II-PACKAGE PLANS AND FEATURES:

Total Audience Plan: (7 Consecutive Days)

Wkly	"AA"	"A"	"B"	"C"	EA	Min. WKLY	EA	30 WKLY
15	3	3	5	4	36	540	29	435
20	4	4	7	5	32	640	26	520
30	5	5	11	9	28	840	23	690

ROS Plans (7 Consecutive Days)

KLY		EA	Min WKLY	EA	30 WKLY
5	ROS 5:30 am-MID. — Mon.-Sun.	25	625	20	500
0	ROS 5:30 am-MID. — Mon.-Sun.	22	1100	18	900

Helicopter Traffic Reports:

7:30-8:30 am/4:45-5:45 pm, Rotating AM-PM Weekly. Sold in multiples of two (2) weeks.

Per Week	Cost Each Min.	30
2	75	60
3	73	58
5	70	56
10	65	52

5 MINUTE NEWS

"AA"	"A"	"B"	"C"	"D"
97	80	55	38	15
88	73	50	34	13
79	65	45	30	10

TIME CLASSIFICATION

"AA"	— 6:00-10:00 am	Mon.-Fri.
"A"	— 3:00-7:00 pm	Mon.-Fri.
	— 6:00 am-7:00 pm	Sat.
"B"	— 5:30-6:00 am	Mon.-Sat.
	— 10:00 am-3:00 pm	Mon.-Fri.
	— 5:30 am-7:00 pm	Sun.
"C"	— 7:00 pm-Mid.	Mon.-Sun.
"D"	— Mid.-5:30 am	Tues.-Sun.

Fig. 5 Rate Card

more than routine record keeping, calculation and data processing. It is entirely feasible to forsee a time when many stations will be able to link up their program automation systems with computers in such a way as to allow the computer to use carefully designed "judgment" in actually sequencing and logging the broadcast schedule. In this sophisticated system, for example, a computer could even be programmed to work out the selection and scheduling of appropriate musical recordings with which to "fill" to the second the unused time following a baseball game or live news event. A computer might also be able to "scrutinize" pre-recorded commercial announcements to decide whether or not a particular copy theme was "logical" in a certain broadcast context. If the computer had been informed that it was a cold, rainy day outside, it would scan and reject a soft drink commercial which was pitched to listeners suffering from heat and sun, substituting one which played up the virtues of flavor or price.

BIBLIOGRAPHY

Barnouw, Erik, *A Tower in Babel*, 1966; *The Golden Web*, 1968; *The Image Empire*, 1970. New York: Oxford University Press. The definitive history of broadcasting. Well written, scholarly, includes critical analyses and the human element.

Coleman, Howard W., *Case Studies in Broadcast Management*. New York: Hastings House, 1970. Fictionalized accounts of problems in operating radio and television stations provide practical problem-solving exercises.

Foote, A. Edward and George L. Hall, eds., *"The Selling of the Pentagon" Papers: CBS vs. Congress*. Columbus, Ohio: Ohio State University, 1971. A comprehensive collection of the official documents, legal briefs, correspondence, and testimony arising from the dramatic and legally far-reaching confrontation of CBS president Dr. Frank Stanton and Congressman Harley Staggers over the airing of the highly controversial documentary program about the Pentagon. While the program in question was done for television, the legal and ethical issues also pertain directly to radio.

Quaal, Ward and Leo Martin, *Broadcast Management*. New York: Hastings House, 1968. A comprehensive exploration of all of the management aspects of U.S. broadcast stations.

Shaw, Arnold, *The Rock Revolution*. New York: The (MacMillan) Paperback Library, 1971. A knowledgeable history of the most important "pop arts" form to engulf radio's mass programming.

Steinberg, Charles S., ed., *Mass Media and Communications*. New York: Hastings House, Rev. Ed. 1972. A collection of essays by experts in all mass media areas, concentrating on their sociological impact and significance in a mass society.

Practical information about developments and trends in radio programming may best be found in the following trade publications: *Billboard, Broadcasting Magazine, Radio-TV Daily, Sponsor, Variety*. Scholarly reports may be found in *AV Communication Review, Journal of Broadcasting, Journalism Quarterly, Public Telecommunications Review*. Criticism relating to radio programming may occasionally be found in such publications as *Atlantic Monthly, The Nation, New Republic, The New York Times, Saturday Review*. Program schedules, published by many radio stations, can serve as a means of concrete investigation into contemporary programming.

5

WRITING

BY ROBERT L. HILLIARD

RADIO has been called the art of the imagination. The radio writer is restricted only by the breadth and depth of the mind's eye of the audience. The writer has complete freedom of time and place. He or she is not limited by what can be presented visually. The radio audience cannot select what it wants to hear (or "see" in its imagination). The writer, through effective combinations of sound, music, dialogue — and silence — can create whatever stimuli is desired and may place the audience in any physical relationship to any character. A vivid illustration of this and, appropriately for this chapter, an example of good script writing is Stan Freberg's award-winning spot announcement, "Stretching the Imagination."

MAN: Radio? Why should I advertise on radio? There's nothing to look at . . . no pictures.

GUY: Listen, you can do things on radio you couldn't possibly do on TV.

MAN: That'll be the day.

GUY: Ah huh. All right, watch this. (AHEM) O.K. people, now I give you the cue, I want the 700-foot mountain of whipped cream to roll into Lake Michigan which has been drained and filled with hot chocolate. Then the Royal Canadian Air Force will fly overhead towing the 10-ton maraschino cherry which will be dropped into the whipped cream, to the cheering of 25,000 extras. All right . . . cue the mountain . . .

SOUND: GROANING AND CREAKING OF MOUNTAIN INTO BIG
SPLASH!

GUY: Cue the air force!

SOUND: DRONE OF MANY PLANES

GUY: Cue the maraschino cherry...

SOUND: WHISTLE OF BOMB INTO BLOOP! OF CHERRY HIT-
TING WHIPPED CREAM.

GUY: Okay, twenty-five thousand cheering extras...

SOUND: ROAR OF MIGHTY CROWD. SOUND BUILDS UP AND
CUTS OFF SHARP!

GUY: Now... you wanta try that on television?

MAN: Well...

GUY: You see... radio is a very special medium, because it
stretches the imagination.

MAN: Doesn't television stretch the imagination?

GUY: Up to 21 inches, yes.

Courtesy of Freberg, Ltd.

Unfortunately, the writer does not have complete freedom. While the medium itself provides wide aesthetic flexibility, the organization and control of the medium create restraints. Because commercial radio broadcasting is dependent upon advertising revenue for its existence, the content of radio has been traditionally oriented toward the widest possible audience in order to provide the maximum number of potential customers. The sponsor and producer frequently searched for and often found the broadest common denominator — a euphemism for the lowest common denominator. Basing programming solely upon quantitative measurements, as represented by ratings, tends to adversely affect the qualitative aspects of the medium.

On the other hand, the intense competition in radio following World War II, as the growth of television forced radio to re-evaluate itself, resulted in a direct interplay between the rating game and the search for and creation of new formats. The increase in specialization in the late 1960's and early 1970's turned station orientation away from the largest general audience to a consistently faithful largest possible specialized audience.

The radio writer is restricted by censorship of various kinds. The rules of the FCC and the pressures of public attitudes combine to bar material that may be considered by the general audience to be profane, obscene or otherwise in bad taste. In the early 1970's, for example, the FCC, with

Congressional prodding, forced abandonment of the so-called "topless" radio format (see Chapter 3). Although stations using this format had found it to be highly successful in attracting audiences, there were virtually no public objections from either the industry or the public to the FCC's actions. Another form of censorship is that of sponsor control. If any piece of material might tend to alienate any potential customer anywhere, almost always that material will be deleted before the script or program is finalized. Censorship also occurs because of a sponsor's personal prejudices, which may range from attitudes about modern art to intolerance of specific religious or political ideas. No wonder we so often hear complaints that the content of radio, with rare exceptions, is bland and squishy!

The various forms of censorship create ethical as well as artistic problems for those writers who believe that they and their medium are a part of the world and that material dealing with the realities of life, including issues of significance to the community that may be of a controversial nature, should be a vital and integral part of a given script.

For standards of practice and overt areas of content regulation as voluntarily practiced by the stations themselves, the prospective writer should obtain a copy of *The Radio Code* from the National Association of Broadcasters, 1771 N Street, N.W., Washington, D.C. 20036. The Code's program and advertising standards can be found at the end of this chapter.

It is true that the practical considerations of keeping a job sometimes create a dichotomy for the writer between the potentials of radio and the restrictions imposed by the industry. Yet, even if conforming to the latter in order to continue working in the field, the writer should not lose sight of the capabilities of the medium or of his or her own role and responsibility in affecting — as only the mass media can — the minds and emotions of the audience.

What are the areas of radio writing today? More and more they have become limited as television has taken away the more popular entertainment-art features that dominated early radio. For practical purposes, radio is no longer a source for drama or for variety shows. The radio playwrights, who for a time in the 1930's and early 1940's were among the most creative writers in America — the Norman Corwins, the Archibald MacLeishes, the Arthur Millers, the Ernest Kinoys and others — went into television, the theatre and film or disappeared from the field entirely. (The revival of some dramatic programming in late 1973 and early 1974, including replays of some "old-time" radio shows, is at this writing not far enough along to indicate a trend.)

At the same time, certain areas of radio writing have become more significant. Foremost of these are commercials and news. As noted in Chapter 1, although radio faltered after the rise of television, it came back and is stronger than ever in terms of audience, stations, advertising and profits. The commercial announcement is at least as important as it ever was. The growth of the all-talk station in the early 1970's has resulted in a re-emphasis on news, discussion and interview shows. The good stations, ranging from large city stations to regional stations to exceptional local stations, make an effort to go beyond the platitudinous ad-lib and try to prepare their recorded musical programs with taste and originality. The competition among formats and within each format, as described in Chapter 3, requires creativity and, hopefully, uniqueness.

The primary areas of concern to the radio writer today and the areas with which this chapter will primarily deal are: commercials, news and sports, special events, documentaries, music, interview and discussion programs. The drama, however, is not ruled out as an area of study. Indeed, it is the base for all other writing. The radio writer of any program type should, as much as possible, be steeped in the techniques of good dramatic writing, for drama is an integral part of all other forms, from the dramatized commercial to the semi-documentary presentation. Accordingly, a brief overview of radio dramatic writing is included here.

Basic Production Elements

Just as the painter must know the tools for expression on canvas, the radio writer must know the tools of the sound medium. The writer must have a basic knowledge of the potentials and limitations of the technical aspects of radio in order to know just how far he or she can go in creating a mind's eye picture for the audience. The writer must also have command of the terms designating various production aspects in order to clearly state in the script the device or action called for. The elements of production that directly affect writing technique include use of the microphone, sound effects, music and the special devices of the control room.

The microphone. The writer should know the five basic microphone positions: a) on mike, where the performer speaks directly into the mike and the audience is put in the same physical setting as is the performer; b) off mike, where the performer is some distance away from the mike, and the audience in its imagination sees the performer as some distance away from its own place in the setting; c) fading on (or coming on), where the performer gradually approaches the mike while speaking, and the audience "sees" the performer coming toward it in the imaginary setting; d) fading off (or going off), the exact reverse of fading on; and e) behind an obstruction, where either through an electronic or manual device it sounds as if there is a barrier, such as a wall or door, between the performer and the center of audience orientation.

Sound Effects. Sound effects, also designated by the writer in the script, serve seven major purposes: a) to establish locale or setting; b) to direct the audience attention to emphasis on a particular sound; c) to establish time; d) to establish mood; e) to signify entrance and exits; f) to serve as a transition between program segments or between changes of time or place; and g) to create unrealistic effects.

Music. The writer must know how and where to indicate the use of music in the script to achieve any one or more of five major purposes: a) as content for a musical program; b) as the theme for any program type; c) for the bridging of divisions in a program; d) as a sound effect; and e) for background or mood.

Techniques and terms. When designating how sound and music are to be employed, the writer must use terms universally understood by radio production people. Essential terms are: a) segue (seg-way), the following of one sound immediately by another; b) cross-fade, the disappearing of one sound even as the next one is being heard and growing stronger; c) blending, the combining of two or more sounds at the same time; d) cutting or switching, the instantaneous and abrupt movement from one sound source to another; and e) fade in and fade out, the gradual appearance of a sound, and the reverse.

More detailed descriptions of how production elements are achieved and utilized may be found in Chapters 2 and 6 of this book.

Audience Orientation

The radio medium permits a subjective as well as objective orientation of the audience. That is, the writer can, through proper designation of technical elements to be used, take the audience along with a performer or situation in the radio script. For example, in a public service announcement on safe driving, the audience may be with a character riding in a car. The car approaches the edge of a cliff. The writer must decide whether to put the sound of the character's screams and the noise of the car as it hurtles down the side of the cliff "on mike," thus keeping the audience with the car, or to fade these sounds into the distance, orienting the audience to a vantage point at the top of the cliff, watching the character and car falling downward.

THE DRAMA

Although, as previously indicated, there is little outlet for the play on radio at this time, the basic form of dramatic structure applies to other forms of radio writing, including the oft-used dramatic commercial and the potentially highly artistic documentary.

Although the genius and inspiration of playwriting cannot be taught, the proven principles of good dramaturgic technique, which apply to the structures of all plays whether written for the stage, television, motion pictures or radio, can be utilized as tools for the construction and development of effective radio drama.

The writer of radio drama must be as familiar with the basic techniques of playwriting as is the person who writes the Broadway play. It must be remembered always that drama is heightened life, not a literal interpretation of it, and that the comparatively short broadcast time allotted to a single drama on radio requires a special heightening and condensation. Sources for the play are several: an event or happening, a theme, a character or characters, a background. No matter what the source, however, it is important to remember that all dramatic action is expressed as manifestations of the needs and purposes of the characters of the play. The characters in a drama are not carbons of real life, but are most effectively developed from a quintessence of many characters from the actual world. Perhaps the best continuing series on radio where drama is still produced is " The Eternal Light," which effectively illustrates the combining of dramatic form and characters of real life, approaching what shall be described later as a semi-documentary or fictional documentary form.

The writer who would write plays for radio would do well to concentrate first on the elements of dramaturgy as taught in a course on playwriting. For purposes of practical application in the commercial radio field today, it is sufficient here to note the special dramaturgical characteristics of radio that are important to the writer who would apply these principles not necessarily to the play, but to the other forms of writing that are most often produced.

Foremost, the writer must remember that he or she is dealing in mental images, with an "art of the imagination." The writer is not restricted by *unities* of time and place, as is frequently the writer for the theatre. Radio may present a character in one setting and in a twinkling transport that character — and the audience — to an entirely different setting. Radio may move us from a polar ice cap to the moon to a battlefield to a jungle to the depths of Hades, creating without restriction the settings for our imaginations. Radio has no visual limitations and the writer's own imagination should not be restricted by what he or she can "see." Radio has no physical limitations and can accommodate a conventional battlefield — or peace conference — with tens of thousands — or dozens — of participants, or, within seconds, a dozen celestial battlefields — or meeting places — with millions of interplanetary participants. No matter how loose the unities of time and place, however, the unity of action must be inviolate: that is, the dramatic script must have a consistency and wholeness of purpose and development; each sequence must be totally integrated with every other sequence, all contributing to the total goal or effect the writer wishes to create.

The radio play must have a *plot* structure approximating that of the good play in any medium: exposition, a conflict, complications, a climax and, if necessary, a resolution. It must have rising action which creates suspense and holds the interest of the audience. Because of the limitation of time, exposition may be revealed even as the action unfolds, the conflict may come at the very opening of the drama, and the play may be limited to one simple plot line.

Character should be the motivating factor in the drama. Time limitations prevent development of character in great depth, however, and sometimes plot, not character, becomes the motivating force. The characters, in any event, should be consistent with themselves and appropriate with reality, although heightened from real life. Character is revealed by what a character does and not principally through what is said; this creates a difficulty in radio, where actions, not descriptions, must be presented through dialogue and sound. Because too many voices may become confusing to a radio audience, the writer should limit the number of roles in the play and the number of characters in any one scene.

Dialogue must be consistent with itself and with the character, appropriate with the situation and the characters, and dramatically heightened. Because everything on radio is conveyed through dialogue and sound — and silence — dialogue on radio serves to forward the situation, reveal character and uncover the plot line even more than in other media. The dialogue should clearly indicate all the action taking place, introduce the characters and tell who they are and even describe them. But it must be done subtly and not through trite description of oneself or another character.

Exposition is difficult in radio because of the time limitation and because it must be presented solely through dialogue and sound. To solve this problem, radio drama utilizes a narrator more frequently than do other media.

Preparation must be valid and presented subtly. The writer must be sure that the audience is prepared for whatever the character does at the end of the play. Because of the lack of visual cues, radio frequently requires an overabundance of preparation.

Setting is extremely important in radio, since it must serve as a visual base for the audience. The writer faces the difficulty of creating visual images solely through dialogue and sound, but, on the other hand, is limited only by the audience's imagination. The mental picture created must be the right one for the situation; the locale and environment must be believable for the characters and must forward the psychological and aesthetic purposes of the author as well as the plot of the play. Sound effects and music are highly important in clarifying movement, setting and action. Transitions of time and place, and exits and entrances must be clear.

ANNOUNCEMENTS AND COMMERCIALS

Spot announcements may be commercial or non-commercial materials. Messages may be of varying lengths. A station break, usually 10 seconds, may consist entirely of the ID (station identification) or it may have a 2-second ID accompanied by an 8-second announcement. Other announcements within the "break" time may include a public service announcement, a station "cross-plug" for one of its other programs, a news flash, a service announcement — combining public service information with a sponsor identification — and, of course, a commercial.

Word counts sometimes may be used to determine time lengths for straight verbal messages. Approximate counts are: 10 seconds — 25 words; 20 seconds — 45 words; 30 seconds — 65 words; 45 seconds — 100 words; 60 seconds — 125 words. Commercials may be inserted within programs purchased by a sponsor and may be of longer lengths, with a 90-second announcement including about 190 words and a 120-second message containing about 250 words. Sometimes an entire 5- or 15-minute segment of programming may consist entirely of a commercial. The FCC has found that program-length commercials are not in the public interest, and in early 1974 was considering specific rules dealing with this practice.

Public service announcements frequently are given as part of the I.D. The local radio station usually receives such announcements in a form already prepared by the writer for the distributing organization.

20-SECOND RADIO ANNOUNCEMENT

The lost Colony's population in 1587 was 118, before it vanished mysteriously. In North Carolina last year, 21,000 persons died from heart disease—"a Lost Colony of Heart casualties every 48 hours." The North Carolina Heart Association urges regular "Health and Heart Checkups" for you. See your physician.

Courtesy of North Carolina Heart Association

Some special service announcements are written for specific programs, to be inserted at appropriate places in the format. The following illustrates how the writer not only can go beyond the general spot announcement, but orient it toward a particular station and locality.

DISC JOCKEY PROGRAM (30 SECONDS, RADIO)
(AFTER MILLION RECORD SELLER)

DISC JOCKEY

_____(title and artist)_____ ...a record that sold a million copies. Easy listening, too. But here's a figure that's not easy to listen to: Over 1,000,000 American children are seriously emotionally ill. During National Child Guidance Week, the _____ PTA, in cooperation with the American Child Guidance Foundation, is holding a special meeting to acquaint you with the problems faced by children in___(town or area)___. It's to your benefit to attend. Be there...___(date and address)___...learn what you can do to help.

Prepared for American Child Guidance Foundation, Inc., by its agents, Batten, Barton, Durstine & Osborn, Inc.

The public service announcement, although not selling a product, nevertheless attempts to persuade the listener to support some cause. It must, in that sense, follow the purposes and techniques of commercial writing. At the same time, it must be in good taste and appeal to the audience's highest attitudes and feelings.

Commercial Formats

The *straight-sell* format is a simple, direct statement about the product. The straight-sell frequently uses a slogan or a gimmick that is repeated for a relatively long period — weeks, months and even years. The *educational* commercial usually uses logical, rather than emotional appeals, and reflects institutional as opposed to product advertising. The *testimonial* varies from the endorsement of a product by a celebrity to the asserted use of the product by ordinary people with whom the audience can most readily identify. *Humor* may vary from gentleness to outright satire. *Musical* commercials have long been popular. From the early jingle, musical commercials developed in some instances into presentations by entire orchestras and by the early 1970's the song had replaced the jingle. *Dramatizations* are very effective, particularly if they can be incorporated into the action of the program itself. Through the use of the dramatization the writer can easily apply the five steps of persuasion, described below, for the solving of a problem by one or more of the characters involved in the action of the commercial.

The radio commercial may be either live or recorded (on record, tape or cartridge).

Writing Techniques

At one time the art of persuasion was practiced primarily in speech making. Today it is effected largely through the writing of advertising copy, including broadcast commercials. The relationship between persuasive speaking and advertising can be found in the application of Aristotle's principles of rhetoric. Aristotle noted three appeals: logical, ethical and emotional. The three, particularly the last one, emotional, apply to the writing of commercials today. An emotional appeal is not used to make one laugh or cry; rather, it plays on the basic needs and wants of the person or persons to whom it is addressed. Analyze the next few commercials you hear. You will notice that in all probability they will appeal to the non-intellectual, nonlogical aspects of the prospective customer's personality. The automobile commercial, for example, most often appeals to the need for power and prestige. Most commercials are not so overt, however, and the good writer uses subtlety in making the appeal. Other basic emotional appeals are self-preservation, love of family, patriotism, good taste, reputation, religion, loyalty to a group and conformity to public opinion.

In order to use appeals effectively, the writer must know the audience as intimately as possible. Because the audience of the mass media is so diverse, accurate analysis is almost impossible. However, depending on the content of the program in or around which the commercials appear, and the location and coverage of the station, the writer can come to some conclusions concerning the needs and wants of the audience. Before writing the commercial, the writer should attempt to determine, as far as possible, the following about his potential audience: age, sex, size, economic level, political orientation, primary interests, occupation, fixed attitudes or beliefs, educational level, knowledge of the product, and geographical concentration.

One of the techniques that has largely eluded writers except as an occasional flash of inspiration has been that of knowing which approach best motivates which audience group. Demographics — the analysis of the audience makeup as a base for specific commercial content and technique as well as for the station format and sound — is a relatively new element, although the principle of audience analysis has always been a basic factor in all writing. In the early 1970's demographics began to become critically essential to agency operations. In 1972 the Radio Advertising Bureau analyzed the frequency of occurrence of elements in 100 Clio Award commercial entries. RAB notes that no definitive conclusions can be drawn from its analysis, that a larger sample needs to be used, that there is no indication whether the commercials were liked by the listeners or not, or that the writers were correct in their choices of creative elements. The following chart, however, does provide an indication of what elements the writers *thought* would be effective and which they put into commercials for the different listening groups.

Commercial elements — frequency of occurrence

ELEMENTS	TOTAL SAMPLE	ADULT MEN	ADULT WOMEN	ADULT WOMEN & MEN	TEENS
Singing	45%	45%	23%	47%	75%
Instrumental music only	18	10	27	17	15
Announcer/primary role	47	50	37	50	55
Announcer/secondary role	32	15	40	37	30
Celebrity announcer	5	5	10	3	0
Humor	46	35	70	47	20
Dialogue/interview	39	40	53	37	20
Sound effects	33	45	33	37	15
Base	100	20	30	30	20

The five steps in persuasive technique (Dewey's, Borden's and those of many recognized authorities who have examined the subject are similar in almost all instances) are found in the organization of the well-written commercial. These steps, in chronological order, are a) getting attention, b) holding interest, c) creating an impression that a problem of some sort exists, d) planting an idea of how the problem may be solved, and e) getting action — in this instance, the purchase of a product. An analysis of the script below delineates the five steps of persuasion. First, attention is obtained by the talking of an inanimate object. Interest is held through the presentation of a conflict: "It's cold out and we're going to try to get started," and through the sound effect of the hard starting of a motor. The impression that a problem exists occurs in the above and is further verified by the groaning and the statement that the pistons "can't get moving." Because of the brevity of the commercial — just 30 seconds — the subtle planting of an idea of how the problem may be solved is bypassed for the direct statement: adding a can of the advertised product. That the product solves the problem is made clear through the starting of the motor and is followed up by the statements designed to get action from the listener: purchase of the product.

MR. MOTOR: Now hear this... this is Mister Motor talking to the moving parts in this engine. It's cold out and we're going to try to get started.

SOUND: HARD STARTING

MR. MOTOR: Sounds like groaning among you pistons.

PISTON: It's so cold down here we can't get moving.

MR. MOTOR: Then we'll add a can of Wynn's Friction Proofing.

SOUND: GLUG, GLUG, GLUG

MR. MOTOR: It makes cars start fast in cold weather... eliminates the need to warm up a cold engine. Let's try again.

SOUND: MOTOR STARTING SMOOTHLY

MR. MOTOR: Smooth!

ANNCR: Wynn's Friction Proofing makes starting easier, eliminates the need for cold engine warm up. Guaranteed to satisfy or your money back!

Courtesy of Wynn's Car Care Products; and Erwin Wasey, Inc.

The persuasive technique approach varies according to the form of the commercial and its length. The longer the commercial, the easier it is to make each step of persuasion more effective. In some forms it is difficult to see just how the process is being used — but it is there. See if you can trace the use of the persuasive technique in the following examples of different commercial formats: straight-sell, testimonial, humor, musical and dramatization. All of these commercials, incidentally, are Clio (for creative excellence) or Effie (for marketing excellence) award winners.

STRAIGHT SELL

SFX: Clock gonging. Horse & carriage.

ORSON WELLES: It's 3 a.m. in the French Quarter of New Orleans. How'd you like
                  the best cup of coffee in town? And a beignet. That's a square
                  donut without a hole.

SFX: People talking, doors opening & closing, plates rattling.

ORSON WELLES: This is the place. Morning Call. Find a stool at one of the
                  elbow-worn marble counters and while you're waiting for your order,
                  take a look around.

MUSIC: Eastern theme fade up and throughout.

ORSON WELLES: The place hasn't changed much in the past 100 years. Same counters
                  same foot rail. Same mirrors where you can watch and be watched
                  sipping coffee and sprinkling powdered sugar on hot beignets,
                  that still cost a nickel. Only in New Orleans...one of the places
                  that make Eastern what it is...the second largest passenger carrier
                  of all the airlines in the free world...the Wings of Man.

Created by Young & Rubicam International for Eastern Airlines.

TESTIMONIAL

Hello, I'd like to tell you something about myself. I used to be a drunk,
and a chronic drunk driver. In the ten years between my first arrest and
having my license revoked I racked up 19 major traffic violations, I caused 6
serious accidents, injured 3 people besides myself and had my license suspended
twice.

I was still driving and drinking.

Then one night I was driving home after work and I had a few and I hit this kid
on a bicycle. He died before they could get him any help. He was just 11 and
a little younger than my oldest boy. I'm living with that now. I was too drunk
to see him then, but, I can see him now...and I remember.

ANNCR: This message was brought to you by The General Motors Corporation

General Motors Corporation "Safer Driver Radio series. Created by Robert
Dunning, N.W. Ayer & Son, Inc., New York

<u>HUMOR</u>

AUDIO:

HUSBAND: I can't believe I ate that whole thing.

WIFE: You ate it Ralph.

HUSBAND: I can't believe I ate that whole thing.

WIFE: No Ralph, I ate it!

HUSBAND: I can't believe I ate that whole thing.

WIFE: Take two Alka-Seltzer.

ANNCR. V.O.: For headache and upset stomach, no aspirin or antacid alone relieves you in as many ways as Alka-Seltzer. For headache and upset stomach.

WIFE: Did you drink your Alka-Seltzer?

HUSBAND: The whole thing.

<u>Courtesy of Miles Laboratories and Wells, Rich, Greene, Inc.</u>

<u>MUSICAL</u>

<u>Song:</u>
I'd like to buy the world a home
and furnish it with love. Grow
apple trees

and snow white turtle doves

I'd like to teach the world to sing
(sing with me) in perfect harmony
(perfect harmony) and I'd like to
buy the world a Coke and keep it
company
It's the real thing.

I'd like to teach the world to
sing (what the world wants today)

In perfect harmony (perfectly)
I'd like to buy the world a Coke.

and keep it company

It's the real thing. (Coke is)

What the world wants today Coca-Cola.
It's the real thing. What the
world wants today Coke is.
Coca-Cola.

<u>Courtesy of The Coca-Cola Company. Words and music by Roger Cook, Roger Greenaway, William Backer and Billy Davis. McCann-Erickson, Inc.</u>

DRAMATIZATION

ANNCR: Hi audience.

AUDIENCE: Hi Bill.

ANNCR: Welcome to "Win or Lose," and now here's our contestant, Frank Mather

FRANK: Hi, Bill.

ANNCR: Your question, Frank is (DRUM ROLL) figure out your bank checking

            statement.

FRANK: Oh...

            (TICKING OFF TIME BEHIND FRANK)

FRANK: Let's see...Thirty-two dollars...that was my gasoline bill. I think.

            Twelve dollars and eight cents...that was...can I use my check stubs?

ANNCR: Go right ahead, Frank.

FRANK: Let's see. That amount must be my car payment...No...Yes!

ANNCR: Time's running out, Frank.

FRANK: Well all these amounts all over my statement...how can anybody figure

            it out?

ANNCR: (BUZZER SOUNDS) Oh, sorry Frank. You lost.

ANNCR 2:   Figuring out a checking statement can be a problem. So Bank of Americ

            has done something about it. We've introduced the Timesaver Statement

            We put your check numbers on it and list them in numerical order. We

            indicate any checks still outstanding. A glance down the column tells

            you which checks haven't come in yet. It's that simple and there's no

            charge to customers using our scenic checks. Drop by and ask for

            our Timesaver Statement. Bank of America. Member F.D.I.C.

Courtesy of Grey Advertising, Inc.

The non-commercial commercial and the anti-commercial commercial were phenomena of the 1970's. Prompted in large part by the anti-smoking spots, which stations continued to carry even after cigarette commercials went off the air, these public service announcements (PSA's) contained the best writing techniques of the most persuasive commercials. Clearly differing from the PSA examples noted earlier in this chapter, the following musical PSA began to achieve the status of a popular folk-rock song.

JANIE SONG:	I want to watch the sun come up another fifty years.
	I want to write a novel that will bring the world to tears
	And I want to see Venice
	I want to see my kids have kids
	I want to see them free
	I want to live my only life I want the most of me
	I want to dance I want to love
	I want to breathe
ANNCR. VO:	Janie died On an endless road in America
	Because a lonely man was driving drunk out of his mind
	Problem drinkers who drive are responsible for more than 40 deaths every day.
	Get the problem drinker off the road.
JANIE SONG:	I want to know what's out there beyond the furthest star
	I even want to go there is we ever get that far
	And I want to see Venice
TAG VO:	Help. Do something about the problem drinker. For his sake. And yours.

Courtesy U.S. Department of Transportation

One of the classic statements on radio commercials came from Maurice B. Mitchell in 1949 as director of broadcast advertising for the National Association of Broadcasters. The continuing validity of the five points presented by Mr. Mitchell, since 1967 Chancellor of the University of Denver, was emphasized by *Broadcasting Magazine* on September 10, 1973 when it reprinted Mr. Mitchell's 1949 statement under the headline: "Second time around: words about radio still ring true." Although Mr. Mitchell's comments related to radio advertising in general, they are in some instances specifically and in other instances by implication oriented toward the job of the commercial continuity writer. Mr. Mitchell stated, in part:

How can you use radio more effectively? What are the things you can do to get greater results from radio? I would tell you five simple things — the five points into which all our study and all our research can be boiled down.

No. 1. Before you can use radio for maximum effectiveness, you have got to understand your objectives. Before an advertiser, before a retailer sets up his radio advertising budget or buys any time, he should know what he expects to advertise and to whom he expects to address his advertising message. What do you want from radio and whom do you want to talk to? It's just that simple . . . .

No. 2. The retailer should take advantage of a technique we have found to be overwhelmingly successful — the beamed program technique. If you know what you want to say and you know whom you want to say it to, you can buy a vehicle that will, without waste, talk directly to the people you want to address. It's a rifle shot at a target, not a buck-shot at a barn door . . . .

No. 3. We think the retailer who wants maximum success from advertising should advertise his strong departments and his strong lines, advertise his in-demand merchandise and advertise it on the radio regularly . . . .

No. 4. You've got to have the kind of copy that will do the selling job right. Not just "copy" — not just the stuff you poke out with one finger on the typewriter for your newspaper *and* your radio advertising . . . sometimes. One of the things we've never been able to understand is why an advertiser will put phrases in his advertising copy that people would never say aloud. Did you ever hear of a woman who called her husband on the phone and said to him, "Would you mind stopping in at Jones's Department Store today and buying me a pair of slippers because, there, quality and variety go hand in hand?" A lot of advertisers are saying that sort of thing every single day of the week. Don't you think perhaps she might actually say, "I wish you'd buy me a pair of slippers at Jones's because their sale ends today and I can't get downtown?" She is telling her husband specifically what she wants, specifically why she wants it, and she makes a decision to buy for a specific reason.

One of the best examples I've seen is the copy of an advertiser who used the radio recently to advertise purses. In his early advertising, he was using this kind of copy: "Stop in here for a purse because we have purses that will help complete a smart costume ensemble at budget prices." Now, nobody buys "a smart costume ensemble at budget prices." But when he later began to say, "Here's where the working girl will always find a purse at $8.98," or "Here's where you'll find plastic bags that wash as easily as your face," or "Here's where you'll find plastic bags and purses in bright colors that will go with your dark suit," he was talking to people in the terms in which they thought of his merchandise. He was talking specifically to the listeners about the specific things his merchandise could do for them, and he wasn't being vague and saying, "This merchandise which we have to sell has this attribute." He was saying "*You* ought to buy this because this will do this for *you.*"

We also think the kind of copy that produces the maximum results for a retailer is truthful, believable copy. If you will sit down and take the trouble to find out those things that you can say about your goods that are truthful and that are believable, then you have taken a step towards greater success in radio. That kind of copy sticks in a person's mind for a long time. It doesn't always produce results *today,* but continual repetition will cause people to remember the store that uses that kind of advertising. Joske's (of San Antonio) continual repetition of "the largest store in the largest state," and similar slogans used by other great stores, stay in the minds of many people who aren't planning a purchase the first time they hear it. The fact that when they do get around to buying they'll remember that here's where they've wanted to shop — that's the real effect of that kind of copy. Truthful copy, like truthful clerks, is a lot more convincing. Very few retailers would instruct their clerks to deliberately lie to a potential buyer. Yet many retailers don't deliberately lie but — let me say — deviate somewhat from the bare facts in their advertising.

Most important of all, invite your customers to take direct action. Don't say: "You should buy a pair of slippers because they're wonderful," but say: "Come on down to our store tomorrow morning at 10 o'clock and go into the entrance just off Main Street. You don't even have to go upstairs — the slippers are right near the door. You can buy them and be out in five minutes." You've given a direct invitation to take direct action.

I've heard some taxi-cab advertising recently that impressed me. Typical was a line of taxi cabs that said, "Here's where you can have dependable, clean, efficient taxi service." Now I don't particularly care if the taxi cab company is run efficiently. If it isn't, I assume they'll go bankrupt and somebody else will come around when I call. Dependability is certainly not the key customer advantage for a taxi-cab company to promote as a basic reason for calling a cab. On the other hand, I have heard another taxi company say, "It's raining out today! Don't get wet! Call a taxi. Call this number. Be sure you call this number if you need a taxi. And if you need a taxi, call this number." They're talking to me about a service I'm liable to need right then in terms of why I might need it, and they make sure I can find it if I do.

One of the things I get a big kick out of, and I'm sure many other advertising men do, is the Christmas approach — "Be sure you bring something home to your wife that will put the lovelight in her eyes." I can put the lovelight in my wife's eyes without the help of any advertising. But there are some other reasons why I might buy her a Christmas present. Some pretty good, sound selling reasons. "Put the old lovelight in your wife's eyes" looks wonderful on a typewriter, but it sounds silly in advertising and doesn't persuade anybody. The direct-action copy approach, talking to people in terms that they understand, in the terms in which they think of the use of the merchandise themselves, will sell.

No. 5. Coordinate your advertising. . . . How do you coordinate your advertising? It's very simple. You display radio-advertised merchandise at the place where you said it could be bought. . . . Make sure you promote your radio programs in all of your other advertising media. . . . Conversely, use radio to make your other media work better. . . . Let radio give emphasis and increased publicity to all of your other advertising purchases.

It is important for the writer to try to keep the commercial in good taste. It should be sincere, direct and simple. It should fit the personality of the performer delivering it. It should be grammatically correct. In persuasion, action words are very effective. Important ideas should be repeated, usually in different words or phrases unless the writer wishes to present a slogan. Avoid false claims and superlatives; unfortunately, in some instances pressures are put upon the writer to write in that manner.

NEWS AND SPORTS

Any real happening that may have interest for people is news. In some instances the radio newswriter has to gather the material; in most instances he or she rewrites the material as it comes from the newsgathering sources. Writing radio news is basically the same as writing newspaper news: the five W's — Who, What, When, Where and Why — apply. Special considerations of the radio medium, however, necessitate some important modifications in their use.

Sources

On most stations news is obtained from the wire services. Networks and larger stations use, in addition, special reporters and correspondents. The writer for a specific program frequently needs only to adapt and rewrite in terms of the format of that news program. In some instances a staff writer may do no more than prepare a basic format with introduction, ending and transitions, and leave the actual newswriting to a special staff. In some local stations the writer frequently seeks, writes and delivers the local news.

Styles

The writer, in utilizing the five W's, must remember that the audience does not have a chance to go back and re-hear the news, as the newspaper reader has a chance to re-read. Therefore, broadcast news must be presented concisely, clearly, simply and directly. Transitions between news segments must be smooth. The material should be thought of in terms of dramatic action, but at the same time should be scrupulously accurate. The nature of radio permits presentation of news almost as it happens, something that newspapers cannot do. The broadcaster is entering the home at all hours of the day, and the selection of material should be in keeping with the composition of the audience and their actions as far as can be determined by the writer. The criteria in the NAB code concerning the treatment of news provide a good guide for the writer.

Broadcast Types and Content

The 5- and 15-minute straight news broadcasts are the most common. The writer may, however, be required to prepare the same news material for other broadcast types, including the news analysis, the personal opinion of the news, the news in depth technique and the editorializing approach. The writer should be aware of whether the news really is being written straight or whether it is being colored or oriented toward a special purpose. In addition, there are special categories of news broadcasts, such as financial news, garden news, campus news and so forth.

Organization

The proper organization of the radio news program is at least as important as is an effective layout for the front page and the placement of stories on the subsequent pages of a newspaper. No matter what special organization is used, the writer should be certain that it is clear and logical and easily understood. News broadcasts are developed around one or a combination of several major organizational forms. The most commonly used approach is to put the most important story first and the others in descending order, as does the newspaper, and to divide the remaining stories of lesser importance into international, national, state and local groupings, and into special content areas, such as sports and weather. Sometimes a geographical grouping, in which stories occurring in the same geographical location are put together, is used. Topical groupings (stories with the same subject area) and size groupings (international down to local) are sometimes used independently.

The physical format of a news program may vary. It may begin with the announcer giving the headlines, followed by a commercial, and then the commentator coming in with the details. It may start with the commentator beginning directly with the news. Radio frequently presents news roundups, usually from various parts of the country or from various parts of the world, thus requiring a format suitable not only to the purpose and content but to the various reporter personalities involved. The following is an example of a 5-minute local news script for a metropolitan area station, WMAL, Washington, D.C. WMAL general manager Harold Green notes that "the Agnew story has national impact, but was used because of the obvious area interest."

```
The vice president said it again today--he is not stepping down.

Spiro Agnew talked to newsmen after lunching with ten liberal senators
on Capitol Hill.

GNEW    "...Possibility of resigning."
:08
```

Just a short time before Agnew said that...The White House was acknow-
ledging that the subject of the vice president's resignation WAS among
the things discussed when Agnew and President Nixon met yesterday. But
Warren said Nixon neither encouraged nor pressured Agnew to take any
particular course.

Meantime...there will be no House action at present on Agnew's request.
for an investigation of the charges that he was involved in Maryland
political corruption. The word came from House Speaker Carl Albert.

ALBERT "...at this time."
:14

Albert's decision today did not stop a flurry of House floor speeches...
some in favor...some against granting Agnew's request.

Republican Paul Findlay introduced a resolution calling for appointment
of a special committee to recommend whether impeachment proceedings should
be instituted.

Today's Senate Watergate hearings featured a course in the art of
political campaigning. The big question: What political tricks are
dirty...and what are acceptable?

                                    ***

A 26 year old Laurel, Maryland man is being held on 75 thousand dollars bond...
charged with the slaying of 13 year old Audrey Blaisdell. WMAL's Bud Steele has
the story.

STEELE :50

                            STEELE TEXT

Prince Georges Country police worked on the case non-stop...from the time Audrey'
parents reported her missing Monday night from a bowling alley near Laurel.
Searchers found the girl's strangled body the next morning in a wooded area
across the street from the bowling alley. Police Lieutenant Colonel John Rhodes
told me the response to broadcast appeals for information was fantastic.
                                    ***
Rhodes says indications are the girl was killed a short time after she and the
suspect were last seen together...and that evidence found during a search of
the suspect's home links him to the crime. Rhodes says the suspect has made a
statement...which he declined to make public at this time. Bud Steele, WMAL News

Two bandits pulled off what may be the biggest bank job in Maryland history.

They got away with more than 500 thousand dollars from the Maryland National
Bank Branch at Friendship Airport. Bank officials say the large amount of cash
was on hand because it was pay day at the nearby Westinghouse Defense Center.

                                    ***

Those challenges to the petitions of four DC School Board candidates have been
thrown out.

The challengers had claimed the petitions submitted by candidates Charles Cassell
Ernestine Saxon, Teresa Jones and Michael Wheeler lacked registration numbers nex
to the names. But Norval Perkins of the city elections board says that doesn't
matter.

KINS   "...would have been September the 17th."
:14

In Prince Georges County...the elections board also came up with a decision.   It
ruled Mrs. Leslie Kreimer CAN be a school board candidate after all.   First she
was disqualified because she's a school employee.   But the Board says a new state
law makes it legal for such employees to serve on the Board.

***

Republican Mills Godwin...running for Governor of Virginia...repeated his charge
today that his opponent--Independent Henry Howell--once favored cross-Potomac
school busing in the Washington area.   Godwin says he has documentary proof.

But three elected officials in Northern Virginia--who support Howell--denounced
the Godwin charge as false.   Everard Munsey of Arlington, Jean Packard of Fairfax
and Charles Beatley of Alexandria say Howell never advocated busing across
jurisdictional lines.

***

Though it returned no indictments...a Prince Georges County grand jury issued
a report today...blistering the suburban sanitary commission.   It charges neglect
in the handling of sewer permits.   And it calls for a further investigation of
what it calls "improprieties" in the granting of sewer rights in violation of
a state-wide moratorium.

***

Prince Georges County has come up with a new program to combat child abuse.

A four member child abuse consultations team is being set up at Prince Georges
General Hospital.   All children who are found to be abused will be admitted
there automatically.   The team will determine whether the child should be
returned to his parents...or placed in a foster home.   The new program was
announced by County Executive William Gullett.

LETT 2   "...on that hotline as well."
:15

***

They still haven't been able to select any jurors for the trial of 19 year old
Tyrone Marshall.   He's accused of shooting and robbing Senator John Stennis
outside his home last January.

The entire day today was spent trying to agree on jury members...and they've yet
to pick the first one.

Courtesy of WMAL, Washington, D.C.

Rewriting

One of the newswriter's duties, particularly on the local level, is *re-writing*. A smaller station without a newsgathering staff is sometimes almost totally dependent on the newswire. The announcer, given sufficient time and energy, edits those stories that can be appropriately adapted to include a local angle, evaluating their impact on the community. In effect, the announcer *re*writes the news. As noted above, news broadcasts are organized into homogenous groupings. Finding a unifying thread that means something special to the listener in that community frequently requires rewriting. For example, segments in a topical grouping of stories dealing with the economy might be rewritten to reflect their relationship to the local unemployment figures.

Perhaps the most common form of rewriting is updating. An important story doesn't disappear after it is used once. Yet, to use exactly the same story in subsequent newscasts throughout the day is likely to turn off those listeners who hear it more than once and conclude that the station is carrying stale news. Updating is an important function of the network newswriter. There are several major areas to look for in updating news stories. First, the writer determines if there is any further hard news, factual information to add to the story. Second, if the story is important enough it is likely that investigative reporting will have dug up some additional background information not available when the story was first broadcast. Third, depending on the happening's impact on society, it will have been commented upon after its initial release by any number of people, from VIPs to ordinary citizens. In addition, a story may by its very nature relate to other events of the day, that relationship being made clear in the rewriting.

Format

Even when the wire services are used exclusively, a format must be prepared containing an opening, a closing and transitional lead-ins for the specific organizational parts of the newscast, including the commercials. Here is a typical format:

FIVE MINUTE NEWS FORMAT - SUSTAINING

OPEN: Good (morning) (afternoon) (evening).

The time is_____.

In the news_____.

(Note: use 4 stories..mixing national, world and local by order of importance).*

ANNCR: More news in just a moment.

TAPE: COMMERCIAL (if logged)

ANNCR: In other news_____.

(NOTE: use 2 stories..national, world and/or local).

ANNCR: WGAY weather for the Washington area_____.

(NOTE: use complete forecast, including temperature, humidity and winds).

CLOSE   That's news and weather ... I'm (anncr. name) .

*Total local news content: 3 stories in entire newscast.

Courtesy of WGAY FM & AM, Washington and Silver Spring.

Sports

The straight sports program is much like the straight news program except that in sports broadcasting one can use colloquial phrases and technical terms which are familiar to sports fans. Most sports programs are of the recapitulation type which gives results of contests. The most-important-to-least-important story approach usually is used, presenting the results first of the most important sport of the particular time of year and gradually working down to the coming events of the least important sport. Local sports news is coordinated with national sports news on most local stations. As with all news broadcasts, however, the most important story, regardless of the sport or season, is the lead story. The sports feature program is one in which interviews, anecdotes and background stories on personalities and events are incorporated.

The live on-the-spot sports broadcast is the most popular form of sports program and, although essentially a special event, will be mentioned here. The writer for live sports coverage is concerned with transition continuity, including opening, closing and filler material. This includes information relating to pre-event color and action, statistics, form charts, the site of the event, the participants and human interest anecdotes. More and more on-the-spot broadcasters provide their own filler material to accompany their or their partner's live description of the game or contest. Where this material is prepared by the writer, the writer's function is primarily that of a researcher, and the script may be little more than an outline and/or a series of statistics, individual unrelated sentences or short paragraphs.

SPECIAL EVENTS AND FEATURES

Special Events

As a result of public interest group and citizen pressures, rulings of the FCC and, in circular fashion, media-induced increased interest in public affairs by young people, the special event became increasingly significant in broadcasting in the past decade.

The special event is usually under the direction of the News Department of the station and is essentially something that is taking place live and is of interest — critical or passing — to the community. These on-the-spot presentations are similar to live sports coverage in that they are narrated rather than announced, and the writer must prepare continuity accordingly. Sometimes interviews or features are taped beforehand for insertion at the proper time during the reporting of the event. Special events ordinarily originate independently and include such happenings as parades, dedications, banquets, awards and the opening of new supermarkets. More significant kinds of special events, perhaps, are political conventions and astronaut launchings. The assassinations of John F. Kennedy, Martin Luther King and Robert F. Kennedy were covered fully by radio, though, of course, unanticipated; the first human landing on the moon and the Watergate Hearings were also fully covered, but as planned events with time for preparation in depth.

Where possible — as in an anticipated special event such as election night coverage — the writer must study news stories, press releases, historical documents, books, locales and all other material that may be pertinent and helpful in preparing opening, closing, transition and filler material that may be needed by the broadcasters. Because the form of the special event is extemporaneous, the material, though prepared as fully as possible, should be simple and sound as though it were ad-libbed. In some instances, where the coverage is of a special event that does not require commentary by the broadcaster, the writer needs to prepare only an appropriate opening and closing. The following illustrates continuity that may be used for a continuing special event that is broadcast more than once.

PRGM: FCC HEARINGS

DATE:

TIME:

_ _ _ _ _ _ _ _ _ _ _ _ _ _ _ _ _

ANN: Good morning.
        Good afternoon.
        In just a few moments, your city station will bring you the
        _____ day of the Federal Communications Commission
        hearings on network television policies and practices.
            The hearings are taking place in the Interstate Com-
        merce Building in Washington, D.C., before the entire Fed-
        eral Communications Commission.

        We take you now to Washington, D.C.

                            * * *

            That concludes this (morning's) (afternoon's) session
        of the FCC hearings on network television policies and
        practices. Your city station is bringing you these impor-
        tant broadcasts direct from Washington, D.C., in their
        entirety, through the week of February 5th. We are inter-
        ested in your reaction to these broadcasts. Write, FCC
        Hearings, WNYC, New York 7. And join us again (at 1:45)
        (tomorrow morning at 10) for the next session.

            Courtesy of the Municipal Broadcasting System—
        Stations WNYC, WNYC-FM, WNYC-TV—New York City.

Coverage in depth of a special event requires considerable preliminary work. Russ Tornabene, Vice President and General Manager of the NBC Radio Network, states: "Extensive research goes into the preparation of material to be used as background for broadcasting special events. For example, the research document prepared for the 1972 Olympics ran to about 500 pages. For the 1972 primaries and political conventions there were several books prepared, each with several hundred pages. They were even tabbed for quick reference, with color-coded sections, for various categories such as candidates, issues, etc. The job of the writer, therefore, in preparing background material for special events is an important one. In addition, the correspondents doing the broadcasts add to the basic book with research, interviews and materials of their own."

Special Features

The special feature differs from the special event in that the former is prepared beforehand and is controlled by the station as a planned program. In addition, the special feature usually is pre-recorded. The writer does a complete script. Special features usually are short — two to five to 15 minutes in length; the former for fillers and the latter for full programs of a public service nature. The subject matter for the special feature varies. Some sample types: the presentation of the work of a special service group in the community, a story on the operation of the local fire department, an examination of the problems of the school board, a how-to-do-it broadcast, a behind-the-scenes story on any subject — from raising chickens to electing public officials. The special feature offers the writer the opportunity to create a program of high artistic quality closely approaching the documentary. Although the script is of a public service nature, it does not have to be purely informational or academic. It may include forms of variety and drama, as well as the more common news and discussion materials. Special features customarily are oriented around a person or thing or situation.

The following is from a regular special feature series on NBC entitled "Emphasis":

```
Even if you go to Washington with a closed mind, keep your eyes open.  Bill
Cullen, At Ease.  More after this for Best Western Motels.

Just about anybody who gets to Washington sees the Lincoln Memorial...most get
to the Smithsonian Institution...and some even manage to find Ford's Theater...
where Lincoln was shot.

But there are hundreds of monuments in the nation's capital that hardly any
visitor notices...and that most Washingtonians themselves know little about.
For instance, there are thirty statues of men on horseback...which may be one
or two too many.  Some of the riders...like Ulysses S. Grant...you may have
heard of...but there are a lot of other generals there that no one now remembers.
```

In the middle of DuPont Circle there is an elegant marble fountain held up by
some partly draped ladies. The fountain honors a Union admiral in the Civil
War named DuPont. The man who designed the fountain was Daniel Chester French.
one of this country's great sculptors. French also did a lovely statue of a dea
girl learning sign language. It's at Florida Avenue and Seventh Street.

If your taste runs more to nostalgia, there are relief sculptures of 1926 automobiles on the Capital Garage...and, for modernists, a lot of strictly abstract
sculpture will go on display at the new Hirshhorn Museum next year.

When somebody wants to put in a piece of decoration or sculpture, Washington
is where they want to do it...and you can spend weeks there just looking around.

Bill Cullen, Emphasis, At Ease.

Now a word for Best Western.

Courtesy of NBC News

THE DOCUMENTARY

Although the documentary on the network level has moved, by and
large, from radio to television, occasional first-rate radio documentaries are
still being broadcast. Many regional stations have contributed importantly
to the public interest by creating and presenting radio documentaries on
controversial and vital subjects, and even small local stations originate
documentaries from time to time on local issues. With drama gone from
radio, the occasional documentary remains the writer's principal form for
artistic creativity on the highest level. Writing a documentary sharpens the
writer's ability in using the radio medium to its utmost; therefore, as with
the earlier material in this chapter on radio drama, documentary writing is
treated here to a greater proportionate extent than it actually is used in
commercial radio. Many noncommercial radio stations, however, produce
dramas and documentaries as significant parts of their schedules.

The documentary not only combines many of radio's forms, including
news, special events, special features, music and drama, but at its best
makes a signal contribution to public affairs by interpreting the past, ana-
lyzing the present or anticipating the future — and sometimes it does all
three in a single program.

Type and Form

The documentary falls into three basic classical patterns: the strength
and nobility of people in a difficult or hostile environment, as exemplified
by the father of the modern documentary, Robert Flaherty, in *Nanook of
the North;* the socio-economic-political problems facing society and the
ways in which they can be solved, as seen in some of Pare Lorentz's films
of the New Deal era; and the details, artistically expressed, of seemingly
ordinary, everyday existence, as presented by John Grierson in *Night Mail.*

Any given radio documentary can — and frequently does — combine more than one of these approaches.

Although the documentary is dramatic, it is not a drama in the sense of the fictional play. It is more or less a faithful representation of a true story. This is not to say, however, that all documentaries are unimpeachably true. Editing and narration can make any series of sequences seem other than what they really are. The semi-documentary or fictional documentary has achieved a certain degree of popularity, presenting a story based on fact, but fictionalizing the characters involved in a true event; or changing the happenings to make the true characters more exciting; or even taking several situations and characters from life and creating a semi-true composite picture. Some of Norman Corwin's semi-documentaries raised radio to its highest creative levels. It should be remembered by the writer that though the documentary essentially deals with the issues, people and events of the news, it is not a news story, but an exploration behind and beneath the obvious. It presents not only what happened but, as far as possible, the reasons for the occurrence, the attitudes and feelings of the people involved, and the implications and significance not only for some individuals, but for the whole of society.

Ordinarily, the documentary is put together in the field on tape. Occasionally, a good documentary can be done in the studio with already existing material and good transitional narration. Interviews and commentary, as well as the actual voices and sounds of the happenings, are important elements in the creation and editing of the radio documentary.

Procedure

Essentially, the documentary contains the real words of real persons (or their writings, published and unpublished, including letters, especially if the persons are not living or cannot possibly be reached and there is no record of their voices) and the sounds of the event. These materials, sometimes seemingly unrelated, must be put together into a dramatic, cohesive whole and edited in terms of a script.

First, the writer must have an idea. What subject of public interest is worthy of documentary treatment? The idea for the program frequently comes not from the writer, but from the producer. The writer (and/or others on the production team) must decide on the point of view to be presented. Then the real work starts, from thorough research in libraries, to personal visits to persons and places, to investigations of what audio materials on the subject are already available. When the research is completed, the writer can begin to prepare a detailed outline.

From the outline the writer can determine the specific material to be accumulated and selected. After hearing — perhaps many times — all the potential program materials, the writer can prepare a final outline and write the script. During the process of gathering materials the writer constantly revises the outline, as new, unexpected material becomes available and as anticipated material turns out to be unavailable or unusable. The final script is used for the selection and organization of the specific materials for the final taping or editing of the program. It is significant, in terms of the high degree of coordination and cooperation needed to complete a good documentary, that in a great many instances the writer also serves as the producer and even as the director.

Technique

Human interest is a key to good documentary writing. Even if you want to present only facts, even if the facts seem stilted and dry, make them dramatic, develop them in terms of the people involved or, if the subject is inanimate, in terms of live attributes. The documentary script is developed in a dramatized fashion: the exploration of character, the introduction of a conflict (the problem which created the happening that requires documentary treatment), and the development of this conflict through complications until a crisis is reached.

A narrator is almost always used in the documentary. Use the narrator judiciously. A narrator who plays too great a role may distract from the "live" material. Avoid the possibility that the program will sound like a series of taped interviews or lectures. Make the points clear and concise. A narrator frequently can crisply summarize on-the-spot materials that would otherwise seem long and drawn out.

One of radio's finest documentaries is CBS' *Who Killed Michael Farmer?*, an exploration in depth of a murder, the murderers and their environment. Although more than ten years old, it is not only a classic but an excellent example of how to write documentaries for current and would-be writers. The beginning of the documentary is presented here, with analysis of the organizational approach and some of the techniques used.

"WHO KILLED MICHAEL FARMER?"

OPENS COLD:

MURROW: This is Ed Murrow. Here is how a mother and a father remember
their son — Michael Farmer.

ET: **MR. AND MRS. FARMER:**

MRS. FARMER: Michael was tall and very good looking. He
had blond hair and blue eyes. Maybe I'm prejudiced as a mother,
but I thought he had a saintly face.

MR. FARMER: He was always laughing and joking. He was a
very courageous and spirited boy. He was athletic, even though he
walked with a limp from an attack of polio when he was ten years old.
He was an excellent student who had great plans for his future. It's
a hard thing to realize that there is no future any longer.

MURROW: Michael Farmer died on the night of July 30, 1957. He was fifteen
years old. He was stabbed and beaten to death in a New York City
park. Boys in a teenage street gang were arrested for this crime.
Ten gang members — under fifteen years of age — were convicted
of juvenile delinquency and committed to state training schools.
Seven other boys — fifteen to eighteen — stood trial for first degree
murder . . . were defended by twenty-seven court-appointed lawyers.
Their trial lasted ninety-three days; ended last Tuesday. This was
the verdict of an all male, blue ribbon jury.

ET: **JUROR:**

We found Louis Alvarez and Charles Horton guilty of murder in the
second degree, and we also found Lencio de Leon and Leroy Birch
guilty of manslaughter in the second degree. We found Richard Hills
and George Melendez not guilty because we believe these boys were
forced to go along with the gang the night of the murder. We also
found John McCarthy not guilty because we were convinced, beyond
a reasonable doubt, that this boy was mentally sick and didn't know
what was going on at any time.

MURROW: It would seem that this case now is closed. All that remains is for
a judge to pass sentence. Under the law, the gang alone is guilty
of the murder of Michael Farmer. But there is more to be said.
More is involved here, than one act of violence, committed on one
summer night. The roots of this crime go back a long ways. In the
next hour — you will hear the voices of boys and adults involved in
the case. This is not a dramatization.

The tragedy first became news on the night of July 30, 1957. At
6:30 on this steaming summer evening in New York City, the
Egyptian Kings and Dragons gang began to assemble. They met
outside a neighborhood hangout — a candy story at 152nd Street and
Broadway, in Manhattan's upper West Side. They came from a
twenty-block area . . . from teeming tenements, rooming houses and
housing projects. One of their leaders remembers the number of boys
present this night.

A standard method of effectively opening a radio documentary is to select carefully out of the mass of taped material several short statements by persons involved and present them immediately in order to get the audience attention and interest as well as to tell, sharply and concretely, what the program is about. This is especially effective here in the opening statements of Mr. and Mrs. Farmer. The stark nature of the beginning of the program — it opens cold, no introduction, no music — lends force to the opening. Short opening quotes are not usually sufficient, however, to provide enough background information. The narrator condenses and states in terse terms the necessary additional material. The type of documentary is suggested close to the beginning. The statement: "But there is more to be said. More is involved here . . . the roots of crime go back a long ways" indicates the line of development: not only will the event and the people involved be explored in depth, but a problem will be presented and solutions will be sought.

ET: GANG MEMBER:

We had a lot o' little kids, big kids, we had at least seventy-five — then a lot of 'em had to go home before nine o'clock; we was supposed to leave at nine o'clock but then we changed our plans to ten o'clock, you know. So I told a lot o' little kids I don't wanna see them get into trouble, you know, nice guys, so I told them they could go home. So they went home. That left us with around twenty-one kids.

MORROW: People sitting on the stoops and garbage cans along this street watched them . . . grouped together, talking excitedly. They called each other by their nicknames: Magician, Big Man, Little King, Boppo. No one bothered to ask what they were talking about. This boy remembers.

ET: GANG MEMBER:

They were talking about what they were going to do and everything. They were going to fight and everything. But they'd never planned nothing. They just said we were gonna go to the fight and we were just gonna get some guys for revenge. They said we ain't gonna let these Jesters beat up any of our guys no more.

MURROW: The Jesters are a street gang in an adjoining neighborhood — Washington Heights, where Michael Farmer lived. The two gangs were feuding. Boys on both sides had been beaten and stabbed. There is evidence that this night the gang planned to surprise and attack any Jesters they could find. They came prepared for a fight.

ET: GANG MEMBER:

Some picked a stick and some had got some knives and chains out of their houses and everything. One had a bayonette. No, a machete.

MURROW: Holding these weapons they lingered on the corner of a brightly lit street in the heart of a great city. A police station was one block away. One gang leader went to a candy store . . . telephoned the President of a brother gang . . . requested guns and cars for the night's activity . . . was told: "We can't join you. We have troubles of our own tonight." Shortly after nine PM, the gang walked to a nearby park . . . was followed there by some girl friends. A gang member, 14 years old, continues the story.

ET: GANG MEMBER:

We went down to the park and sat around for a while. Then we started drinking and we drank whiskey and wine and we was drunk. Then we started talkin' about girls. We started sayin' to the girls that if they get us to bring us some roses an' all that — that if we get caught to write to us and all this.

MURROW: In one hour, Michael Farmer would be dead. The gang prepared to move out. Some had doubts.

Suspense is an important ingredient of the documentary. But it is not the suspense of finding out what is going to happen. The documentary is based on fact: we already know. The suspense is in learning the motivations, the inner feelings, the attitudes of the persons involved even as the actual event is retold. This is implied in the narrator's previous speech.

ET: GANG MEMBER:

I didn't wanna go at first, but they said come on. So then all the big guys forced me to go. I was scared. I was worried. I realized like what I was doing I'd probably get in trouble.

MURROW:

They left the park and headed for trouble at about ten PM. They walked uptown toward the neighborhood of the rival gang — the Jesters. They walked in two's and three's to avoid attention. Along the way, they met, by chance, this boy.

ET: GANG MEMBER:

I was walkin' uptown with a couple of friends and we ran into Magician and them there. They asked us if we wanted to go to a fight, and we said yes. When they asked me if I wanted to go to a fight, I couldn't say no. I mean I could say no, but for old-times sake, I said yes.

MURROW:

He was a former member of the gang—just went along this night, "For Old-times Sake." Next stop: Highbridge Park . . . within the territory of the Jesters. Michael Farmer lived one block from the park. In the summer, the Egyptian Kings and Dragons fought the Jesters at the park swimming pool. This pool is closed at ten PM but not drained. Boys in the neighborhood frequently slip through a breach in the gate to swim here late at night. The Egyptian Kings and Dragons regrouped near the pool. Two gang members continue the story.

ET: GANG MEMBERS:

FIRST BOY: We were waiting over there, in the grass. Then two guys went down to see if there were a lot of the Jesters down there. To check. I was kind of nervous; felt kind of cold inside.

SECOND BOY: They sent three guys around the block. We walked around the block to see how strong the club was we was gonna fight. To see if they had lots of guys and what-not. What we saw, they had lots of big guys. I'd say about nineteen, twenty or eighteen, like that. And we figured it out so we kept on walking around the block.

MURROW:

While their scouts prowled the neighborhood, Michael Farmer and his friend, sixteen year old Roger McShane, were in Mike Farmer's apartment . . . listening to rock 'n' roll records. This is Mrs. Farmer.

We can see the use here of D. W. Griffith's technique of dynamic cutting: switching back and forth between two or more settings and two or more persons or groups of people who are following a parallel course in time and in action. The actions of the gang have been presented in chronological order. Now time is moved back and the actions of Michael Farmer and Roger McShane will catch up in time and place.

ET: MRS. FARMER:

They stayed in his room playin' these new records that they had bought and Michael came out to the kitchen, just as I asked my husband what time it was, to set the clock. It was then five after ten. He asked for a glass of milk and as he walked from the kitchen, he asked, "I'm going to walk Roger home." And that was the last time I saw him.

MURROW:

Both boys had been warned by their parents to stay out of Highbridge Park at night. But, as they walked along the street on this steaming July evening, they decided to sneak a swim in the park pool. At this pool, the Egyptian Kings and Dragons were waiting for their scouts to return. Here is what happened next; first in the words of Roger McShane; then in words of the gang members.

ET: McSHANE AND EGYPTIAN KINGS:

McSHANE: It was ten-thirty when we entered the park; we saw couples on the benches, in the back of the pool, and they all stared at us, and I guess they must 'ave saw the gang there — I don't think they were fifty or sixty feet away. When we reached the front of the stairs, we looked up and there was two of their gang members on top of the stairs. They were two smaller ones, and they had garrison belts wrapped around their hands. They didn't say nothin' to us, they looked kind of scared.

FIRST BOY: I was scared. I knew they were gonna jump them, an' everythin' and I was scared. When they were comin' up, they all were separatin' and everything like that.

McSHANE: I saw the main body of the gang slowly walk out of the bushes, on my right. I turned around fast, to see what Michael was going to do, and this kid came runnin' at me with the belts. Then I ran, myself, and told Michael to run.

SECOND BOY: He couldn't run anyway, cause we were all around him. So then I said, "You're a Jester," and he said "Yeah," and I punched him in the face. And then somebody hit him with a bat over the head. And then I kept punchin' him. Some of them were too scared to do anything. They were just standin' there, lookin'.

THIRD BOY: I was watchin' him. I didn't wanna hit him, at first. Then I kicked him twice. He was layin' on the ground, lookin' up at us. I kicked him on the jaw, or some place; then I kicked him in the stomach. That was the least I could do, was kick 'im.

FOURTH BOY: I was aimin' to hit him, but I didn't get a chance to hit him. There was so many guys on him — I got scared when I saw the knife go into the guy, and I ran right there. After everybody ran, this guy stayed, and started hittin' him with a machete.

MURROW: The rest of the gang pursued Roger McShane.

ET: McSHANE:

I ran down the hill and there was three more of the gang members down at the bottom of the hill, in the baseball field; and the kids chased me down hill, yelling to them to get me.

MURROW: Members of the gang remember.

ET: EGYPTIAN KINGS AND McSHANE:

FIRST BOY: Somebody yelled out, "Grab him. He's a Jester." So then they grabbed him. Mission grabbed him, he turned around and stabbed him in the back. I was . . . I was stunned. I couldn't do nuthin'. And then Mission — he went like that and he pulled . . . he had a switch blade and he said, "you're gonna hit him with the bat or I'll stab you." So I just hit him lightly with the bat.

SECOND BOY: Mission stabbed him and the guy he . . . like hunched over. He's standin' up and I knock him down. Then he was down on the ground, everybody was kickin' him, stompin' him, punchin' him, stabbin' him so he tried to get back up and I knock him down again. Then the guy stabbed him in the back with a bread knife.

THIRD BOY: I just went like that, and I stabbed him with the bread knife. You know, I was drunk so I just stabbed him. (LAUGHS) He was screamin' like a dog. He was screamin' there. And then I took the knife out and I told the other guys to run. So I ran and then the rest of the guys ran with me. They wanted to stay there and keep on doin' it, so I said, "No, come on. Don't kill the guy." And we ran.

ET: FOURTH BOY: The guy that stabbed him in the back with the
                   bread knife, he told me that when he took the knife out o' his back, he
                   said, "Thank you."

                   McSHANE: They got up fast right after they stabbed me.
                   And I just lay there on my stomach and there was five of them as
                   they walked away. And as they walked away they . . . this other big
                   kid came down with a machete or some large knife of some sort, and
                   he wanted to stab me too with it. And they told him, "No, come on.
                   We got him. We messed him up already. Come on." And they took
                   off up the hill and they all walked up the hill and right after that they
                   all of 'em turned their heads and looked back at me. I got up and
                   staggered into the street to get a cab. And I got in a taxi and I asked
                   him to take me to the Medical Center and get my friend and I blacked
                   out.

MURROW: The gang scattered and fled from the park. This boy believes he is
                   the last gang member who saw Michael Farmer this night.

ET: GANG MEMBER:

                   While I was runnin' up the footpath, I saw somebody staggering in the
                   bushes and I just looked and turned around, looked up and kept on
                   runnin'. I think that was the Farmer boy, he was staggerin' in the
                   bushes.

   The suspense has been built and a climax reached. The selection and editing of taped
materials to tell the story of the assault and murder are done magnificently. Excerpts from
the taped interviews were selected to follow a chronological pattern and to present the
actions, feelings and attitudes of the gang members in terms of increasing tempo and
violence. Various physical and emotional viewpoints are presented, all relating to one
another and building the suspense into an ultimate explosion. The documentary should be
dramatic. Is there any doubt about the existence of drama in the preceding sequence?
The audience is put into the center of the action, feeling it perhaps even more strongly than
if the incident were fictionalized and presented, as such incidents frequently are, on a
"private-eye" series. Could any line of a play be more dramatic than, in context, "That
was the least I could do, was kick 'im," or "(LAUGHS) He was screamin' like a dog," or
"The guy that stabbed him in the back with the bread knife, he told me that when he took
the knife out o' his back, he said 'Thank you'."?

MURROW: He left behind a boy nearly dead . . . continued home . . . had a glass
                   of milk . . . went to bed. But then.

ET: GANG MEMBER:

                   I couldn't sleep that night or nuthin' cause I used to fall asleep for about
                   half an hour. Wake up again during the middle of the night. My
                   mother said, "What was the matter with you? Looks like something
                   is wrong." I said, "Nothin'."

MURROW: That boy used a baseball bat in the attack. This boy used a bread
                   knife.

ET: GANG MEMBER:

                   First I went to the river to throw my knife away and then I went home.
                   An' then I couldn't sleep. I was in bed. My mother kept on askin' me
                   where was I and I . . . I told her, you know, that I was in the movies.
                   I was worried about them two boys. If they would die . . . I knew I
                   was gonna get caught.

MURROW: At Presbyterian Medical Center, Roger McShane was on the critical
                   list. Before undergoing major surgery that saved his life, he told
                   about the attack in Highbridge Park. The official police record re-
                   veals what happened next. The speaker: New York City's Deputy
                   Police Commissioner, Walter Arm.

The remainder of the script, after detailing what happened, deals with actions and attitudes following the crime, indicating that there is more to the story than overt events and that the persons involved are not the two dimensional characters of a television fiction series. The script explores motivation and gets behind the problem. Interviews with experts provide the transition into the establishment of the problem as one that goes beyond the specific incident and area. After investigating the reasons for the problem, the documentary explores some possible solutions, those already attempted and those still to come.

It is not necessary to have a network budget and a plethora of personnel to do a good documentary. The following is the first part of an award-winning documentary put together by students without a budget and relying heavily on library research and interviews with persons locally available. In this composite of script and verbatim description, the final script is shown in capitals, and the material in parentheses is that actually recorded and incorporated into the program with the narration.

THE PIEDMONT NORTH CAROLINA FARMER AND POLITICS, 1961

OPEN COLD: TAPE #1, CUT 1, DUPREE SMITH: "I WOULD LIKE VERY MUCH . . BEST PLACE TO WORK."

(I would like very much to spend my entire life here on the farm because I feel like being near the land and being near the soil and seeing the operation of God on this earth is the best place to live and the best place to work.)

MUSIC: IN, UP, AND UNDER

NARRATOR: THIS IS THE SMALL FARMER IN THE PIEDMONT OF NORTH CAROLINA.

MUSIC: UP AND OUT

NARRATOR: YOU ARE LISTENING TO THE "PIEDMONT, NORTH CAROLINA, FARMER AND POLITICS   " THE VOICE YOU JUST HEARD WAS THAT OF DUPREE SMITH, A FARMER IN PIEDMONT, NORTH CAROLINA. IN RURAL AMERICA A CENTURY AGO THE FARM PROBLEM WAS AN INDIVIDUAL ONE OF DIGGING A LIVING OUT OF THE LAND. EACH FARMER SOLVED HIS OWN INDIVIDUAL PROBLEMS WITHOUT GOVERNMENT AID. NEARLY EVERYONE FARMED. TODAY, BECAUSE OF INCREASING COST OF MAIN - TAINING CROPS, LARGER SURPLUSES, HEAVIER STORAGE COSTS AND LOWER FARM INCOME, THE SMALL FARMER IN NORTH CAROLINA, AS WELL AS ACROSS THE NATION, HAS BEEN UNABLE TO DEPEND ON HIS LAND FOR A LIVING. PRODUCTION CON- TINUED TO GROW. SURPLUSES MOUNTED. FARM INCOMES FELL AND THE GOVERNMENT SUBSIDIES NECESSARILY GREW.

PROFESSOR
KOVENOCK: TAPE #2, CUT 1: "THE COMMON PROBLEMS . . . ARE THESE."

(The common problems shared by almost all national farmers today and, at the same time, most North Carolina farmers, are these.)

NARRATOR:	YOU ARE LISTENING TO PROFESSOR DAVID KOVENOCK OF THE POLITICAL SCIENCE DEPARTMENT OF THE UNIVERSITY OF NORTH CAROLINA.
KOVENOCK:	TAPE #2, CUT 2: "FIRST OF ALL . . . SHELTER FOR HIS FAMILY."
	(First of all, a decline in the income going to the farmer—a problem of—this is particularly for, let us say, the marginal farmer, the farmer with a small operation in North Carolina and the rest of the country—the problem of obtaining employment off the farm, that is, some relatively attractive alternative to continuing an operation on the farm that is becoming insufficient for feeding, clothing, and buying shelter for his family.)
NARRATOR:	THIS IS DUPREE SMITH'S PROBLEM.
SMITH:	TAPE #1, CUT 2: "YES, THAT WAS MY DESIRE . . . PART TIME AND WORKING."
	(Yes, that was my desire after returning from service, was to go back to nature and live and raise a family where I felt that I would enjoy living to the fullest. For several years, on this same amount of land, I was able to support my family and myself adequately. For the last year or two, this has been on the decrease. The decline has been to such extent, that I've had to go into other fields—my wife helping part time and working.)
NARRATOR:	WHAT SPECIFICALLY ARE DUPREE SMITH'S PROBLEMS?
KOVENOCK:	TAPE #2, CUT 3: "THE COMMON PROBLEM . . . OCCUPATIONAL PURSUIT?"
	(The common problem shared by the North Carolina farmer and by the national farmer would be, first of all, the condition of agriculture, the relationship of the supply of agricultural commodities to the demand and, of course, consequently, the price that the farmer receives which, of course, now is somewhat depressed. The second major problem is the condition of the rest of the economy as a whole— that is, is it sufficiently good so that the farmer has some alternatives to continuing his, currently, rather unsatisfactory occupational pursuit?)
NARRATOR:	FARMERS ARE MARKETING MORE, BUT ARE RECEIVING LOWER PRICES FOR THEIR CROPS AND PRODUCE. DR. PHILLIPS RUSSELL, A FORMER COLLEGE PROFESSOR AND RETIRED FARMER, HAS THIS TO SAY:
PHILLIPS RUSSELL:	TAPE #3, CUT 1: "THE FARMER HAS BEEN LOSING . . . IN AN UNPROTECTED MARKET."

WUNC, University of North Carolina

Issues of the day and important people of the day provide ready-made material for documentaries, combining interviews with statements already on the record. The beginning of NBC's March 11, 1973 award-winning documentary series, *Second Sunday,* illustrates this approach:

MAN: The accepted use of executive power compelled the Congress and the
United States to re-examine itself and its role ...

MAN: ... The dislocations and the frictions between the Congress and the
White House has been exaggerated ...

MAN: ... Nineteen seventy-six will either be 200 years of the glorious
republic, or else it's going to be the year two or three of the Executive
Monarchy in the United States ...

MAN: ... To the extent that Congress hasn't exercised the full scope of its
authority in the past, it really doesn't have the President to blame; it has
itself to blame ...

JACOB JAVITS: ... Who made the bargains? The Congress and the President.
One cannot undo the bargain ...

GERALD FORD: The American people are on the side of the President.

(MUSIC)

ANNOUNCER: Second Sunday, the award - winning documentary series presented
each month by NBC News. Our subject for March: Congress and the President --
A Constitutional Crisis. Here is NBC News Correspondent, Paul Duke.

PAUL DUKE: We're going to examine what may be the most serious confrontati
between two branches of Government this century. It's a clash which may have a
major impact on the American system, and perhaps, even affect the future of
representative democracy. It's a clash of strong opinions, and strong wills.
And it's producing a crescendo of comment and criticism across the country.

But most of all, as voiced by Washington satirist Mark Russell on Capitol
Hill.

(PIANO MUSIC)

MARK RUSSELL: You know, we go to the trouble in our country of electing
Senators and Congressman. Then we send them out in the cold, to Washington. It
a lonely place, and it's a lonely place for the bills they pass, too. Because t
passed, and they see the light of day, and then they're cut off. Yes, Washingtc
is a lonely town, for our Congressmen and our Senators sometimes sing: Nixon
doesn't love us anymore.

DUKE: If love means doing what Congress wants, then President Nixon is a
rejecting suitor. Mr. Nixon is doing what he wants, and what he believes is bes
for the country. He is making the White House more of a center for Federal
power, and policy making. In the process Congressional power is being eroded an
diminished. The irony is that the President's declared goal is to reduce the
authority of the Federal Government, including his own authority. He struck
the central theme in his inaugural address in January.

PRESIDENT RICHARD NIXON: We have lived too long with the consequence
of attempting to gather all power and responsibility in Washington. Abroad
and at home, the time has come to turn away from the condescending policies of
paternalism; of Washington knows best. In trusting too much in government, we
have asked of it more than it can deliver. This leads only to inflated
expectation, to reduced individual effort, and to a disappointment and frust-
ration that erode confidence both in what government can do, and in what
people can do.

DUKE: It's not the President's goal, but the President's tactics which
have precipitated the gathering fury on Capitol Hill. Mr. Nixon has refused
to spend money appropriated by Congress. In some instances, after Presidential

vetoes were overridden. He has moved to close out Federal programs without
Congressional consent. He has named three super-secretaries of the Cabinet,
without Congressional confirmation. He has drawn a cloak of executive privilege
around his top aides, to prevent them from testifying before major committees
on issues of war and peace. In all of this, Democratic leaders believe the
President has gone too far, exceeding his authority under the Constitution, and
the result, as House Speaker Carl Albert sees it, is a crisis that goes to the
heart of the American system.

CARL ALBERT: The issue here is where do we draw Constitutional lines,
and do we believe what we say when we say that we will support and defend the
Constitution of the United States. That's the overriding issue.

DUKE: Senate Democratic leader Mike Mansfield is concerned, not just by
the erosion in Congressional authority, but that a fundamental alteration may
be taking place in the checks and balances built into the Constitution by the
Founding Fathers.

MIKE MANSFIELD: If that document is ever undermined, and one of the three
branches of the government becomes too subordinate, as we are on the way to
becoming at the present time, then all I can say is, "God help the Republic"
because the foundations will have been broken, and perhaps broken down at least
in part.

DUKE: To some extent, President Nixon is only accelerating a trend which
began when Franklin Roosevelt came to office during the Great Depression of the
1930's. Since then, power has steadily flowed down Pennsylvania Avenue from the
Capitol to the White House. Accordingly, as Democratic Representative Morris
Udall of Arizona observes, the country has grown accustomed to Presidents
exercising strong commands.

MORRIS UDALL: I credit this to two unusual coincidental incidents in
the life of our nation. One was the Depression. All of a sudden the whole
free enterprise system has failed, and a third of the people out of work, and
anything the President wanted, he set up a bill in the morning and the Congress
would pass it that afternoon. Or let the President fill in the details. We
were just recovering from that and Congress, you will recall, in the late
thirties, was beginning to assert itself again, and saying "Hold on, now, we
make the policy in the Congress," when along came World War II-- the whole free
world threatened with extinction by two powerful dictators. And we said to the
President, whatever he wants--bombers, ships, selective service--turn it over to
the President. And so we've developed a whole generation of leaders in the
Congress who are sort of conditioned to stand back and let the President make
decisions.

DUKE: The country's growth, and the emergence of the United States as a
great world power has established the President as a pre-eminent world leader.
The people have come to look to the President as the country's principal
protector. Speaker Albert believes the wars of the Twentieth Century made it
inevitable that the White House would gain added stature, with Congress less
involved.

ALBERT: I think that the tendency is for the President to be strengthened in
time of crisis, because faster action is required. I think the Congress --
the Congress enjoyed its greatest period of prestige between the War of 1812 and
the Civil War, and that was the longest peace-time period we ever had. And that's
when the giants who overshadowed the President appeared on the scene: like
Craig, Webster, Calhoun, and Haines and others.

DUKE: But some critics, such as Democratic Congressman John Conyers of
Detroit, believe the President has seized upon the dangers of the Atomic Age
as justification for seizing more power than is warranted.

JOHN CONYERS: The use of nuclear weapons required that we vest unprecede
power in the executive office, along with the decision-making right that goes
along with it. This was the natural base for the executive to balloon in this
power far beyond anything conceived by the framing of the Constitution. Now,
many instances, it was perfectly rational and logical. But the whole question
these powers being not only taken by the executive, but then being used as a b
to go even further afield. And then we move of course into the questions of
impoundment, the right of the executive to legislate after we have, in effect;
on the questions of executive secrecy, in which the White House now literally
instructs anyone that is invited to testify before Congressional Committees tha
their testimony may in some way disclose the secrets of the executive branch
that are not ready for public disclosures that this point, which all now goes f
beyond the historical reasons that the executive began to gain power over the
Congress and at the expense of Congress.

DUKE: If there was any catalyst that stirred Congress to ponder the
trend toward Presidential government, it was the Viet Nam War. As the nation
was torn over the American policy, so was Congress torn. But more than that,
the critics began to question the President's power to commit U.S. forces to
faraway places. Thus, today's outcry is directed at the expansion of the Presidential power both at home and abroad. The man who is leading the Congression
counterattack is Senator Sam Ervin of North Carolina. For 18 years, Ervin has
been the principal Congressional custodian of the Constitution. The 76-year-ol
Democrat's stubborn convictions about the Constitution have led him into many
lonely and unpopular battles. But now, quite suddenly, he is the man of the
moment. Ervin has long believed the greatest threat to the country's freedoms
comes from the government, and the men who run the government.

SAM ERVIN: I think that most public officials, including the President a
including some of us, and including Congress, have an insatiable thirst for
power. And I think the reason the Constitution was written was to keep them fr
being able to indulge their insatiable thirst for power. And this kind of conflict has gone on throughout the history of the Republic to a more or less exte
but it's been very much accentuated of late by the wholesale impoundments,
and I think the conflict will go on more or less forever. I think it was
Justice Brandeis who said that Our Constitution wasn't written to make the
most efficient government; was written to insure liberty and also to put in
its place the forces of friction; as to keep one department of government
from trespassing upon the domain of another. And that was the same idea
George Washington expressed in his farewell address.

DUKE: Nothing has aroused Congress so much as the President's refusal
to spend money appropriated by Congress. Senator Ervin and other critics conte
that the President's impoundment of 12 billion dollars in funds for Government
programs presents a theft of legislative power. President Nixon has defended
the action by claiming an absolutely clear Constitutional right to hold up the
funds. But Senator Ervin contends the Constition does not give the President
so much as a syllable of such power.

At a Senate hearing, Deputy Attorney General Joseph Snead argued the
administration's case in a confrontation with Ervin, who insisted the
President's Constitutional responsibility is limited to executing the laws.

ERVIN: Now, this word execute has several meanings. For example, the law
used to say a person shall be executed for certain crimes. They have had laws
like that. The word execute does not mean that his life will be exterminated.
Now, with this provision of the Constitution, the President shall take care that
the laws be faithfully executed does not contemplate that the President should
kill those laws.

JOSEPH SNEAD: Senator, I don't think the word executed as used in the
Constitution, Article II, Section III, is used in the same sense as it is used
in phrasing of sanctions for penal purposes.

ERVIN: Doesn't it mean that he shall take care to see that the laws that are in force are carried out, and made effective, according to their terms?

SNEAD: Senator, he has the responsibility, under the Constitution, as we have said, and as you have indicated, to see that the laws be faithfully executed. He has, however, at all times, to consider all the laws. And it has been our position, as my statement indicated, that he is confronted, and was confronted in the '73 budget issue, with laws consisting of appropriation acts; laws consisting of the 1946 full employment act; laws consisting of the debt ceiling; and laws consisting of the Economic Stabilization Act. And above and beyond that, he was looked to in part by Congress and certainly by the public, as one having a very profound responsibility for price stability. But when we put all that together, the problem is how best to faithfully execute the laws.

ERVIN: Well, now, the President doesn't have the responsibility in a governmental sense, for anything except the things that the Constition and the laws force on him. Isn't that true?

SNEAD: Yes, sir.

ERVIN: And the fact that the people look to him to do something doesn't give him either Constitutional effect or authority to do it, does it?

SNEAD: No. I'm merely injecting the political realities...

ERVIN: Yes, but the political realities are supposed to bow to a Constitutional government.

SNEAD: Indeed they do.

ERVIN: Yes.

Courtesy of NBC News

Talks Programs

"Talks" is an all-inclusive term that covers such diverse program types as interviews, discussions, quizzes, panel and audience participation shows, and speeches. Most of these programs do not use complete scripts, partially because the program is in many cases more or less extemporaneous and partially because the non-actors who appear on many of these programs cannot make a script sound ad-libbed as can the professional performer. Yet, in order to make certain that the program is as good as it can be, the writer has to prepare each script as thoroughly as possible beforehand. In many instances a detailed routine sheet is used — that is, a script which is written out as fully as possible with as much of the dialogue and description of the action as can be prepared, at the same time leaving gaps for the non-memorized dialogue or action of the participants. Frequently, a key phrase or a question or a description of an action or routine suffices, with the master of ceremonies or principal performer or participants filling in extemporaneously during the program.

The Interview

The completely prepared interview is too risky because the interviewee, if not a professional performer, may sound too stilted and be embarrassing. The completely ad-lib interview is also too dangerous and is rarely used. The most frequently used form of script or routine sheet for the interview consists of carefully and fully prepared questions and, through pre-interviewing, general lines of answering. The writer of the interview, after research on the subject and on the interviewee, prepares preliminary questions. A pre-interview conference is held with the interviewee, during which time the preliminary questions are discussed and anticipated answers are set. On the basis of this information, the writer can prepare a rundown and routine sheet. The rundown sheet — used for many types of programs — lists the program segment and the elapsed time for that segment (see page 205); the routine sheet — also used for many program types — contains more detailed material, as described earlier.

The interview program may vary from strictly questions and answers to discussion. In many instances a pre-interview is not possible. In that case the producer will try to get the interviewee to the studio before the program for a rehearsal or at least a warm-up session. In any case the writer must at least prepare the opening and closing, the introductory material about the interviewee and some transition material between program segments for lead-ins and -outs for commercials.

Types. There are three major interview types. For the *opinion* interview the writer may prepare only an introduction, a question and follow-up questions. When the opinion interview is with a prominent person, the *personality* interview may be combined with the opinion type. The *information* interview has as its purpose the eliciting of factual material of a public service nature from relatively unknown or well-known persons. Because the presentation of information is the object, the routine sheet may be more detailed than for other types of interviews. The personality interview is perhaps the most popular kind in radio because of its orientation toward the human interest or feature story. In all cases the writer should obtain full background information on the interviewee and in addition to the usual opening, closing, introduction and transition material should have ready a series of follow-up and probe questions developed in light of probable answers elicited during the pre-interview. An interview may take place with one or more interviewees and with one or a panel of interviewers.

The following is an example of the routine sheet-outline script, omitting the formal opening and closing, prepared and used by Duncan MacDonald for her 30-minute interview program on WQXR, New York.

```
Today is the anniversary of the signing of the United
Nations Charter in San Francisco. In observance of this
anniversary our guest today is Dr. Rodolphe L. Coigney,
Director of the World Health Organization liaison office
with the UN in New York City.
```

Dr. Coigney was born and educated in Paris. His career in international health began in 1944. In 1947 he became director of health for the International Refugee Organization. In his present post at the UN he represents WHO— the World Health Organization—at Economic and Social Council meetings, the Committee of the UN General Assembly, and other bodies of the UN.

1) Dr. Coigney, as one of the 10 specialized agencies of the UN, what is WHO's specific function?
   a) Is it included in the Charter of the UN?
   b) Active/passive purpose?
   c) Is WHO affected by various crises within UN? Financial/political? Your own crises in health?
   d) Do you have specific long term goals, or do you respond only to crises in health? Earthquakes/Floods/Epidemics?

2) How does the work of WHO tie in with other UN organizations?
   UNICEF/ILO/Food and Agriculture/UNESCO/International Civil Aviation/International Bank/Reconstruction and Development/International Monetary Fund/Universal Postal / International Communications / World Meteorological.

3) Background of WHO.
   a) How started? Switzerland?
   b) Headquarters for all international organizations?

4) How much would the work of WHO differ in a country medically advanced, such as Sweden, as opposed to developing countries: Africa, Far East?
   a) Religious or social taboos?
   b) Witch doctors?
   c) Birth Control?

5) Can you give an example of a decision made at Headquarters and then carried out in some remote area of the world?

6) What do you consider WHO's greatest success story in fighting a specific disease: malaria, yaws?
   a) Ramifications of disease? Economic/Disability for work?

7) Your secretary mentioned on the phone that you were going to Latin America. What specifically takes you there now?

8) How does a country get WHO assistance?
   a) Invited?
   b) Matching funds?

9) We are aware of the shortage of doctors and nurses in the United States. What is the situation world-wide?
   a) Do you think Public Health is an important career for young people? Now? For the future?

Courtesy of Duncan MacDonald,

Discussion Programs

Discussion programs are aimed toward an exchange of opinions and information and should not be confused with the interview, in which the purpose is to elicit and not to exchange. The writer of the discussion program has to walk a thin line between too much and not enough preparation. It is not possible to write a complete script, partially because the participants frequently cannot know exactly what specific material is to be presented at any given time. On the other hand, a complete lack of preparation would likely result in a program in which the participants would ramble and would present the moderator with the impossible task of getting someplace without knowing where they were going. A detailed discussion outline distributed to all participants some time prior to the program and altered as they respond to it, also before the program date, is the most effective kind of script. In addition, the writer should prepare opening and closing material, introductions of the participants and general summaries for the moderator.

There are several types of discussion programs. The *panel* discussion — not to be confused with the quiz-type or interview-type panel — is the most often used and the most flexible. It presents a number of people in a more or less formal exchange of ideas on some topic of interest, with the participants having done as much or as little background preparation as they desired. A moderator attempts to keep the discussion on the track and frequently summarizes. The routine sheet consists of the moderator's opening remarks, the introduction of the panel members, a statement of the problem by the moderator, a flexible outline of the topics to be discussed and developed, and the closing. The *symposium,* now infrequent, but once made famous by the long-running "Town Meeting of the Air" radio series, is more structured, with participants given equal time for opening statements and closing summaries, questions from the audience occupying a center portion of the program, and the subject a highly controversial one with clearly opposing opinions represented among the participants. *Group discussion,* where the participants come to mutually agreeable solutions to the problem, and the formal *debate* are rarely heard on radio.

The following is the beginning and end of a script-routine sheet prepared for a panel discussion program. Note the use of sub-topics to reinforce the discussion of the principal question. The script repeats the "principal question-subtopics" outline four times.

WUNC "CAROLINA ROUNDTABLE"

"The Berlin Crisis"

Thursday, 7-8 P.M.

MODERATOR (GEORGE HALL): (OPEN COLD) West Berlin—to be or not to be? This question has been reiterated thousands of times by the peoples of the world. With the erection of physical barricades between the Eastern and Western zones of Berlin, conflict between the East and West German regimes has become one on which may very well hang the future of the entire world.

This is your Moderator, George Hall, welcoming you to another "Carolina Roundtable."

All of us are by now fearfully aware of the critical importance of West Berlin. Most of us recognize that the East Berlin limitations on inter-city travel and the West Berlin opposition to negotiation with and recognition of the East have created an impasse that demands a response from both sides. What is that response to be—not only that of the West and of the United States, but that of the Communist East and of the Soviet Union? How will the choice of a course of action determine not only the fate of both Berlins, but of mankind? Are there any areas of compromise that would be satisfactory to all parties?

This evening, with the aid of our guests, we will attempt to seek answers to these questions.

Dr. Charles B. Robson is a professor of Political Science at the University of North Carolina and an authority on Germany. Dr. Robson teaches in the fields of German government and in modern political theory. He recently spent a year in Germany studying that country's political affairs. Good evening, Dr. Robson.

ROBSON: (RESPONSE)

MODERATOR: Dr. Leopold B. Koziebrodzki is an associate professor of Economics and History at the University of North Carolina. His special field is Russian foreign relations in the twentieth century, and he has observed first-hand governmental policies of eastern European countries in relation to the Soviet Union. Good evening, Dr. Koziebrodzki.

KOZIEBRODZKI: (RESPONSE)

MODERATOR: Dr. Samuel Shepard Jones is Burton Craige Professor of Political Science at the University of North Carolina. His area of specialization is United States foreign policy and international politics. He has served as cultural attache with the U.S. State Department, and has lectured before the National War College. Good evening, Dr. Jones.

JONES: (RESPONSE)

MODERATOR: I'd like to remind our participants and our listeners that questions are encouraged from our listening audience. Any one having a question for any or all of our panel members is invited to phone the WUNC studios at 942-3172. Your question will be taped and played back for our panel to answer at the first opportunity. That's 942-3172.

With the East German government having seized the political offensive, it seems as if the next step is up to the West. In view of the growing power and influence of the small and uncommitted countries in the United Nations, what concessions, if any, should the West be prepared to make in the interest of peace in Berlin? Dr. Jones, would you start the discussion on this matter?

(BRING IN OTHER PANELISTS ON THIS QUESTION. THROUGH PRE-DISCUSSION, DETERMINE
TENTATIVE AGREEMENT ON SOME AREAS, AS BELOW.)

(SUB-TOPICS, AS NEEDED)

    1.   Berlin to be a free city under U.N. jurisdiction, as proposed by Soviet
        Union?

    2.   Recognition of East German government?

    3.   Demilitarization with foreign troops withdrawn?

    4.   Admission and roles of West and East Germany in U.N.?

MODERATOR: (REMINDER TO AUDIENCE ON PHONE CALLS)

* * *

MODERATOR: (IF ABOVE TOPICS NOT CONCLUDED BY 8 MINUTES BEFORE THE
END OF THE PROGRAM, SKIP TO FOLLOWING:)   Of all of the possibilities discussed
on the program, which, if any, do you think have the most chance of acceptance?

(IF FEW OR NONE, ASK ABOUT ALTERNATIVES AND POSSIBILITIES OF WAR.)

MODERATOR: (SUMMARY AT 3-MINUTE MARK.)

    1. Possible concessions by West.

    2. Attitudes and actions of East Germany and the East.

    3. Attitudes and actions of West Germany.

    4. Future of Berlin.

    5. Chances of war.

MODERATOR: (AT 1-MINUTE MARK) Dr. Charles Robson, Dr. Leopold Koziebrodzki,
and Dr. Shepard Jones of the University of North Carolina, we thank you for being our
guests this evening on this "Carolina Roundtable" discussion of the possible solutions to
the Berlin problem.

GUESTS: (MASS RESPONSE OF GOOD NIGHT, ETC.)

MODERATOR: We thank you all for listening and invite you to join us next week at this
same time when "Carolina Roundtable's" guests, _____, _____, and
_____ will discuss _____ .

        This has been a presentation of WUNC, the FM radio station of the
Department of Radio, Television and Motion Pictures, in the Communication Center of the
University of North Carolina. Continuity was written by Gilbert File, and the program was
directed by Reno Bailey. Your moderator has been George Hall.

Quiz, Panel and Audience Participation Shows

These mainstays of radio in the pre-and post-World War II years have
virtually all migrated to television. The goal in these formats is for someone
to solve a problem, stump an expert or successfully perform some feat that
is somehow embarrassing and humorous at the same time. The writer does

not create a full script because these shows should communicate an extemporaneous quality; there is, however, a routine sheet. Because the program must seem spontaneous, yet professional in quality, as much material must be prepared beforehand as possible. As far as the non-professional participants are concerned, the material cannot be in dialogue form. The routine sheet should consist of the opening and closing, the introductions of the participants, the presumably ad-libbed gags, the questions and similar material, and the transitions between program segments. The writer tries to find a "gimmick" which will involve the audience in the proceedings, such as being phoned to share in a prize.

Speeches

Most speeches are prepared outside the station and the staff writer usually has no concern with them except for the opening and closing of the station's part of the program. In some instances, usually on the local level, speakers unfamiliar with radio's time requirements may have to be advised how and where to trim their speeches so that they are not cut off before they finish. In other instances it may be necessary to help the speaker re-write in terms of legal, FCC or station policy concerning statements made over the air, including libel, obscenity and fairness doctrine considerations.

A sample basic format, containing "intro," "outro" and transitions, is the following used for speeches during a political campaign:

```
ANNCR:  In order to better acquaint Virginia voters with the candidates
        and issues in the upcoming general election...the WGAY Public
        Affairs Department presents ... "Platform '73"

        Now ... here is _____
                        _____.
                        (play cart)
        You've just heard_____
                        _____.

        Now ... here is _____
                        _____.
                        (play cart)
        You've just heard _____
                        _____.

In the public interest, WGAY has presented "Platform '73" ... a look
at Virginia general election candidates and issues.  The opinions
expressed are those of the candidates and do not necessarily reflect
the feelings of WGAY or it's sponsors.  Stay tuned for other candidates
and their views throughout the campaign.  (PAUSE)

From atop the World Building .. WGAY FM & AM, Washington & Silver
Spring.  (WGAY-FM in Washington.)
```

WOMEN'S PROGRAMS

A program type that began to undergo a complete about-face in approach in the 1970's is the women's program. Until the efforts of various organizations on behalf of equal rights and opportunities for women (including correction of prejudicial and demeaning practices in programming and broadcast employment), women's programs were principally those which primarily attracted women listeners because of the time of day during which they were presented and those which carried content traditionally deemed of interest primarily to women regardless of the time of presentation. Commercials, which did not change as readily as program formats, were frequently the blatantly sexist "My wife, I think I'll keep her" type. The new kind of women's program concentrates on matters that *affect* women and, consequently, affect men and children as well.

Some of the most commercially successful programs on radio have been women's programs on the local station. These have usually consisted of non-controversial material such as announcements of club meetings, advice on interior decorating, information on fashions and interviews with local personalities; depending on the intelligence and perception of the writer-producer-announcer they have also contained material relating to youth problems, consumer needs, environmental affairs, civic development and similar subjects. Many of these programs have reinforced campaigns of interest to the principal listening target, the housewife, such as promoting higher budgets for schools and referendums for better municipal services. Recently, however, women's programs have begun to add or substitute topics that are even more vital to women and to society, such as equal opportunities, job training, rape, abortion, birth control, financial dependence and legal discrimination. Some of these programs serve as a consciousness-raising tool for women and men both.

The womens' program has unlimited commercial opportunities. In a format which includes a number of subject areas relating to consumer products and services, there need be no dearth of advertisers. A sponsor may be found for the portion of the program dealing with whatever he or she is selling. The women's program is usually written in magazine format to accommodate different topics and their concomitant sponsorship potentials. Programs dealing with just one subject often require a single sponsor for the entire time period. The format within any given program may be flexible and may include interviews, discussions, speeches, news, music, special features and other forms. The writer of the women's program, particularly on the local station, is usually a woman who also MCs and sells time for the show. The writer's work varies, with the content of each particular portion of the program indicating the extent to which a brief routine sheet or a detailed script should be prepared. The approach should be informal without being condescending. Involving listeners in the program — through phoning in questions or comments, for example — is an effective way to build an audience.

Music Programs

Music comprises the bulk of radio programming today — almost exclusively on what has become known as the disc jockey show — through records, transcriptions and tape. Independent stations rely primarily on music for program content and even network affiliates devote most of their non-network time to music shows.

Music Types and Formats

In recent years the prepared script for the disc jockey show has virtually disappeared, especially for the pop program. Some disc jockeys can grab a batch of records at the last minute and somehow spontaneously organize them into a program with continuity, but such a haphazard procedure usually is reflected in the final result. This means, then, that even without a formal script, organic unity must somehow be created for the music program — that is, a central theme, a focal point around which all the material is organized and from which the program grows and develops. Even without the traditional script, preparation must be made. On good stations, such preparation, equivalent to actually writing a script, is arduous and time consuming. On page 285, Harold Green, general manager of WMAL, Washington, D.C., details the kind of preparation required by his announcers, including the gathering and development of material to be used as continuity on the disc jockey show.

The central theme of the music program may be oriented around an event, a type of music, a holiday, a composer's birthday, a visit to town by a rock star — anything that can give the show unity. Clear transitions should be developed from number to number so that the program builds, moving from a good opening selection through careful variation to avoid boring repetition, until a high point is reached at the climax of the program. The idea of a unifying theme, in microcosm equivalent to the station's image, is important in all formats, as described in Chapter 3.

Two examples of central themes in classical programs are illustrated in the following opening statements from scripts. In each case, of course, the full continuity expounds on the themes in detail.

ANNCR: The three greatest masters of the Viennese classical school are Ludwig von Beethoven, Wolfgang Amadeus Mozart and Franz Joseph Hayden. Today we will hear works by each of these three masters.

ANNCR: Today's program is devoted to musical works that
deal with the supernatural. One of the three selections is from an
opera, one is a suite from a ballet, and the third is a symphonic
poem, later used for a ballet.

Reprinted by Permission of Radio
Corporation of America (RCA
Victor Records Division.)

Style

It is important to get variety into the music program, notwithstanding
the fact that in many popular disc jockey shows the teen-ager audience may
seem to appreciate only the same seemingly repetitious sound and incom-
prehensible lyric. Be conscious of the ever-changing fads and fancies of the
young D.J. audience. The disc jockey, in great degree, molds and determines the tastes in popular music. In the classical program the writer must
be more of an "expert" than in the pop music show. The classical music
audience expects more than cursory introduction and closing notes, and
appreciates analysis on a mature level. The writer cannot simply say "This
is the finest example of chamber music written in the 19th century," but
should give the reasons why. In certain pop music forms, such as acid rock
and jazz, the D.J. is expected to be highly knowledgeable; the serious innovative approach to music by the Beatles educated an entire generation to
the intricacies of some types of modern music.

Continuity should not play down to what one thinks may be a low
level of taste, either in the popular or classical program. The D.J.-producer-
writer must analyze the potential audience, and though giving the listeners
what interests them should nevertheless present the best type of music. The
writer must adhere to the purpose of the given program; the audience tunes
in because it likes that particular format, which may be for relaxation, for
education, for dancing or for any number of other purposes. This suggests
an adherence to a single type or homogenous types of music. Although
there are exceptions, the mixing of Beethoven and "bop" or of rock with
string quartets is not likely the most effective way of building an audience.

Continuity should be fresh. In most disc jockey programs continuity
sometimes seems to be limited to phrases where orchestras always "render"
and singers always give "vocal renditions of," where pianists always play
"on the 88" or are given to "impromptu meanderings," and where songs
and singers are interminably "ever-popular" and "scintillating." If it is
impossible to think of something new and fresh and not trite, the best style
is to keep it simple. Because music itself makes up the bulk of the program
content, continuity is comparatively short. Learn how much continuity is
needed by first outlining the program and noting the time of each musical
selection to be played. Rundown sheets, such as the following, are commonly used.

THE JIM LOWE SHOW, AUGUST 28, 10:10-10:30 A.M.

1. S'WONDERFUL   SHIRLEY BASSEY   MGM

        LIVE: COMMERCIAL (60)

2. PUT AWAY YOUR TEARDROPS
                      STEVE LAWRENCE   COL

        LIVE: COMMERCIAL (30)

3. VOLARE   ELLA FITZGERALD   VERVE

        LIVE: PROMO, NEWS (15)

4. THE JOLLY PEDDLER HARRY SOSNICK   MERCURY

        ET: COMMERCIAL (60)

5. I LOVE PARIS   ANDY WILLIAMS   CADENCE

6. COMIN' HOME BABY   JACK LAFORGE   REGINA

        OFFTIME: 29:55

        Courtesy of WNBC-AM/FM, New York

Rundown or format sheets such as the following may be prepared for an entire evening's schedule, containing the timing for each musical piece and the listing of non-musical program segments.

```
9:00      yes we can can/pointer sisters  6:00
          half moon/janis joplin  3:50
          water song/hot tuna  5:17
news      #21 roller coaster/bs&t  3:25
          brandy/looking glass  3:07
          sylvia/focus  3:32
9:30      something so right/paul simon  4:34
          let's get together/youngbloods  4:39
          so what/monty alexander  10:29 (FADE)
*news     #14 too high/stevie wonder  4:35
          out in the country/three dog night  3:08
10:00     hollywood/chicago  3:53
          ooh la la/faces  3:35
          jessica/allman brothers band  7:00
news      #2 angie/stones  4:30
          dolly/nicky hopkins  4:42
10:30     brandenburg/walter carlos  5:05
          aquarius/ronnie dyson & company  2:55
          aubrey/grover washington, jr.  3:40
          lady honey/pan  4:07
**news    #9 all i know/art garfunkel  3:50
          super strut/deodato  8:55
```

*BACKGROUND REPORT #1   Courtesy of WMAL-FM, Washington D.C.
**EDITORIAL

Live — that is, non-recorded — music programs and variety shows have just about completely disappeared from radio. Where they do exist, the writer usually orients them to a type of performance such as a vocalist or a twin-piano team or a novelty group or an orchestra. Writing the live program is essentially the same as writing the D.J. show, except that in the live situation the writer can include material of a variety program nature by inserting live personalities in the dialogue portion of the script.

The Radio Magazine

One of the interesting experiments of post-television radio has been the magazine format, in which a continuous stream of different kinds of materials — music, news, interviews, discussions, human interest, features, sports, special events, skits, and a voluminously interspersed series of commercials — is presented over a given, extended time period. This format seems oriented toward the person on-the-go, the listener who may be occupied primarily in other things and who will listen with one ear most of the time and with both ears some of the time and who can be held with a well-produced, interesting variety of short program segments.

The writer's job is two-fold: research and organization. The writer must prepare a routine sheet which clearly delineates the time length for each presentation and which accurately schedules the commercial announcements. Accurate background material must be provided for introductions to the differing sections of the program and sometimes complete script materials are written for a prepared and rehearsed segment. Much scripting is done by local people in the "field," for most of the material on the program is usually "remote." Perhaps the most difficult job is total arrangement of the program over many hours to provide continuity and variety in subject matter and length at the same time.

The most successful of such programs has been the National Broadcasting Company's *Monitor*. Examine the following excerpt from one of its routine sheets (more akin to the "rundown" sheet described earlier) and the accompanying script for the same time period. The opening of each hour of *Monitor* is a five-minute "news package." Note that the final script substitutes a sports feature for the "Movie Critic" scheduled for 9:12:45.

BUD DRAKE	MONITOR ROUTINE SHEET	PAGE
CHARLES GARMENT		DATE
MELANIE TURNER	HOST: BILL CULLEN	TIME

```
9:00:00  BEEPER

         BILL:              INTRO

         CART:              RCIA COMMERCIAL              (1:00)

         CART:              LYSOL COMMERCIAL            (0:30)

9:05:25  BEEPER
```

```
9:05:30  DISC/BILL          SOUL MAKOSSA
                            MANU DIBANGO
                            RUNS 3:00
                            PLAY TOP & FADE ON CUE

9:07:40  BEEPER
```

```
9:07     CART:              THEME #5F                   (0:11) FADE
                                                             AT :111
9:07:55  BILL:              BB & ID                     (0:30)

9:08:25  DISC/BILL:         LOVES ME LIKE A ROCK        (2:55)
                            PAUL SIMON
                            RUNS 2:55 SNEAK :08 - ID OVER

9:11:20  CART/BILL:         SOUNDER & TIP               (0:15)

9:11:35  CART:              DUTCH BOY COMMERCIAL        (1:00)

9:12:35  BILL:              INTRO                       (0:10)

9:12:45  TAPE:              MOVIE CRITIC                (2:00) APX.

9:14:45  BILL:              OUTRO                       (0:10)

9:14:55  CART:              ARMOUR COMMERCIAL           (0:30)

9:15:25                     BEACON CUE                  (0:05)
------------------------------------------------------------------
         BEEPER

9:15:30  CART:              "B" - CUT #1                (1:10)
```

NEWS PACKAGE

BEEPER

DISC: SOUL MAKOSSA
             (ESTAB AND UNDER ON CUE FOR ID)

BILL (OVER) You take a heaping helping of "soul...add a measure of "makossa"
             ...get Manu Dibango to stir it all up...and what have you got?
             I don't know what you've got...but Monitor has a couple of minutes
             of "Soul Makossa"...that's wot.

DISC:	UP AND TO FADE ON CUE
CART:	THEME # 5F (UNDER AFTER :11)
BILL:	Yes...Bill Cullen and Monitor 73 are back...and I trust we're a bit more welcome than something else that's back again...namely ...talk about raising the income tax...which is what the President's counselor, Melvin Laird, brought up a couple of days ago. However...Congressional reaction seems to be negative... so we can now proceed into our weekend with a positive, cheerful attitude...and music to match.
DISC:	LOVES ME LIKE A ROCK (ESTAB FOR :04 UNDER UNTIL :08)
BILL (OVER)	This is Paul Simon's big hit..."Loves Me Like A Rock:
DISC:	UP AND TO END
CART:	TIP SOUNDER
BILL:	A Monitor Household Tip: Material leftover from making slipcover can be cut into strips and sewed onto the tapes on Venetian blind to add a decorative note to the window treatment. Now something else for the home-maker:
CART:	DUTCH BOY COMM (:60)
BILL:	Now...a Monitor Sports Feature. The bill ending the professional football TV blackout of home game went into effect yesterday. Doing some "Saturday-morning quarterbacking" on the reasons and effects of this legislation are the Commissioner of football, Pete Rozelle, and Monitor Sports Editor Len Dillon.
TAPE:	PETE ROZELLE O: COMMISSIONER PETE ROZELLE C: FOR MONITOR SPORTS (1:56)
BILL:	I would imagine that among the other avenues to be explored... which the Commissioner did not mention...would be pay TV. But that's getting way ahead of the game. How about some football type food now?
CART:	ARMOUR COMM (:30)
BILL:	Dom De Luise...a very funny fella...who got rave reviews for his brand new NBC show..."Lotsa Luck"...will prove that it wasn't luck...by being funny here, too...in a couple of minutes as a guest on the Monitor beacon.
BEEPER	
CART:	CUTAWAY

Material provided by the NBC Radio Division

BIBLIOGRAPHY

Bliss, Edward, Jr. and John M. Patterson, *Writing News for Broadcast*. New York: Columbia University Press, 1971. Analysis of newswriting for radio and television, including comparative examples between the two media.

Dary, David, *Radio News Handbook*. Blue Ridge Summit, Pennsylvania: TAB Books, 1971. Oriented toward local station news personnel.

Gordon, George N., *Persuasion: The Theory and Practice of Manipulative Communication*. New York: Hastings House, 1971. An historical and psychological analysis.

Hall, Mark W., *Broadcast Journalism*. New York: Hastings House, 1971. Covers the basics of radio and television newswriting styles and sources. Emphasizes "writing for the ear" and includes a "Style Guide."

Hilliard, Robert L., *Writing for Television and Radio*. New York: Hastings House, Second Ed., 1967. Comprehensive analyses and examples of non-dramatic forms of mass media writing, with emphasis on "bread-and-butter" approaches. Section on the play based on new concepts of dramaturgy for television.

PROGRAM AND ADVERTISING STANDARDS OF THE RADIO CODE
OF THE NATIONAL ASSOCIATION OF BROADCASTERS
(SEVENTEENTH EDITION):

I. PROGRAM STANDARDS

A. News

Radio is unique in its capacity to reach the largest number of people first with reports on current events. This competitive advantage bespeaks caution — being first is not as important as being right. The following Standards are predicated upon that viewpoint.

1. *News Sources.* Those responsible for news on radio should exercise constant professional care in the selection of sources — for the integrity of the news and the consequent good reputation of radio as a dominant news medium depend largely upon the reliability of such sources.

2. *News Reporting.* News reporting shall be factual and objective. Good taste shall prevail in the selection and handling of news. Morbid, sensational, or alarming details not essential to factual reporting should be avoided. News should be broadcast in such a manner as to avoid creation of panic and unnecessary alarm. Broadcasters shall be diligent in their supervision of content, format, and presentation of news broadcasts. Equal diligence should be exercised in selection of editors and reporters who direct news gathering and dissemination, since the station's performance in this vital informational field depends largely upon them.

3. *Commentaries and Analyses.* Special obligations devolve upon those who analyze and/or comment upon news developments, and management should be satisfied completely that the task is to be performed in the best interest of the listening public. Programs of news analysis and commentary shall be clearly identified as such, distinguishing them from straight news reporting.

4. *Editorializing.* Broadcasts in which stations express their own opinions about issues of general public interest should be clearly identified as editorials and should be clearly distinguished from news and other program material.

5. *Coverage of News and Public Events.* In the coverage of news and public events the broadcaster has the right to exercise his judgment consonant with the accepted standards of ethical journalism and especially the requirements for decency and decorum in the broadcast of public and court proceedings.

6. *Placement of Advertising.* A broadcaster should exercise particular discrimination in the acceptance, placement and presentation of advertising in news programs so that such advertising should be clearly distinguishable from the news content.

B. Controversial Public Issues

1. Radio provides a valuable forum for the expression of responsible views on public issues of a controversial nature. The broadcaster should develop programs relating to controversial public issues of importance to his fellow citizens; and give fair representation to opposing sides of issues which materially affect the life or welfare of a substantial segment of the public.

2. Requests by individuals, groups or organizations for time to discuss their views on controversial public issues should be considered on the basis of their individual merits, and in the light of the contributions which the use requested would make to the public interest.

3. Programs devoted to the discussion of controversial public issues should be identified as such. They should not be presented in a manner which would create the impression that the program is other than one dealing with a public issue.

C. Community Responsibility

1. A broadcaster and his staff occupy a position of responsibility in the community and should conscientiously endeavor to be acquainted with its needs and characteristics in order to serve the welfare of its citizens.

2. Requests for time for the placement of public service announcements or programs should be carefully reviewed with respect to the character and reputation of the group, campaign or organization involved, the public interest content of the message, and the manner of its presentation.

D. Political Broadcasts

1. Political broadcasts, or the dramatization of political issues designed to influence an election, shall be properly identified as such.

2. They should be presented in a manner which would properly identify the nature and character of the broadcast.

3. Because of the unique character of political broadcasts and the necessity to retain broad freedoms of policy void of restrictive interference, it is incumbent upon all political candidates and all political parties to observe the canons of good taste and political ethics, keeping in mind the intimacy of broadcasting in the American home.

E. Advancement of Education and Culture

1. Because radio is an integral part of American life, there is inherent in radio broadcasting a continuing opportunity to enrich the experience of living through the advancement of education and culture.

2. The radio broadcaster, in augmenting the educational and cultural influences of the home, the church, schools, institutions of higher learning, and other entities devoted to education and culture:

(a) Should be thoroughly conversant with the educational and cultural needs and aspirations of the community served;

(b) Should cooperate with the responsible and accountable educational and cultural entities of the community to provide enlightenment of listeners;

(c) Should engage in experimental efforts designed to advance the community's cultural and educational interests.

F. Religion and Religious Programs

1. Religious programs shall be presented by responsible individuals, groups or organizations.

2. Radio broadcasting, which reaches men of all creeds simultaneously, shall avoid attacks upon religious faiths.

3. Religious programs shall be presented respectfully and without prejudice or ridicule.

4. Religious programs shall place emphasis on religious doctrines of faith and worship.

G. Dramatic Programs

1. In determining the acceptability of any dramatic program containing any element of crime, mystery, or horror, proper consideration should be given to the possible effect on all members of the family.

2. Radio should reflect realistically the experience of living, in both its pleasant and tragic aspects, if it is to serve the listener honestly. Nevertheless, it holds a concurrent obligation to provide programs which will encourage better adjustments to life.

3. This obligation is apparent in the area of dramatic programs particularly. Without sacrificing integrity of presentation, dramatic programs on radio shall avoid:

(a) Techniques and methods of crime presented in such manner as to encourage imitation, or to make the commission of crime attractive, or to suggest that criminals can escape punishment;

(b) Detailed presentation of brutal killings, torture, or physical agony, horror, the use of supernatural or climatic incidents likely to terrify or excite unduly;

(c) Sound effects calculated to mislead, shock, or unduly alarm the listener;

(d) Disrespectful portrayal of law enforcement;

(e) The portrayal of suicide as a satisfactory solution to any problem.

H. Responsibility Toward Children

The education of children involves giving them a sense of the world at large. It is not enough that programs broadcast for chil-

dren shall be suitable for the young and immature. In addition, programs which might reasonably be expected to hold the attention of children and which are broadcast during times when children may be normally expected to constitute a substantial part of the audience should be presented with due regard for their effect on children.

1. Programs specifically designed for listening by children shall be based upon sound social concepts and shall reflect respect for parents, law and order, clean living, high morals, fair play, and honorable behavior.

2. They shall convey the commonly accepted moral, social and ethical ideals characteristic of American life.

3. They should contribute to the healthy development of personality and character.

4. They should afford opportunities for cultural growth as well as for wholesome entertainment.

5. They should be consistant with integrity of realistic production, but they should avoid material of extreme nature which might create undesirable emotional reaction in children.

6. They shall avoid appeals urging children to purchase the product specifically for the purpose of keeping the program on the air or which, for any reason, encourage children to enter inappropriate places.

7. They should present such subjects as violence and sex without undue emphasis and only as required by plot development or character delineation. Crime should not be presented as attractive or as a solution to human problems, and the inevitable retribution should be made clear.

8. They should avoid reference to kidnapping or threats of kidnapping of children.

I. General

1. The intimacy and confidence placed in Radio demand of the broadcaster, the networks and other program sources that they be vigilant in protecting the audience from deceptive program practices.

2. Sound effects and expressions characteristically associated with news broadcasts (such as "bulletin," "flash," "we interrupt this program to bring you," etc.) shall be reserved for announcement of news, and the use of any deceptive techniques in connection with fictional events and non-news programs shall not be employed.

3. The acceptance of cash payments or other considerations for, including identification of commercial products or services, trade names or advertising slogans, including the identification of prizes, etc., must be disclosed in accordance with provisions of the Communications Act.

4. When plot development requires the use of material which depends upon physical or mental handicaps, care should be taken to spare the sensibilities of sufferers from similar defects.

5. Stations should avoid broadcasting program material which would tend to encourage illegal gambling or other violations of federal, state and local laws, ordinances, and regulations.

6. Simulation of court atmosphere or use of the term "court" in a program title should be done only in such manner as to eliminate the possibility of creating the false impression that the proceedings broadcast are vested with judicial or official authority.

7. Quiz and similar programs, that are presented as contests of knowledge, information, skill or luck must in fact, be genuine contests and the results must not be controlled by collusion with or between contestants, or any other action which will favor one contestant against any other.

8. No program shall be presented in a manner which through artifice or simulation would mislead the audience as to any material fact. Each broadcaster must exercise reasonable judgment to determine whether a particular method of presentation would constitute a material deception, or would be accepted ·by the audience as normal theatrical illusion.

9. Legal, medical and other professional advice will be permitted only in conformity with law and recognized ethical and professional standards.

10. Narcotic addiction shall not be presented except as a vicious habit. The misuse of hallucinogenic drugs shall not be presented or encouraged as desirable or socially acceptable.

11. Program material pertaining to fortune-telling, occultism, astrology, phrenology, palm-reading, numerology, mindreading, character-reading, or subjects of a like nature, is unacceptable when presented for the purpose of fostering belief in these subjects.

12. The use of cigarettes shall not be presented in a manner to impress the youth of our country that it is a desirable habit

worthy of imitation in that it contributes to health, individual achievement or social acceptance.

13. Profanity, obscenity, smut and vulgarity are forbidden. From time to time, words which have been acceptable, acquire undesirable meanings, and broadcasters should be alert to eliminate such words.

14. Words (especially slang) derisive of any race, color, creed, nationality or national derivation, except wherein such usage would be for the specific purpose of effective dramatization, such as combating prejudice, are forbidden.

15. Respect is maintained for the sanctity of marriage and the value of the home. Divorce is not treated casually as a solution for marital problems.

16. Broadcasts of actual sporting events at which on-the-scene betting is permitted should concentrate on the subject as a public sporting event and not on the aspects of gambling.

II. ADVERTISING STANDARDS

Advertising is the principal source of revenue of the free, competitive American system of radio broadcasting. It makes possible the presentation to all American people of the finest programs of entertainment, education, and information.

Since the great strength of American radio broadcasting derives from the public respect for and the public approval of its programs, it must be the purpose of each broadcaster to establish and maintain high standards of performance, not only in the selection and production of all programs, but also in the presentation of advertising.

This Code establishes basic standards for all radio broadcasting. The principles of acceptability and good taste within the Program Standards section govern the presentation of advertising where applicable. In addition, the Code establishes in this section special standards which apply to radio advertising.

A. General Advertising Standards

1. A commercial radio broadcaster makes his facilities available for the advertising of products and services and accepts commercial presentations for such advertising. However, he shall, in recognition of his responsibility to the public, refuse the facilities of his station to an advertiser where he has good reason to doubt the integrity of the advertiser, the truth of the advertising representations, or the compli-

ance of the advertiser with the spirit and purpose of all applicable legal requirements.

2. In consideration of the customs and attitudes of the communities served, each radio broadcaster should refuse his facilities to the advertisement of products and services, or the use of advertising scripts, which the station has good reason to believe would be objectionable to a substantial and responsible segment of the community. These standards should be applied with judgment and flexibility, taking into consideration the characteristics of the medium, its home and family audience, and the form and content of the particular presentation.

B. Presentation of Advertising

1. The advancing techniques of the broadcast art have shown that the quality and proper integration of advertising copy are just as important as measurement in time. The measure of a station's service to its audience is determined by its overall performance.

2. The final measurement of any commercial broadcast service is quality. To this, every broadcaster shall dedicate his best effort.

3. Great care shall be exercised by the broadcaster to prevent the presentation of false, misleading or deceptive advertising. While it is entirely appropriate to present a product in a favorable light and atmosphere, the presentation must not, by copy or demonstration, involve a material deception as to the characteristics or performance of a product.

4. The broadcaster and the advertiser should exercise special caution with the content and presentation of commercials placed in or near programs designed for children. Exploitation of children should be avoided. Commercials directed to children should in no way mislead as to the product's performance and usefulness. Appeals involving matters of health which should be determined by physicians should be avoided.

5. Reference to the results of research, surveys or tests relating to the product to be advertised shall not be presented in a manner so as to create an impression of fact beyond that established by the study. Surveys, tests or other research results upon which claims are based must be conducted under recognized research techniques and standards.

C. Acceptability of Advertiser and Products

In general, because radio broadcasting is designed for the home and the entire family, the following principles shall govern the business classifications:

1. The advertising of hard liquor shall not be accepted.

2. The advertising of beer and wines is acceptable when presented in the best of good taste and discretion.

3. The advertising of fortune-telling, occultism, astrology, phrenology, palm-reading, numerology, mind-reading, character-reading, or subjects of a like nature, is not acceptable.

4. Because the advertising of all products and services of a personal nature raises special problems, such advertising, when accepted, should be treated with emphasis on ethics and the canons of good taste, and presented in a restrained and inoffensive manner.

5. The advertising of lotteries is unacceptable. The advertising of tip sheets and other publications seeking to advertise for the purpose of giving odds or promoting betting is unacceptable.

The advertising of organizations, private or governmental, which conduct legalized betting on sporting contests is acceptable, provided it is limited to institutional type advertising which does not exhort the public to bet.

6. An advertiser who markets more than one product shall not be permitted to use advertising copy devoted to an acceptable product for purposes of publicizing the brand name or other identification of a product which is not acceptable.

7. Care should be taken to avoid presentation of "bait-switch" advertising whereby goods or services which the advertiser has no intention of selling are offered merely to lure the customer into purchasing higher-priced substitutes.

8. Advertising should offer a product or service on its positive merits and refrain from discrediting, disparaging or unfairly attacking competitors, competing products, other industries, professions or institutions.

Any identification or comparison of a competitive product or service, by name, or other means, should be confined to specific facts rather than generalized statements or conclusions, unless such statements or conclusions are not derogatory in nature.

9. Advertising testimonials should be genuine, and reflect an honest appraisal of personal experience.

10. Advertising by institutions or enterprises offering instruction with exaggerated claims for opportunities awaiting those who enroll, is unacceptable.

11. The advertising of firearms/ammunition is acceptable provided it promotes the product only as sporting equipment and conforms to recognized standards of safety as well as all applicable laws and regulations. Advertisements of firearms ammunition by mail order are unacceptable.

D. Advertising of Medical Products

Because advertising for over-the-counter products involving health considerations are of intimate and far-reaching importance to the consumer, the following principles should apply to such advertising:

1. When dramatized advertising material involves statements by doctors, dentists, nurses or other professional people, the material should be presented by members of such profession reciting actual experience, or it should be made apparent from the presentation itself that the portrayal is dramatized.

2. Because of the personal nature of the advertising of medical products, the indiscriminate use of such words as "Safe," "Without Risk," "Harmless," or other terms of similar meaning, either direct or implied, should not be expressed in the advertising of medical products.

3. Advertising material which offensively describes or dramatizes distress or morbid situations involving ailments is not acceptable.

E. Time Standards for Advertising Copy

1. The amount of time to be used for advertising should not exceed 18 minutes within any clock hour. The Code Authority, however, for good cause may approve advertising exceeding the above standard for special circumstances.

2. Any reference to another's products or services under any trade name, or language sufficiently descriptive to identify it, shall, except for normal guest identification, be considered as advertising copy.

3. For the purpose of determining advertising limitations, such program types as "classified," "swap shop," "shopping guides," and "farm auction" programs,

etc., shall be regarded as containing one and one-half minutes of advertising for each five-minute-segment.

F. Contests

1. Contests shall be conducted with fairness to all entrants, and shall comply with all pertinent laws and regulations.

2. All contest details, including rules, eligibility requirements, opening and termination dates, should be clearly and completely announced or easily accessible to the listening public; and the winners' names should be released as soon as possible after the close of the contest.

3. When advertising is accepted which requests contestants to submit items of product identification or other evidence of purchase of products, reasonable facsimiles thereof should be made acceptable. However, when the award is based upon skill and not upon chance, evidence of purchase may be required.

4. All copy pertaining to any contest (except that which is required by law) associated with the exploitation or sale of the sponsor's product or service, and all references to prizes or gifts offered in such connection should be considered a part of and included in the total time limitations heretofore provided. (See Time Standards for Advertising Copy.)

G. Premiums and Offers

1. The broadcaster should require that full details of proposed offers be submitted for investigation and approval before the first announcement of the offer is made to the public.

2. A final date for the termination of an offer should be announced as far in advance as possible.

3. If a consideration is required, the advertiser should agree to honor complaints indicating dissatisfaction with the premium by returning the consideration.

4. There should be no misleading descriptions or comparisons of any premiums or gifts which will distort or enlarge their value in the minds of the listeners.

WILLIAM HAWES

Associate Professor
Department of Communications
University of Houston

● In addition to his teaching responsibilities, Dr. Hawes is former manager of KUHF, the FM radio station of the University of Houston. Previously he was faculty director of WUNC, the FM radio station of the University of North Carolina at Chapel Hill, and adviser to KTCU, Texas Christian University, which he developed from carrier current to an FM station.

He received the A.B. degree from Eastern Michigan University, where he majored in English and Speech. He has the A.M. and Ph.D. degrees from the University of Michigan. After teaching at Eastern Michigan for four years, he became director of the Division of Radio-Television-Film at Texas Christian University, where he produced numerous radio and television programs for commercial stations in Fort Worth and Dallas, in addition to his duties with KTCU. After a brief period at WTOP-TV, Washington, D.C., he spent a year as a visiting assistant professor in the Department of Radio, Television and Motion Pictures of the University of North Carolina. He has also served on the staffs of the University of Michigan and the National Music Camp, and as a consultant to Maxwell House and *The Houston Post*.

Originally interested in art and theatre, Dr. Hawes has directed, designed and acted in university and community theatres. In 1956 he made an official tour of European theatres, and the following year won a major Hopwood Award in drama. In a joint venture with Eastern and Central Michigan Universities and WJRT, Flint, he taught the first television course in drama for those educational institutions, and subsequently taught courses in educational television and in radio at Texas Christian University and at the University of North Carolina. He has also produced various films, including three on ballet. He has been a speaker and panelist at conventions of professional organizations, and a frequent contributor to media publications. Dr. Hawes is listed in a half dozen national and international biographies.

6

PRODUCING
AND
DIRECTING

BY WILLIAM HAWES

ENTERTAINMENT, information, commercials and announcements are the substance of radio programming. To a degree every moment
of the broadcast day requires the services of a producer and a director, although in modern radio these titles as such are virtually non-existent.
The functions of the producer and director have been absorbed by other
members of the radio production team — the program director, the news
director, the disc jockeys, and other people who double as producer-director
and talent. For these people, producing and directing is just *part* of a day's
work. It is, therefore, desirable, if not essential, for a novice to understand
the diverse responsibilities of producing and directing so that person is prepared to share these assignments. The purpose of this chapter is to examine
in detail the philosophy, place and application of producing and directing in
a modern radio station.

PHILOSOPHY

Producing and directing is a mixture of the ideal and the expedient. A
producer and a director must have the ability to lead people and sufficient
self-discipline to get the job done on time. Each must be familiar with legal
restrictions and the industry's self-imposed rules of good practice. Each
must have a temperament that will endure the most exasperating circumstances, and must have self-confidence.

A producer and/or director must be a man or woman of many talents, and must be constantly alert to new ideas and to the changing world. This is especially important from a financial viewpoint. So often, being able to do several different tasks makes the difference between staying in the same job indefinitely or advancing in the radio organization.

Producing. Producing is the task of bringing programs, commercials and announcements into existence. Its goal is to make the creative process possible. To do this, a producer may assemble artists, technicians, financiers and administrators from all over the world. He or she has a keen memory for talent, and is an originator of ideas. A New York producer once said that producing is a matter of getting people to believe in your ideas. A producer sells ideas: program ideas, ideas for commercials, ideas concerning how to utilize talent. A producer has wide experience and many contacts in show business and finance, constantly looking for new ideas, new talent, new sources of money. What does the public want to hear? What does the industry need? A producer attempts to answer these questions. He or she is a businessperson. Although every venture involves an amount of risk, he or she is cautious with the money of investors. That is the reason a producer selects highly competent, dependable people — in other words, "professionals." As accurately as possible he or she determines the cost of the production of a program or commercial, so that lawyers, accountants and sponsors can appreciate the ideas in terms they understand. Every moment on the air, even sustaining spots, is paid for by someone. In that sense each moment is a risk to someone. A producer attempts to minimize that risk. He or she works with talent agents, advertising agencies, unions and station executives. A producer may hire talent directly, or may work with the talent's representative or agent. A producer negotiates contracts, which are often long and complex. A contract describes in detail the conditions under which a performer will work, and how much he or she will be paid. It is an agreement which protects both the producer and the performer. Large markets are highly unionized. Union membership adheres strictly to the contract; infringement may result in cancellation of the contract and/or a legal suit. A producer may be a salaried employee of a radio station or free lance. He or she may get a commission on each program or be reimbursed at the end of a series. He or she may have "residual rights," that is, he or she may receive money each time the program is repeated on the air, or may sell all of the interests to the station at one time.

Directing. Directing is the process of artistically arranging sounds in a meaningful order. A director is a student of sound. He or she may be versatile enough to work in radio, recordings, television or film. Technically competent, he or she is equally at home directing a program from an acoustically treated radio studio, from a large auditorium, from a golf course or from a mobile unit. A director is an artist. He or she realizes that every sound has aesthetic value. How useful a sound is depends upon how sensitive a director is to it. A director uses speech, music and special effects the way a painter chooses colors from his palette. A director knows that a performer never utters just a word, rather a sound that ignites a multitude of stimuli in the brain of the listener. Years ago the news commentator Gabriel Heatter sometimes began his program with "There's good news tonight" — a line which, by its very inflection, raised and lowered the blood pressure of a war-conscious nation. A skillful performer can take a nonsense syllable and by sheer inflection make it vibrate with suggestive overtones, such as in a recent novelty recording consisting mainly of two people laughing. A classic case occurred during the 1930's when Mae West played Eve in a sketch on the Edgar Bergen show. As a result of the broadcast, Ms. West was not heard on radio for many years. A good director remembers voices, their nuances and their dialects, so he or she can use them whenever necessary. Sounds, like colors, have many shades of meaning and expression. Listening to a symphony orchestra, a director hears the exotic lilt of Rimsky-Korsakoff's *Scheherazade*, the delightful rhythms of Saint Saëns's *Carnival of the Animals*, the piercing notes of Paganini's *Caprices*, the majesty of Schubert's *Ave Maria*. A director keeps a mental notebook of sounds. Someday a few measures from Moussorgsky-Ravel's *Pictures at an Exposition* may provide a theme for a newscast, or a pastoral sequence from Debussy's *Prelude to the Afternoon of a Faun* may cast the proper mood for a moment in a documentary. Just as the length of a single note is important to a conductor, the duration of each sound is significant to a director. He or she also seeks the sound that is precisely correct.

Directors are continually finding new sounds. These days monaural sound is being replaced with stereophonic sound — sound that is, in a sense, bigger than life itself. One thing which the rock-and-roll era has taught the modern director is that *no sound should be overlooked.* Clever directors have styled relatively unattractive voices into a composite of highly popular sounds. What is a microphone to a director but a means of amplifying an irresistable sound? . . . The mellifluous harmony of the Beatles, the raucous screams of Mick Jagger and The Rolling Stones, the semi-spoken delivery of Johnny Cash, the incoherent lyrics of Elvis Presley, the breathless clear volume of Barbra Streisand, the hand clapping of Joan Baez, the whispers of Peggy Lee are superb uses of sound. Show business consists of people who have mastered sound, who have made an artistic use of their vocal gifts. Such an artist may seem larger than life itself because his or her "sound" is a *composite* of the skills of many people, including those of an imaginative director. A voice may succeed or fail because of the decisions a director makes. Noise is disorganized sound. But what is organized and what is not? Some composers are working with garbage can covers in their compositions. Strange? Yet, washboards have been used for years. Remember Spike Jones? What about the Nitty Gritty Dirt Band? Isn't Oriental music dissonant to people in the Western Hemisphere? Explain the popu-

larity of Ravi Shankar. Radio directors have just begun to use sounds from
other countries, to replace tired commercials with fresh, new sounds. Wind,
heartbeats, engines running and fire were among the old sound effects;
rockets, sonar devices, voices from outer space are the current ones. But
what are the sounds of starvation? the sounds of learning? the sounds of the
joys and sorrows that forge the will of humanity? A director hears these
sounds, remembers them, knows where to get them and when to use them.
A director conducts an orchestra that embraces all of the sounds the human
ear can detect.

Basic Functions

From time to time nearly every employee shares the producer-director
functions, although these duties are included primarily in the programming
category. A radio station's staff ranges from less than a dozen to more than
40 people. No radio station is quite like any other; furthermore, it is
constantly changing. One representative 250-watt station has about eight
people involved in program production: a program director, a continuity
writer, and a half-dozen announcers who operate their own audio consoles.
One representative 50,000-watt network affiliate has 19: nine people in
programming, one newsman, six in traffic-continuity, and three secretaries.
The size of the staff depends upon the demands of the market and the sol-
vency of the station.

Initial Conferences. Anyone at a radio station may originate an idea
for a program or a commercial, but ultimately it will involve several people.
Inasmuch as a lack of audience interest and high production costs have
forced radio networks and stations to omit, for all practical purposes, dramas
and documentaries from their schedules, radio production is a relatively
simple task. It begins with three or four people — the program director, the
talent, perhaps a continuity writer, and someone from promotion or sales —
sitting in an office or conference room, where they develop a new idea for a
program. They discuss the proposal from every point of view: content,
talent, schedule, promotion, sales. If they agree that it is a good idea, each
of them assumes part of the producing and directing function. They are
primarily interested in keeping their ratings up and in selling as many
commercials as possible. The program director usually coordinates all activities and sends out memoranda confirming their plans. He or she often
assumes the chief producing responsibility or delegates it to a performer,
who then develops the program. The entire process is informal.

Rehearsal or Practice Sessions. The directing functions are commonly
shared by the talent and engineer, who are often the same person. Each
should be a master craftsman and be acquainted with the aesthetic objectives
of directing.

Establishing Purpose and Mood. The talent determines what the mood
of the program should be according to the consensus established in the initial

conference. He or she may consult further with the continuity writer, although a knowledge of the station's library should enable a person to establish the appropriate atmosphere without much difficulty. All music and sound effects are carefully filed. The talent locates the records, tapes and cartridges. He or she may have to reserve studio facilities.

Timing. Radio's time limitations require strict control over the length of program material. Optional cutting is one method. There are two kinds of cuts: structural and line omissions. Both are useful. The former refers to entire segments or scenes; the latter to lines, phrases or words. Every segment of a program is timed with a stop watch before a broadcast or recording. A few extra seconds are allowed for music bridges, elaborate sound sequences, and so on. A set amount of time is specified for ad-libbed sections. Long scripts are immediately cut to the proper length. Paragraphs that can be omitted without destroying the intention or mood of the program are marked. These optional cuts are carefully timed and used as "pads" to lengthen a program on the air, if necessary. Timing and cutting are frequently handled outside of the studio during an early rehearsal or, for example, in the newsroom.

The Control Room. Anyone who wishes to direct should know how to operate tape recorders, turntables, a patchboard, a console, microphones and a cartridge machine. Regardless of whether the program is live or recorded, there is a basic, standard directing procedure followed by the director in the control room. The following is a chronological rundown of a typical sequence of control room procedure for the director.

To talent over the intercom: "Level check, please."

The engineer adjusts his "pots."

To talent over the intercom: "30 seconds to air."

To talent 10 seconds to air: "Stand by — quiet."

To engineer (in the control room): "Hit theme. Music to background."

To announcer (in announcer's booth): "Cue announce."

The announcer reads the copy.

To engineer: "Music up." (It plays for a few more seconds so as to establish the sound.) "Sneak music out."

To talent (gesturing from control room): Stand by and cue.

Talent performs. (During the broadcast the director gives whatever additional hand signals are essential. A smile or gesture may show that the program is going well. The director watches the time carefully. In long programs talent prefers cues at 15, 10, 5, 4, 3, 2, 1, and one-half minutes.) The talent finishes.

To engineer: "Theme. Fade to background and cue announcer."

The announcer reads the closing copy.

To engineer: "Theme up and fade out."

Everyone remains silent until the director indicates that the program is over. Speaking over the intercom: "That's it. Thanks, everybody. That was fine."

HAND SIGNALS

The following standard hand signals must be known by the performer and
staff, obeyed virtually as reflex actions.

Signal	*Meaning*

The director points
directly at the per-
former.

Start what you are
supposed to do.
Cue.

The director's hand
is held up, palm to-
ward the *perform-
er* with a pushing
motion.

Move away from
the microphone.

The director's hand
is held up, palm to-
ward the body with
a pulling motion.

Move closer to the
microphone.

The director's index
finger moves in a
rapid clockwise
motion pointed
straight ahead.

Speed up.

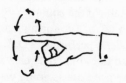

The director's hands
pull away from
each other in a re-
peated stretching
motion.

Slow down.

Fig. 1: Signal Chart.

Prepared by Earl Wynn

The director moves
the hand upward,
palm open and up.

Raise volume.

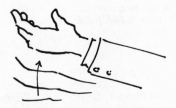

The director moves
the hand down-
ward, palm open
and down.

Lower volume.

The director's
thumb and index
finger form an "O"
with the other fin-
gers stretched up.
The colloquial
"okay" sign.

In position. Every
thing satisfactory.

The director's index
finger touches the
nose.

On time or "on the
nose."

The director draws
the index finger
across the throat in
a slashing motion.

Cut or stop.

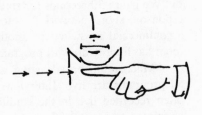

The director holds
the index finger
straight up.

One minute.

| The director crosses the index finger held vertically with the index finger of the other hand held horizontally. | One-half minute. | 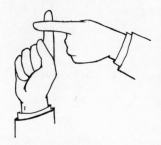 |
| The director shows a closed fist. | Wrap-up. Often indicating thirty seconds to the end of the program. |  |

The longer the staff works together, the fewer signals are needed. Electronic devices such as "on-air" lights sometimes cue talent. Once a program is in progress, a director depends upon visual signals to contact the performer. Hand signals for cueing, for regulating the talent's relationship to the microphone, and for timing are commonly used. The signal chart (Fig. 1) indicates the appropriate, standard signals for all situations. Remember that not only the director and other production staff members, but also the performers (see Chapter 7) must be able to give and respond to these signals without a moment's hesitation.

Live Broadcasts or Taping Sessions. At most radio stations newscasts, disc jockey programs, a few commercials and announcements, and an occasional public service program are live. At some stations newscasts originate from the news room, at others from the control room or studio. Live sports programs are broadcast from remote locations. The microphones in these various locations are activated by merely throwing the proper switch in master control. In actual practice performers time their own programs and use specific verbal cues — "This is (name), (call letters) news, (location)," or "We pause 30 seconds for station identification. This is (call letters), the (sponsor) sports network." — to alert the one at the audio console to insert a commercial or switch to another program. The engineer in the control room has little to do with program content unless he or she is also the talent.

Much radio broadcasting is pre-recorded, but at some time or other all programs are live. Interviews, feature programs, political speeches are often recorded live in the studio and broadcast later. A director may be appointed to assist in the production of these programs. For example, the program director might serve as director-moderator for a panel discussion. Time limitations on busy participants, economic factors, long-playing tapes, programs distributed by tape production companies, and pre-recorded commercials and announcements indicate a trend toward automation. A program may be — and frequently is — taped in segments and then spliced together. Every director should know how to edit tape. (See Chapter 2.) After the tape is ready, it is played for the program director and a salesman. If it gets their approval, it is heard by the sponsor. If approved, the program is broadcast.

Evaluation Conference. After several people, especially top management, have heard the program, mail has come in and ratings have been tabulated, it is evaluated. Improvements may be made or the program may be dropped.

ENTERTAINMENT PROGRAMS

Traditionally, a producer and director were associated particularly with the entertainment aspects of radio programming: network dramas, musical programs, variety-comedy programs, quizzes, and similar formats. Even though radio drama has declined in the United States, it finds occasional revival at independent radio companies. Shakespearean plays, children's programs, serials and mysteries are frequently redesigned in highly abbreviated, segmented forms to attract radio listeners of the present generation. One firm, for example, divided three-hour Shakespearean plays into six half-hour segments. In 1965 the ABC Radio Network initiated *Theatre 5*, a half-hour dramatic series for radio. "Unless radio tries original programming methods," said Robert R. Pauley, president of the ABC Radio Network, "we can never become anything more than a news and music medium."[1] Radio dramas are being produced by educational groups and by foreign radio networks, such as the British Broadcasting Corporation and the Canadian Broadcasting Corporation. In Germany, where radio drama thrives, the Hans Bredow Institute for Radio and Television of the University of Hamburg seriously studies it as a literary art.[2]

Although the radio producer-director of entertainment programs in the United States is less concerned with drama, as a practical production assignment, than with musical programs, contests, some forms of variety programs, and public service entertainment, drama is enjoying a resurgence in the 1970's. After a successful syndication of nostalgia favorites such as *The Shadow, The Lone Ranger, Gangbusters,* and *Fibber McGee and Molly,* the CBS Radio Network introduced original dramatic mysteries during 1974. The newcomer to the field, the student, therefore, has a need to study the producing and directing of drama programs. The drama often encompasses most, if not all, of the elements found in other forms of radio production, and knowledge of and familiarity in producing and directing the drama provide a firm base for creative and effective work in all other forms of radio production. The following material on the drama, therefore, is not meant to suggest an area for immediate application in the field, but a base for applicability and adaptation to other forms.

[1] For Notes, see end of this chapter.

Dramas

The schedule for a producer and a director of a radio drama includes preliminary program planning, an off-mike rehearsal, an on-mike rehearsal, a dress rehearsal, and the on-air performance.

Preliminary Program Planning. The producer plans the program or series. He or she selects the director and the writer. He or she may contract some of the leading players, and may take care of the legal and promotional aspects of the program. He or she often tries to interest an advertising agency or network or station in the idea while the program or series is still in the planning stage. The producer usually estimates budget requirements.

The director, meanwhile, studies the script in detail. He or she depends upon one's imagination and understanding of it to create the sound image necessary for complete visualization by the radio audience. The director consults with the writer, if possible. Some passages may need clarification and changes. For timing purposes, the director and writer decide where the script can be cut judiciously, if that should be necessary in production. Opinions may differ between the writer and the director. These differences should be resolved before rehearsal. Although a radio production is a composite effort, the writer's vision tends to prevail during this period. The director holds conferences with the composer and the sound technicians. If special sound effects are required or a new musical score must be composed or arranged, this will take time. The director must allow for its completion.

The director may select the entire cast. He or she may wish to be in on the choice of each voice, or may let a competent casting director do the screening. It is common in radio dramas for a single actor to play two or three minor roles in a production. The judgment necessary for picking out such a versatile actor is another reason for the director's attendance at tryouts. Often a director is already acquainted with people who have ability and with whom he or she can work effectively. He or she tends to hire them if one can. A stimulating working atmosphere must exist between the director and the cast, if excellent results are to be obtained. The director may have to reserve space and studio facilities for specific time periods. Production space is limited and talent time is expensive. The director has to work out a well-planned rehearsal schedule, and may also have to allow for special technical rehearsals.

Off-mike Rehearsal. The director calls the actors and technicians together for a reading of the script. He or she assigns parts and discusses the approach to be used by generally describing the characters and the sound effects as he or she hears them. The cast reads the entire script aloud. This reading rehearsal establishes overall continuity and a sense of the total dramatic effect of the script. The director times the reading. Each elapsed minute is noted in the script so that it can be used as a check point during the on-air production. This read-through enables the director and the cast to become acquainted. It also establishes the director as the organizational and artistic leader upon whom everyone depends for judgment and, practically speaking, for cues.

A competent talent contributes immeasurably to the role he or she is portraying; however, if the interpretation is not consistent with the director's concept, the director probably will correct it during an off-mike rehearsal. It is equally important he or she encourages the good aspects of the reading by giving some praiseworthy attention to each talent. Establishing a working rapport with an actor is one of the director's most delicate and difficult tasks.

On-mike Rehearsal. The director calls a production rehearsal in the studio, where the drama is rehearsed, scene by scene, from the beginning. The director attempts to integrate all elements — actors, music and sound. No attempt is made to time these segments.

This is the creative period for everyone. The director concentrates on the content of the script, interpreting it in terms of the sound medium. The actors' voices, the music and the sound effects require detailed attention. The director will stop and start the production many times. The director's skill is needed in proportioning the right amount of time to each production obstacle. Rehearsal time is very limited, and there are about twice as many things as he or she is able to do. The director must be highly selective. One thing the director works on is pacing. A script usually consists of a series of minor crises leading to the climax or turning point in the life of the protagonist. Often these moments of crisis alternate with moments that are relatively placid. The director tries to manipulate the internal rate at which the scenes progress, and is concerned more intimately with each characterization. The director describes the total character first and then discusses the performance of each actor. The sound person, too, is considered an artist. The degree that the director can get the cast and crew to do what he or she wants is the essence of his or her contribution to the program. The psychology of human motivation, artistic sensitivity and technical skill are prerequisites to successful radio directing.

The director must also work with the engineer. The engineer will control, mechanically at least, the volume, the placement of microphones and special electronic sound effects; he or she may pick out some recorded music. The engineer's job can be complex. The on-mike rehearsal will indicate whether the engineer can manage all of the sound sources as rapidly as the script demands. A sensitive engineer can assist in making artistic decisions. Each microphone, for example, brings out certain qualities in an actor's voice. An engineer can alter these qualities. To some extent, he or she can regulate the relative loudness of voices and of other sounds by "riding gain." The engineer can assist in determining actor "presence" by suggesting the relative position of the actor to the microphone. Standard "on-mike" distance for most scenes is about one foot.

Dress Rehearsal. The dress rehearsal is a facsimile of the on-air performance. The director, therefore, runs through the complete performance even though there may be obvious errors. The script, moreover, is accurately timed by the director or by an assistant. The director takes notes on every aspect of the entire production, giving every cue to the cast, technicians, and engineer just as they can expect to get them during the final on-air performance. During this period the director also must listen to the program as a whole, as the listener will hear it.

After the dress rehearsal, the director goes over notes with the respective members of the cast and crew, and rehearses any weak spot in the production. If a new cue is to be used, the director makes certain everyone knows what it is. Generally speaking, it is too late to change characterizations during the dress rehearsal, for such changes might endanger the final performance.

The producer, some members of the advertising agency and the sponsor may sit in on the dress reheasal. They may even have a conference with the director prior to the on-air broadcast, especially if the sponsor disapproves of something in the program. The producer tries to keep both the sponsor and the director happy. Ability as a diplomat in moments of conflicting opinion is an important attribute.

On the Air. The strain and excitement of a production reaches its height just prior to air time; nevertheless, the director attempts to radiate confidence and composure. The director gives those cues which were clearly established in rehearsal, following the script carefully, looking ahead to warn the engineer (and anyone else) about a difficult passage that is coming up.

Many directors give as meaningful a performance in the control room as the actors do before the microphone. This responsiveness on the part of the director to the performance of the actors is infectious. Some radio actors, especially comedians, prefer live audiences so that they can have the stimulation of a "live" reaction from them. The feeling that someone is paying attention creates a response within the performer which is invigorating. The director controls the mechanics of the program, too. He or she constantly checks the time to make sure it compares favorably with that recorded during the off-mike rehearsal. The director lets the cast know whether the tentative cut will be deleted or not; the director continues to indicate to his cast that the program is going well, even if mistakes are made. The director should not show displeasure during the program because this might create a bad psychological effect on the entire cast and crew, resulting in more errors. Besides, mistakes seem smaller in retrospect. The director blends the sound elements by listening and responding with the subjectivity of an artist and the objectivity of a member of the audience.

The producer, the sponsor, advertising agency representatives, network or station personnel and a few guests may attend the program. The producer attempts to point out some of the positive features and benefits of the program to the group. In short, he or she serves skillfully in public relations, listening carefully, however, to the opinions of the others. When the program is over, the producer dutifully thanks everyone. Later, the producer discusses the program with the director privately. The producer often has a more detached point of view which may be helpful to the director.

The history of radio has indicated that some dramas are particularly well suited to the sound medium. These programs stimulate the imagination — "the theatre of the mind," as Erik Barnouw called it — by suggesting scenes of horror, mystery, fantasy, and romance.[3] *Lights Out, I Love a Mystery, Let's Pretend,* and the "soap operas" were some of them.

With the advent of audio tape, the production techniques changed. Nowadays, dramatic productions are recorded on bits and pieces of audio tape, and they are so skillfully spliced together that every element blends with every other imperceptibly. For a WUNC (Chapel Hill, North Carolina) radio production of Charles Dickens' "A Christmas Carol," the director taped many elements out of sequence: first, the narrator; second, scenes with Scrooge and the cast; third, scenes with Scrooge only; fourth, crowd scenes. Some sounds (the phantom's chains, for example) and background music were added last. The director, producer and engineer heard all of the segments and arranged them in order. Then they began the long process of editing them and splicing them together. After 15 hours of recording the scenes and about 46 man hours of editing and splicing, "A Christmas Carol" was finally assembled for broadcast. The final, two-hour production consisted of over 250 splices. A vast difference from the days of the *Lux Radio Theatre,* which was presented live in one continuous performance.

Musical Programs

Music is the staple of modern radio. Recordings on cartridge, tape and disc are readily available and inexpensive. Popular musical taste is capricious. "Pop music creates potent symbols for its literature. In 1967, it was Black Panther leader Huey Newton sitting in a rattan chair with an automatic rifle. In 1970, it was the smiling face of Bob Dylan on the cover of *Nashville Skyline,* which marked the entry of country music into rock's lexicon. In 1973, pop stars seemed to admit summarily that what they did was trivial. Nobody wanted to be caught with a 'message song.' The creed of '73 was 'goodtime,' diversion for its own sake. It was a populist judgment that brought top-40 back to life."[4] A producer must anticipate trends. Complicating the music scene for radio programmers is a major shift of listeners away from AM radio to FM stereophonic sound and emerging quadraphonic broadcasting.[5]

The Program Director as Producer. The principal producer of musical programs is the program director. Usually the program director is in charge of all programming — its scheduling and its composition. On the one hand the program director is challenged to create new ideas or to improve established techniques. On the other there is the operational problem of translating ideas into action. The program director is hired to maintain or establish the entertainment image of the station. Selection of talent and authority over programs give the program director the key responsibility for program innovation. Perhaps the main duty of a program director is to devise an attractive sound image for the station. A station image is a blend of all the programming elements — music, news, production techniques, promotional spots, announcements, jingles, talent, and its services to the community. It is the total concept a listener has of the station.

Stations are classified in various ways: foreground, middle of the road, traditional, special interest, educational and free form. A popular classification is by dominant music: top-40, progressive rock, middle-of-the-road (MOR), beautiful music, country, classical and religious. At many foreground or top-tune stations the program director controls what is played on the air by purchasing records for the station's library and by restricting the list of records that can be broadcast. The program director does this in consultation with talent and the music librarian. Records are chosen generally by personal taste and by published surveys. *Billboard, Variety,* local sales in records and juke boxes are among the many sources. In Los Angeles, radio station record libraries range from 3,000 to 900,000 selections. Playable records at a top tune station may be as few as 100 or 200, however. Many program directors go a step further than the list by using a formula or order in which the records are to be played. For example, an ideal quarter-hour of popular songs might include two current hits and two standards, done as a group vocal, a male vocal, a female vocal, and an instrumental.[6] Frequently, a disc jockey works within the list, but the DJ selects the order for playing the music. At various middle-of-the-road or easy-listening stations, the program director merely reviews what the disc jockey decides to put on the air. The station may have thousands of records to choose from, and so there is no list or formula so long as the disc jockey keeps within the basic philosophy of the MOR station. "We are trying to gear ourselves backwards," says Bob Henley, program director of Chicago's WGN. "The audience can do nothing but grow older. And what we're trying to do is not grow older with them; we're trying to keep our age constant. That means you have to continually go back and review your music policies and start including those things that were appealing to youngsters who are now older." Middle of the road radio is adult radio, programmed for a 25- to 49-year old audience. "Music is only one part of a mixture necessary to hold an adult audience. Music, news and information are almost equal in importance to the adult mind and must be given credibility and cohesion through presentation by personalities. That has been the tried and true method for more than 20 years now."[7]

In addition to top tune, easy listening, and traditional or classical music stations, some stations broadcast to social or ethnic groups. One station specializing in black audiences bases its philosophy on a survey indicating that blacks prefer rhythm and blues, news, spirituals, daytime serials and variety,

in that order. Consequently, two-and-a-half hours daily are devoted to spirituals. WLIB-FM, New York, is programmed as much by "feel" as anything,
according to Frankie Crocker: "We choose records by feeling. Sure, we look
at the charts but we're usually so far ahead of the trades that it takes time
for them to catch up."[8] In 1972 nearly 20 radio stations were wholly or substantially owned by blacks. Over 400 stations were programmed entirely or
partly in a foreign language such as Spanish or even Japanese. A further
kind of radio operation is the automated station. It is commonly an FM
adjunct to an AM-FM combination. Its stereophonic and popular music is
recorded on three-hour tapes, and its news is simulcast from its AM counterpart. In effect, the AM staff produces the FM programming, too, duplicating
within the limits set by the Federal Communications Commission.

An expansion of FM broadcasting during the 1960's and into the
1970's to about 2500 FM radio stations in the United States provided the
opportunity for experimenting with new format ideas that were being discussed but not attempted on AM. Out of this radio laboratory some relatively
new styles of commercial broadcasting developed. The free form progressive
stations, which were also called underground, became important in reaching
the 18- to 34-age group. At the same time the opportunity for innovative
broadcasting attracted some exceptional young talent. Communicators interested in an alternative to AM top-tune programming found outlets for a
different kind of creativity in the free form approach.

Program (Music) Director Pat Fant, of KLOL(FM), Houston, explains:

> Selection of music for stations broadcasting a free form format is done
> almost entirely from album product. Each announcer or programmer selects
> his own music and arranges his sets of selected cuts in sequences of his own
> choosing. Establishment of a mood is effected by seguing musical tracts
> smoothly. Sets can be of any length, but usually average 12 to 15 minutes.
> The flow of music is stopped only for a commercial set which sometimes
> begins with either a live or taped station promotion or a PSA. Announce-
> ments of this type are usually short and to the point and are kept to an
> effective minimum. When selecting music, the length of the cut is not as
> important a consideration as the mood needed to be set musically at the
> moment. Segments flow smoothly from one to the other, but limited use of
> purposefully jarring transitions are effected, and they solicit yet another
> variety of listener reaction. The call letters or station logo is given as the
> most important element of programming, and should be inserted in some
> creative way upon each opening of the mike. The station identification
> should also be given at the end of each musical set. The importance of
> station identification cannot be overstressed.
>
> The programmer is free to air any material he chooses at any time of
> the day. Generally, the only restriction on what is aired is that the material
> must come from the station programming library. In this way the music
> director, representing station management, controls objectionable material

to prevent its airing. The programmer selects his music using his own ear and good musical taste as his guideline.

The extensive variety of music includes without a doubt the routes of nearly all musical expression. The free form sound is built around the central core of high quality rock music which includes many progressive artists having had exposure on "top 40" outlets. We find a strong influence of progressive jazz, representing both new performers and many of the traditional greats of the jazz world enjoyed by some generations for years. With the mixture of rock and progressive jazz came the powerful child of this new marriage . . . progressive jazz rock, which received the public acceptance it demanded.

At the same time the acoustic folk artists multiplied and the exceptionally talented among this group soon emerged to the surface to also be included in progressive programming. Acoustic country music, with enough of a rock beat to be accepted, evolved into numerous styles. Some of these pastoral-flavored songs would tell the story of the beautiful and peaceful life in the country and held special appeal for those who felt urban American pressures too great. The flashy sound of over-produced music using majestic strings and multi-tracked vocals gave way to a simpler more honest approach to music that could be reproduced live on stage. Groups sang about ecology, war, political and social disorders, peace, love and brotherhood, and religions of all forms. The music simply reflected a changing life style that many young Americans were experiencing. The progressive stations tried simply to serve this new public need.

The exceptionally wide variety of music that free form radio covers also includes blues. This helped cause a revival of old black-roots blues music and artists. The free form format also allowed some experimental music to be aired. This broad classification includes the electronically synthesized sound, which incorporates highly sophisticated gear to alter either an external sound input or produce its own sound through actual wave shaping. It is this experimental material, sounding at times very harsh and non-melodic and at other times very strange and ethereal, that alienated, disgusted and sometimes even frightened those who were not ready to accept this experimental music for its own sake. Finally the classics have also found a place in progressive radio. Used as transitions or aids in setting special moods they added further to the variety of sound.

The listener really doesn't know what to expect when he tunes his environmental control system, i.e. radio, to the free form station. The new and unusual is an important part of progressive programming. In free form radio, the only constant is *change*.[9]

The program director, consequently, produces a sound image that is consistent with the philosophy of the station: foreground, middle of the road, traditional, special, educational or free form. The PD may even program two stations, where one is dependent upon the other. Commercial radio station philosophy is based on providing attractive entertainment programs that will sell products to a particular audience. The program director never forgets this concept.

The Talent as Producer. The program director may delegate the responsibility for the development of individual programs to the talent, such as a disc jockey or master of ceremonies. The program director is thus placed in a supervisory capacity, leaving the internal production of the program — its continuity and its music selection (within limits) — to the talent.

Typically, these stations encourage "personalities." The program director has the job of deciding what personalities best convey the image of the station throughout the broadcast day. The program director may divide disc jockey shifts into the morning, early evening, and late night tours, using an entirely different personality for each. A Fort Worth top-tune station rotates six disc jockeys throughout the day. Each person has a unique style. The early morning man is a mature, veteran announcer playing top tunes and talking to housewives in an easy manner. As the day progresses other men pick up the pace slightly. During the evening hours, a young fellow playing the same records shouts and jokes in breathless delivery to attract the teen-agers; and late at night another young man changes the pace and speaks in a mellow voice. Each man tries to project his own personality — mature, moderate, boisterous, smooth. Personalities lend variety to top tune stations, where the record selection and order are relatively constant, by ad libbing continuity in a jargon peculiar to the disc jockey. The basic procedure:

1). The disc jockey arrives at the station in time to study the program log. It will list all of the commercials, PSA's and ID's that must be played on the program. There may be 20 or 30 separate items in addition to music. The DJ checks to be certain that they are in the control room, probably in the tape cartridge rack or "tape deck" or record rack. He or she also pulls records from the station's library, if necessary.

2). The disc jockey is an expert in the operation of the audio console, having practiced long hours before going on the air. He or she is thoroughly familiar with the layout of the control room. The disc recordings, audio tapes and cartridges are within about an arm's length from where he or she sits at the console, and so are the machines to play them.

3). On the console desk is the program log which he or she follows. Nearby is the continuity book containing all announcements that will be read live. If there is any extra copy such as gags from magazines or newspapers, it will be near also.

4). The disc jockey might begin the show with theme, program ID, transition to first record, first record, comment and lead to first commercial, first commercial, comment, second commercial, and lead to second record. Disc jockey comments are commonly under 10 seconds, pacing is lively with tight cueing at top tune stations; and easier style is used with other formats. If the disc jockey works his or her own board, the disc jockey frequently has a third-class radiotelephone operator's license issued by the Federal Communications Commission. It should have a broadcast endorsement.

At many middle-of-the-road stations the program director prefers anonymous announcers. He depends upon the total programming of the station and its reputation to attract an audience, not personalities. Some stations are a combination of both philosophies.

The Radio Team as Producer. At large stations in highly unionized markets talent and engineering duties are well defined and tend not to overlap as much as they do in small markets. That is to say, one person does not perform as many different services. The program director determines the composition of the program; the program operations manager schedules it; a continuity writer provides copy; the talent reads it; and an engineer controls the audio console. The modern radio production team at work consists of several professional people producing and directing a single moment on the air. The basic procedure:

1). After the initial conference described earlier, the talent, a continuity writer and the program director meet a second time to talk about the program's content and other details. Most radio stations specialize in some kind of music, so the tunes they play are restricted to the format. An easy-listening station, for instance, might develop a program of Latin American music. The talent is asked to brush up on Spanish and Portuguese pronunciation. The continuity writer will get short feature items about Latin America. The program director suggests a program title, theme music, and what the announcer's opening and closing remarks should include. They list the order for playing records (instrumental, vocal, novelty) and approximately where the spot announcements will go. This outline is called a "run down." The session is informal, and these plans are tentative.

2). The writer polishes all of the continuity before it goes on the air, and the talent reads it over many times. Numerous commercials are developed in cooperation with the sales department.

3). On the day of the broadcast, the talent arrives early enough to have an informal rehearsal with the director — who may be the engineer. The program director and writer listen to the first few programs and continue to make improvements, which gradually become the responsibility of the talent and the engineer, although the writer continues to update commercials.

Contests

Occasionally, radio programs which are involved with talent, guests, audiences, prizes, judges, accounting problems and contracts have a producer and/or director who function in the traditional sense. They meet with the talent and guests, plan the format of the program, rehearse it if necessary, work with sponsors and perform other traditional duties. These programs often duplicate a program already on network television. They no longer originate very frequently on the local level. Producing and directing the contest requires several special considerations:

1). The producer-director (or program director) must be thoroughly familiar with the complex laws concerning contests. No advertisement of or information concerning any lottery, gift enterprise, or similar scheme, offering prizes dependent in whole or in part upon lot or chance, are permitted on radio.

2). The producer-director may be required to obtain legal opinion before entering into any contracts, if there is the slightest doubt concerning the details of the contest. The Storer Broadcasting Company, for example, requires this of its managing directors.

3). After the program is approved, the producer-director gives full information to all contestants so that they can compete fairly. Contestants may also be rehearsed in the mechanics of the game, but they must not be provided with information which gives one contestant an advantage over another.

4). The producer-director reads the continuity to be sure that the rules for judging entries are explicit. The producer-director determines the dates of the contest, and where, when and how entries must be submitted. The producer-director decides the number and nature of the prizes and the order in which they are to be awarded. Finally, he or she must be responsible for the prompt awarding of prizes, and must be certain that the contest is conducted in accordance with the rules.

Contests are among the most difficult programs to produce because they arouse keen public interest and, as a result, bring the station's policy of fairness and responsibility under intense scrutiny.

Simple quiz formats and contests have been tried by local stations. They are a mainstay of top-tune stations. These programs consist of playing records and placing telephone calls to homes in the listening area, sometimes selected at random from the telephone directory, sometimes drawn from postcards sent to the radio station by listeners. After the talent draws the name, the talent calls the listener. If the listener is at home, he or she is asked a question. If the answer is correct, the listener, of course, wins the prize; if not, the prize often gets bigger. Such programs are attractive to listeners and furnish the station with some feedback concerning the audience. Record hops, treasure hunts, mystery voices, talent searches, word and number games are the bases for other contests. The list is unlimited. The basic procedure:

1). After a standard opening, the talent may play a record or two, and give a clue or answer to the day's question.

2). The talent draws a name at random and makes the call, relating every step to the listener: "While I play the next tune, I'll make the first call on today's *Telequiz.*"

3). The talent gets the party: "This is WXXZ Telequiz calling. To whom am I speaking? Hello, (name). Have you listened to our program, and do you know the magic word?" The talent is friendly, but usually specifies the allotted time in which the listener must answer the question. Frequently the talent repeats the question once.

4). The talent may have a winner, or may have to call someone else. After the program the names of all prize winners are usually submitted to the Promotion Department. Prizes are often mailed to winners. Occasionally, the talent awards them in person because the ceremony publicizes the station.

Variety Programs

In recent years "magazine" formats have become more difficult to identify in radio programming. In the mid-1960's segments of music, comedy and conversation were heard regularly on NBC's *Monitor* and on the CBS equivalent, *Dimension*. These programs are virtually non-existent in the 1970's. Inasmuch as radio formats are cyclic — being updated and repeated at intervals — the variety program is being briefly referred to here. A producer has the overall responsibility of integrating pre-taped program material, pre-taped commercials, and live newscasts. Each segment is scheduled to the second so that local stations can insert local spot announcements, if they wish. Even the 20-year-old *House Party* began to reflect this trend in the early 1960's. It changed from strictly light fare concerning children, adults, games and prizes to some serious moments concerning special problems and other issues. It developed a "magazine-like" concept, according to its master of ceremonies, Art Linkletter. The antics and music of *Grand Ole Op'ry* were among the few survivors of radio's yesteryear.

On the local level, the producer of a variety show is often the talent. Listeners may provide some of the continuity either by letters or by calling the station while the program is on the air. Sometimes two people are talent and producers for this kind of a program. The job of collecting material is substantial. When they are before the microphone, one person can be assembling material or answering the telephone while the other is speaking on the air. One Hollywood commentator obtains part of the copy for a casual variety-talk format from an information service. In all practical respects, the service dictates its "inside" reports over the telephone to the talent's secretary, who types them up. Subsequently, the talent reads these reports over the air. The secretary may also schedule interviews with celebrities, may research the guest's background and, in fact, may literally produce the program for the talent. Well known commentators are flooded with promotional materials from all areas of show business. Most celebrities are just as eager to be interviewed by disc jockeys or commentators as the local performers are glad to have them on the program.

The directing function for such a program, after an informal preliminary rehearsal, is principally a matter of cueing talent, riding gain, and playing music or sound effects as needed. The engineer does this at large "local" stations, such as WTOP, the CBS affiliate in Washington, D.C.

Public Service Entertainment

Special entertainment programs are broadcast by schools and civic groups for educational or fund raising purposes, historical ceremonies and holiday celebrations. The programs are produced and directed without charge by the group concerned. The station furnishes air time and technical skill through its program director. A typical example is a campus talent program that is sent to local stations on a regular basis. The program may be prerecorded at the institution or at the station. Virtually every local radio station is willing to accept such programs on a limited basis. Numerous universities have standing agreements with commercial stations for broadcasting student programs. Programs from educational institutions and civic groups vary in quality and frequency; nevertheless, these programs are a valuable supplement for educating students in broadcasting. They are also important to stations that could not afford to produce these programs and yet need them to round out their local program responsibilities. The basic procedure:

1). The producer-director (who is often an educator or civic leader) goes to the program director of the local commercial station. He or she explains the idea for a program or series. The program director usually asks what the station has to furnish in regard to personnel, facilities and air time. The program director may offer suggestions concerning the content of the program. If the idea is a good one, and air time is the only request made of the station, chances are that the program will be accepted. Radio stations usually are cooperative and generous.

2). The producer-director plans the entire program in detail, enlisting the assistance of the talent needed. A telephone call may be sufficient. In some cases, governing boards must be consulted before students, teachers or public servants may participate as representatives of the institution where they are employed. Rehearsal times are agreed upon and coordinated with everyone.

3). The producer-director forms the radio team. An assistant and an engineer may be all the staff required. The fewer the better. The program-director should obtain the most competent people he or she can find. Many high schools have students who are capable engineers.

4). If possible, the producer-director should follow a procedure similar to that of the radio drama: off-mike rehearsals, on-mike rehearsals, and performance. Inasmuch as the producer-director would be working with inexperienced people, instructions have to be explicit, consistent, and perhaps repeated often. Practically speaking, people tend to be too busy to devote much time to complex programs. The producer-director therefore keeps the requirements on the talent to a minimum. He or she sets deadlines and takes nothing for granted. The producer-director rehearses the program as much as time will allow. Most of the talent are devoting their spare time to the project; therefore, the producer-director should appreciate whatever they contribute.

5). The program may be recorded at the radio station or on other high quality equipment. The producer-director should have access to the equipment for several hours at a time because the editing and splicing process is a tedious one. After all of the segments are recorded, they are assembled in accordance with the script. Swift pacing, fast action and many voices maintain audience interest. The producer-director previews the tape in sufficient time to allow for changes. Some industrious producer-directors do all of the technical work themselves.

6). The producer-director delivers the tape to the station by placing it in precisely the right spot at the agreed-upon time. Program directors rarely play these tapes on the air themselves; the disc jockeys or engineers do. In order to avoid confusion, pickup and delivery times should be carefully coordinated with the program director.

7). If it is a series, the producer-director should meet with the program director occasionally for a critical evaluation. Both parties should consider the series as a serious contribution to the community. The station may wish to assist in promoting it.

Informational Programs

Informational programming is perhaps the fastest growing area in radio. Immediate or "hard" news and news-in-depth are its two principal categories. Both utilize several techniques — reporting, talking, interviewing and discussing — to reveal current happenings. Both are commonly divided into areas. Immediate news includes international, national, regional, local weather and sports events. Feature news runs the gamut from a one-minute editorial to an hour-long documentary. Broadcast journalism has gradually tended to reduce broadcast entertainment. When WNUS, Chicago, became the first all-talk AM-FM radio combination in the country, Gordon McLendon, president of the McLendon Broadcasting Corporation, announced: "No city in the world except Chicago can immediately tune news — on either band — at any hour of the day or night."[10] WINS, New York, a Westinghouse station, also adopted an all-news format shortly thereafter.

Informational programs have developed steadily from broadcasts of news, weather and market reports by pioneer stations KDKA, Pittsburgh, WHA, Madison, and WWJ, Detroit, to the intensive coverage of events in space by the networks. NBC Radio, for instance, began its coverage of the Gemini space mission claiming "the largest, most elaborately equipped mobile unit ever designed and built especially for radio reporting of space projects." The network initiated its broadcast an hour before scheduled launch time, continued its coverage through the first orbit, then issued ten-minute progress reports every half-hour. It broadcast the third orbit and recovery of the space vehicle completely. Extensive coverage along with documentaries before and after the flight were also on ABC and CBS radio.

News

News or "hard" news, as it is referred to in radio, is the day to day, minute to minute compilation and dissemination of current events. Providing the public with fair and comprehensive news coverage is a difficult job. Due to increased demands on newspeople, there is a trend toward hiring those with college degrees in journalism, broadcasting, government, history and political science. Despite increasing salaries, expanding radio news departments have difficulty obtaining good news personnel. This is particularly true at smaller stations.

The Local Newsman as Producer. The backbone of a news operation is the man or woman on the scene, whether it is in a small town in the South or in the jungles of Asia. A News Department at a local station may have one or two people. One typical small station in Texas has two newsmen, with the diverse producing and directing responsibilities of one of them a graphic illustration of the situation in many small stations; he is a newsman, chief announcer, audio engineer, and program director (although most decisions are made by the station manager). He reads the news, checks the weather instruments, makes tape recordings of incoming news from the mobile units, or covers wrecks, fires and special events himself; he plays records, reads commercials and announcements, produces promotional spots, jingles and special effects; he purchases stock, helps in the office with the log, is in charge of the music library, carries out a multitude of engineering duties, and opens the station in the morning if the announcer fails to show up.

At larger stations several reporters may be "on assignment" anywhere in the world. These stations may have free-lance or part-time reporters, called "stringers," who report significant news items whenever they occur in their vicinity. Each of these reporters is, in fact, the producer of a news segment that may be used on a radio program.

The News Director as Producer. The principal producer of news programs is the news director and/or news editor. He or she works in cooperation with the program director on all matters, especially those involving program policy. The news director knows the station philosophy and so emphasizes the news accordingly. The news director has the responsibility for molding the staff into a news team. Multi-station news operations like those of the McLendon chain require an executive producer for news. The executive producer oversees and coordinates the activities of all the stations. Whether the responsibilities are placed with an executive producer for news, a news director or a local reporter, the newscast is produced essentially in four steps; planning the news, gathering news, assembling news, and presenting news.

Planning the Newscast. The news director must make several preliminary decisions in news programming. Length, frequency, emphasis and staff assignments are among them. Radio newscasts last from five to 30 minutes.

Some stations give "headlines" and "the top story of the hour," both brief reports. Major newscasts are commonly presented at times which coincide with meals, driving to and from work, or going to bed. Minor news summaries are customarily presented on the hour or half-hour, although there are variations. Stations and networks broadcasting "the news when it happens" interrupt programs any time an important story breaks. The news director and program director determine the length and frequency of newscasts.

Most news directors emphasize the news of the locality. A low-power station has local coverage and local emphasis, whereas a powerful station may cover several counties and have regional coverage and regional emphasis. An extremely powerful station may be heard over many states. Emphasis in the news depends upon the nature of the station. Most newscasts carry international, national and local news along with weather and sports. Often they are in just that order. It makes little sense for a network affiliate to concentrate its staff on national news, if the network is already providing it. For major events, however, a station that can afford it will send a reporter to the scene for a story with a local viewpoint. The Republican and Democratic conventions draw many local station newscasters as well as those from the networks.

At the network level, news is radio's most marketable program service. For over a quarter of a century CBS produced *World News Roundup*, which illustrates the duties of a producer-director. Its current variation — CBS *News-on-the-Hour* — is produced in a similar way. The producer of *World News Roundup* began planning the program at CBS News Headquarters on the afternoon before the broadcast. During this period the producer determines which stories will have direct reports from all over the world. The producer sends wire and transoceanic orders to appropriate correspondents for reports. A correspondent, moreover, may originate a report by notifying CBS News Headquarters. The chief newscaster or "anchor" shares the producer-director responsibility, checking the lineup of stories hours in advance of the newscast. The anchorperson and the producer are, of course, constantly on the alert for late-breaking stories that may replace or affect the apparent lineup. Overseas and national spots are carried live, if possible; if atmospheric conditions do not permit it, the producer has the stories pretaped. Prior to air time, the anchorperson at the microphone gives the lineup a final check. A news editor, sharing the director function, meanwhile, sits alongside the engineer in the control room. The editor speaks to the overseas correspondents and coordinates their reports with the newscast. The editor accurately checks the lead-in and -out cues, story content and length of the reports. The anchorperson must be prepared to give ad-libbed introductions to live spots on a moment's notice; changing circumstances may require updating some reports. A anchorperson must have planned in advance to have sufficient information on all news items. The CBS news team with its news editor and engineer share modern producer-director functions by carefully organizing each newscast in advance.[11]

Gathering News. The reporter, particularly in the smaller station, will obtain copy from a wire service. In fact, he or she may literally rip the copy from the machine and read it over the air — hence, the expression "rip and read." This kind of news operation is looked down upon because the newscaster neglects to shape the material to the audience. The newscaster will make a few routine calls around town for additional items of local interest. At a large station the news gathering sources multiply and so does the staff. The news director assigns certain areas of city government to reporters on the staff. They telephone their stories to the station, or report them from any one of several mobile units. These reports are recorded at the station on audio tape and at an appropriate time the news director or anchorperson on duty inserts them into the newscast.

The most dramatic news gathering event in recent times occurred in Dallas, Texas, when President John F. Kennedy was assassinated. An account of how Dallas radio station, KLIF, and Fort Worth radio station KXOL, gathered the news on November 22, 1963 is illustrative of the efficient use of local radio news facilities and of the complex assignment many news directors have.[12] The Dallas radio and television stations had agreed that two reporters, one representing radio and the other television, would cover the President's arrival at Love Field. Joe Long, news director of KLIF, and Bob Walker, of WFAA-TV, represented each medium, respectively. The two newsmen stood on the roof of WFAA's mobile television unit, where they made a 45-minute broadcast of the landing. The President's motorcade was to travel more or less in a loop from Love Field to downtown Dallas and back again. KLIF newsmen Roy Nichols and Glen Duncan were positioned in two mobile units along the parade route, while Gordon McLendon (president of the McLendon stations) awaited Kennedy's appearance at the Dallas Trade Mart, where he was to make a luncheon address. The motorcade consisted of the President's car, followed by Secret Service men, and the Vice President's car. A fourth vehicle was the bus containing the White House correspondents. One was Bruce Neal, assistant news director of KXOL. As the President's car passed the Texas School Book Depository, Neal, who was near the front of the bus, recalled hearing "what sounded like firecrackers. . . . We didn't know what had happened. The bus speeded up and we went immediately to the Trade Mart, thinking the shots had missed."

In another part of Dallas, Joe Long was returning to KLIF when he heard a "Signal 19" police call, indicating a shooting. It was followed by the words, "The motorcade is involved." Long states: "Apparently the button stuck on a policeman's radio — probably someone on motorcycle — because I could hear sirens screaming. A voice said, 'We're Code 6 (have arrived) Parkland. There is a shooting. Two persons have been rushed to Parkland. No identification.' "

Both the Dallas and Fort Worth stations geared for action. They abandoned musical programming and commercials and switched to continuous news. Their approaches to covering the series of events were quite different, however. The news director at the Fort Worth station concentrated his staff at Parkland Memorial Hospital; the news director of the Dallas station placed his newsmen at key positions throughout the city. KXOL depended heavily on the Associated Press to amplify its stories; KLIF used United Press primarily for non-local events. Both stations set up a small staff and special facilities for feeding other stations.[13] A make-shift press room was prepared at the hospital. Within an hour four newsmen, two mobile units, a portable tape recorder, a walkie-talkie and a teletypewriter enabled the KXOL newsmen to switch from telephone communication (which was overloaded) to continuous two-way radio communication with their station in Fort Worth. Neal directed the operation, assigning Russ Bloxom in one mobile unit to the front of Parkland, Jerry Hahn to the emergency entrance, Bill Hightower to the medical briefing room, and Bill Hicks to a second mobile unit that served as liaison and back up. At KLIF, Joe Long took over as anchorman and directed the operation. He called in extra reporters and dispatched them to key places in Dallas. Nichols and Duncan, who were in mobile units along the parade route, went to Parkland and police headquarters, respectively. At the book depository Gary DeLaune got an eyewitness account of the shooting; Nichols reported from Parkland that President Kennedy and Texas Governor John Connally were both struck; McLendon described the confusion at the Dallas Trade Mart; and Duncan made reports from police headquarters. "By one o'clock we had two reports from each man in addition to interviews from Jim Wright, Ralph Yarborough, and others."[14] In approximately one hour the KLIF news director had activated a ten-man news staff to cover the city. In the control room at each station the news director immediately defined the situation, decided how to cover it for his station, assigned his personnel, mobilized his facilities, and actually participated in the newscast as anchorman.

Because of the growing complexity and expense of covering important news events, networks, individual stations, and wire services have consolidated their efforts. Memo #2 (See Appendix, page 265) from Russ Tornabene, "pool" producer for Pope Paul VI's visit to New York City in 1965, illustrates the enormous amount of advance planning that such an event requires. Temporary phone lines between pool control and each location, and radio relay between control and the helicopter gave the pool producer command over the entire operation. Explicit "end" cues are especially noteworthy for they signal the next program segment. Notice that pool reporters were in eight locations only; therefore, networks and individual stations were assigned space at other key locations where they provided their own reporters.

Assembling News. The gathering process will bring in much more news than the news director will need for any broadcast, even on a "slow" news day. He or she must evaluate what is news from what is not, and then determine just which facts are essential for a clear understanding of what is happening. After every story is condensed to the irreducible minimum length, the news director arranges the stories in a meaningful order, and times them. The news director also determines where — in the studio or on location — each newscaster will read the story and where tapes, telephone reports and commercials will be inserted in the program. A complete run down is then typed up, duplicated, and distributed to all concerned. This sample format for *Communique 30 — The News at Ten,* produced for WUNC, Chapel Hill, shows how the news director has organized the program: [15]

Report	Time	Newsman	Location
Opening Headlines (AP)	00:30	Buddine	Announce Booth
Introduction (Cartridge)	00:30	Engineer	Master Control
National/International (AP)	04:00	Buddine	Announce Booth
Promo "The Musician" (Cartridge)	01:00	Engineer	Master Control
National/International (AP)	03:00	Buddine	Announce Booth
NASA Report, "Gemini" (Tape)	03:35	Engineer	Master Control
National/International (AP)	02:00	Buddine	Announce Booth
State News (AP)	05:00	Neiburg	Studio
Weather Report (AP and Local Airport Tape)	03:00	Freakly	Announce Booth
Sports	02:30	Coates	Studio
Promo "Peace Corps." (Disc)	01:00	Engineer	Master Control
Sports	02:30	Coates	Studio
Wrap-Up	01:00	Buddine	Announce Booth
Closing (Cartridge)	00:15	Engineer	Master Control

Presenting News. A news director listens for a particular kind of voice or style of reading that fits the station's image. No criteria have been successfully established. The selection of a newscaster is highly subjective, but news directors seem to agree that a solid education and a good voice are both desirable. Newscaster David Brinkley has said that broadcasting hopefuls should "stop wasting their time with speech courses because it doesn't matter that much."[16] It is true that a man with a message does manage to communicate it in most cases. But the dynamic, compelling voices of an Edward R. Murrow, a Lowell Thomas and an Edward P. Morgan certainly have done a great deal to present the news in a listenable fashion. Inasmuch as newscasting is so highly competitive, there seems to be a trend toward greater perfection in its presentation vocally as well as in other aspects. Few   nationally famous newsmen have noticeable dialects or speech defects. Many news directors, anchorpersons and major correspondents have virtually flawless speech; in fact, they not only report the news but they tend to set the national standards for enunciation and pronunciation. Furthermore, most of them read with great fluency. When a young person looks for employment as a newscaster, he or she will be screened through the submission of an audio tape.

The news director frequently uses production aids. Some journalists believe that these aids tend to destroy the basic reason for tuning in the news: that is, to hear accurate, immediate, unbiased reporting. Many news directors agree with production people, however, that production techniques help to attract larger audiences to radio. Many directors augment the news with "beeper" phone reports, remote reports and taped interviews. They use special effects such as a teletype machine, rockets blasting off and musical inserts to focus attention quickly on the scope, dependability and immediacy of the newscast and, therefore, on the station. They employ these devices to give the station a unique sound for the opening, closing and transitions during programs. Special effects are mass produced and sold by various companies. They are heard typically on top-tune stations, where news directors strive for a dynamic sound image.

The following routine for a typical 5-minute local newscast summarizes the duties of a news director. The news director:

1). Assigns and dispatches all news personnel.

2). Edits wire service copy.

3). Obtains local stories by calling hospitals, government offices, educational institutions, churches, businesses and athletic departments, and by listening to police, fire and sheriff department monitors. The news director may rewrite an article or two from a newspaper, giving credit to it for originating the story.

4). Tapes incoming calls from reporters on assignment, special interviews, statements from public officials and reports from the weather bureau.

5). Rewrites and assembles each item, being wary of remarks that are inaccurate, libelous, or contrary to good taste.

6). Practices reading copy.

7). Takes cues from the engineer on duty.

8). Reads the newscast on the air.

9). Updates all stories for the next news report.

The news director's work is never finished. At many local stations the news director reads the newscast from a newsroom where microphones, telephones, tape recorders, monitors and teletype machines are located. The task, then, becomes noisy as well as hectic.

Sports Programs

Sports newscasting often consists of reading excerpts from the wire services. The biggest stories of the day are summarized and the scores of major contests are read. Sports news is treated as another news sequence in the routine newscast, particularly at a small station.

A sports director or sportscaster comes into his own during the play-by-play radio coverage of an entire sports event. Women are rarely hired as sportscasters, although they occasionally do "color" and feature reports. Football, baseball, basketball and boxing receive the most complete coverage, primarily those contests of national interest but frequently on a local level, too. The national Indianapolis 500-mile auto race and the more locally oriented Fort Worth Colonial Golf Tournament both get full attention on radio stations. The sportscast can be programmed as a special event of the station; it can be sold as an entire program or as spots. It not only brings valuable extra revenue to the station, but is welcomed by tournament entrepreneurs as a source of promotion and money for the event. Interest in high school and regional contests has increased, and local rivalry provides as great a potential audience for the local station as do some national contests.

A sports director may undertake the role of producer-director and commentator. He will know in advance when and where the contest will take place and that he will probably broadcast from a remote location such as a press box, a mobile unit or a gymnasium. He must do a great deal of planning:

1). He obtains clearance from the university athletic department, country club, stadium or arena officials to broadcast the event. Broadcasting rights are restricted and must be cleared ahead of time. Accessibility to players is sometimes limited. Usually a public relations man representing the club and/or athletes handles arrangements for radio coverage. He is the contact man for the sports director.

2). The sports director advises the program director about the event and how extensively he would like to cover it. The program director schedules the sportscast by preempting the regular programs.

3). The sports director carefully plans what he will do with his equipment (microphones, cables), where he will park his mobile unit, where the power supply is located, where telephones are if needed. He anticipates every contingency regarding the physical setup of the program.

4). He discusses the organization of the program with his assistant, or "color" man, and if it is a big game he may line up interviews with local celebrities because they add background information, insights and personal rapport with listeners. He studies the contest and the players thoroughly. He memorizes the players' names and numbers. "Pre-game preparation is 90 per cent of the broadcast," according to Bill Currie, sports director for WSOC, Charlotte.

5). For football, the sports director must obtain good spotters. No one can spot by himself because he can not see the game that well. A sports director may place a spotter on either side of him. Each spotter observes one team, and records his observations by sticking pins into a cork-backed chart called a "spotting board." The spotting board — one for each team — lists each player's number, last name, age, weight, height and home town. The spotters give silent signals to the sportscaster concerning substitutions and other changes, while he is on the air. In basketball, spotters are too slow. The sports director must remember the names of the players, and must be able to see the game clearly. Baseball action is so relatively slow that the sports director needs to fill with a great deal of additional information about the players and previous games. Again, separate charts are used for keeping track of the team at bat and the team in the field.

6). On the day of the game the sports director and his assistants are at the site early enough to set up properly and to check out all equipment. There is always the possibility that they will have to return to the station for an emergency item, even though possible breakdowns have been anticipated. The sports director has an easier set-up if he broadcasts from a permanent press box, with an assigned area. He must, nevertheless, arrive soon enough to check his lines with master control at the station, where an engineer on duty will take the sports director's signal or "feed" and broadcast it to the fans. Occasionally, a game does not start as scheduled. A rule-of-thumb one sports director uses is to ad-lib a delay of ten minutes or less, but to return to the station disc jockey if the delay is longer.[17]

7). The sports director is sometimes responsible for promotional materials and for attending numerous athletic functions (dinners, pre-season activities) to stimulate interest in the team. He must travel a great deal.

The Houston Astros Principal Announcer, Gene Elston, has described his producer-director functions for the first regular season baseball game in the Harris County Domed Stadium, the "Astrodome."[18]

1. He spent about two hours at home preparing for the game by reviewing the history of the Astros' opening day games and starting line-ups each year.

2). He arrived at the Astrodome about three hours before the game. He checked the broadcasting booth, the largest one used for radio. The items needed by the announcers were a scorebook, binoculars, record books, statistic sheets, the visiting team roster, pens and pencils. He made certain a Western Union machine giving up-to-date scores was working properly. Elston was to do the play by play of the first three innings and the last three innings along with putting together both the pre-game and post-game shows. Harry Kalash and Loel Passe did the other innings.

3). He talked to his engineer, Bob Green, about a tape of the last out at Colt Stadium that they would be running on the pre-game show. The engineer was checking the audio console, 3 tape recorders (1 large semi-permanent unit and 2 portable units) 7 microphones (4 for the announcers, 1 for the crowd, 1 in the dugout, 1 behind home plate), and a tape cartridge machine for commercials.

4). He went to the field to check the starting line-ups and talk with some of the players.

5). Returning to the broadcast booth, he found that Passe had interviewed Warren Giles, president of the National League, as the guest on the pre-game show. Elston also noted the itinerary for the pre-game ceremonies with the Astronauts.

6). During the three middle innings when he was not on the air, Elston watched the game and kept up with the scores off the wire service. Throughout the game the announcers would check the commercial book to see if the upcoming spot was live or on tape. On the post-game show Kalash interviewed Richie Allen whose two-run homer won the game for the Philadelphia Phillies. Elston ended the program with a look at all of the scores of other games in the American and National leagues.

Weather Programs

Weather programs are produced at the weather bureau, at a station or on location. If the local weather bureau is the producer, the process is simple: the announcer on duty calls the weather bureau, the person at the weather bureau makes a report over the telephone, and the report is either broadcast live or is taped for replay later. If the weather report is assembled at the station, the procedure is the same as for any newscast, except that the announcer may check a few instruments (thermometer, barometer, rain gauge, radar) at the station.

Expected seasonal changes in the weather are not very exciting perhaps, but all listeners are influenced by them. Even the casual reassurance that tomorrow will be sunny and warm is important to listeners. Weathercasts reporting temperatures throughout the nation and the world are useful to those who have relatives in distant locations or who intend to fly. Weather forecasting is a fascinating study thoroughly researched by radio meteorologists. Severe snow storms, premature warm weather causing floods, drought, tornadoes, hurricanes and dust storms are frequent occurances throughout the United States.

If the weather requires a direct report, the station weatherperson (or reporter) goes to the scene. The basic procedure:

1). The weatherperson packs two kinds of gear — emergency broadcasting equipment (audiotapes, batteries) and survival supplies (flashlight, first aid kit, blankets, matches, even food) — in the mobile unit.

2). The weatherperson drives to the location and sets up the headquarters at an affiliated station, if there is one.

3). The weatherperson observes conditions, checks with the local weather experts, and gets on-the-scene interviews.

4). The weatherperson telephones reports to the home station at predetermined times unless an important story breaks. The reports are recorded by the engineer on duty in the control room, or by the news director.

Gathering information can be hazardous work. Porter Randall, veteran KFJZ (Fort Worth) newsman, gave this description of a hurricane that ravaged the Texas coast. Whether the hurricane is Cindy, described here, Beulah (1967) or Celia (1970), the characteristics are similar. Randall and Gene Duncan of KOLE, Port Arthur, Texas, attempted to reach High Island during the height of the storm:

> The highway from this little town to High Island on the coast was — as we had been warned — impassable. And yet, somehow we got through. We maneuvered the car around the bodies of cattle that had died — drowned — in the storm. Great piles of brush had blown onto the roadway. The most pitiful thing was the birds. I saw thousands of dead ones. Others — still alive — would try to get out of the way of the car, but couldn't. Maybe they were halfdrowned — or maybe they couldn't fly in that screaming wind — but anyway our wheels have crushed dozens of them; perhaps hundreds. There was not any way we could miss them.
>
> At High Island, on the coast, only about six people had remained. We were the only reporters on the spot. No one else had been able to get through. . . .
>
> High Island was a nightmare. Its fishing vessels had been carried up into the streets by wind and water. Its fishing dock was half destroyed. Stores and houses lay strewn about in pieces; like crushed match-boxes. But the tiny telephone exchange was still standing, and I learned it had just managed to restore service on emergency power.
>
> . . . I managed to get through two reports to KFJZ from High Island, and then I called A.P., the U.P.I., and finally the weather bureau at the Jefferson County Airport.[19]

Both novice reporters and veterans have sometimes gained local or national prominence by being on the scene when a hurricane struck.

In modern radio, weather information may be produced as on-the-spot coverage by two reporters from local stations. As with the hurricane disaster, coverage of the Alaskan earthquake of March 27, 1964 also illustrated how radio stations and wire services cooperate with each other. The owner of Radio Station KBVU, Bellevue, Washington, was talking to his brother in Anchorage when he heard his brother shout: "My God, we're having an earthquake!" The telephone went dead. The station owner quickly relayed his brother's words to The Associated Press in Seattle. This was the first report of the great, widespread disaster. At least 50 newspaper and broadcast members combined to help report that story.[20] Reporting natural disasters is another dimension of the news. Great personal risk to newspeople is often involved. Foresight, daring and ingeunity are combined with succinct reporting ability.

Feature Programs

Informational, and some entertainment programs, may examine a subject in depth. There are several ways to do this. Talks, interviews, discussions and documentaries are the most commonly used methods. Programs derived from these methods may be of interest to the public generally or to specific audiences such as women, farmers, children or other groups. Broadly speaking, a talk involves one person, an interview two or more, and a discussion three or more. The content of a talk focuses on the beliefs of a single person such as a politician making a speech or a teacher giving a lecture. The interview is usually a study of the interviewee's knowledge, attitudes or personality. The discussion explores a subject ostensibly from many points of view. The documentary is a collection of these techniques assembled or edited by an outside party so as to express a certain point of view on a particular topic. Often the editor of a documentary assembles non-fictional or actuality materials as though they were fiction; that is, in the classic pattern of a beginning, middle and end. An individual (or group) has a problem, he seeks a solution, he does (or does not) solve it, he looks at the prospects for the future. The feature or news-in-depth type of programming has become increasingly popular during recent years. Talks, interviews and discussions are rather inexpensive. The documentary may vary greatly in cost, from a simple local program to a complex study of a world crisis.

The Talk. Speeches, commentaries, editorials and lectures are among the principal talk programs. The prime example of a talk program is introduced by the famous line, "Ladies and Gentlemen, the President of the United States." Then, for the next several minutes the President, alone, talks about issues of national significance. Such talks received national acclaim during the 1930's when President Franklin Delano Roosevelt had a series of warm, intimate conversations with the public concerning the complex problems of the Depression. These effective talks were termed "Fireside Chats." Perhaps the longest running "talk" program on radio is *The World Tomorrow*, which began in 1934 by pioneer broadcaster Herbert W. Armstrong. In many instances the talent produces the programs, and the engineer on duty gives the talent basic cues. If a greater degree of perfection is desired, the talent will probably have someone in the control room listening critically and functioning as a producer.

Politicians frequently use a campaign aide as producer. The political speech should be written and delivered with great care, concentrating on a vocabulary that is easy to understand and on conversational delivery that makes the most of simple, direct sentences. Many newspapermen record commentaries for the broadcasting media. In the early days of radio some newsmen won international fame by broadcasting their opinions to the world. The commentator is often his own producer-director and controls the entire program. He may seek outside help during the initial broadcasts so that he can make the transition from writing for print media to writing for broadcasting media more rapidly. On some occasions the commentator will simultaneously record a video tape for television and an audio track for radio. Editorials reflect the station's viewpoint and are usually no more than five minutes in length. The news director usually is the producer, although higher station executives sometimes assume that responsibility. Because of the fairness doctrine issued by the Federal Communications Commission, stations are supposed to seek and encourage opposing points of view. Sometimes an opposing view is presented in person, other times through letters read over the air. The basic procedure:

1). The producer files a request for air time with the station. A special form is provided for political candidates. It states that the candidate is legally qualified and that he or his representative will appear on the program. It designates other details about the broadcast such as payment, length, frequency and time. The station may require a statement releasing it from liability for remarks made by a political candidate.

2). The producer must arrange to have the script, records or transcriptions of the proposed broadcast ready for review by the station prior to air time. The station's program director will call attention to material that cannot be broadcast legally: obscene, indecent or profane language, language that advocates the violent overthrow of the Government, that incites to riot, that is libelous or slanderous. The producer can then expect the program to be broadcast in accordance with all aspects of the equal treatment of candidates regarding rates, sponsorship and announcements.

3). If the broadcast originates at the station, a director will probably be assigned. He or she may be the engineer on duty. In any event, the director makes the candidate or speaker comfortable in the studio, and follows standard directing procedure. The director may wish to have a read-through rehearsal; however, for simple talk programs this is seldom done.

The lecture is usually an educational program. A producer and/or a director are needed. For such programs the educational institution may provide both of them. Programs involving direct instruction are broadcast over educational radio stations almost exclusively. These stations provide staff members who assist the teacher in designing the lecture series. The producer may also direct the program and assume full responsibility for the production. He or she coordinates the broadcast schedule with the administrations of the schools using the programs, and will suggest various production aids that may improve the lectures. A teacher's personal approach to teaching must, of course, be respected; but the producer-director should seek ways to skillfully enhance the studio presentation. The basic procedure:

1). A producer-director is assigned to the series by the program director.

2). The producer-director schedules a conference with the teacher and with an administrator who coordinates the program on behalf of the school systems. Sometimes the producer-director must coordinate the program directly with the schools involved, which can be a very difficult and time-consuming task. More often, scheduling problems are handled at the highest administrative level so that uniformity can be assured. School supervisors and the teacher outline what must be covered, and the teacher develops it in detail. The producer-director suggests how the teacher's objectives might be more beneficially fulfilled using radio. He or she assembles all sound and music effects which the teacher needs.

3). The producer-director meets the teacher in the studio for a rehearsal that resembles the complex procedure of a drama: read through, on-mike rehearsal, dress rehearsal and performance. He or she will probably have a complete staff. The teacher reads through the script and the director times it, including ad-lib remarks and sound effects. Educational programs often involve large groups, especially children. The director and teacher may have difficulty in getting participants to speak naturally on microphone. Children are very good as a rule, but adults are often artificial. A large group also increases the possibility of studio noise, and injects the danger of miscuing because of inattention. Explicit, polite instructions are among the director's more helpful tools. Another problem may be condensing the teacher's vast amount of material into the length of the program.

4). During the on-mike rehearsals, the director tries to correct any problems he or she might have on the air. Can everyone see the director? Will the teacher need a glass of water? No detail is too small. Hand signals are reviewed, levels are checked. Basic instructions are thoroughly discussed several times because non-professionals (children, guests) tend to become nervous and confused.

5). During the performance the director concentrates on encouraging and reassuring the teacher and the guests that the program is going well. This heightens everyone's spirits: if the talent enjoys the program, the listeners will.

6). After the performance, the director praises everyone, even though perfection is seldom obtained; an atmosphere of good will should be preserved for all succeeding broadcasts. As the teacher and director become better acquainted, they depend upon each other in numerous minor ways that strengthen the program.

The Interview. The producer-director of an interview must decide upon a subject, obtain a guest to interview, schedule a production date and work out the details of the program. He or she can begin with a topic or an interesting person. For example, if the community has a campaign for safe driving, the police chief may be the natural person to interview. Popular today is the interview conducted initially by a radio host who then opens the telephone lines for audience participation. In effect, the audience gets a chance to interview the celebrity, a person whom the listeners would not have an opportunity to talk with otherwise. Politicians, film stars, authors and others who want to promote themselves and their books or films are frequent guests. In some cases the producer may host the program.

The producer schedules the program through the news director, if it is part of a news program, or through the program director, if it is a special series. Once the guest and the subject have been determined, the producer plans a list of questions that explore the topic thoroughly and effectively. The questions should blend from one to another without repeating themselves. A good interview takes consummate skill. The interviewer works under the pressure of limited time. He or she must get to the heart of the topic quickly and at the same time must not appear to rush the guest. The producer's responsibilities for an interview differ somewhat from those for a talk:

1). The producer-interviewer visits the guest on several occasions before the program, reads what the guest has written or has had written about the guest, and then prepares a routine or run-down sheet, as described in the chapter on Writing. This is distributed to the director and production staff.

2). On the day of the program the producer-interviewer greets the guest well in advance. He or she assures the guest of the importance of the interview and attempts to make the guest comfortable in a brief warm-up session. The director explains the program procedure to the interviewee so the latter will not become annoyed or confused during the program. The producer-interviewer has the duty of getting the broadcast on and off the air on time.

The Discussion. Technically, discussion programs have many forms — panels, which enable anyone to speak out at any time informally; symposiums, which give everyone an opportunity to make a formal presentation first, then include questions and cross discussion; audience participations, which are basically question and answer situations between the guest and the audience; and forums, which are formal presentations of several points of view. A discussion has two main characteristics: several participants and a sincere desire on the part of all of them to solve or work toward solving a problem. Topics frequently deal with air and water pollution, mass transportation, preservation of the natural environment, racial conflict, school integration, law enforcement and unique local problems. At KQED, San Francisco: "More than 30 local groups and organizations take part, together representing a cross-section of San Francisco's community interests. They produce their own programs, providing costs, talent and format, while KQED broadcasts their productions to the groups' built-in audiences and to the public at large."[21] A debate, to the contrary, is a formal presentation of opposing points of view without attempting to reconcile the opposing sides. Instead, it is an effort to persuade a third party, the listening audience.

The producer's task in the discussion program is to get the right guests together to discuss only those aspects of a given subject which create excitement and enlightenment. Once the producer has an idea for a program, he or she selects a moderator who has insight and knowledge of the subject (or is willing to become informed). The moderator should have an understanding of human beings, an ability to listen attentively and a keen sense of organization. The producer and moderator outline the program. They decide which guests would be most effective. A guest who is responsive, intelligent and willing to speak candidly is rare. The producer and moderator may visit personally each potential member of the discussion group to discover where the individual stands on each issue, and whether he or she will talk about it on the air. Essentially, only those questions where there is disagreement are discussed, and these provide the base for the program outline. The moderator must maintain a neutral position during the program, although he or she may play the devil's advocate if the occasion calls for it.

Guests on discussion programs frequently do not wish to be controversial — to be involved in any situation where they might lose face or suffer embarrassment. The moderator must create an atmosphere that allows the free exchange of ideas, but which also protects the dignity of the participants. The procedure for the discussion is similar to that of the talk and the interview except that its complexity is multiplied by the number of guests:

1). During the program the producer and/or moderator keeps the discussion moving at a lively pace by asking the most controversial questions first, by including all of the guests in the conversation, and by striving toward greater understanding for the listening audience. Four guests with voices that are easy to distinguish are about maximum for radio.

2). In the control room the director gives the usual signals, knowing that it is more difficult to stop a stimulating discussion than an interview with a single person. At a prearranged time, perhaps two or three minutes before the end of the program, the director will expect the producer-moderator to end the discussion and to read a prepared, pre-timed summary or to ad-lib one that will fit the time requirement. Well-prepared openings, closings and summaries add clarity and smoothness to the discussion program.

The Documentary. There are two basic types of documentaries: the actuality program, with on-the-spot reports involving real people and real events, and the dramatized or semi-documentary, which uses actors to recreate a real happening. The producer and director have a complex responsibility resembling that of the radio drama.

"With the advent of television, radio's function altered so drastically that the latter lost much of its significance as a documentary instrument. While sporadic individual efforts in a documentary style are still made by local stations, it is fair to observe that one of the central conditions we have established for documentary — to create a massive impact upon great audiences — has ceased, in radio, to exist."²² Nevertheless, the artistic and informational impact of the documentary and its occasional production in many stations make it worth-while examining. Lyn Salerno, of KPRC, Houston, sees a resurgence of the documentary in the seventies: "Documentaries are becoming more and more popular today and are, at times, some of the most controversial programs on the air." In the early 1970's Public Affairs Director Frank Haley of KILT, Houston, developed a series of hour-long documentaries, some with the assistance of student producers studying communications at the University of Houston. Drug addiction, rock stars, and what it is to be an American provided some of the content. The artistic and informational impact of the documentary and its occasional production in many stations make it worth-while examining.

The producer sees a need to explore a certain theme or topic in depth. He or she (or the writer) does extensive research, organizes a script outline, arranges a budget and obtains clearances, as necessary. Next the producer assembles a production unit consisting of a director, a narrator, an engineer and, depending upon the complexity of the project, other artistic, production and technical personnel. (He or she may do two or three of these jobs himself.) They tape-record the events on location and bring them back to the station for editing. The tape is evaluated and assembled. WBT, Charlotte, for example, has produced a series called *Project 60*. Each hour-long program is a composite of interviews, discussions, comments by individuals and announcer narration concerning such topics as the lost continent of Atlantis, extrasensory perception, and sounds of the city. Numerous local stations have documentaries concerning civic issues, especially around election time. Although all creative radio personnel would like to produce documentaries, the factors of money, time and mass sales appeal discourage most from doing so. The basic producing-directing procedure is essentially the same for all types of stations and subjects:

1). The producer-director drafts an outline of an idea for a program or series. He or she gets approval from the program director to produce it.

2). The producer-director assembles all of the actuality tapes, transcriptions and sound effects that the program will need. This process may take several months. In addition to live taping, he or she may depend on library resources of the station and of national and even international broadcasting organizations. Gathering material may require an extensive amount of preliminary listening as well as a great deal of time clearing copyrights.

3). The director re-records all of the assembled pertinent material on audio tape approximately in the order it will be used on the program. He or she edits and times each segment.

4). Next he or she carefully splices the segments together, checking each one for fidelity, length and relevance to the script.

5). After all of the editing and splicing is done, the director duplicates the "master" or final tape. The duplicate will be played on the air.

International Programs

International radio programming is limited mainly to news events of unusual worldwide concern such as the assassination of President Kennedy or the activities of celebrities like Pope Paul VI, previously mentioned. Exceptional international interest and participation is illustrated in the space missions of the United States, particularly man's first flight to the moon. Apollo 11 attracted over 3,000 journalists, including the writer, who spent much of his time before liftoff to splashdown at the Manned Spacecraft Center of the National Aeronautics and Space Administration (NASA) in Houston, now called the Lyndon B. Johnson Space Center.

The Johnson Space Center is an austere collction of black and white rectangular buildings surrounded by lush green lawns. Several of the 27 major structures encircle a rocky pond where brown ducks find sanctuary, and several overlook a sprawling residential area called Clear Lake City. The press was located in the main public auditorium and exhibit hall known as "Building 1." The auditorium held the last press conference for Apollo 11 Astronauts Neil Armstrong, Edwin Aldrin, Jr. and Michael Collins. The surrounding exhibit area was cleared for 150 tables with four to six chairs at each, 40 individual studios for radio and TV, video monitors and 33 Western Union Telex machines that sent messages throughout the world. A typical domestic radio station newsman-producer placed a remote console on top of a table and broadcast from there. Westinghouse Broadcasting and KPRC Radio, Houston, pitched tents over their tables to screen out extraneous noise.

International broadcasting — the most comprehensive to date — was done principally from 5 x 7 foot studios which ran along one side of the building. A typical studio contained an audio control unit, a microphone, two headsets, a telephone and a TV monitor. The standard interior included an equipment shelf, a foam rubber mat on the floor, a velveteen drape over the doorway, two chairs and an ashtray. Each studio was identified by country and station call letters.

Southwestern Bell Telephone Company had a message desk. In service areas behind the auditorium were the network TV pool, rotated to CBS this time, an ABC office and studio, small NBC and CBS offices (CBS, NBC, AP, UPI and local newspapers maintained newsrooms across the highway from NASA), additional tables and facilities for Voice of America which broadcast in 11 languages.

Outside, three support vans were for the European Broadcasting Union, the International Pool and a bus for weary technicians and international personnel. The EBU van was divided into three sections: a switching area, an AT&T order desk and the international line terminals. CBS provided about 40 employees and the international group about 100. AT&T had four men on duty receiving messages confirming broadcast times worldwide. Inasmuch as the Atlantic satellite was not working properly, video signals were fed from Houston to New York to Oakland, California to the Pacific satellite to Tokyo to an Indian Ocean satellite to Goonhilly, England to Brussels for EBU distribution. Asian distribution was from Tokyo. Audio signals were routed in the same way or via cable/microwave directly to England. In the second trailer were offices for the International Pool, including guide tracks (audio cues) in Japanese and English. Here producers planned coverage and exchanged messages. The third unit contained direct Telex communications with Geneva where EBU programs were coordinated.

The four principal reasons radio producers cited for being in Houston for Apollo 11 were involvement, association, international interest and competition. "Listeners want involvement in a more direct personal way with your emotions. You feel as if you are part of the crew. You want a material proximity. You want to be near somebody near to them. Every step you can meet somebody who knows something. Even to get a can of Heinz soup out of a machine, there was an astronaut telling you how it works," said Danilo Colombo, RAI Italian Radio. "Our company is one of the largest in South America," William Restrapo, Todelar, Columbian Radio, said ."We have one of the biggest news teams. We can go anywhere."[23]

The Johnson Space Center provided continuous air-to-ground audio "feed" within Building 1, and KMSC (Clear Lake City) broadcast this feed in its entirety, its news staff providing interpretation and significant summaries periodically. According to Gordon Bassham, KMSC news anchorman, "John" 'Shorty' Powers, recognizing a need for comprehensive reporting of space flights, assembled a team of veteran newsmen, technical writers and producers whose 'mission' was the development of a format of space news coverage that was technical enough not to alienate those familiar with the intricacies of space flight, yet comprehensive enough to be easily understood by the non-space-oriented listener." Bassham outlines his radio procedures, which were typical of those used by many news producer-directors:

1). Research. Material includes official NASA documents and publications as well as material distributed by manufacturers of equipment and hardware.

2). Formulation of coverage format.

3). Setting up of remote equipment including telephone lines, remote console, microphones and reel-to-reel and/or cartridge tape machines.

4). Pre-arranged out-cues that were part of but separate from the format.

5). Coverage of in-flight change of shift press briefings indicating contingency planning and last minute developments.

6). Breakdown remote site. This follows the post mission press conference held after splashdown or in the case of Apollo 11, 12 and 14 after the crewmen were released from their quarantine at the MSC Lunar Receiving Laboratory.

COMMERCIALS AND ANNOUNCEMENTS

Radio today caters to the local community. According to FCC radio financial figures, advertisers spent over $1.5 billion on radio in 1972. Local advertising was again by far the biggest money source, contributing $1.098 billion (up 15.1%). Network advertising accounted for only $65 million (up 18%). National and regional spot sales were up slightly (1.7%) over 1971, with a total of $384.3 million. Radio is largely a daytime medium, with prime time being "drive time" when motorists are driving to and from work. "Radio's audience is bigger than television's throughout the entire day — television is bigger only after approximately 6 p.m." During the hours of 10 a.m. to 3 p.m. men represent more than 43% of the adult audience.[24] "...65% of our gross is built on a seven-hour period, between 6:30 and 1:30," Daytime AM-FM Station owner Robert T. Olson, WMPL, Hancock, told small market radio station managers at the NAB Convention in 1971. "We have an all-news and information talk format at WMPL in Hancock, Michigan, which has enabled us to bill $300,000 in our first full year of operation in a city of 5,000 people."[25] In order to make such sales possible, the production of commercials and public service announcements thrives at local radio stations.

Stations like those mentioned earlier seeking young listeners identifying with new and outrageous musical programming changed their commercials. Low key delivery, comparative absence of station and on-air promotions, and fewer commercials are characteristic. The ideal commercial load for a free form FM station is 8 minutes maximum per hour; this compares with 16-18 commercial minutes per hour on AM stations.

The creative genius of people in advertising is sometimes overlooked. Poetry, original music, original sound effects, comedy, attention-getting devices and audience research are some of the ways advertisers stimulate listeners to purchase products and services. Commercials and some promotional spots are the most expensive moments on the air. Many sponsors believe that radio can give a product more exposure than any other medium for each dollar invested. Because of the high investment in radio advertising, many employed in radio spend part of their time producing and directing commercials. The business is so lucrative and complex that several major manufacturers, department stores, and some non-profit organizations have their own promotion departments which design commercials and public service announcements for all media. Radio stations and advertising agencies either produce their own commercials or hire a production company to do them.

Station Production. Many local sponsors work directly with the station. As a result the station makes money on selling the air time and on producing the commercials. In many instances two of the station's personnel

— the operations manager and the sales director, for example — might spend a couple of hours in the evening after their daytime-only station goes off the air to produce a one-minute commercial. They might read all the roles themselves, operate their own console, and change the copy as they go along. Procedures differ, of course, for different stations:

1). Unless a sponsor dictates what his commercial shall include, the salesman and a continuity writer assume the chief responsibility for producing the commercial. If a sponsor wishes to put on an entire campaign or several different commercials involving a great deal of production work, the campaign may go through the several steps typical of a major radio program, beginning with an initial conference examining the product or service from every point of view.

2). Once the copy is written, it is sent to the program director who assigns it to someone on the production staff, probably an announcer. After his board shift is over, the announcer finds production orders accompanied by sales copy in a studio available for the production of commercials. One radio station, used as an example here, has two production studios. Studio A is used for most everyday production. Studio B — the larger of the two — is the commercial production room with an array of microphones, three turntables, two tape recorders, a disc recorder, a record library and recorded sound effects. The station may have over 1,000 sound effects on file in addition to many commercial lead-ins and jingles. All production copy is initially recorded on tape. This work is done by the program director and the five station announcers. (At some stations audition copy is written, produced on tape and then played for a prospective client over the telephone. If the client buys the spot, it is then placed on the disc.) Because of the constant turnover in announcements, the production work is never finished.

3). Radio announcers are generally familiar with editing techniques and with unique sounds which will draw and hold the attention of listeners. The announcer reads and records the copy as it is written, integrating the sound and music that he or she believes will be effective. Recorded music typically is used. Live music is easier to pace and usually results in better spotting and more exact duration. Small combos and vocal groups can be hired. Good effects are achieved by such instruments as guitars, drums or even slide whistles. Electronic filters, reverberation synthesizers and delayed impulse echo equipment are useful devices. Experimentation pays.

4). As a final step the announcer-producer duplicates the completed audio tape of the commercial on a cartridge and puts it in master control. The production order is marked complete.

Although the process is not easy, many commercials and announcements are frequently done in a day. One station, for example, tries to give sponsors "same day" service, that is, it broadcasts the commercial the same day the order comes in! The writer has to constantly dream up ways of selling products over radio. The production people have to find new ways — attention getters or "gimmicks" — that will intrigue listeners. The problem is complicated further by a desire on the part of the radio station and the sponsor to have the listener indicate that the commercial was heard on radio, as described in the section on "feedback" in Chapter 4.

Advertising Agencies. An advertising agency is a business consisting of specialists who create and plan a company's entire marketing program. Nearly all national advertising (that is, other than retail) in newspapers, magazines, outdoor displays and broadcasting media is placed through advertising agencies. Radio stations in major markets like Washington, D.C., do not as a rule produce their own commercials. They receive them from agencies. Agencies also place most of the advertising in the professional, technical and business publications. An agency handles a number of accounts. Its function is to select, recommend and contract those it feels are best-suited to advertise a client's product or service. The radio and television department of an agency is one of its exciting and challenging divisions, because of the amount of money involved and the skill, judgment and taste entailed in selecting the radio and television programs and for producing the commercials. Radio and television production calls for a high degree of talent and experience and the ability to work long hours under pressure.

Joel Raphaelson, one of the three creative people reporting directly to David Ogilvy, of Ogilvy & Mather, Inc., makes these comments and observations about radio advertising and commercials in a 1970 memorandum:

Brand identification is more difficult in radio than in other media. Most radio commercials are deficient in brand identification. The brand name must be repeated often and clearly. It helps to *spell* the name.

Radio commercials are *heard* — not seen. In developing radio copy, never judge a commercial by reading it silently to yourself. *Listen* to it. Spoken copy should be colloquial. Copy that *reads* well will often *sound* stiff and unnatural.

Although radio is not a visual medium, the best people writing for it think visually. The mind's eye can go anywhere. You can produce a Cecil B. DeMille extravaganza for little more than the cost of stand-up announcer. Good diction is vital — particularly in jingles. Many radio commercials simply cannot be understood.

Repeat important points. The ear alone cannot grasp as much as the eye alone — and not nearly as much as eye and ear together (television). You should *repeat* whatever you want people to remember.

Radio is the most flexible of all media. You can do anything. You can go anywhere. You can jump around in time and in place to your heart's content. Few writers use the medium fully.

Too many radio commercials try to be funny — and fail. Avoid a joke at the end of a radio commercial. The joke tends to obliterate brand identification. Don't write too many words — no more than 140 for a straight announcement in a minute. You can squeeze more in but you will force the announcer to go at an unnatural pace, faster than the listener can grasp.

Don't relegate radio to your most junior writers. Since the advent of television this has been the practice in agencies. It accounts for the low quality of so many radio commercials.[26]

If an advertising agency has studios, they are similar to those at a radio station, and the procedure for producing the spot is basically the same. Agencies send cartridges, tapes and discs to the station after the agencies have purchased air time through the station's sales department.

Agency Production. Small agencies consisting of two or three account executives or salesmen do not have studios. The account executive functioning as a radio producer-director coordinates the production of a commercial or public service announcement.

1). The account executive convinces the client to advertise through radio because it is the best medium to buy for the client.

2). The account executive writes the copy, usually a 20, 30 or 60 second "spot" announcement.

3). The account executive hires an announcer to record the copy on audiotape at a small studio which is leased for an hour or so specifically for that purpose. At the studio an engineer records the announcement exactly as the account executive dictates. The account executive decides when the spot is air quality.

4). The account executive delivers the taped commercial to the radio station, hoping that within a few days there will be sufficient new business generated for the client that the agency will be asked to produce more radio commercials.

SUMMARY

Producing and directing radio programs have changed greatly since the advent of television. The producer and director functions have been absorbed by individual members of the radio team: the program director, the news director, the talent, the continuity writer and other production people. Nevertheless, producing and directing will always be a vital function of a radio station. Someone has to do it. There would be no radio otherwise.

The emphasis in this chapter has been purposefully oriented to local station operation because the bulk of the opportunities in radio are on the local level. A clear understanding of what a station expects of its programming personnel, as delineated in Chapter 4, should be of benefit to the aspiring radio employee. Good radio is more than just a voice over the airwaves. It requires skill, artistry, and knowledge of the technical aspects of the medium, of writing, of production, of performing. It is also a complex process of knowing people — what they like to hear and what they will buy. A radio producer and director or one who serves these functions must have an intimate knowledge of all of these aspects of the radio business, if he or she hopes to be successful.

ADDITIONAL DIRECTING TECHNIQUES AND VOCABULARY

Commercials. A director often records commercials and promotional spot announcements at a higher volume than the programs; as a result, the commercials receive greater prominence while they are on the air. Fewer radio spots are merely read today; most require production.

Cues. A director calls cues aloud when working in the control room so that technicians there can hear them. The director may use the expression "from the top," which means from the beginning of the script. As a psychological device, some directors smile prior to cueing, and periodically signal "on-the-nose" and/or "thumb-forefinger circle" to assure talent that the program is on time and/or going well.

Gain. Most programming can be properly recorded if the needle on the volume unit meter on the console remains in the black. Louder, more forceful sound is obtained when it "peaks" in the red. A director should watch the meter, for it is the only accurate gauge. A control room monitor can be deceptive at times.

Microphones. A director should not encourage performers to touch microphones. A director should explain the beam pattern to the talent. Maximum "presence" and clarity are established when the talent speaks directly into the beam in a normal tone. Voices positioned at various distances from the beam give the production "perspective." Performers should never be allowed to yell, tap or purposefully blow into a microphone to test it. Microphones in auditoriums should be placed so as not to detract aesthetically from a concert or recital.

Mixing. A director may find taping the music, sound and voices separately is desirable, if he or she can combine them more easily by electronic than by live means. A director should remember that the qualities of a soft voice can be easily amplified without strain on the performer. "Dubbing" is the process of filling in a missing segment on a tape or of duplicating it.

Music. For bridges and transitions, a director generally looks for passages that are not easily recognized. He or she allows about 10 seconds to establish a musical segment. "Fades" should occur at the end of musical phrases. Decreasing volume imperceptibly is referred to as a "sneak out."

A "segue" is usually a transition from one musical selection to another. A "stinger" or "stab" is a brief, intense note(s) inserted for emphasis. If a director hopes to have amateurs sound like professional performers, he or she tapes them utilizing every electronic aid available.

Noise. A director should warn performers about script rattle. A disc jockey "wows" a record when he prematurely increases its volume before it is up to proper speed. Microphones used outside should be covered with a moderately light cloth to avoid unwanted noise.

Script Marking. A radio script can be marked in any manner that is meaningful to the director, but clear notations are essential because there is little time to figure them out during the performance.

Sound Effects. To deaden a room, a director may surround the talent with a "gobo," a two-fold covered with heavy material such as velvet. When additional dimension is needed in a sequence, the director uses reverberation or filter. Slight reverberation or filter is sufficient, otherwise it is difficult to understand the talent. A "sound truck" is a movable bench containing turntables and storage space for live sound effects. A simultaneous fade out of one element and fade in of another is a "crossfade."

Voices. The closer a performer is to a microphone, the softer he or she should speak and the more intimate the sound becomes. Words with plosive sounds should be spoken gently, if a "pop" is to be avoided.

NOTES

Grateful acknowledgements for revisions in this chapter are made to my former students who are now in commercial broadcasting: Gordon Bassham, KXYZ News; Pat Fant, Music Director, KLOL; Lyn Salerno, Traffic Department, KPRC; Steve Barcus, who assists Gene Elston; Producers Terry Jastrow, of ABC Sports, and John Tracy, of CBS, for my 1973 tour of network facilities in New York. My appreciation is also extended to Michael G. Turner, managing director, Ogilvy & Mather, Inc.

[1] Robert R. Pauley, " 'Creativity', Not 'Conformity', Radio Necessary Says Pauley," *Radio-Television Daily*, Vol. 96, No. 54 (March 22, 1965), p. 23.

[2] Roger L. Cole, "European Radio Drama Still Lives," *NAEB Journal*, Vol. 24, No. 1 (January-February 1965), pp. 3-7. Martyn A. Bond, "Radio Drama on North German Radio and the BBC: 1945 to 1965," *Journal of Broadcasting*, Vol. 17, No. 4 (Fall 1973), pp. 475-492.

[3] Erik Barnouw, *Handbook of Radio Production* (Boston: D. C. Heath and Company, 1949), p. 9. Mutual Broadcasting System's Black Network planned a soap opera for 1974.

[4] *Broadcasting*, December 17, 1973, p. 50. See also Michael Shain, "Now, we're into music . . . it's a family affair," *Broadcasting*, December 27, 1971/January 3, 1972, p. 31-48.

[5] The FCC has not set a standard for FM quadraphonic broadcasting. In the matrix system four signals are picked up, encoded into two, and decoded back to four signals at the receiver. The discrete method is a 'pure' four-channel system. See "Problems peculiar to FM broadcasting," *Broadcasting*, September 24, 1973, p. 33.

[6] J. Leonard Reinsch and Elmo I. Ellis, *Radio Station Management* (New York: Harper & Row, Publishers, 1960), p. 126.

[7] Shain, Michael. "There's still magic in the middle of the radio road,' *Broadcasting*, June 12, 1972, pp. 37-38.

[8] "Growth Market in black radio," *Broadcasting*, January 24, 1972, p. 17. Black stations include WEBB (AM), Baltimore; WJBE (AM), Knoxville; WRDW (AM), Augusta; KWK (AM), St. Louis; WCHB (AM), Inkster, Mich.; WEUP (AM), Huntsville, Ala.; KPRS (AM), Kansas City, Mo.; WGPR (FM), Detroit; WTLC (FM), Indianapolis; WMPP (AM), Chicago Heights; WORV (AM), Hattiesburg, Miss.; WWWS (FM), Saginaw; WVOE (AM), Chadbourn, N.C.; WSOK (AM), Savannah; KOWH-FM, Omaha; and WBLK-FM, Buffalo.

[9] At this writing, station using the free form format are KLOL, Houston; KFML, Denver; KSAN, San Francisco; WABX, Detroit; KZEL, Eugene, Oregon; WMMR, Philadelphia; KINK, Portland; KADI, St. Louis; WNCR, Cleveland; KFIG, Fresno; KPRI, San Diego; KPPC, Los Angeles; CHUM, Toronto.

[10] "WNUS Expands to FM, 24-Hour, 'All-News'," *Radio-Television Daily*, Vol. 96, No. 54 (March 22, 1965), p. 4.

[11] CBS Radio Network news services include in 1973 *Weekend Specials, All-Night News, Early Morning Sports, Spectrum* (commentaries), and news feeds, in addition to CBS *News-on-the-Hour*.

[12] Interviews with Joe Long, Vice President of News, The McLendon Stations, and News Director for KLIF, Fort Worth; and with Roy Eaton, News Director, and Bruce Neal, Assistant News Director, KXOL, Fort Worth.

[13] KLIF fed 75 different radio stations in addition to Radio France, the BBC, and the Voice of America. Roy Eaton estimates that KXOL fed over 100 stations.

[14] Interview with Joe Long.

[15] This "run down" happens to be for an educational radio station, but it serves equally well as an example of a segmented format for a commercial broadcast. *Communique 30 — The News at Ten* was developed by Bill Jennings, Producer, and Richard Buddine, News Director for WUNC radio, University of North Carolina at Chapel Hill.

[16] "Here and There," NAEB *Newsletter*, Vol. 30, No. 4 (April, 1965), p. 4.

[17] From a speech by Bill Currie, Radio and Television Sports Director, WSOC, Charlotte, at the University of North Carolina, June 16, 1965.

[18] The Houston Astros played the Philadelphia Phillies in a night game, at 8:00 C.D.T., on April 12, 1965. The Phillies won the game 2 to 0.

[19] Porter Randall, My Date with Cindy, Radio Station KXYZ (Ft. Worth: KXYZ, 1963), pp. 5-6. Several radio stations issue "Hurricane Tracking Charts" in coastal areas where hurricanes are prevalent.

[20] *Earthquake in Alaska*, The Associate Press (New York: The Associate Press,

1964).

[21] Bernard Mayes, "Tribal Radio in San Francisco," *Educational Broadcasting Review*, Vol. 5, No. 5 (October 1971), pp. 3-6. A similar use of facilities is provided by the BBC according to Winifred Von Thomas, in discussion on KUHF (FM), University of Houston, on January 16, 1974.

[22] A. William Bluem, *Documentary in American Television* (New York: Hastings House, Publishers, 1965), pp. 71-72.

[23] Interviewed at the Manned Spacecraft Center, Houston, July, 1969.

[24] *CBS Radio Network Affiliate Research Promotion Reference Guide*, May, 1973, p. 16.

[25] Robert T. Olson, "Programming News for Profit," Small Market Radio Session, National Association of Broadcasters Convention, Chicago, March 31, 1971.

[26] Ogilvy & Mather has done extensive research in advertising for television and newspapers. In anticipation of similar research for radio, these notes are drawn from a memorandum dated December 7, 1970, indicating suppositions by its writer, Joel Raphaelson.

BIBLIOGRAPHY

Chester, Giraud, Garnet R. Garrison and Edgar E. Willis, *Television and Radio*. New York: Appleton-Century-Crofts, 1963. Rev. Ed. A comprehensive view of broadcasting, including reference and background material on radio programming.

Fang, Irving E., *Television News*. New York: Hastings House, Publishers, Rev. & Enl. Ed., 1972. Includes a chapter on radio news and much practical material on preparing broadcast news programs.

———, *Television/Radio News Workbook*. New York: Hastings House, Publishers, 1974.

Hilliard, Robert L., *Writing for Television and Radio*. New York: Hastings House, Publishers, Inc., Second Ed., Rev., 1967. Analyses and examples of non-dramatic radio scripts illustrate the relationship of writing to producing and directing.

Jackson, Allan, "You Have to Write, Too!" New York: CBS Radio Network. A concise, brief statement about writing news programs.

Johnson, Joseph S. and Kenneth K. Jones, *Modern Radio Station Practices* (Belmont, California: Wadsworth Publishing Co., Inc., 1972). Up-to-date information on operations of representative radio stations, with basic radio techniques.

McCoy, John E. (ed.), *Storer Broadcasting Company Program Manual*. Storer Broadcasting Company, 1960. Some legal considerations and precautions the company takes in programming for the media.

Nisbett, Alec, *The Technique of the Sound Studio*. New York: Hastings House, Publishers, 3rd Ed., Rev. & Enl., 1972. The use of sound as a medium of expression in addition to technical information.

Oringel, Robert S., *Audio Control Handbook*. New York: Hastings House, Publishers, 4th Ed., Rev. and Reset, 1972. An introductory text filled with clear illustrations and explanations of audio facilities and procedures.

Skinner, George, *The Nuts and Bolts of Radio*. New York: The Katz Agency, Inc., 1959. Top-tune radio from an agency viewpoint.

Willis, Edgar E., *A Radio Director's Manual*. Ann Arbor: Ann Arbor Publishers, 1961. A collection of exercises that illustrate technical and artistic problems in production.

APPENDIX
TO CHAPTER 6

TO: Those Concerned   September 23, 1965

FROM: Russ Tornabene   MEMO #2 Pope Paul VI Radio
                              Coverage

This second memo to all interested parties of radio pool operations of Pope Paul's visit to this country will recap all planning to this date.

The pool will consist of the following members:

ABC—Dick Dressel, 39 W. 66th St. SU 7-5000
CBS—Sheldon Hoffman, 524 W. 57th St. 765-4321
WCBS—Marvin Friedman, 51 W. 52nd St., 765-4321
NBC—Jim Holton, 30 Rockefeller Plaza, CI 7-8300
MUTUAL—Jack Allen, 135 W. 50th St., LT 1-6100
WOR—Les Smith, 1440 Broadway, LO 4-8000
WNYC—Allen Levin, 2500 Municipal Building, 566-2283
WMCA—Barrie Beere, 415 Madison Ave., MU 8-5700
WINS—Stan Brooks, 19th Floor, 90 Park Ave. (39-40th St.), 867-5100
UPI AUDIO—Scott Peters, 220 E. 42nd St. Room 1216, TN 7-3995
RPI—Bill Scott, 604 5th Avenue, LT 1-6444
WBNX—C. Carroll Larkin, 801 2nd Avenue, 889-6880
WRUL—(RADIO N.Y.) Mitchell Krauss, 4 W 58th St., PL 2-3322
WABC—Robert Kimmel, 1926 Broadway, SU 7-5000
RADIO PULSEBEAT NEWS—Jay Levy, 340 E. 34th St., 686-6850
WNEW—Gerald Graham, 565 Fifth Avenue, YU 6-7000
USIA—Robert Rudine, 205 W. 57th St., 971-5641
WADO—Sydney Kavaleer, 205 E 42nd St. LE 2-9266

Events will be divided into two main areas: United Nations and outside the United Nations. United Nations facilities for unilateral feeds will be handled by Josef Nichols, PL 4-1234, ext. 2997. Outside United Nations activities will be handled by Papal Visit News Center, 866 United Nations Plaza, Radio and Television Public Relations: Jack Slocum. 421-1494. The news center has copies of the Pope's itinerary.

The pool will operate in the following manner: I, as pool producer, will be in control room 5B, 5th floor, NBC, 30 Rockefeller Plaza. All subscribers listed above will be linked with me by a producer's PL. This PL, which is being ordered by NBC Traffic Department, will have a phone installation, jack, head set and speaker box. This Command PL will be used to provide all cueing information. For example, the pool producer will say on the PL, "Coming up in two minutes from now, a report from Lester Smith in the helicopter, to run about two minutes, ending with the normal end cue. Starting in one minute and thirty seconds . . . starting in one minute, a two minute spot by Lester Smith from the helicopter." and so on, with the countdown going to "five seconds from now." I will then cue Les for a spot which I have pre-arranged with him.

The pool producer invites all members to suggest spots to be done by pool reporters, if at all possible.

The following are the termination points for the PLs:

CBS—Studio 1—524 West 57th St.
WCBS—Control A—51 W. 52nd St.
ABC—Studio 1A—39 W. 66th St.
WABC—Tie in with ABC network.
MUTUAL—Control A—16th Floor, 135 W. 50th St.
WOR—Control 6—1440 Broadway, 24th Floor
WNYC—Master Control—25th Floor, 2500 Municipal Building
WMCA—Master Control—415 Madison Ave.
WINS—19th Floor Broadcast Control, 90 Park Ave. (between 39 and 40 St.)
UPI Audio—Room 1216—220 E. 42nd St.
NBC—Control 5C—30 Rockefeller Plaza
RADIO PULSEBEAT NEWS—1st. Floor Suite 1-H—340 E. 34th St.
WNEW—Control room, 2nd floor, 565 Fifth Ave.
WBNX
RPI—Master Control—604 Fifth Ave.
WADO—Master Control—205 East 42nd St., 8th floor.

FEEDING ARRANGEMENTS

The pool will feed sound from all major events involving the Pope's visit, in the following manner:

Each of the remotes will be fed into NBC control 5B, mixed and sent on a landline to WNYC, which will re-feed the composite programs to all members of the pool listed previously.

WNYC will feed all members by pre-arranged lines. If any member does not have a line from WNYC, he must make this arrangement.

Each member of the pool is reminded that he must order all unilateral lines, though the pool producer is requesting broadcast positions from the Press Office and the Police Department.

Pool reporters will be at the following locations:

1. Helicopter
2. Mobile Unit
3. United Nations entrance
4. United Nations Reception
5. St. Patrick's Cathedral
6. Church of the Holy Family
7. Vatican Pavilion
8. Waldorf Towers for meeting with Johnson

In addition, the feed by the pool to the WNYC line of the Mass at Yankee Stadium will have a running commentary by a priest. This priest will make occasional theological explanations of what is occurring in the Mass. He also will briefly describe the departure of the Pope from the Stadium, so we may have a smooth close-out to this event.

We will offer clean sound, without reporters, from the following locations:

1. Airport Arrival.
2. Statements from White House and Vatican or Diocese spokesmen
   from Waldorf.
3. United Nations speeches and remarks by the Pope in the following manner: The major address to the General Assembly by the
   Pope will be in French. This feed and a simultaneous U.N. provided English translation will be mixed at Pool control and fed
   to the pool. The Pope's remarks to assembled groups in the
   three Council Chambers and to the UN staff later in the General Assembly, to be spoken by him in English, will be fed on
   the pool line.
   NOTE: The pool producer may, for the Pope's remarks other
   than the major address, be able to give very short notice on the
   Command PL. Therefore, it is strongly advised that all producers refer to live television picture to aid in cueing their commentators.
4. Yankee Stadium. The mass, with priest (name to be supplied)
   providing occasional comments.
5. Airport Departure.

POOL REPORTERS

Following is the list of pool reporters and their positions; a
name or two may change before airtime, but the position and the
reporter's instructions will remain the same:

HELICOPTER—Lester Smith. End cue will be "This is Lester
    Smith in the Helicopter."

ST. PATRICK'S CATHEDRAL—Joseph Michaels. End cue will be
    "This is Joseph Michaels at St. Patrick's Cathedral."

UNITED NATIONS: Public entrance of the General Assembly ter-
                 race position—Frank Singeiser. End cue will
                 be "This is Frank Singeiser at the entrance to
                 the United Nations."

                 Exception: Frank also will cover the departure
                 of the Pope from the UN Building, reporting
                 from his terrace position. With the help of a
                 TV monitor, he will describe the departure
                 from the building which will take place at the
                 Delegate's entrance (on the West side of the
                 General Assembly).

                 North Lounge—This is the site of the major
                 reception in the UN.—correspondent to be an-
                 nounced. End cue: "This is_____
                 in the reception at the United Nations."

MOBILE UNIT—   Definitely in the motorcade from the airport
                 in the morning. Hopefully in all movements
                 from one point to another during the day and
                 into the night, ending at the airport for the de-
                 parture—Dallas Townsend. End cue: This is
                 Dallas Townsend in the mobile unit." OR upon

occasion, where it is important editorially, "This is Dallas Townsend at _____ in the mobile unit," to describe for example, "in the heart of Harlem," or "entering the World's Fair Grounds." But in all cases, the last words will be "... mobile unit."

HOLY FAMILY CHURCH —Meeting of Pope with other religious leaders—Harry Hennessy. End cue will be: "This is Harry Hennessy at the Holy Family Church in Manhattan."

WORLD'S FAIR VATICAN PAVILION—Paul Parker. End cue will be: "This is Paul Parker in the Vatican Pavilion at the World's Fair."

IN ALL CASES, AND IN ALL CIRCUMSTANCES, NO POOL CORRESPONDENT SHOULD SPEAK FROM HIS POSITION WHILE HE IS ON THE AIR AND THE POPE OR ANY DIGNITARY IS ABOUT TO SPEAK. WE MUST HAVE CLEAN FEEDS OF ALL STATEMENTS.

The pool producer will have individual PLs to each of the pool correspondents (except the helicopter and the mobile unit, which are RF) for coordination and cueing to air.

REHEARSAL

Because the Pope arrives on Monday morning, the pool rehearsal must be on Sunday, Oct. 3. Therefore, the following facilities must be checked out on Sunday, Oct. 3, in a runthrough scheduled from 11 a.m. to 1 p.m.

Both United Nations pool reporters' position.
Vatican Pavilion.
WNYC feeding line.
Command PL.

It is not absolutely necessary that the assigned reporter be at the rehearsal, but is desired to acquaint him with the position he will work the next day.

We do not expect to rehearse the helicopter, the mobile unit and St. Patrick's and the Holy Family churches.

Would all producers have someone on deck Sunday at 11 a.m. to answer the command PL?

UNITED NATIONS SCHEDULE

Here are the highlights of the announced schedule of events for Pope Paul within the United Nations:

3:20 to 3:30 p.m. Arrival by Canadian Doors, at Public Entrance (north end of building) of the General Assembly. Goes to Visitation Room.

3:30 to 4:00 p.m. Address to the United Nations, in General Assembly, speaking in French.

4:00 to 4:30 p.m. Visit to the three Council Chambers. Speaks briefly in each one.

4:30 to 5:15 p.m. Reception in North Lounge, 400 dignitaries will file past and meet him.

5:15 to 5:45 p.m. Private reception by U Thant on 38th Floor (no coverage of any kind permitted).

5:45 to 6:00 p.m. Remarks to UN staff members in General Assembly.

6:00 p.m. Departure for Church of the Holy Family.

NOTE: All remarks except major address will be in English.

MEETING WITH PRESIDENT JOHNSON

The Pope will leave St. Patrick's after his blessing there (approximately 12:30 p.m.) and go to the Waldorf, entering the Waldorf Hotel via the Towers entrance on 50th Street side. He will be greeted by President Johnson at street level, either outside the doors or immediately inside. They will take the Towers elevator to the 42nd floor. There, they enter the suite of Ambassador Goldberg, going immediately into the den for a private meeting. The length of this meeting is not known at this time, but it is estimated that the entire visit of the Pope, portal to portal, will last about one hour. After the private meeting, the two men will walk from the den into the living room, where they will pose, it is estimated, about five or ten minutes. The Pope probably will be accompanied by the President down the elevator to the spot where the two met, the street level exit of the Tower's side. The radio pool will have a reporter inside the apartment, and be able to describe the arrival in the apartment, and the picture taking. IF the Pope and the President speak in the living room, it will be fed as part of the Pool. If they do not speak, there will be statements by a White House and by a Vatican or Diocese spokesmen, at a larger room, probably on the ground level of the hotel. There, unilateral arrangements must be made for reporters; the pool will feed clean sound of these statements.

POOL-ARRANGED UNILATERAL POSITIONS

The pool was requested by the Papal Visit News Center to coordinate the requests for working positions of networks and stations where there is limited space. These include:

AIRPORT ARRIVAL
ST. PATRICK'S CATHEDRAL (EXTERIOR ONLY)
HOLY FAMILY CHURCH (EXTERIOR ONLY)
YANKEE STADIUM—MEZZANINE BOXES WILL BE ALLOCATED
VATICAN PAVILION (EXTERIOR ONLY)
AIRPORT DEPARTURE

I have received to date (10 a.m. Sept. 23) requests for positions from:

UPI	ABC	MUTUAL
WABC	RADIO NEW YORK (WRUL)	RADIO PULSEBEAT NEWS
CBS	WMCA	WNEW
NBC	WOR	WBNX
RPI	WINS	

Therefore, I have not heard from USIA, WADO, WCBS and WNYC.

Reminder: all members using unilateral positions must order their own lines after allocation of work space is made.

NOTE: The Papal Press office has provided two warnings: mobile units and/or reporters cannot expect to move from one major event to the next. Also, credentials for the airport departure will be different from those used for the airport arrival.

SHARE OF COSTS.

As you have noted, the pool requirements are rather basic and have not entailed great cost. Each network or station providing a correspondent and engineering to the pool will pay for these items. Therefore, the only expected costs to be borne by the pool are the special broadcast lines and PLs from each pool position, and the command PL system. Networks (there are eight) will be charged a greater share of the total cost than local stations (there are eight, with no charge to USIA and WNYC). These divisions will be made by Business Affairs experts.

AIRPORT ARRIVAL AND DEPARTURE

Today I surveyed the airport and have allocated all radio positions. No other radio positions will be set up except those listed below. As you know, the Pope arrives aboard ALITALIA airlines plane at 9:30 a.m. OCT. 4, at the International Arrival Building, and departs from the same spot sometime after 11 p.m. aboard TWA plane.

All radio positions will be on the OBSERVATION DECK as noted on the sketch below and in the attached drawing. Positions running WEST along the Deck from the corner will be even-numbered. Positions running SOUTH will be odd-numbered. Now you may order your own lines, PLs and production facilities from the telephone company.

The numbering was done alphabetically, with Vatican Radio getting a favored position, then three groupings: major networks, network-type services, and local stations. From all positions, it is possible to see the Pope easily. The spaces are easily identifiable: it is the space between the posts of the metal mesh fence on the OBSERVATION DECK. Each space is about eight feet wide. We will be permitted to use about 3-and a half feet deep, or away from the fence.

EARL R. WYNN

*Professor of Radio, Television and Motion Pictures,
University of North Carolina*

• Professor Wynn has taught at the University of North Carolina since 1938, except for the years 1942-1946, when he produced films as a civilian for the United States Army and later as a Lieutenant in the Naval Reserve. During the World War II period he worked with several of the major motion picture companies in Hollywood and had an opportunity to study first hand the educational uses of the mass media by the armed forces.

Professor Wynn received the A.B. degree from Augustana College and the M.A. degree from Northwestern University. Until 1942 he taught in the Department of Dramatic Art at the University of North Carolina and introduced courses in radio into its curriculum. His radio work included the producing and directing of two thirteen-week series of Carolina Playmaker plays for the Mutual Broadcasting System network. In 1945, as a result of Professor Wynn's proposal, the University established a Communication Center for the purposes of bringing together radio, television, motion pictures and photography in order to extend education more effectively to the people of the State. In 1947 he proposed the establishment of a new academic department, that of Radio (subsequently Radio, Television and Motion Pictures), and was appointed the Department's first chairman. He served as Director of the Communication Center and Chairman of the Department of Radio, Television and Motion Pictures until his resignation from administrative duties in 1963. He continues to teach as a full professor. He has taught all phases of the mass media, including speech and performance.

During the formative years of educational television, Professor Wynn acted as a consultant to the Joint Committee on Educational Television and later served several terms as a member of the Board of Directors of the National Association of Educational Broadcasters. In North Carolina he was Executive Director of the Educational Communication Study Commission under Governor Kerr Scott, and Executive Secretary of the Educational Television and Radio Commission under Governor William Umstead. Professor Wynn is an experienced performer. In addition to extensive work in university theatre and summer stock, he has acted major roles in outdoor dramas, *The Lost Colony, Unto These Hills,* and *The Legend of Daniel Boone.* His 40 years of radio performing experience includes the narration, in the 1960's, of nationally distributed recordings by Erwyn Productions, his own company. In addition to his teaching, he produces and performs in television educational program series for the cable and cassette markets through Network Premium Productions.

7

PERFORMING

BY EARL R. WYNN

RADIO communicates by sound alone: the sound of human voice and speech, the sound of music and the sound of sound effects. These create the illusion of reality, fantasy or varying aspects of either for an audience that cannot see. The radio performer may create any character or situation within the scope of the listener's imagination — a mature, resonant voice with careful speech may establish the image of a strong, generous patriarch; a dramatic scene enhanced by the music and sound effects of the orient and in the dialect of the country may produce a mental picture of setting and mores oriental and magnificent. There is no limit to the imagination of people. They are led by voice, sound effects and music to envision what the radio artist creates. This limitless aspect of radio applies to public speeches, commercials, dramas or any broadcast in which the imagination of the listener is free to soar. Radio fertilizes an aspect of humanity far beyond the cold reality of seeing things as they are — the possibility of achieving perfection inevitably present in the human mind.

Opportunities for "unseen" performers today vary from those of a few years past. They occur not only in local, regional and clear channel radio stations and in networks, but often in advertising agencies, religious denominational offices, national public service agencies and in narrated films for television and the general public, or wherever effective voice and speech are needed in the complex of today's interrelated media. Excellence in performance is fundamental no matter who the employer may be or what the performer's title: announcer, disk jockey, on-the-air salesman, news reporter or analyst, interviewer, master of ceremonies, narrator, actor or sports broadcaster.

In all of these positions there is a pattern of vocal excellence required, reflecting a sound mastery of the fundamentals of voice and speech. It is imperative, therefore, that a knowledge of these precedes any discussion of special radio performance techniques.

THE FUNDAMENTALS OF VOICE AND SPEECH

Voice

A full, strong voice is supported by the whole person: the mental emotional attitude toward what is being read or spoken, the entire nervous system, and all the muscles of the body. Voice is not just one part of the performer, or an isolated factor; it represents the entire performer and is the product of the physical self times the mental-emotional self, plus the performance of the organs that produce it. The voice can be made more effective through attention to those muscular functions that cause it to be weak, metallic, harsh, husky, breathy or nasal in quality and to those mental-emotional attitudes of personality which cause it to be raspy, melancholy or cold in tone. The muscles which initiate the tone, the state of mind and feelings which determine the nature of it, and those organs which amplify and color it must function together with precision, accuracy and ease. They are responsible for the basic fundamentals of voice: attitude, breathing, phonation, resonance, and variety.

Attitude. Voice is affected by the nature of thinking and feeling. The performer knows from experience that temporary states of mind, such as excitement, fear or anger, affect the nervous system, the emotions and, consequently, the voice. The nature of one's disposition and attitudes governs tones of voice. Experiences and the intensity of one's reaction to them always register in the quality of a voice. Contrast the voice of the person who is embittered or beaten with the one who assumes a hopeful attitude; the known "crank" with the unassuming person; the conceited man or woman with the humble one. Their attitudes are reflected by their tones of voice. Voice, then, is the channel through which character, attitudes and emotions are communicated.

Breathing. Breath is the control for voice and speech. Its power is located in the central abdominal region — the upper abdomen and the lower chest. Central control in breathing results in clarity of tone and the ability to produce sensitive variations in volume and intensity. There can be no effective speech performance without controlled breathing. This is especially true for radio, since the performer speaks close to the microphone where every nuance of voice and speech is amplified.

Breathing is a basic biological function for sustaining life. Its control is vital for producing voice and continuous speech. Knowledge of how the breathing mechanism functions to produce voice and to support and control it provides a clearer understanding of phonation, resonance and articulation. Although the muscles of the lower rib structure, which encases the lungs and heart, may be responsible for inhalation and exhalation of ordinary breathing, a quick and adequate supply of air for energy and control in continuous speaking is governed by the muscles of the diaphragm and upper abdomen. The diaphragm, the convex structure of muscles and tendons in the concave surface below the lungs, forms a partition between the chest and abdominal cavities. These muscles are attached to the sternum (breast bone), the lower ribs and the spinal column in such a way as to give a forward-diagonal thrust when they are contracted. The muscles of the upper abdomen, primarily responsible for the strength and control of an out-going speech breath, are located in the triangle described by the sternum (as apex) and the right and left lower side rib areas. These muscles must relax as the diaphragm contracts (pulls down) in order to provide for expansion. The intestinal fullness of the abdominal cavity will impede if not obliterate the forward-downward pull of the diaphragm if this forward relaxation of the upper abdomen does not take place.

The spinal column is the only skeletal connection between the bony structure of the upper body and that of the lower. The ability to stand, walk and sit easily and without tension depends upon the weight balance relationship between the upper and lower body as adjusted by the flexible spinal column. *The key to this balance and adjustment is the pelvic basin,* the bony, basin-like structure of the hips. The pelvic basin may tip forward, backward or to the sides. The spinal column and upper body adjust to this "tipping" in order to maintain a balance of weight. When the pelvic basin is tipped to the front, the whole weight of the viscera is thrown forward against the abdominal wall, straining, if not preventing controlled breathing; the natural curve of the spine is also exaggerated in order to maintain balance. When the pelvic basin is tipped toward the back, the muscles of the abdomen become loose and cramped; the spine loses its natural curve, and arches forward into a "C." Good standing and sitting posture for all purposes is dependent upon keeping the pelvic basin at "even keel," the upper body at ease and the shoulders relaxed in a downward position.

Phonation. Vocal tones are initiated in the larynx by the breath stream passing over approximated vocal folds (cords), causing them to vibrate. This process is called phonation. The larynx, in which is located the sound-producing vibrators of the voice, is a skeletal structure of resilient cartilages resting on top of the wind pipe (trachea) and suspended from the base of the tongue. The length and thickness of the vocal folds vary from person to person; in men, they are about an inch long; in women, a little shorter and thinner. These physical differences account in general for variations in pitch level between the sexes. Variations in pitch and loudness while speaking take place within the vocal folds by means of changes in their length, thickness and span of vibration. When the folds lengthen and thin, the pitch rises; when they shorten and thicken, the pitch falls; and when their span of vibration increases or decreases, the volume rises or falls.

In the production of vocal tone, the throat, mouth and nose should be open channels, free of unnecessary tension. The muscles of the throat are often tense in order to communicate intense emotions such as fear, anger, or hate; but the throat must never be closed or squeezed shut. The throat should be open, the muscles responding normally to thoughts and feelings. If all passages are open and free of unnecessary tension and squeezing, the mouth, nose and, particularly, the throat amplify and give emotional meaning to the vocal tone.

Functionally, faulty tones such as huskiness, stridency, hoarseness, breathiness and throatiness are the result of poor breath control, a squeezed throat or both. Controlled breathing and an open, functionally relaxed throat are always essential to effective voice production. In radio, no faulty quality of voice goes unnoticed.

Resonance. Initial vocal tones are weak and colorless. They must be amplified to be heard and given color (quality or timbre) for richness and to communicate emotional meaning. Vocal tone amplification and changes in quality take place within the resonators of the human voice. The process is called resonance.

In the amplification of any initial musical tone, including that of the human voice, there may be two types of resonance: "sounding board" and cavity. A tuning fork held free cannot be heard with ease except at close range. When its stem is touched to a table top, however, the tone may be heard throughout the room; the whole table is set to vibrating in "sympathy" with the exact number of vibrations of the fork. The tone is amplified because the size of the vibrator has been increased. The quality of the amplified tone will change from table to table depending upon the size and composition of the table. This is an example of "sounding board" resonance. The violin is another. When the vibrating tuning fork is held inside one end of an open pipe and the hand cupped over that end, its tone will be amplified and projected through the open end. The encased air column is set to vibrating sympathetically and the concentration resulting from enclosure produces amplification. Again, the quality of the tone will vary from pipe to pipe, depending upon its diameter, length, shape, openings and internal texture. This is an example of cavity resonance. The clarinet is another.

All vibrators, including the human vocal folds, vibrate as a whole and in harmonic segments *ad infinitum.* The vibration of the whole produces the fundamental tone; the segmented vibrations produce harmonics, partials or overtones. Depending upon those factors already mentioned, resonators will select particular overtones for emphasis. Thus, one violin produces a richer tone than another; one clarinet is thinner in tone than another; and one voice is metallic while another is mellow and full.

For cavity resonance, the more open and softer textured the resonators, the greater the emphasis upon the lower, richer overtones (those next in number of vibrations per second to the fundamental); and the smaller and more tense the resonators, the greater the emphasis upon the higher, thinner, less pleasant overtones (those farthest away from the fundamental). Since, in the human voice, tone quality is established primarily in the throat, this principle means that *an open, functionally relaxed, flexible throat will emphasize richer overtones; a tense, squeezed, inflexible throat will emphasize thinner overtones.*

There are three principle cavity resonators of the voice: the throat, the mouth, and the nose. All are located above the vibrators. The mouth is most variable; the nose most invariable. Below the vibrators are the invariable trachea and bronchial tubes, cavity resonators which, according to their size, openness and health, may emphasize certain overtones. Since these are fixed and untrainable, the only control over them is to keep them healthy and free of infection. The bones, cartilages and muscles of the chest, neck and head are "sounding boards" of the human voice. They vibrate in varying degrees during speech and influence both amplification of tone and selection of overtones. They, too, must be kept healthy and free of infection.

The throat must be kept open, free of unnecessary tension, and with sufficient flexibility to respond to any shade or degree of feeling. A healthy throat is capable of responding to any emotion which the performer feels or attitude he possesses. It should lengthen, narrow and change the texture of its muscle walls in response to feelings, but it must never be closed. Just as a muted cornet or reversed megaphone diminishes projection, so does a closed throat.

The sounds "m," "n" and "ng" are resonated in the mouth, nose and bony structure of the head. Adequate resonance of these sounds adds musical body to the spoken word; too much produces nasality; too little, denasality. Balance of nasal-head resonance depends upon a healthy, open nasal passage and a free-functioning soft palate. A lazy soft palate, one which is slow in opening and closing the nasal passage, causes too much nasal resonance or nasality. When the nasal passages are clogged with swelling from a cold, an allergic condition or by growths, the result is too little nasal resonance or denasality.

All vowels and diphthongs are shaped, given their recognized tone quality in the mouth by means of particular sets of jaw, tongue and lip positions. The tone quality of "AH" is different from that of "AW," for instance. For "AH" the jaw is open, the lips are relaxed on the teeth and the tongue is flat and forward. For "AW," on the other hand, the jaw is open, the lips openly rounded and the tongue slightly arched toward the back of the mouth. Accuracy in shaping every vowel and diphthong is vital to correct and precise speech. A regional dialect, for example, is mainly due to incorrect shaping and production of certain vowels and diphthongs. Amplified vocal tone is finally projected to the listener through mouth resonance. If the jaw is held rigid and closed or the tongue bunched toward the back of the throat, no matter how open and flexible the throat resonator may be, the final projected tone will be impeded and squeezed. Jaw openness and flexibility and tongue forwardness and mobility are essential to the strength and richness of the final projected tone.

Balanced resonance requires a careful blending of throat, mouth and nose resonance. Without it the voice is inefficient and frequently disturbing. With a lazy soft palate, for instance, the whole tone may become nasal; when the throat is squeezed and inflexible, the tone seems thin, high-pitched and harsh: or, if the tongue is bunched toward the back of the throat, the projected tone sounds flat and thick. Normally, balanced resonance is achieved when the throat and jaw are functionally relaxed, flexible and never closed, and when the soft palate performs accurately its role of opening for the sounds of "m," "n" and "ng" and closing for all other sounds.

Variety. The radio performer must possess a voice which adapts easily to the mood and meaning of the assignment. No matter what the situation or copy, the performer must communicate to the listeners sincere belief in the subject matter and a natural excitement for it. All meanings must be clear. Monotony should never mar a natural vitality. All subtle changes in mood and feeling, dictated by the words and the situation, should occur as easily as they do in a conversation with a close friend. Such changes appear most naturally in the voice when they are *actually present*, when they are *felt* by the announcer or actor.

The human voice with speech is capable of reflecting every conceivable shade of mood and meaning. Variations in vocal pitch, time, force and quality make this possible. Speech without thoughtful variation communicates only a shade of the full mood and meaning, and it may be monotonous and inaccurate. The performer must *feel* a mood and *know* a meaning if it is to be reflected in his voice with sincerity.

Pitch. Pitch inflections (glides) are of three kinds: upward, downward, and circumflex (curved downward and upward or upward and downward). An upward inflection communicates uncertainty, question or partial expression with more to follow. A downward inflection reflects certainty, definiteness or authority. A circumflex provides an ironic, sarcastic, double or uncertain meaning. For instance, the word "really" inflected upward asks a question, inflected downward communicates understanding, and inflected with a curved circumflex (depending upon direction and lilt) provides any one of several ironic, sarcastic or double implications.

The vocal step or leap is a sudden change in key or pitch level either upward or downward. It is used to tell of a shift in subject, to make an item or series stand out or to place a phrase in apposition. For example, "The boys slithered off their sleds in all directions. *You saw it, didn't you, Joe?* Oh, it was a terrifying sight!"

Time. Changes in the rate of speech and the use of pauses while speaking are essential to understanding. Normal speech rate varies from 80 to 175 words per minute. A constant of any rate produces monotony. In general, rate variations reflect the importance of the subject matter. Important aspects are slowed; less important ones may be speeded.

The vocal pause is an oral punctuation mark. It makes possible the separation of thoughts and segments of thoughts. Without the vocal pause, meaning would be jumbled and difficult (frequently impossible) to follow. The vocal pause also provides a time for replenishing one's breath naturally and unobtrusively.

Force. Variations in the force (volume and/or intensity) of the voice provide a further dimension for vocal emphasis. A louder or more intense and slower passage is made more important than a quieter and faster one. Upon occasion, however, for reason of contrast, a quiet statement following a longer and highly intense one will be heightened in importance. Extended sameness of volume or intensity will cause monotony.

Vocal force combines with a form of time (duration) in producing another most essential means of achieving emphasis. The correct pronunciation of a word results from this combined emphasis on an appropriate syllable or syllables. The intended meaning of a phrase or sentence is made clear by giving more time and force to a particular word or words. This form of emphasis is called stressing or pointing. For example, "Jerry announces at the local station" may communicate the following several meanings depending upon which word is stressed: *Jerry* announces at the local station (Jerry, not Ralph); Jerry *announces* at the local station (announcing is his specialty); Jerry announces *at* the local station (he is there physically); Jerry announces at *the* local station (the most important station); Jerry announces at the *local* station (not the regional station); Jerry announces at the local *station* (not at the local ball park).

Quality. Thoughtful variations of pitch, rate and force in large part make intellectual meanings clear. Variations in the quality (or timbre) of vocal tone communicate variations in mood, attitude and feeling. The performer should possess the desired feeling, mood or attitude in order best to communicate it. Otherwise, insincerity may result. Such desirable personality characteristics as warmth, vitality and believability are communicated by radio entirely through tonal qualities of the voice. Coldness, fear, boredom and insincerity may likewise be projected if these are the attitudes and feelings of the performer. In radio, every subtle shade of feeling is transmitted by voice and voice alone. The performer must not only possess such feelings but develop a highly flexible vocal instrument capable of communicating them.

Speech

Voice is the controlled sound of speech. Speech is the *articulation* of this sound into units and words and the blending of words into phrases and sentences.

Vowels, diphthongs and consonants. Vowels and diphthongs, the resonant sounds of speech, carry the tone of the word; the consonants, the obstructed sounds, give it frame. In the English language there are 15 separate vowel sounds, 5 major diphthongs and 27 consonants, 10 of which are voiceless. Recognition and accurate use of these is essential for easy articulation, correct pronunciation and smooth blending.

It is important for the radio performers to develop a full and flexible command of all vowel and consonant sounds. A course in voice and speech in which there is application of the voice requirements and standards stated in this chapter is essential for all potential radio performers.

The organs of articulation. Speech is produced by the action of the articulators: the tongue, the lips, the soft palate, and the jaw, with the teeth, upper gum-ridge, hard palate and upper throat as anchors. Of these, the tongue does the most work. The function of the articulators is to shape the vowels and diphthongs, articulate the consonants and blend them all into conventional patterns of pronunciation. Each sound has a particular and precise shaping or position which may become modified as it blends with other sounds in syllables, words and phrases. Distinctness and accuracy depend upon correct shaping of each vowel and diphthong, precise articulation of each consonant and easy blending of all sounds.

The moving articulators — tongue, lips, jaw and soft palate — must be flexible, mobile and free of restricting tension. During speech the tongue is in continuous movement from one sound to another with its back, middle, tip and sides playing separate but related roles in the shaping and blending of sounds. During one minute of moderately paced speech the tongue may take as many as 200 separate positions. The tongue is an integrated set of many muscles. It can be trained, as any other healthy muscle of the body, to perform with precision, accuracy and mobility.

The lips as constrictor muscles extend and vary the opening of the mouth. For the back vowels, variations in lip opening and extension are required. The lips, too, may be trained to be accurate and precise. The same is true of the jaw, which must vary in its openness among sounds, and of the soft palate, which must be open for "m," "n" and "ng" and closed for all other sounds.

Pronunciation. For the correct pronunciation of any word, a particular syllable is given *major* stress. In polysyllabic words, one or more additional syllables may be given *minor* stress. For instance, "hotel" and "idea" must be pronounced with the accent or stress on the second syllable. In the word "inseparable" (five syllables) there is also only one stress. For "inarticulatory" (seven syllables), however, there are two stresses, one major and one minor. Some words have one major and two minor stresses: "autobiographic." Occasionally a word will have two major stresses: "backbone."

Spoken languages are always in the process of growth and change. A pronunciation acceptable 15 years ago may be second choice or incorrect today. Such changes are brought about by those men and women in the public view who use the language day in and day out. The only sure guide to correct pronunciation is a current edition of a standard dictionary or pronunciation handbook. There is no excuse for a performer being incorrect. Frequently a word may have more than one acceptable pronunciation. Shifting from one correct pronunciation to another, however, is poor practice and, particularly in announcing, gives the impression of uncertainty.

PERFORMANCE TECHNIQUES

Microphone Techniques

The microphone is the radio performer's technical means of communication with the audience. Correct use of the microphone is vital to the effectiveness of a performance. Microphones have various directional patterns or characteristics: *non-directional* microphones pick up sound with equal intensity around their full circumference; *bi-directionals* on two (opposite) sides; and *uni-directionals* pick up from one direction only. Chapter 2 of this book includes an analysis of microphone characteristics that the performer needs to know.

General usage. For virtually all performers, the following principles need to be understood and effectively put into practice:

1. Speak in a normal, conversational voice, neither too quiet nor too loud. For such average volume the speaker should be approximately the distance of two stretched hands from the microphone. A weak voice will need to be a little closer, a stronger voice farther away. It is good practice to have the control engineer check the performer's volume "level" to determine his proper microphone distance. Balance among voices is essential when several people are using the same microphone. The director or control engineer will fix distances from the microphone for proper balance.

2. Never puff or blast directly into a microphone. A disturbing, explosive sound may result. This is especially true if a bi-directional, ribbon or velocity microphone is being used.

3. Maintain effective microphone distance. Moving toward and away from a microphone will produce noticeable variations in volume.

4. Handle scripts noiselessly. Be certain the pages are unstapled and in order. A good procedure is to read to the bottom of one page, meanwhile quietly sliding it to expose the first few lines of the next page. When the

new page is begun, either drop the completed page to the floor or carefully move it in a large sweeping motion to the back of the script. Heavy, soft paper produces the least noise, thin paper, such as onionskin, the most.

Special acting techniques

1. To give the illusion of moving into a conversation, start speaking five to seven feet away from the microphone and, still talking, move into the fixed distance position; to give the illusion of leaving, move away from the microphone while still talking.

2. The illusion of one person speaking to a second from another room may be created by the distant person speaking five to ten feet off mike. Both performers should raise volume slightly.

3. Actors may vary their distances from the microphone in accordance with the mood and intensity of the scene. For instance, a whispered love scene plays best three to four inches from the microphone, while an intense political speech may need to be as much as several feet away.

4. Know the standard hand signals, used by the director and other production staff members. They are illustrated on pages 222 – 224.

5. The five basic microphone positions, on mike, off mike, fading on or coming on, fading off or going off, and behind an obstruction are defined on page 160.

PERFORMANCE TYPES

The professional performer through analysis and rehearsal, knows exactly what is required before going on the air. In addition to interpretation, mood, technique and relationships to other performers, the audience must be envisioned. It is always a small audience, seldom larger than two or three in any one place, frequently just a single person. The performer "sees" the audience where they are: in the study, in the kitchen, in the family room, in the bedroom, in an automobile; and knows who they are: the teenage boy or girl, the housewife at her work, the salesman driving from one town to the next, the sports fan, the father interested in trading cars.

In a real sense, all radio performers are actors, using the actor's tools and techniques in whatever mode of on-the-air presentation they are engaged. It is appropriate, therefore, to consider the needs and potentials of the actor as a base for all other forms of radio performance.

The Actor

Acting is an art, and as such requires extensive study for adequate understanding. However, certain basic principles and suggestions which may be helpful can be presented here. Acting demands control of the mind, the feelings, the body and the voice. Such control comes only from practice and experience under sensitive guidance. The only way to learn to act is to act!

The mind. Every character to be acted, no matter how few lines there are, must be analyzed. This is an intellectual process and should take place prior to rehearsal, if at all possible, and always after conferring with the director who must see that the script has unity and who will have visualized the kind of characterization desired. Certainly, it is permissible and desirable for the actor to evolve a concept of character which is different from that of the director, but these must be melded and agreed upon by both. The director is always the final authority.

What takes place during this analysis? First, a clear mental picture of the character to be acted must be established: What is his or her function in the script? What relationships to other characters? What feelings? What general moods and attitudes? What does the character look like? How does the character walk, stand and sit? What quality of voice? Is it resonant, high pitched, strident or nasal? Is the speech slow, rapid, hesitant or monotonous? Does the character have a dialect? When these factors are determined and clearly in mind, the actor is ready to develop the role, to transfer these definitions into actuality.

The feelings and attitude. An actor may understand a character's feelings and general attitude, but to communicate feelings and attitude is often difficult. Since the voice responds naturally to actual, real feelings, the best approach is for the actor to feel anger, pity, remorse, love or any of the varying shades of these and other emotions. Lines spoken with real feelings present will usually result in the vocal communication of the feelings. Many trials and much experimentation may be necessary alone and with the use of a tape recorder before the desired effect begins to show.

The body. When an actor is seen, the body conveys a significant part of characterization: the strength of stride; the movement of head or mouth when speaking; the quick or slow movements of fingers and hands; habits such as touching the ear lobe when nervous. The use of the body, is, strangely, no less important for the radio actor. True, the actor is "chained" to a microphone. But if a scene takes place while two people are walking down a gravel path, actual walking in place at the microphone will better establish the illusion of walking. When one climbs, a ladder or lifts a heavy stone, there is a sound of strain in the voice. This must be duplicated at the microphone. Twiddling the lobe of an ear, although it cannot be seen, may help emotionally to establish nervousness. In a covert way, the body must be used at the microphone to assist the voice in communicating the illusion of reality.

The voice. For radio, voice and speech alone communicate a character to the listener. There may be shuffling footsteps or other recognizable sounds made through movement of the body; the intellect and emotions, too, come into play to produce a full and well-rounded character. But it is voice and speech that communicate, that build in the mind's eye of the non-seeing audience an image of how this "real" person speaking to them thinks, feels, acts, reacts and moves. For this kind of real communication, a radio actor's voice must be versatile, sensitive and completely under control. The fundamentals of voice and speech must be automatic.

Rehearsal. For theatre, television and the motion picture, an actor memorizes lines and normally has adequate time for rehearsal and the development of characterization. Once rehearsals begin, a half-hour radio play, for example, is frequently completed and taped or aired in four hours or less. Of course, a radio actor reads lines from a script, but the characterization must come to life in the brief time of the rehearsal period. Every moment at a radio play rehearsal must count. During this period the play is read once or more with the cast and director sitting around a table. Voice quality, speech rate and intonation, general characterization, even dialects are established and tentatively set at the table rehearsal. The next rehearsals are on microphone. The director usually will set the actor's positions, placement, and approaching and leaving the microphone at the first "mike" rehearsal. During these rehearsals the character must come to life: inflections, voice quality, dialect, tempo and all subtle aspects of interplay with other characters are firmly established. The director must now concern himself with coordinating the final production. There is time for only quick suggestions which must be adopted immediately. In a real sense the actor is responsible for maintaining the role as it was established.

Radio acting requires quick judgments, the ability to respond instantly to direction, and firm control of body, feelings and voice. Such attributes come only from experience and intensive practice.

The Straight Announcer

This performer may be required from time to time to handle almost every radio-speech assignment at a station. A straight announcer must be prepared to introduce speakers, announce classical and popular music programs, read commercials of all types, prepare and conduct interviews, present the news, deliver public service announcements, make station breaks and report on the weather, perhaps do color or even play-by-play for local athletic events, and even serve as master of ceremonies for special broadcasts such as the local beauty contest finals. On the spur of the moment the announcer may be asked to extemporize the narration of an event which is immediate news but may in several hours have lost its importance and interest.

The straight announcer must be versatile, adaptable, quick-thinking and indefatigable, possessing variety, honest vitality and an ability to adapt quickly to the mood of the copy or the situation. A large vocabulary and a facility for its use that will bring to mind and tongue the appropriate word for the occasion are essential. The straight announcer is really all announcers in one. Today it is mainly in the smaller radio stations that such a person may be found or, more often, needed. Usually, in larger stations the varied announcing responsibilities are divided among a staff of announcers, taking advantage of and building special talents and abilities.

Harold Green, general manager of radio station WMAL, Washington, D.C., offers an excellent analysis of the requirements for a good announcer — an analysis which applies to the other categories of announcing in succeeding sections of this chapter, including the disc jockey, commercials announcer, newscaster and so forth. Mr. Green writes:

The day of the "limited" announcer is about over. Just a beautiful voice, or just a snappy, witty, or attractive personality, is not enough for today's successful radio station. All the tricks, gimmicks, formats, points of view have been tried in one form or another. Some are quite successful in a limited way. The danger that the individual suffers is the strong possibility that he will remain submerged or anonymous. This is particularly true in a station that depends strongly on a particular "format." We feel that the stations that matter in the community don't limit themselves to a format, or other gimmick. The key is community involvement . . . information with a purpose . . . and a continuity of sound (in music and personality) that will continually serve — and please — the audience that particular station has cultivated.

This type station requires a special person as an air personality. He may possess one of the unique abilities: voice, humor, style, wit, intelligence . . . any one of which is a big help . . . but he must have a think-box as well as voice box. He must be truly interested in his community. He must be completely alert to the world around him. He reads at least two newspapers every day, reads three or more quality magazines every week. He is probably taking a course or two at one of the universities. He has a natural, and genuine, interest in people. He realizes that he is in a highly sophisticated communications business . . . and he'd better have something to communicate.

Our announcers go on the air each day with a thick folder of clippings, personal observations, letters from listeners, and tears from all the news and sports wires.

By the time a man actually goes on the air each day, he is fully briefed on all that is happening that is significant in the news, in sports, special events in the community, special broadcasts of more than routine interest scheduled for that day and week, or anything else that amounts to information *with a purpose*. He has spent a minimum of two hours in the music library. Generally, each day's music preparation time amounts to approximately 50% of air time. A 4-hour program requires about two hours to prepare musically. This is for one who is thoroughly familiar with the library. Otherwise, it becomes a 1:1 ratio, or even longer. This is because the music list must reflect variety and balance: up-tempo music, boy vocal, lush orchestra, girl vocal, combo or variety, group vocal, and back around again. Specialty, novelty, or other types that break the pattern must be showcased by the DJ. There must be a reason for playing these "extras," and it must be explained.

It is safe to say that when a man does a smooth, informative, professional 4-hour show — one that teased the imagination, and piqued the curiosity — he did an equal four hours of preparation. If he doesn't, he'll know it in about an hour. I'll know it in about an hour and a half, and the listener will know it before noon the next day. Without preparation, background, genuine interest in the world around him, and diligent attention to getting informed and staying informed, a broadcaster sinks instantly into mediocrity. He is then relying on tricks . . . he is ordinary . . . he is short-changing his audience. He won't last long.

The Disc Jockey

The disc jockey program, which occupies a large portion of the small station schedule and serves as a personality or special audience program in the larger station, requires special talents. It is a one-person program which, in simple essence, introduces, talks about and plays popular music recordings with announcements, occasional interviews and commercials interspersed. There is much more required, however, for its success. The disc jockey should have a keen, vital sense of humor with a talent for meaningful comment and not just unrelated patter. Superior disc jockeys develop individual program formats and styles of delivery which become their trademarks. Such styles evolve from creative experiment based on the personality of the announcer and quite often with a selected segment of the audience. Every good disc jockey program is prepared in depth.

The-On-the-Air Salesperson

American commercial radio exists through the selling power of the medium. Announcers persuade listeners to buy the product or subscribe to the service. These commercial messages, group themselves into several types; "punch" — in which the style is vital, intense and emotional for purposes of a quick sale; "institutional" — in which a straightforward, more reserved style is usually employed to create an image of the business organization and develop goodwill toward it; and "personality" — in which the known and popular style of a particular announcer is appropriate to the product being advertised. The announcer must be able to adapt to each type with sincerity. As the spokesperson for the sponsor the sales announcer must believe in the product for its potential customer.

There are also varying forms of commercials: the "ad lib," in which one knows the product and talks about it conversationally and with complete ease; the "straight," which is read from written copy with which the announcer should be thoroughly familiar; the "dual or multiple voice," in which the selling is shared by two or more announcers who are acquainted with the product; the "jingle," which titillates the ear with an intriguing verse set to music; and the "dramatic," in which a scene is quickly set, a dramatic twist is established, and focus is emphatically placed on the product. All commercials require vocal variety, vitality and an ability to establish mood and believability.

The News Reporter

In addition to vocal talents, those who broadcast the news should possess background qualifications in depth: they should be college educated in the liberal tradition with specialization in political science, radio-journalism and history, with a vital interest in current events; should know how to edit the news with a disciplined knowledge of what is newsworthy; and should be able to communicate confidence to the listeners.

A station newscaster has access to the news wire services, but these services should be only the beginning. Responsibility resides with the individual newscaster and the station, not with the wire services. Careful judgment, knowledge and responsibility must always be present in editing the news and delivering it to those many listeners who depend on radio for accurate and rapid reporting. The news wire services provide a serious temptation to the busy station announcer to rip the news from the teletype and read it "cold." What happens? Mispronunciations, misreadings, inclusion of items of unimportance to the region, and failure to communicate the meaning of the news. The responsible newscaster must prepare the newscast, editing it when necessary, reading it for meaning, rehearsing it aloud for proper phrasing and tempo, and determining the correct pronunciation for any unfamiliar words and names of persons and places. In delivery the newscaster should communicate with quiet vitality, warmth, ease and authority.

For the *news analyst*, who interprets the news, a greater amount of preparation is obviously required, a wealthier background of knowledge and experience is *imperative*, and a more highly developed vocal maturity is essential. Success is dependent upon the audience following, and the news analyst's responsibility in forming public opinion is grave.

The Sportscaster

Normally, sportscasting is a specialized position in radio. The director of sports at a station is responsible for all programming in the sports area: play-by-play broadcasts of athletic events; the color or descriptive matter about the game, the teams, the fans and visiting celebrities before and after the game and during normal and special intervals; interviews at the time of the game; and sports news and interviews at the studio. The sportscaster (often the director of sports at the smaller station) usually has a "color" person along at athletic events for relief and variety.

The sportscaster must know in depth the events to be broadcast and the terminology peculiar to the sport. He or she should be completely familiar with the rules but must avoid any on-the-air disagreement with the judgments of the officials. The sportscaster must possess a talent for extemporary speech in which the appropriate words flow easily and rapidly, permitting easy description of the action as it is happening. This allows for little or no hesitation, and even when action is temporarily halted, the sportscaster — as the eyes of the listener — must continue to describe what is happening. Normally a station sportscaster follows a "home" or special team and should memorize the names and numbers of players before the season opens. The names and numbers of visiting team members may be procured prior to the contest and should be memorized before game time. For the complex team sports and for those which involve many players, such as football, the sportscaster will employ a "spotter" and a "spotting board" to assist in identifying substitutions and players involved in a particular action. One who is interested in sportscasting should observe at length a capable and experienced sportscaster at work. Should one wish to change from straight announcing to sportscasting, a fine opportunity to gain experience would be to do "color" with a good play-by-play sportscaster and eventually provide "relief" during a broadcast as the situation permits.

The "color" announcer is extremely important. Play-by-play work demands absolute attention; relief is necessary. The "color" announcer is responsible for the pre- and post-game introductions and summations and for filling the natural breaks for innings, halves, time-outs and official delays. The "color" job is to set the mood of the occasion and to fill the allotted time with pertinent information which will interest the listener. This may include announcements of the line-ups, information about the team or individual players, appropriate comments about surroundings, special occurrences and statistics, interviews with visiting guests and sports figures, and frequent responsibility for delivery of commercials.

Both must bring to sportscasting an exciting, varied, vital and believable style of delivery.

The Interviewer

An interviewer must be at ease, knowledgeable, vitally interested in the work of the person being interviewed, and professional in the conduct of his interview. The principal types of interviews are personality, opinion, and information. Basically, an interview follows a question-answer format with an introduction, a main segment or body of information, and a conclusion. In style of performance it must be natural, straightforward, and conversational.

The interviewer should find out as much as possible about the interviewee through pre-interview talks, if possible, and prepare a detailed question and answer outline. More questions should be planned than seem necessary for the length of the program, for it is poor practice to complete an interview with air time remaining. In planning, the interviewer should organize the material to rise to an informational climax and fall briefly into a wrap-up conclusion, making it necessary to refer to notes as infrequently as possible on the air.

During the show-time, a feeling of casual spontaneity should exist, a give and take between the interviewer and guest, with the interviewer taking the responsibility of keeping the program moving in a conversational but vital atmosphere.

The Panel or Roundtable Moderator

A panel or roundtable program is comprised of a moderator and several participants. The subject is usually controversial but may be simply informational. The moderator introduces the subject and the participants, often identifying the viewpoint of each panel member. During the program he or she guides and paces the discussion, avoiding serious digressions from the central theme and working for a balanced presentation of the material. A good moderator must be well-informed on the subject, adept in asking appropriate questions, and gifted in extemporaneous expression. At the close of the program the moderator summarizes the salient points.

The Master of Ceremonies

Occasionally an announcer must serve as a "master of ceremonies," or m.c., for a high school rally, for a "meet the candidate" public forum, or in a variety of public situations where speech continuity must be provided in the mood of the gathering. A master of ceremonies should possess a sense of humor, be able to adapt quickly to the mood of the situation, know how to keep the program moving with variety and vitality, and be especially talented in picking up cues and taking advantage of what occurs. A personal extemporaneous or "ad lib" style is most valuable.

The Narrator

For regular radio program fare, narration is the running, descriptive presentation of an actual event, such as a parade, a funeral cortege, or a four-alarm fire; for radio drama it is the expository passages which set the scenes and tie them together; and for the documentary it is the commentary which links and underscores the actual events and gives them meaning. The first is extemporized, the latter two are read. The narrator is a combination of both announcer and actor, making the listeners not only "see" but also "feel" by setting the mood for the actual event. The narrator's voice must be vital, varied and highly sensitive to the emotional implications of the material.

The Outside Speaker

Many lay citizens perform as speakers or interviewees. If they are accomplished speakers, but lacking in radio experience, there is little to advise except in the use of the microphone. For the totally inexperienced, however, the following principles should be helpful.

1. Know and follow the suggestions on microphone use.
2. Outline the speech, giving it an introduction, a main body of information and a conclusion. Write out the speech from the outline, using simple,

concrete words that create pictures. Read the speech aloud, timing it accurately with a *stop watch*. Cut or add to it until it fits the exact, allotted time segment.

3. Rehearse the speech aloud several times, possibly using a recorder for self-criticism. Work for a natural, conversational quality. Remember that any given audience will be a small one, one to three people at each receiver. Speak to them, not as from a platform, but with as much ease, naturalness, vitality and quiet enthusiasm as in talking directly to the same small group.

4. An interviewee will be briefed by the interviewer and the questions to be asked will be agreed upon prior to the broadcast. Approach the actual program with as much ease as possible, remembering that the area to be discussed is your field. Speak conversationally, but with natural enthusiasm, answering the questions fully without launching into a lengthy speech. If interruptions by the interviewer occur from time to time, take them in stride, helping always to make the program what it should be — a vital conversation. Be acquainted with the basic signals and microphone techniques.

PERFORMANCE OPPORTUNITIES IN RADIO TODAY

Radios, often two or more, are tuned in regularly in most American homes. Millions of automobiles are equipped with radios. In the early 1970's over 7,000 radio stations were operating throughout the United States, with the number steadily increasing. There is a large radio audience, a growing radio industry and a need, therefore, for competent men and women to staff these stations and to supply them with regular and public service program material. The voice of radio — the performer and what he or she does on the air — is radio's most important single element. A listener *tunes in* or *tunes out* because of the performer and the program. What are the performer's opportunities?

Stations

The basic jobs have been discussed under PERFORMANCE TYPES. However, certain additional information should be explored. In the small or local station, for instance, most of the performance work will be carried by the disc jockey, who will do news, interviews, ad lib, read commercials and frequently help with sports events. Salaries in the small station will not be large, although these vary, depending upon talent, experience and station locality. In the small station, however, because of the wide variety of performance experience, the young, learning performer will have fertile opportunity to grow and move up.

A typical day and individual program hour for the announcer-disc jockey at a small station is described by Wayne Pond of WCHL, Chapel Hill, North Carolina:

My day at the station usually begins by checking in with the program director. Our chats range from a brief "hello" to lengthy and detailed discussions of format, spots, special programs which the station might be running, performance, or changes in the routine yet important machinery of how things get done. I spend the majority of my time prior to an air shift, however, on copy and production. Usually I have from three or four to upwards of a dozen spots to cut, the copy comes from any one of the station's copy people (one full time copy writer, with several others, secretaries or salesmen, filling in when needed). I spend a few moments looking over the continuity and getting to "know" it; then I try to find accurate and complementary background music. Most of the time, my main responsibility is simply to cut the copy on tape and leave it for dubbing onto cartridges for airing (this is usually done by the all-night man). At any rate, when I cut the spots, regardless of who does the dubbing, there are several standard procedures that I follow: before cutting the spot itself, I inform the dubber as to (1) the length of the spot, (2) the exact closing words of the spot — the out-cue — so that he in turn can place secondary, or trip-cue, on the cart (this helps make for tight air sound, with less — hopefully no — dead air), and (3) any specific production instructions (for example, occasionally a spot will run only half a day, or have to be updated — and consequently recut — or changed).

At any rate, all of this is done for several reasons, the most obvious of which is the accuracy of the information which gets onto the cart label. This label (again, part of the process of standardization at WCHL) must contain the following information: (1) the exact length of the spot; (2) the exact out-cue of the spot; (3) the exact length of any musical introduction to the spot, so that a jock can talk over it if he wishes to; (4) the name of the announcer who voices the spot (this in order to mix voices in on-the-air spot sets); (5) the date(s) when the spot is to run; (6) if necessary, some explanation as to the content of the spot (for example, occasionally a tire company will pitch bicycles instead of tires, or a department store will be selling tires instead of clothing or household wares; what we are trying to avoid, in short, is embarrassing sponsorship conflicts); and (7), the name of the account, of course.

Another of my concerns at the station is music. Although I am not directly responsible for the type of music that finds its way onto the air (which is the dubious chore of the music director, who must try to please an extremely diverse audience, not to mention the program director and the clients), I am responsible for the flow or pace of the music which has been selected. This is to say that I have to watch the mixture of music during my shift; the "don'ts" more or less sum it up: don't play two instrumentals back to back; don't play two of a genre back to back (rock, soul, country); don't, in short, force musical redundancies on the listener. To this end, we follow a musical rotation system at the station, which goes more or less as follows: one record from the current top forty charts; one recent top forty hit; one "memory" or gold record that was big before 1968; another current top forty hit; a cut from a current and popular album (this is the most distinctively "middle of the road" piece to get on the air); another "memory," this time dating between 1968 and the present; and here the cycle begins anew. What I have to do is familiarize myself with what *is* new on our music list from week to week; this includes checking, among other things, the intro time on each piece of music, the out-cue, and the viability of any piece of music in the context of the jingles which the station uses (more on this later). Since all of the music at WCHL — with the exception of some of the oldies — is on tape, this information is included on the label of the cart onto which the music has been dubbed. Another element which helps me to be comfortable around the music is frequent reading of the musical trade magazines, including *Billboard* and the Hamilton *Radio Report*; I try to keep up with these on a weekly, if not daily, basis.

On any given day at the station we might have an announcers' meeting; generally these meetings take place only two or three times a month, but occasionally we get together more often than that. Announcers' meetings are "rap" sessions, very informal, but quite helpful. Topics range from new music, to information from the people in sales about new commercial promotions, to discussions of proposed changes in format — in short, we talk about the entire operation. I have found that the announcers' meetings provide an opportunity to talk frankly about my own and others' performance; to hear someone else who does what I do make suggestions may be a strain on the ego, but it's good, nevertheless, largely because most of the suggestions that we make to one another are valid. In any event, this freedom and exchange pay off.

The three hour air shift I do is, of course, the focal point of my work at the station. In a sense, the man on the board *is* the entire radio station as far as the listener is concerned, and that responsibility is a serious one, even though disc jockeys are proverbially carefree. Indeed, a good disc jockey should sound carefree or refreshing to the listener, but in my opinion this is ideally a highly calculated and planned lightness. The quality of a disc jockey's air performance stems largely from how much he controls what he does; if he doesn't know his music, commercials, jingles — his format — the sound that results is choppy or uneven, filled with unnecessary talk or verbal bumbling. On the other hand, solid control of format can result in a smooth and listenable sound. Regardless of its nature — middle-of-the-road, top forty, country, whatever — format is at least as important as personality, since the former is the vehicle of the latter. Suffice to say that a *sense* of format carefully executed is important for me. The programming of WCHL aims at an interesting, entertaining and coherent sound. Let me discuss a sample hour of my shift in an attempt to illustrate these generalities:

The hour begins with a newscast, a combination of network and local elements. Following a commercial "time tone" and station identification exactly on the hour, we feed approximately 90 seconds of MBS news. Upon a pre-determined cue from the network I start a 60-second locally-oriented (and generally, therefore, station-produced) spot; upon its completion, I go back to the network for approximately another minute or so. At this point, our own newsman runs what we call a "minicast" of regional or local news; most often this is live, but from time to time it is done on tape just before air time. Here follows a 20-second news spot (same account as 60-second), and a weather forecast. As the newsman reads the forecast, he is free to "walk" whatever instrumental intro there may be on the first record of the hour. At the end of the first record of the hour (usually an upbeat tune, depending on the category which has come up in the record rotation), I play the disc jockey intro, a kind of orchestrated choral rendition of my name. This is immediately followed by another record; according to the availability of an instrumental intro, I will walk the music and utter something profound such as "Good afternoon, it's three-oh-eight at WCHL, and here's so-and-so to (sing) (dance) (play) (gargle) for you." The point is that it's terribly difficult day in and day out to say or do something original and fairly distinctive in those few moments before and after records, when a disc jockey has the air all to himself. This is not by way of complaint so much as lament. Working within the confines of a highly calculated and well defined format is good insofar as one has some idea of what to strive for. Realizing that desire concretely is the challenge, and whether you've done it or not is something that your intuition, rather than the program director, will tell you. Probably the most desirable elements in these moments of talk before and after records are credibility, warmth, sincerity and a sense of personableness with which the listener can identify or relax, since it is the disc jockey who gives direction and continuity to the mixture of spots, music and talk.

After the second record, I go into the first spot of the hour. The commercials, like the music, are programmed. This doesn't mean that they necessarily get onto the air in the exact order that they are listed on the program log, but that we try for as much continuity with spots as with anything else. A typical set will include one 60-second spot, one 30-second spot, and/or some kind of non-commercial announcement (Community Chest, basketball promo, or whatever). Or a set will consist of three 30-seconds, or two 60-seconds. If and when live spots come up, they precede the recorded ones, on the theory that it's best to keep the talk together; for example, a live 60-second or live 30-second followed by recorded spots. Spots which have commercial jingles or upbeat music, if not preceded by live commercials, are placed first in the set to maintain pace. An average is between one and two minutes per set, on the theory that this represents a good mixture for the 14-minute commercial hour at WCHL. At least twice an hour (at roughly 20 minutes past and 15 minutes before the hour), I will begin the spot set with a live public service announcement, then go directly to the commercials, and then I do a weather forecast.

The schedule which I have been describing permits me to play approximately 10 to 12 or 13 records an hour (most of them average about three minutes) with approximately seven or eight spot sets per hour. One of the challenges inherent in such a system is timing — not just in the spot to spot or music to music sense, but in terms of moving toward the top of the hour with the proper mix of spots and music so as to come out at the end, rather than the middle, of the hour's last record. This is tricky because most of the time we run commercial time-tones and pre-recorded station IDs immediately before the network news feed, which commences exactly on the hour and is itself preceded by an instrumental logo. One of the things which helps to time out the hour exactly is the jingle package we use at WCHL. The jingles represent a number of musical tempos, from slow to fast, and are useful, therefore, in more than timing. Frequently I will have time enough to play two or more records back to back, and the jingles facilitate these sequences largely in terms of tempo (moving from a fast to a slow record, or between two fast or slow ones). I even have my own drive time "going home" jingle; this is great not just for the help it gives in timing out the hour but also — let's be honest about this — for the kick I get when I hear it!

And so the hour moves on. Sometimes we will have special bits to run (parades, interviews, news drop-ins, bulletins, etc.), but ideally these are generally a part rather than interruption of a pre-established format.

I suppose what appears to be a routine could become rather boring, but somehow it never has. A three hour shift on the air demands a good deal of concentration; there is not time to be bored. You know, of course, that disc jockeys do more than "play records"; how much more is almost entirely up to the disc jockey, since I know of few professions which allow an individual as much freedom or creativity. There are those few extremely routine chores which must be attended to (log and transmitter readings, for example), but these are certainly the exception to what I feel to be a fun and fascinating job.

In the larger regional station, duties become more specialized and salaries larger, again depending upon the station and its market. In addition to regular duties, announcers will frequently have their own programs. There may be positions for on-the-air news announcers, sports announcers, even farm director-announcers. Frequently a woman will handle programs for women.

Ty Boyd, one of the best known radio personalities in the South, writes about his experience and duties as an announcer-disc jockey at WBT, a 50,000 watt regional station in Charlotte, North Carolina:

What is a regional disc jockey, and how does he get that way? I've been a broadcaster for 26 years, having started at the age of 15 in my home town of Statesville, North Carolina. I don't know what is typical or average for a DJ in my kind of job, but I would guess that the average age and experience are less than mine, and that non-broadcast involvements are fewer. I'm not sure there is a "typical' regional DJ.

I started work for free. Our local station wanted a volunteer nighttime announcer for FM baseball broadcasts. I wanted to get into broadcasting. After six months I was budgeted for $5 a week "carfare." That early experience gave me a foothold into the business. For 14 years I worked at a number of local stations and 12 years ago came to WBT-AM-FM-TV, a regional station in Charlotte, North Carolina. Each experience helped me to learn and grow. I helped put one station on the air; we all pitched in and painted, strung wire, nailed sound board and prayed that it wouldn't fall apart. At another station I got exposed to programming, sales and management. At one station I got the opportunity to do some national commercials and to host some regional sport shows and a statewide beauty pageant.

What does a regional disc jockey do? What are his responsibilities? First, I detest the term "disc jockey." It connotes for me a not-necessarily responsible individual who plays a few records and gets his kicks rapping. But the person on the air today is a skilled professional who has planned and executed with finesse his broadcast chores. I prefer to be called an entertainer-air salesman.

A typical day for me is to get up at 5 A.M. for my 6 A.M.-10 A.M. "Ty Boyd Show." The nighttime security officer at the station (one of 300 employees at Jefferson-Pilot Broadcasting) phones me at home to be sure that I get to the station at least 15 minutes before show time. When I arrive I go immediately to some of the source material we will be using during the day. A newspaper is the best investment for a broadcaster who wants to be on top of contemporary subjects. It gives you a whole team of responsible news people who are doing your research for you *every day*. I can lace my morning raps with references from the newspaper alone. We also use periodicals, regional publications and listener mail. I also subscribe to a comedy materials service. My producer arrives at the station about the same time I do and we plan our day, decide where we are going to use any pre-produced bits, and generally outline the four hours of our program.

The show is really a team effort. In addition to myself, the producer, and a resident newsperson, we draw on the talent of the entire news and announcing staff of WBT Radio and Television. Because WBT is a 50,000 watt station we feel a responsibility not only to our local community but to the larger regional coverage area which blankets about 52 counties in North and South Carolina. Before dawn and after dusk we reach from Canada to Cuba. We've had mail from every continent.

We believe that *time, temperature, weather* and *news* need to be delivered succinctly, frequently and interestingly. We use a number of program aids such as jingles, background music and sound effects. We try to stay on top of traffic bulletins, though our market does not seem to require a helicopter traffic service. (Other stations have used helicopter reports, but each has dropped them after the original contracts expired.) A typical hour of our show includes news at the top and bottom of the clock, sports raps maybe three times, weather capsules about six-eight times, a phone call, short info bits, a story or two, plus 16 units of commercials (maximum 14 minutes). We try to be informative but tight. It's gotta flow!

Our music selection is contemporary MOR. Our mix has varied over the years, but is currently one hit to one oldie. Our oldies consist of million-sellers which have captured the listener imagination over the past dozen or so years. What we're selling is factual information you can trust, a good music mix and an old familiar voice (mine!). Many listeners have grown up to my "sound," but our market has a fairly rapid turnover in audience makeup, so we are also constantly promoting and selling our station and its personalities to capture the new listeners in the area.

One of the things we do almost every show is to use the "Fun Phone." We've called everybody from Buckingham Palace to the guy who makes the elevator shoes for Sonny of Sonny and Cher. We talk to one, two or three persons every day and get tremendous listener response. Many of these calls are repeated at another hour of the program. About three-fourths of these phone calls are pre-produced (between 10 and 11 A.M. the morning before) so we can edit them for content and duration. You can take a six-minute conversation, whittle it down to about two-and-a-half minutes and its dynamite! We have no time limit on conversations, though I don't believe we've ever gone over five or six minutes. Most of the calls run about two to three minutes.

The responsibilities of a regional station as opposed to a local station differ principally in subtle ways. For example, it's important in the regional situation to stay away from the one-on-one station. If you're honoring only one person (unless that person happens to be a celebrity) you're wasting thousands of listeners' time. Consequently, we don't do birthdays, lost dog announcements, etc. We do make regional and local public service announcements, and try to present them as gutsy, informative and succinct. We usually do these in talk-ups to records. Each day following my morning show we work for about an hour or so producing bits, phone calls, recording materials, etc., for general air play and for the next day's program. The key to a constantly good radio program is *preparation. There's no substitute for it.*

After my four-and-a-half hours of daily broadcast (I also do a half-hour TV news-weather-interview show), I get down to the desk work the job requires. My day is normally in excess of eight hours, usually running about ten. I answer a half-dozen letters a day and about a dozen phone calls. Most of the letters and calls request my participation in civic affairs. A radio personality becomes a public figure and over the past 12 years I've worked for almost every civic endeavor in this city. And I've enjoyed most of them. Some typical projects: cutting promos and being involved in the producing and airing of an auction for Boys Town of North Carolina, as well as serving as vice chairman of the Boys Town Board; developing and promoting a professorial chair in sales and marketing for the University of North Carolina at Charlotte; serving on several university and civic association boards in the State; performing as master of ceremonies for community and charitable activities. In the month as I write this I will have spoken to several thousand people in Cleveland and Cincinnati, flown to Mobile to talk to a conference of sales and marketing representatives (because of the airline schedules, incidentally, I arrived back in Charlotte at 2 A.M., was fast asleep in the Announcers' Office at 2:30 A.M. and up at 5:45 A.M.); five straight nights of the Miss North Carolina pageant; and assorted speeches in four other states as well as locally. The broadcast facility hires the whole person, and the DJ's responsibilities and reputation frequently go far beyond the radio studio.

The company also has a large production house located in our building and produces annually several million dollars worth of commercials and programs. Clients include just about every national advertiser. Mobile units cover the national election scene, hundreds of football and basketball games and numerous location commercial settings for television. I frequently do these commercial jobs, which can take 10 minutes, 10 hours or several days.

Personnel at a regional station with multi-outlets (we have TV, AM and FM) find themselves working cooperatively with all outlets. As noted before, I do a TV show, too, and we help people at all three stations produce sales spots, promos and public service announcements.

But by and large the activities of a regional station DJ are similar to those of the DJ in the smaller facility or market — except on a broader scale. A regional station broadcaster is responsible to a larger segment of the population, has a larger staff and resources, will not be able to act as often in the one-to-one situation and will probably need to be more competitive than his smaller market counterpart.

In the large or clear channel station there will be departments of news, sports, women's programs, farm news and perhaps even one for public service programs, in addition to specialized-personality disc jockey programs for varying audiences at different times of the day. Most performance work will be specialized and of the highest quality. Certain voices will be demanded for certain commercial products and these voices will get extra "talent" fees for their work. The salaries, too, will be much higher. In one typical large station, Announcers earn annually from $12,000 to $40,000, News Reporters from $7,500 to $15,000, Sports Reporters from $10,000 to $20,000, a News Correspondent from $15,000 to $30,000 and a Women's Program Specialist (Home Economist) $20,000.

Advertising Agencies

A variety of materials, including commercials, jingles, dramatic vignettes, public service spots, speeches and political announcements, are written, produced and recorded by advertising agencies for distribution locally, regionally and nationally. Most cities of 50,000 residents and larger support at least one advertising agency. They employ superior announcing, acting and singing talent, usually on a free-lance basis.

Religious Centers

Most religious denominations operate national and sometimes regional radio and television centers. Religious plays, daily devotionals, spot announcements and other religiously oriented programs are produced at these centers. Many programs feature ministers and lay religious leaders, but announcers, singers, narrators and actors are also in demand.

Public Service Agencies

Public service agencies in the areas of health and welfare operate national, regional and often local offices. Such agencies must inform the public of their work; they need support. For this purpose they use modern media of communication, including radio. Stations and artists donate much time and talent to public service agencies, but frequently there are opportunities within the agencies for paid employment.

The Handicapped

The disc jockey and often the radio announcer sit as they speak and operate the turntables and control board. For those who are blind, radio offers a real opportunity. The blind person can learn by touch; the immobilized need not move from their seats.

If you choose radio as a career, choose it wholeheartedly. Work hard. Continue to grow. Never be satisfied with less than your best. Perfect your voice and speech and learn to adapt yourself to any kind of radio-speech assignment. Radio as a medium is expanding and offers many opportunities for the talented performer who is prepared.

BIBLIOGRAPHY

Anderson, Virgil, *Training the Speaking Voice*. New York: Oxford University Press, 1961. Speech oriented, this book provides background in the physical and physiological bases of speech and presents exercises for developing tonal quality and for gaining variety and expressiveness. An excellent book in all areas of voice and speech.

Barnhart, Lyle, *Radio and Television Announcing*. Englewood Cliffs, New Jersey: Prentice-Hall, Inc., 1953. Includes many exercises and drills which need to be carried out under competent supervision and instruction. Particularly helpful is a pronouncing guide to geographical names in the news, plus definitions and pronunciations of numerous musical terms.

Henneke, Ben and Edward Dumit, *The Announcer's Handbook*. New York: Rinehart and Company, 1959. This updated version of the earlier *Radio Announcer's Handbook* uses some material from television and features more than 200 pages of exercises and vocabulary drills, with attention paid to the pronunciation of foreign terms and English words derived from foreign languages.

Hyde, Stuart, *Television and Radio Announcing*. Boston: Houghton Mifflin Company, second edition, 1971. With the first half of the book devoted to all phases of announcing, including technical problems and FCC regulations, and the second half devoted to practice material, this book is extremely helpful to the beginning student. Also contains the International Phonetic Alphabet and a valuable chapter on the disc jockey.

Kingston, W., R. Cowgill and R. Levy, *Broadcasting Television and Radio*. New York: Prentice-Hall, Inc., 1955. Introduces the reader to all phases of radio and television broadcasting, with important emphasis given to performance for the two media.

Lewis, Bruce, *The Technique of Television Announcing*. New York: Hastings House, Publishers, Inc., 1966. "This is the first volume that treats the functions, the skills, the art and the responsibilities of the announcer in a comprehensive manner." (From the Foreword by J. Robert Myers, Vice President, NBC International.)

INDEX